The Limits of Partnership

The Limits
of Partnership

U.S.-RUSSIAN RELATIONS
in the
TWENTY-FIRST CENTURY

Angela E. Stent

Princeton University Press
Princeton and Oxford

press.princeton.edu

Jacket Photograph: U.S. President Barack Obama shakes hands with Russia's
President Vladimir Putin in a bilateral meeting during the G-20 Summit,
June 18, 2012, in Los Cabos, Mexico. Courtesy of AP Photo/Carolyn Kaster.

Library of Congress Cataloging-in-Publication Data

Stent, Angela.
  The limits of partnership : U.S.-Russian relations in the twenty-first century / Angela
Stent.
      pages cm

  Summary: "The Limits of Partnership offers a riveting narrative on U.S.-Russian relations since the Soviet collapse and on the challenges ahead. It reflects the unique perspective of an insider who is also recognized as a leading expert on this troubled relationship.
American presidents have repeatedly attempted to forge a strong and productive partnership only to be held hostage to the deep mistrust born of the Cold War. For the United
States, Russia remains a priority because of its nuclear weapons arsenal, its strategic location bordering Europe and Asia, and its ability to support—or thwart—American interests.
Why has it been so difficult to move the relationship forward? What are the prospects for
doing so in the future? Is the effort doomed to fail again and again? Angela Stent served
as an adviser on Russia under Bill Clinton and George W. Bush, and maintains close
ties with key policymakers in both countries. Here, she argues that the same contentious
issues—terrorism, missile defense, Iran, nuclear proliferation, Afghanistan, the former Soviet space, the greater Middle East—have been in every president's inbox, Democrat and
Republican alike, since the collapse of the USSR. Stent vividly describes how Clinton and
Bush sought inroads with Russia and staked much on their personal ties to Boris Yeltsin
and Vladimir Putin—only to leave office with relations at a low point—and how Barack
Obama managed to restore ties only to see them undermined by a Putin regime resentful
of American dominance and determined to restore Russia's great power status. The Limits
of Partnership calls for a fundamental reassessment of the principles and practices that
drive U.S.-Russian relations, and offers a path forward to meet the urgent challenges facing both countries"— Provided by publisher.

  Includes bibliographical references and index.
  ISBN 978-0-691-15297-4 (hardback)
  1. United States—Foreign relations—Russia (Federation) 2. Russia (Federation)—
Foreign relations—United States. 3. United States—Foreign relations—1989– I. Title.
  E183.8.R9S836 2014
  327.73047—dc23   2013024484

British Library Cataloging-in-Publication Data is available

This book has been composed in Baskerville 120 Pro and Didot

Printed on acid-free paper. ∞

Printed in the United States of America

1 3 5 7 9 10 8 6 4 2

To Danny, Alex, and Rebecca

Contents

Introduction   ix

List of Acronyms   xvii

Prologue
George H. W. Bush and Russia Reborn   1

Chapter One
The Bill and Boris Show   13

Chapter Two
Rethinking Euro-Atlantic Security   35

Chapter Three
Bush and Putin in the Age of Terror   49

Chapter Four
The Iraq War   82

Chapter Five
The Color Revolutions   97

Illustrations following page 123

Chapter Six
The Munich Speech   135

Chapter Seven
From Kosovo to Georgia: Things Fall Apart   159

Chapter Eight

Economics and Energy:
The Stakeholder Challenge 177

Chapter Nine

Reset or Overload? The Obama Initiative 211

Chapter Ten

From Berlin to Damascus:
Disagreements Old and New 235

Chapter Eleven

The Limits of Partnership 255

Acknowledgments 275

List of Interviewees 279

Chronology of Major Events in U.S.-Russian Relations 283

Notes 293

Bibliography 321

Credits for Illustration Section 327

Index 329

Introduction

The two summits were a study in contrasts. In June 2010 Barack Obama invited Russian president Dmitry Medvedev to a favorite eatery, Ray's Hell Burgers, in Arlington Virginia, for a "cheeseburger summit." The two presidents rolled up their sleeves, dined on gourmet burgers, and exchanged jokes in a friendly atmosphere.[1] The summit highlighted the two young post–Cold War leaders, both trained as lawyers, and the new high-tech U.S.-Russian relationship. Obama's reset—his move to improve ties with Moscow—with its relaxed body language was on full display. After the two leaders announced a partnership for innovation, Medvedev flew on to Silicon Valley, where he met with young entrepreneurs, and proudly opened his first Twitter account.

Two years later it was a very different scene. In June 2012 Obama met Vladimir Putin on the sidelines of the G-20 summit in Los Cabos, Mexico, their first meeting since Putin reclaimed the Kremlin.[2] In the words of Russia Today, a government-run TV network, the two leaders sat "poker-faced" as they eyed each other across the table, their body language signaling wariness.[3] Obama said of the meeting, at which they sparred over missile defense and Syria, "We did have a candid, thoughtful and thorough conversation on a whole range of bilateral and international issues." Putin was more sparing. The conversation, he said, was "very substantive and concrete."[4] The reset appeared to be on ice.

Then there was the summit that never was. Obama and Putin were scheduled to meet in Moscow in September 2013. But weeks before the meeting Edward Snowden, a disaffected 30 year-old contractor for the U.S. National Security Agency, landed in Moscow carrying a huge trove of classified information. The Russians took their time assessing the situation, but eventually granted him political asylum, despite repeated U.S. request for his extradition. The White House then lost no time in canceling the summit. Shortly thereafter, Putin said of his relationship with Obama, "We hear each other and understand the arguments. But we simply don't agree. I don't agree with his arguments and he doesn't agree with mine."[5]

These events highlight a basic fact of life since the Soviet Union disappeared on Christmas Day 1991. It has been a constant challenge for Washington to move forward on a constructive and productive agenda with Russia. Periods of dialogue, progress, and optimism have been followed by tense periods, standoffs, mutual criticism, and pessimism. Both Bill Clinton and George W. Bush began their administrations with high expectations about improving ties with Russia, only to acknowledge at the end of their terms that the relationship had seriously deteriorated. The Obama reset was over by the end of his first term. Moreover, Washington's repeated cycles of high hopes followed by disappointments have been mirrored in Moscow. As a close advisor to Presidents Boris Yeltsin and Vladimir Putin put it, "Every Russian President has begun his term with high expectations for the relationship and every term ends in disappointment" because the United States has disregarded Russia's interests.

In fact, U.S.-Russian relations since the Soviet collapse have gone through not one, but four resets. The first, albeit brief and partial, was during the last year of George H. W. Bush's presidency when postcommunist Russia was reborn. The second was President Bill Clinton's more ambitious attempt to refashion the entire relationship in the 1990s. The third reset was Vladimir Putin's initiative when he was the first foreign leader to call George W. Bush after the 9/11 attacks and offer moral and material support for the antiterrorist campaign, with the expectation that Russia would become the United States' full-fledged partner. The fourth reset was initiated by Obama, when he pledged to renew and improve relations with Russia after the 2008 Russia-Georgia War that had brought bilateral ties to a new low. Russia believes that the United States rebuffed its post-9/11overtures during the Bush administration and views the Obama reset as a necessary American course correction, not a joint project.

This book seeks to answer basic questions about the relationship between these two nations: Why has it been so difficult to develop a productive and more predictable post–Cold War U.S.-Russian partnership?

What areas of this relationship have worked best? What have been most problematic? And why? Why are American and Russian priorities so often misaligned? What would it take to redesign this relationship and move it beyond what at best is a limited and selective partnership? These questions—and their answers—have far-reaching global implications.

Moscow's importance for Washington inevitably changed after the Soviet collapse. The United States had viewed the USSR as its major global rival and threat to its national interests. Both countries' missiles had targeted each other, creating a balance of terror and the possibility of nuclear Armageddon. All of that changed after the collapse of the Soviet Union. Its demise ushered in fifteen new independent states of which Russia was by far the largest and the obvious legatee of the USSR. Washington no longer saw Russia as either an ideological or a military rival. But this new reality was a bitter pill for the Russian leadership and the population. Many Russians equated respect with fear and found it hard to accept that the United States no longer regarded Russia as a rival. Since 1992, a central Russian objective has been to regain its status as a great power and be treated as an equal by the United States—a goal that was constantly frustrated. Russia has been indirectly important inasmuch as it is a player in theaters where the United States has vital interests. Even at its weakest in the 1990s, Russia—with its extensive stock of nuclear warheads and weapons of mass destruction (WMD) materials, its substantial albeit weakened military, and its remaining relationships with states that America considered unsavory—possessed the ability to thwart American interests. Every American administration since 1992 has recognized that a key interest in dealing with Russia has been to prevent it from acting as a spoiler in areas where the United States has vital interests—be they Iran, Iraq, Afghanistan, or the Greater Middle East.

It has been more than two decades since the Cold War ended, yet the legacy of that era still shapes the relationship well into the twenty-first century. Another legacy also weighs on bilateral ties—that of the 1990s, the first decade of the independent Russian Federation. Those years, to some degree, have shaped American perceptions that a weak Russia is amenable to acquiescing to a U.S. agenda. By contrast, they have created a visceral Russian determination not to be treated as the United States' junior partner. Russia in the middle of the second decade of the twenty-first century is a very different country than the Russia of the 1990s. Since Vladimir Putin came to power in 2000, its GDP has grown seven-fold. It holds $500 billion of foreign reserves and earns $350 billion a year from oil and gas exports. It still faces challenges in terms of economic growth, innovation, demography and diversification of its economy, and many parts of the countryside are far behind the cities. But, in contrast to the 1990s, there is little of a concrete nature that Russia needs from the United States. Some Americans remember the 1990s as a time of hope, pluralism and freedom of speech in Russia. For most Russians, however, the 1990s were a time of weakness, poverty and uncertainty, of *bezporiadok* (disorder)—a time to which Russians are determined not to return.

U.S. approaches toward Russia have sometimes been internally contradictory. Parts of the policy community and the private sector have stressed the opportunities that a market-oriented Russia offers. But much of the American security establishment continues to view Russia with suspicion through a traditional Cold War lens. The same is true for Russia, where the emerging middle class is eager to do business with West—and invest its money there—while much of the foreign policy and security establishment continues to nurture grievances against a country it still largely views as an antagonist out to minimize its significance. The Cold War may be over but its legacy weighs heavily on perceptions and policies. Senator Sam Nunn, co-author of path-breaking legislation to reduce the dangers of the post-Soviet nuclear legacy summarized it succinctly: "The United States and Russia remain on automatic Cold War pilot."[6]

Although Russia no longer looms as large in American foreign policy considerations as did the Soviet Union, when it was a Cold War adversary, the relationship with Russia still represents a significant priority for the United States. Russia's geopolitical situation straddling Europe and Asia, its large nuclear arsenal, and its permanent seat on the United Nations Security Council give it enduring leverage. It can support or hinder the pursuit of key U.S. national security interests. Similarly, America can influence how successfully Russia can pursue its goal to restore its position as a global player. Russia and the United States share significant interests ranging from counterterrorism and counterproliferation of WMD to working together to stabilize Central Asia and contain the spread of radical Islam, and dealing with challenges from new frontiers, such as the Arctic. Despite these common interests, however, the two countries subscribe to very different views about their respective roles in the world.

Moreover, the relationship is constrained by the two countries' divergent value systems, in particular their contrasting views of the purposes and means of acceptable state behavior at home and abroad. The ideological antagonism between international communism and capitalism has disappeared, but Russia today sees itself as a great power and the guardian of traditional principles of maintaining the international status quo, absolute sovereignty, and noninterference in the internal affairs of other countries. The United States, by contrast, supports the United Nations' principles of the responsibility to protect, humanitarian intervention, and, if necessary, regime change in cases of violent interstate conflicts or civil wars that threaten populations. It also remains rhetorically committed to global democracy promotion, an increasingly neuralgic issue for Russia.

These contrasting worldviews were a source of conflict during the Balkan wars of the 1990s and they have continued to strain bilateral ties since the beginning of the upheavals in the Arab world in 2010. President Obama's second inaugural speech committed his administration to pursuing these goals. "We will support democracy from Asia to Africa, from the Americas to the Middle East, because our interests and our conscience compel us to act on behalf of those who long for freedom."[7]

Much has changed in the decades since the implosion of the USSR. Russia has become a market economy, albeit with its own specific characteristics—"capitalism Russian-style"—and the Russian people enjoy such liberties as the freedom to travel, to use the Internet, and to express their opinions—up to a point. Yet elections are managed, political opposition discouraged, and the rule of law remains elusive. The Russian political system remains a hybrid, and the evolution away from Soviet society will be the work of many more decades than some in the West originally envisaged. Nevertheless, the United States and Russia, with their nuclear arsenals, no longer face each other as antagonists.

Expectations of and preparations for bilateral conflict that were central to the Cold War have disappeared. In their place has come what one former senior U.S. official describes as a "cranky" relationship, for which both sides bear responsibility. America and Russia no longer are antagonists but they remain antagonistic. Could it have been otherwise? How and why did it evolve like this?

During the time period covered by this book, successive U.S. and Russian administrations have faced six major sets of issues that they have jointly sought to manage. As a result, there has been a great deal of continuity in the substance of U.S.-Russian relations, irrespective of who occupies the White House or the Kremlin. The first basket of issues is the nuclear legacy, involving arms control and missile defense. The second, related basket is nonproliferation of WMD, particularly the question of Iran's nuclear program—as well as that of North Korea. The third relates to Russia's neighborhood and the respective roles of Russia and the United States in what, for want of a better word, is called the post-Soviet space and the territories around it. The fourth involves European security, including the conflicts in the Balkans and Euro-Atlantic security architecture, as well as NATO expansion and the role of the Organization for Security and Cooperation in Europe (OSCE). The fifth, most recent set of issues, relates to Russian and U.S. policies toward the upheavals in the Arab world. The final constant has been Russia's domestic situation, including the wars in Chechnya, instability in the north Caucasus, and the state of democracy and human rights.

This is indeed a long and challenging list of issues that both countries have had to confront. They continue to demand both sides' attention more than two decades after the demise of the USSR. There have been some arms control agreements, but missile defense remains highly problematic. Cooperation on dealing with Iran's nuclear program has improved, but the United States and Russia continue to disagree about the severity of the problem—and the way to resolve it. Russia's neighborhood has diminished as an issue of contention since the 2008 Georgia war, but Washington and Moscow continue to subscribe to very different views of how the post-Soviet states should evolve and what their relationship with Russia should be. There has been little progress on the future of Euro-Atlantic security architecture, although further NATO enlargement appears to be on indefinite hold. Russia's refusal to recognize Kosovo's independence, the suspension of its participation in the Treaty on Conventional Forces in Europe, and the West's reluctance to respond to Russian initiatives proposing a new European Security Treaty have highlighted a basic reality: the United States and its allies failed to devise a post–Cold War framework for including Russia in Euro-Atlantic structures, and thus Russia remains outside of the institutions that regulate European security, charting its own path. Cooperation in dealing with the upheavals in the Arab world remains elusive. And the Kremlin has increasingly rejected U.S. attempts to influence its domestic trajectory and support Russian civil society organizations devoted to improving the rule of law, human rights, and democratic practices.

This book examines both the U.S. and Russian perspectives on the relationship, informed by many discussions with former and current officials. Some of the challenges for U.S. Russia policy are intrinsic to the general problems of U.S. foreign policy, such as dealing with Congress and overcoming bureaucratic stove-piping within the executive branch. They also touch on broader determinants of U.S. foreign policy, such as definitions of the national interest and how to promote American values. Others are more specific to Russia and involve the tension between focusing on interests versus values and determining how much Russia's internal developments should affect U.S. foreign policy decisions and how far American actions in Russia's neighborhood should be calibrated to take into account Russian concerns. In order to tell the story, the book is chronological, except for the chapter on commercial and energy relations, since these are less affected by the policies of different administrations.

At the heart of this limited partnership is the difficult question of how far the United States should allow its policies to be shaped by an acknowledgment of Russia's unique post-Soviet preoccupations and continuing conviction that the United States disregards its interests. Russia does not loom as large in American foreign policy priorities as America does in Russian priorities. Russia is instrumentally important to the United States because of its ability to make it difficult—or easier—for Washington to achieve its goals on a range of international problems.

Its veto power on the United Nations Security Council provides it with a key lever to prevent the United States from taking actions where American and Russian interests diverge. This recognition of the reality that Russia is less important per se than indirectly is a continuing source of irritation to Russian officials. In this sense, the various American resets have represented attempts to engage Russia productively by persuading it to acknowledge and accept the asymmetries in the relationship and move forward on that basis. Putin's 2001 attempted reset, by contrast, was a bid to establish a strategic partnership of equals, acting as if these asymmetries did not exist.

The book is based on work I have done over several decades both as a scholar and as a practitioner. In addition to my years at Georgetown University as professor and director of its Center for Eurasian, Russian and East European Studies, I have served in the State Department's Office of Policy Planning in the Clinton and Bush administrations and as National Intelligence Officer for Russia and Eurasia at the National Intelligence Council. Teaching a course on U.S.-Russian relations at the Moscow State Institute of International Relations (MGIMO) gave me insights into the attitudes of the younger, educated generation toward ties with the United States. My understanding of the views of the Russian leadership has been enhanced by my participation in the Valdai International Discussion Club for the last decade. This has provided a unique opportunity to assess the perceptions of key policymakers and opinion-leaders. In these annual conferences, we have met every year with President Putin for several hours. We have also met with other senior officials and have listened to a variety of views on Russia's domestic and foreign policy. The interpretation of the views of American and Russian officials is, of course, entirely my own.

List of Acronyms

ABM: anti-ballistic missile
APEC: Asian-Pacific Economic Cooperation
BRIC: Brazil, Russia, India, and China
BTC: Baku-Tbilisi-Ceyhan (oil pipeline project)
CFE Treaty: Treaty on Conventional Forces in Europe
CFIUS: Committee on Foreign Investment in the United States
CIA: Central Intelligence Agency
CIS: Commonwealth of Independent States
CSTO: Collective Security Treaty Organization
DEFCON: defense readiness condition
EU: European Union
FBI: Federal Bureau of Investigation
FSB: Federal Security Service
G-7: Group of Seven Countries
G-8: Group of Eight Countries
G-20: Group of Twenty Countries
GDR: German Democratic Republic
GUUAM: Georgia-Ukraine-Uzbekistan-Azerbaijan-Moldova
HEU: highly enriched uranium
IAEA: International Atomic Energy Agency
ICBM: Intercontinental Ballistic Missile
IMEMO: Institute of World Economy and International Relations
IMF: International Monetary Fund
KFOR: Kosovo Force
KGB: Committee on State Security
LDPR: Liberal Democratic Party of Russia
MAP: membership action plan

MD: missile defense
MGIMO: Moscow State Institute of International Relations
NATO: North Atlantic Treaty Organization
NDN: Northern Distribution Network
NGO: nongovernmental organization
NIS: Newly Independent States
NRC: NATO-Russia Council
NSC: National Security Council
ODIHR: Office for Democratic Institutions and Human Rights
OIC: Organization of the Islamic Conference
OSCE: Organization for Security and Cooperation in Europe
OVP: Office of the Vice President
P-5: Five Permanent Members of the United Nations Security Council
PfP: Partnership for Peace
PJC: Permanent Joint Council
PNTR: permanent normal trading relations
PSA: production sharing agreement
SALT: Strategic Arms Limitation Treaty
SORT: Strategic Offensive Reductions Treaty
SS-24: class of Soviet ICBMs
SS-25: class of single-warhead Soviet-designed ICBMs
START: Strategic Arms Reduction Treaty
SVR: Russian Foreign Intelligence Service
UN: United Nations
UNMIK: United Nations Interim Administration Mission in Kosovo
UNSC: United Nations Security Council
USAID: United States Agency for International Development
USSR: Union of Soviet Socialist Republics
WMD: weapons of mass destruction
WTO: World Trade Organization

The Limits of Partnership

Map 1. Russia and Its Neighbors.

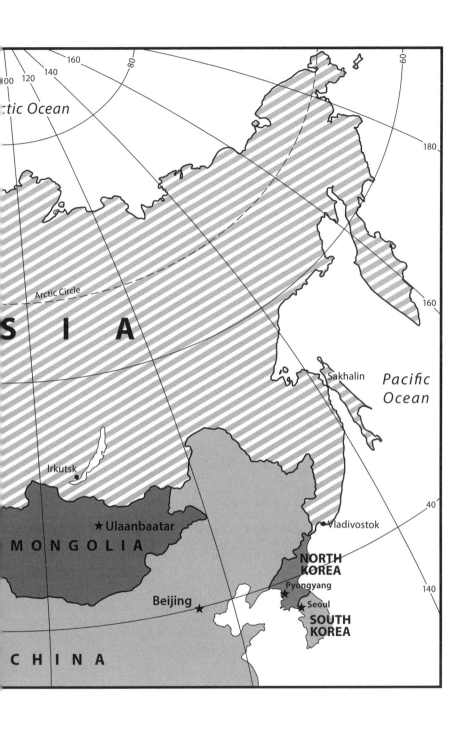

Prologue
George H. W. Bush and Russia Reborn

The Soviet Union ended not with a bang but with a speech. A sober Mikhail Gorbachev appeared on television to announce his resignation—and the end of the USSR—on December 25, 1991. "I hereby discontinue my activities at the post of President of the Union of Soviet Socialist Republics," he said. "There were mistakes made that could have been avoided," he added. He ended his brief speech on an upbeat note: "I am positive that sooner or later, some day our common efforts will bear fruit and our nations will live in a prosperous, democratic society." But he also expressed his worries about the future: "I am concerned about the fact that the people in this country are ceasing to become citizens of a great power and the consequences may be very difficult for us to deal with."[1] Events would prove him prophetic.

As his speech ended, the red hammer-and-sickle Soviet flag was lowered over the Kremlin and the new red, white, and blue Russian tricolor flag was raised. A stunned Soviet population struggled to understand how this could have happened and what life would be like the next day. The 1917 Bolshevik Revolution and the 1991 Soviet collapse bookended a tumultuous century that had seen the rise and fall of some of history's most brutal dictators. Now that both the Cold War and the USSR had ended, and more and more countries were seeking to free themselves from authoritarian rule, how should the international system reconstitute itself to reap the unexpected dividends of the USSR's demise? What did it mean that the United States and Russia no longer would face each other as antagonists whose large stockpiles of nuclear weapons targeted each other? What kind of political system would the new Russia have?

As the outside world began to grapple with the contours of a post-communist world that Christmas day, President George H. W. Bush appeared on television to offer reassurance. Congratulating Gorbachev on having liberated the Soviet people, he officially recognized the Russian Federation as the legal successor to the USSR and described the end of the Soviet Union as "a victory for democracy and freedom, for the moral force of our values." He reassured Americans that the Soviet nuclear weapons were safe and suggested that the events of the day "clearly serve our national interest."[2] "President Bush did not want to antagonize the Russians," said his National Security Advisor Brent Scowcroft. "He emphasized that no one had lost the Cold War, but everyone had won."[3]

COPING WITH THE SOVIET COLLAPSE

Almost three years earlier after coming into office, the Bush administration had begun to consider alternative futures for Russia. Robert Gates, then deputy national security advisor, organized a small high-level group that met regularly in secret to discuss contingency planning for a range of alternative Soviet futures.[4] Moreover, although there were divisions within the intelligence community over the significance of developments within the USSR, some analysts were willing to think the unthinkable—namely that the USSR might actually disappear.[5] U.S. Embassy officials also had inklings of what might happen. One recalls flying to Moscow with Sapurmurad Niyazov, then the communist leader of the Turkmen Republic, at the same time when Gorbachev was trying to negotiate a new union treaty among the fifteen constituent republics of the Soviet Union. "I will never sign this treaty," Niyazov vowed, "I want to control my own oil and gas reserves."[6] Nevertheless, Bush himself was determined not to undermine the embattled Gorbachev.[7] In a speech later dubbed "Chicken Kiev" by critics, Bush warned the Ukrainians to beware of "suicidal nationalism" and said that "Americans will not support those who seek independence in order to replace a far-off tyranny with a local despotism."[8]

U.S.-Russian relations can be understood only in the context of both countries striving to come to terms with the legacy of the Cold War and its aftermath. The United States considered the collapse of the USSR a victory for Western interests and democratic values. But that is not how it was seen by much of the Soviet population. It was difficult for them to accept that the USSR had expired because of its own internal weaknesses. Mikhail Gorbachev had come to power vowing to make the USSR a stronger, more effective global actor, not to preside over its demise. But the economic reforms he introduced were too little, too late, and he was hit hard by the falling price of oil, the USSR's major export commodity, and a neo-Stalinist economic system that was unreformable because the Communist Party feared losing political control.

What ultimately doomed Gorbachev's experiment at greater political openness and economic restructuring (*glasnost'* and *perestroika* as they were known in Russia) was the failure to sustain economic growth and solvency along with the inability to deal with what the Bolsheviks had called the "nationalities question." His attempt to create a federal state that would have devolved real power to the USSR's constituent ethnically based national republics, and which was at the same time acceptable to his more hard-line opponents, failed. In August 1991, disgruntled military and security officials had launched a coup against him. Not only did they want to remove him from power. They also were determined to prevent the signing of a new Union Treaty that would have lessened Moscow's control over its republics. Gorbachev was placed under house arrest in his vacation home in Crimea, while the disheveled putschists held a press conference announcing an emergency committee to save the USSR.

The coup caused considerable consternation in Washington. The administration of George H. W. Bush had developed a good working relationship with Gorbachev for several compelling reasons. He had allowed the Soviet-backed communist governments in Eastern Europe to collapse peacefully, he backed the U.S.-led UN coalition during the first Gulf War to liberate Kuwait from Iraqi occupation, and he supported new U.S.-Soviet arms control efforts. The specter of a group of communists in uniform vowing to put an end to Gorbachev's domestic and foreign policy reforms threatened to revive the worst days of U.S.-Soviet antagonism.

The coup lasted just three days. During those days, the world had its first glimpse of Boris Yeltsin, the newly elected president of the Russian Republic. A provincial party secretary from Siberia, he had initially been a Gorbachev supporter. During the coup, he became the embodiment of resistance to the coup when he stood on top of a tank and read a proclamation defying the putschists. After the coup, Gorbachev was fatally weakened. The Baltic states declared their independence from the USSR, and Yeltsin increasingly challenged Gorbachev's authority and appealed to other republic leaders to follow suit.

The Bush administration was divided over whether to continue supporting Gorbachev or to back Yeltsin. In September 1989, Yeltsin had made his first trip to the United States and made a negative impression on both General Scowcroft and his Russia advisor, Condoleezza Rice. When Yeltsin found out that he would not have an official meeting with President Bush, he initially refused to get out of his car. He only reluctantly agreed to enter the White House's West Wing where Scowcroft sat after it was made clear that protocol did not warrant a meeting with the president. Notwithstanding, George H. W. Bush did a "drop by" with him in Scowcroft's office.[9] At that juncture, the White House viewed Yeltsin as an unpredictable, populist challenger who threatened to unravel much of what Gorbachev was trying to accomplish. By 1991, Bush and Secretary of State James Baker still supported Gorbachev, while Secretary of Defense Dick Cheney led the group that favored Yeltsin and viewed him as a genuine democrat.[10]

After the failure of the coup, Gorbachev was no longer able to assert his authority over the leaders of the individual republics—led by Boris Yeltsin—who wanted independence. He recognized the independence of the three Baltic states in September 1991 (the United States had never recognized their incorporation into the USSR, and from Washington's perspective they were henceforth not counted as "post-Soviet" states). On December 8, 1991, Yeltsin met with the Ukrainian leader

Leonid Kravchuk and Belarussian leader Stanislau Shushkevich in a hunting lodge in the Belovezhskaya Pushcha, a nature reserve outside the city of Brest on the Belarus-Polish border. After a long night of wrangling and libations, they proclaimed the creation of a new entity, the Commonwealth of Independent States (CIS), a paper entity with hazy legal standing that was intended to render the USSR obsolete. It was all over. Gorbachev had lost his country. His resignation came just two and a half weeks later.

By the time that Gorbachev announced his resignation, each of the twelve remaining republics of the USSR had become independent states, although some—particularly in Central Asia—had independence thrust on them rather than choosing it. The impact of the Soviet collapse on U.S. decision makers varied. "I felt a tremendous charge as I watched the final breakup of the Soviet Union," Bush later wrote. "I was pleased to watch freedom and self-determination prevail as one republic after another gained its independence."[11] Robert Gates, by then director of the Central Intelligence Agency, had a different take. Explaining that "the Cold War itself had been waged in shades of grey," it was unclear what the end of the Cold War meant for the United States. Moreover, a host of domestic problems now demanded the attention of the Bush administration. "And so," said Gates, "the greatest of American triumphs—became a particularly joyless victory. We had won the Cold War, but there would be no parade."[12]

The interpretation of how the Cold War ended is still hotly disputed in Russia. Many find it hard to accept that the world's second-largest superpower could have imploded in this way. They suspect that outside agency—primarily the United States—deliberately caused the Soviet collapse. These views have been passed on to the post-Soviet generation, which came of age after the demise of the USSR.[13] If the USSR was not responsible for its collapse, and was not defeated in a war, then it follows that Russia should rightly be restored to its former world role. Of course, all imperial powers have had difficulty coming to terms with the loss of empire. In the twentieth century alone, the tsarist, Ottoman, Austro-Hungarian, British, and French empires came to an end, necessitating major adjustments—albeit very different ones—on the part of the former imperial powers to their reduced international status and their definitions of national identity. There were also major adjustments for the new successor states that had gained statehood, some for the first time in history. The demise of the USSR was bound to present major challenges to the international system. There was no road map for how to deal with this unprecedented situation. In the face of uncertainty and in the absence of institutions to guide this transition, improvisation prevailed in both Moscow and Washington.

The Soviet Union was not defeated in a war; it perished from self-inflicted wounds. How, many asked, did this vast multinational state, a nuclear superpower, which despite its precarious economic situation still possessed enormous natural resource wealth, just disintegrate, literally petering out? Russia's domestic and foreign policy adjustment to its reduced status has, therefore, been more complicated—albeit less violent—than that of the other twentieth-century former empires. Its continuing role as a nuclear superpower—despite its economic weakness—made that transition away from empire more complex. After all, unlike other fallen empires. it still had the military capability to destroy its former antagonist, the United States.

Very few people in the United States—or in Russia, for that matter—anticipated the collapse of the Soviet empire in Eastern Europe or of the USSR. Indeed, as late as 1988 West German chancellor Helmut Kohl believed that he would not live to see Germany reunified.[14] Once the Soviet Union had imploded, Washington struggled to chart a course for dealing with the new Russia and defining American interests in the post-Soviet space.[15]

Moreover, most Western leaders were ambivalent about the disintegration of the USSR. They felt comfortable with a reformist Soviet leader who wanted to move beyond the Cold War. The USSR had cooperated with the Coalition partners during the Gulf War—against its erstwhile ally Saddam Hussein—largely as a result of the Bush administration's artful diplomacy. But there were other reasons to fear a Soviet collapse. Eastern Europe may have overthrown communism peacefully but, as the Soviet Union headed toward dissolution, Yugoslavia had descended into a brutal civil war as its constituent republics declared their independence. The United States and its European allies feared a repetition of the Yugoslav debacle in the former Soviet Union on a far larger scale, involving widespread ethnic violence in a nuclear-armed country spanning twelve time zones. They preferred to deal with Mikhail Gorbachev, the reformist Soviet leader they knew and, by 1991, trusted, and they feared what would happen if the Soviet Union were to fall apart.

A MODEST RESET

In 1992 the White House had to reinvent the U.S.-Russian relationship, with little to guide it from the Cold War era. The Bush administration was careful to react cautiously to the Soviet collapse, eschewing any public triumphal rhetoric. Washington understood that it had to treat Russia with respect during this difficult transition. The administration followed the same policy as it had when the Berlin Wall fell in November 1989, seeking not to exacerbate Russian sensitivities at a time when there was great uncertainty about what would happen next. In place of the familiar Soviet antagonist came fifteen new states, mostly with new borders, and Russia itself was geographically smaller than it had been since the seventeenth century. All of these new states were grappling to understand the new reality and define how they should proceed. A huge and ailing society had thrown off seven decades of communism almost serendipitously, but it was unclear how this vast space would develop. There was no consensus in Washington about what U.S. goals toward a postcommunist Russia should be. One Bush official recalled that "dealing with a wounded rival was just as complex as dealing with a strutting one."[16]

Nevertheless, perhaps because it was an election year and domestic issues took priority, the Bush administration did not embark on a major reevaluation of its relations with post-Soviet Russia. It focused on the most pressing issues—nuclear weapons and economic assistance—but eschewed bold initiatives. In the election year of 1992, there was scant appetite for new policies and considerable apprehension about what could go wrong in the post-Soviet space. Secretary of State James Baker, in an important gesture, insisted on opening embassies in all twelve post-Soviet states—over the objections of much of the State Department's European bureau—to stress the United States' commitment to their continued independence.

The new Russian government immediately came under siege from its opponents. Boris Yeltsin and his team of young market reformers were bitterly opposed by communists and other groups in the Congress of Peoples' Deputies, who dismissed the new team as "boys in pink shorts."[17] Bush's first summit with Yeltsin took place at Camp David on February 1, 1992. Given the previous skepticism on the part of some administration officials about Yeltsin this was a crucial meeting. Yeltsin's advisor subsequently admitted that the Russian president had rehearsed for two or three days for what the realized was his "big exam."[18] He apparently passed with flying colors and managed to convince the skeptics that he was, indeed, capable of leading the new Russia. Bush's colleagues soon concluded that the fate of Russian reform depended on one man—Boris Yeltsin. As one administration official said at the time, "The only alternative to Yeltsin is Stalin—and authoritarian regimes."[19]

Throughout the 1990s there was one mantra in Washington: without Yeltsin the communists would return, and that would be a catastrophe. In the absence of established frameworks between the United States and the new Russia, there was a certain amount of improvisation as both sides contemplated how to institutionalize the relationship. An early example of this was the disposition of the USSR's permanent seat on the United Nations Security Council. It was not clear who would inherit this seat that went back to the founding of the UN in 1945. The Russians with some consternation turned for advice to Richard Gardner, an American professor of international law, who explained to them why legally Russia should be designated the heir of the Soviet Union. His counsel was instrumental in ensuring that Russia indeed took over the USSR's permanent seat. Nevertheless, because there was sufficient ambiguity about whether Russia indeed was the legal heir, the transfer was carried out inconspicuously over a weekend, when the name plate "USSR" over the Soviet seat on the Security Council was replaced with "Russia."[20] Thus, Russia then became the legatee to the USSR and inherited its embassies, its ministries—and its debts.

The U.S.-Russian agenda in 1992 was limited. President George H. W. Bush and his key advisors—General Scowcroft and Secretary Baker—were realists who generally viewed foreign policy through the prism of U.S. interests rather than values. Exporting democracy was not a priority for them in these early post–Cold War days. They also realized that it was important not to humiliate Russia in its weakened state.

SECURING THE NUCLEAR WEAPONS

Washington's most urgent concern in 1992 was the fate of the Soviet nuclear, chemical, and biological weapons arsenal. The USSR had more than eleven thousand strategic nuclear weapons (capable of striking the continental United States) and at least fifteen thousand tactical or battlefield nuclear weapons.[21] Who would inherit them? Who might steal them? Where would they end up? And how might they be used? There were two dimensions to this challenge—dealing with Russia's own nuclear arsenal and denuclearizing the non-Russian post-Soviet states. In place of one nuclear country, there were now four nuclear states—Russia, Belarus, Ukraine, and Kazakhstan. Overnight Ukraine, which had existed as a state for only two brief periods in history, had become the world's third largest nuclear power. Washington's biggest nightmare was the possibility of a threefold nuclear hemorrhage: unemployed Soviet nuclear scientists selling their services to states or non-state actors seeking to acquire their own nuclear arsenal; the theft of nuclear materials insufficiently secured in Soviet facilities that could also be sold to the highest bidder; and illicit technology transfer.

Administration officials worked hard to tackle these three dangers. The first challenge was to ensure that only Russia remained a nuclear state. In May 1992, James Baker—after three months of hectic diplomatic activity—and the foreign ministers of Russia, Ukraine, Kazakhstan, and Belarus signed the Lisbon Strategic Arms Reduction Treaty (START) protocols, which the United States and the USSR had originally signed in July 1991. These stipulated that the non-Russian states would become nonnuclear "in the shortest possible time" and accede to the nuclear Nonproliferation Treaty. Baker also proposed that the United States and Russia commit to drastically reducing the number of strategic nuclear weapons they both possessed.

After the Lisbon treaty, the second major achievement during the Bush administration was the Nunn-Lugar program, whose importance has not subsequently been fully recognized. It was a historic accomplishment and rare example of true bipartisan cooperation. Senator Richard Lugar had been committed to reducing the danger of nuclear war since his time as mayor of Indianapolis when, he observed, he realized that the city would have been a target in a Soviet nuclear strike on the United States.[22]

In November 1991, just before the Soviet collapse, Senators Lugar and Sam Nunn authored the Nunn-Lugar Act, establishing the Co-operative Threat Reduction Program funded by $1.27 billion from the Department of Defense. President Bush signed it into law on December 1991. This innovative program, in the words of Senator Nunn, was "designed to help the states of the former Soviet Union handle responsibly weapons of mass destruction."[23] Its main goals were to secure nuclear materials, providing assistance to the former Soviet states to safeguard and dismantle their stockpiles of nuclear, chemical, and biological weapons, as well as related materials and delivery systems. It also supported retraining unemployed scientists and their families living in formerly closed nuclear cities so that they could find gainful employment elsewhere, as opposed to selling their know-how to states seeking to acquire nuclear materials. This program played an important role in diminishing the post-Soviet threat from "loose nukes."[24]

A major challenge, however, was to create a constituency within Russia that believed that securing its own nuclear weapons and facilities would be in its own self-interest. Frustrated by the slow pace of the American interagency process in advancing the agenda, White House officials not only reached out to the Russian government but also promoted cooperation between American and Russian nuclear laboratories.[25] The Bush administration simultaneously began the process of denuclearizing Ukraine and Kazakhstan.

ECONOMIC ASSISTANCE: NO NEW MARSHALL PLAN

The administration of George H. W. Bush has been criticized by some inside and outside of the government for not doing enough to help post-communist Russia as it struggled to get back on its feet. Yegor Gaidar described what it was like to wake up on January 1, 1992, in the new

Russia: "Everything was in in a terrible, unbelievable mess, he said, "We had no money, no gold, and no grain to last through the next harvest—It was like traveling in a jet and you go into the cockpit and you discover that there's no one at the controls."[26] Advocates for more robust assistance invoked the U.S. post World War Two experience. In 1947 Secretary of State George Marshall announced the Marshall Plan, a $13 billion program to aid the recovery of Western Europe states struggling to rebuild their shattered postwar economies after a particularly bitter postwar winter. The fear was that, without aid, communists would come to power in France, Italy, and possibly elsewhere. Marshall aid was crucial in ensuring the future prosperity—and political stability—of Western Europe. As the Soviet Union was disintegrating, Russia's economic situation became increasingly precarious. Some Americans argued that the United States should follow the precedent of 1947 and offer a substantial aid package to help Russia move definitively away from communism.[27]

This debate became part of the election campaign. In 1992 Bush came under pressure from the candidate Bill Clinton's campaign to put together a robust aid package for Russia, whose economy was reeling from the collapse and where there was concern about possible starvation during the harsh winter. Former president Richard Nixon, in an unusual alignment with Clinton, urged Bush to do more for Russia.[28] In a March 1992 "secret" memo entitled "How to Lose the Cold War" he warned that the volume of U.S. assistance to Russia was "a pathetically inadequate response."[29] Brent Scowcroft believes that the United States should have given more assistance but attributes the modest level of support to severe U.S. budgetary constraints.[30] Richard Armitage, who became the first coordinator for aid to the former Soviet Union, also argues that the United States should have been more generous in its assistance package. But the Congress was reluctant to allocate more than the $480 million initially promised.[31] In Operation Provide Hope, the United States provided food aid and medicines for sixty-two cities. But it rejected the idea of a Marshall plan for Russia and limited its involvement in assistance programs.[32]

This caution about Russia also affected the Bush administration's policies on democracy promotion. Armitage recalls asking German officials how long they believed Russia's transition would take. Their answer: it will take East Germany at least forty years, so it will probably take Russia at least seventy years.[33] Even if some American officials feared the return of communism, there was no commitment to reshaping Russian society. There was relief at the dogs that did not bark—no Yugoslav-type large-scale civil war or ethnic cleansing, no mass starvation, no economic collapse, no nuclear conflict between Ukraine and Russia—but Washington pursued a policy of restraint. In an election year, the White House's attention was focused elsewhere.

Nevertheless, the Bush administration did take some substantive steps. In 1992 it convened an international conference on assistance to Russia, which announced a multilateral aid package of $24 billion, and it hosted three other donor conferences. However, much of what was promised never materialized. Anatoly Chubais, one of Yeltsin's key advisors, argues that, had this $24 billion reached Russia, it would have had a significant impact on Russia and on improving U.S.-Russian relations: "This is a sad story. The United States missed a chance."[34] Congress did pass the Freedom Support Act to provide funds for democratizing efforts. And the United States created the North Atlantic Cooperation Council (a NATO-led forum that included all the postcommunist states) and introduced a proposal for a START-II nuclear arms reduction treaty. But there was scant public rhetoric about prospects for fundamental change in Russia, and expectations for how much could change were modest.

The cautious Russia policy of George H. W. Bush differed from that of both the subsequent Clinton and George W. Bush administrations. Their rhetorical commitment to improving U.S.-Russian relations and support of major policy initiatives raised expectations about the possibility of qualitative changes—expectations that would eventually not be met.

Chapter One
The Bill and Boris Show

Shortly before taking the oath of office in January 1993, Bill Clinton declared that what was happening in Russia was "the biggest and toughest thing out there. It's not just the end of communism, the end of the cold war. That's what's over and done with. There's also stuff *starting*–stuff that's *new*. Figuring out what it is, how we work with it, how we keep it moving in the right direction: that's what we've got to do."[1] Indeed, the challenge of supporting Russia's postcommunist transition and defining its new international role consumed much of the Clinton administration's foreign policy energy during its eight years in office. Along the way, the intense and often turbulent personal ties between the American and Russian presidents came to define U.S.-Russian ties.

The Clinton administration initially raised high expectations about re-creating the U.S.-Russian relationship in what became the second—and more ambitious—reset since the Soviet collapse. By the end of Clinton's two terms, however, these expectations had not been met. They probably could never have been. It became clear that the relationship was, at best, a selective partnership, where cooperation and competition coexisted, albeit in fluctuating proportions. Whatever happened, Russia would not evolve as a Western-style democracy, and American influence on Russia's internal evolution would be circumscribed.

The bilateral framework that was established in these years has in many ways defined how Washington and Moscow have dealt with each other ever since then, in both process and substance. Many of the issues over which Clinton and Yeltsin sparred remain problematic today. Indeed, there has been far more continuity in U.S.-Russian relations over the past two decades than either Democrats or Republicans might admit. That is because, as an official who served in the administrations of Bush 41 and 43 noted, "You can't choose your inbox."[2]

Nevertheless, the outcome of Clinton's policies is still hotly debated. Did the Clinton administration play a major role in bringing democracy and the market to Russia? Or did it, as the Republicans (supported by some on the left) claimed in 2000, "fail the Russian people" and turn a blind eye as the system became increasingly corrupt? Should Washington have promoted less "shock" and more "therapy" for the economy, as Clinton's chief Russia advisor and former deputy secretary of state Strobe Talbott himself at one point suggested? Was it right to enlarge NATO to include Russia's former Warsaw Pact allies and the Baltic states? Should the United States have focused instead on designing a post–Cold War Euro-Atlantic security system that included Russia? Could that have even been done?

"THE RUSSIA HAND"

Bill Clinton seized the unique opportunity to reshape the landscape of U.S.-Russian relations when he entered the White House. It became one of the defining themes of his eight years in office, a relationship beset by constant challenges, yet one in which, despite all the controversy, there were notable achievements. As Strobe Talbott writes, the president quickly became "the U.S. government's principal Russia hand" and remained so for the rest of his presidency.[3] Clinton appointed a team of expert advisors on Russia led by his Rhodes Scholar roommate Talbott, whose knowledge of Russia and its culture was extensive—and to whom Clinton had served tea in their Oxford digs while Talbott was translating the memoirs of Soviet leader Nikita Khrushchev.[4] Talbott persuaded the secretary of state–designate, Warren Christopher, to create a special office that dealt with the post-Soviet states (minus the Baltics) in order to ensure that they received the attention they needed, and he became the first ambassador-at-large for the Newly Independent States (S/NIS).[5] Previously, the Soviet Union had been part of the State Department's European Bureau.

Moreover, the new administration came into office promoting a liberal-internationalist view of foreign policy, one that held that the more democracies there were, the safer the world would be. This required an active U.S. commitment to influencing Russia's domestic transformation. The Clinton administration adopted a far more interventionist policy than did the preceding Bush administration because it believed that Russia's domestic democratic evolution was a prerequisite for a more benign foreign policy. In a 1993 speech on Russia at the Naval Academy in Annapolis, Clinton set out the basic premise. He called for a "strategic alliance with Russian reform," warning that "the danger is clear if Russia's reforms turn sour—if it reverts to authoritarianism or disintegrates into chaos. The world cannot afford the strife of the former Yugoslavia replicated in a nation as big as Russia, spanning eleven time zones with an armed arsenal of nuclear weapons."[6]

The defining idea behind the Clinton policy was that democracies do not go to war with each other. Hence it was imperative for the United States to do as much as it could to nurture the growth of Russian democracy. Moreover, economic and political liberties are inextricably linked, and a market society based on private property would ultimately produce a more democratic polity. The third premise was that the West should promote an American market-oriented economic model, as opposed to a European social democratic one (a view shared by economic liberals in Yeltsin's government). That meant that Russia should move rapidly toward privatization of the economy, greatly reducing the government's role. The Clinton administration believed that the return to power of the communists was the major danger threatening Russia's successful transformation—hence the unquestioning support for Boris Yeltsin, irrespective of his idiosyncrasies.

One issue stood out ahead of all the others. The White House understood that the greatest security danger remained Russia's large arsenal of nuclear weapons and weapons of mass destruction (WMD) materials not under the full control of the central authorities and vulnerable to theft and sale to rogue nations. Hence Washington had to focus on enhancing the Bush administration's nuclear nonproliferation programs and the Nunn-Lugar initiatives. The Clinton administration was committed to supporting continuing sovereignty and independence of the post-Soviet states and encouraging Moscow to move toward a post-imperial foreign policy. Finally, it recognized that it had to offer Russia incentives to accept its diminished international role. The United States led the West in offering Russia some of the trappings of a major power, including association with the G-7—the group of major industrialized nations—along with membership in what became the G-8, and later a partnership with NATO.

Yet Washington may well have overestimated how much influence the United States could have on Russia's economic development. The Clinton economic team supported a prescription for Russia macroeconomic stabilization based on shock therapy, a policy favored by Yelstin's chief economic advisor Yegor Gaidar and his small group of liberal reformers, who believed that a gradual road to capitalism was impossible in Russia's unique circumstances of total state ownership.[7] "We had no money, no gold, and no grain to last through the next harvest," said Gaidar, "It was a time when you do everything you can do, and as rapidly as you can. There was no time for reflection."[8] Yet Russian-style capitalism turned out to be very different from what the American team envisaged.[9] It became apparent as the decade wore on that Russia was developing a form of "Wild East" capitalism that was sui generis, opaque, and involved levels of corruption and patronage unanticipated by Washington. Some American critics have accused the Clinton administration of knowingly aiding and abetting the rise of a form of capitalism that left most Russians impoverished, while a few corrupt oligarchs became stunningly wealthy.[10] However, these charges vastly overestimate the impact of outside agents in determining the unique way in which the Russian economy developed.

Underpinning the Clinton administration's philosophy was a belief in the possibility of a large-scale transformation of Russian society. It was a belief that contradicted much of the Russian and Soviet historical record. For a millennium, Russia had been ruled by men, not laws.

Individuals were always more important than institutions, and informal mechanisms were more important than official structures. Historians of Russia—be they Russian or Western—pointed to centuries of authoritarian rule by competing clans who paid obeisance to an all-powerful tsar or Soviet general secretary, even if at some periods the ruler's powers were more virtual than real and groups around the ruler wielded considerable influence.[11] The tsarist patrimonial state, where the aristocracy was dependent on the ruler's goodwill to maintain its status and property, was replaced by a Soviet patrimonial state, where the Communist Party was in charge of patronage. In neither system were property rights or the rule of law much respected—or even recognized.

The Russia experts in the Clinton administration understood well these persistent factors in Russian history. But they thought that the Soviet collapse offered an opportunity to break with these traditions and to modernize Russia in a democratic way-- for the first time in its history. Given the cycles of the American political system, their time horizon was short—particularly when viewed through the prism of Russian history. They had, at best, eight years to help encourage the beginning of a radical transformation in Russia. Even if they recognized that this was a major challenge, without a bold vision and dogged persistence, they might have accomplished much less.

NEW VISTAS FROM WASHINGTON AND MOSCOW

The greatest successes of the Clinton reset, from an American point of view, were in foreign policy: denuclearizing Ukraine, Belarus, and Kazakhstan, securing Russia's cooperation in the Balkans(albeit at considerable cost in Kosovo), neutralizing Russian opposition to NATO enlargement, and bringing Russia into the G-7 as a stakeholder. Iran remained a significant area of disagreement. But all of the successes were on issues where Washington had persuaded Moscow to take actions it initially resisted.

One of the Clinton administration's first challenges was to tackle the stakeholder problem. The number of American stakeholders in the U.S.-Russian relationship has always been limited—unlike the situation with

China—in part because the bilateral economic relationship was very modest. In the more than two decades since the collapse of communism, there have rarely been substantial groups on either side who have consistently pressed for improved relations. This contrasts sharply with the European relationship with Russia, where the number of stakeholders in Western Europe and Russia rapidly grew during the 1990s because of their burgeoning economic relations. Early in its tenure, the Clinton administration came up with an idea about how to build a group of stakeholders. In 1993 it established a binational commission cochaired by the U.S. vice president Al Gore and the Russian prime minister Viktor Chernomyrdin. The idea initially came from Russian foreign minister Andrei Kozyrev, who saw it as a way to create a more organized interagency process on the Russian side.[12] This binational commission, which lasted until George W. Bush came into office and was subsequently reincarnated under Barack Obama, set up working groups that dealt with a range of issues—including space, energy, and economics—and was designed to create networks of officials that ensured a continuing dialogue and had a vested interest in the success of the relationship.

Another challenge for America and Russia in the 1990s was dealing with their different visions of the post-Soviet space. The United States consistently supported the independence and sovereignty of the countries in the area that, for the first decade, it referred to as the Newly Independent States. It refused to recognize the Commonwealth of Independent States because it viewed the organization as a Russian attempt to continue to exercise undue influence in its neighborhood. Immediately after the Soviet collapse, as already noted, it dispatched officials to open embassies in every new state, which no other Western country had the resources to do. Because a number of these countries had had independence thrust upon them, they were eager for advice on how to set up their own constitutions and solicited American assistance.[13] The United States insisted that Russia had no right to a sphere of influence in the post-Soviet space. The Russian view, even during the early 1990s, was that these countries were part of what they dubbed the "near abroad," as opposed to real foreign countries that constituted the "far abroad," and that Russia had the right to a special relationship with them. In January 1993 Vladimir Lukin, the first post-Soviet ambassador to the United States, said that relations between Russia and the former Soviet states "should be treated as identical to those between New York and New Jersey."[14]

But Washington also remained preoccupied by what would happen inside Russia, from nuclear weapons to a democratic transition, to the risk of violence or starvation. So Clinton focused on cultivating his relationship with Yeltsin. Personal ties between Russian and American leaders have always been disproportionately important, given the existential challenges that the two nuclear superpowers faced and because of the absence of strong institutional ties between the countries. But the Yeltsin-Clinton relationship acquired an intensity and significance all its own, in part because of the outsize personalities of the two men. Yet what comes through in the pages of their autobiographies is that Clinton left office with a more positive view of his Russian counterpart than vice versa—perhaps inevitably, given the disparity in the power and influence of the two countries. "Yeltsin had complicated feelings toward the United States," says one senior Yeltsin-era official, "that were a product of the Soviet times."[15] Clinton said he felt "more confidence in Yeltsin" after their first official meeting in Vancouver in April 1993. "I liked him. He was a big bear of a man, full of contradictions—Compared with the realistic alternatives, Russia was lucky to have him at the helm."[16]

Individuals inevitably interpret other peoples' behavior and motivations through the prism of their own experiences. Clinton often dealt with Yeltsin—particularly in the most difficult moments—by interpreting Yeltsin's actions through the prism of his own stepfather's alcoholism, comparing his relationship with Yeltsin favorably to the one he had with his stepfather.[17] While his willingness to humor Yeltsin no doubt succeeded in avoiding several major showdowns, he may also have underestimated other factors that lay behind Yeltsin's often unpredictable behavior, including the competing domestic political pressures that the Russian president faced. Clinton's concluding assessment of Yeltsin is generous: "For all his physical problems and occasional unpredictability, he had been a courageous and visionary leader. We trusted each other and had accomplished a lot together."[18]

Yeltsin's assessment of Clinton is less fulsome. "Bill Clinton is a notable figure in U.S. history," he writes, admitting that when he first met him, "I was completely amazed by this young, eternally smiling man who was powerful, energetic, and handsome."[19] His chief bodyguard and drinking companion Alexander Korzhakov reports that Yeltsin saw Clinton as a younger brother.[20] He viewed Clinton's struggles with the Congress over his relationship with Monica Lewinsky and his impeachment through the prism of his own struggles with the Duma (the Russian parliament), which likewise tried to impeach him. Indeed, he claims that his intelligence services reported as early as 1996 that the Republicans planned to plant a beautiful young woman in the White House to seduce Clinton and then create a scandal that would depose him—a piece of information that Yeltsin says he decided not to share with Clinton. Nevertheless, as he became increasingly embattled domestically, Yeltsin became more estranged from the United States. By the end of his presidency, he felt betrayed by the Clinton administration because of its bombing campaign against Serbia during the Kosovo war, its enlargement of NATO, and its treatment of Russia—in Moscow's eyes, as a defeated power rather than as an equal.[21] Western observers today often attribute the Russian narrative about condescending and unequal treatment by the United States to Vladimir Putin. But the complaints originated in the Yeltsin era, and indeed with Yeltsin himself, and were widespread by the end of his tenure in office.

KEEPING YELTSIN IN POWER

In the 1990s, Washington believed that, for all his shortcomings, Yeltsin was the leader whom the United States had to support to prevent the return of a Soviet-style regime that could jeopardize U.S. interests and international stability. Almost as soon as he came to power and began to introduce sweeping market reforms, the new Russian president was challenged by a range of opponents, including communists and far-right nationalists. The first major crisis came in the fall of 1993. Yeltsin and the Soviet-era legislature were on a collision course over Yeltsin's proposed economic reforms and the constitutional future of Russia. Yeltsin had promised more far-reaching privatization moves, and he had convened a Constitutional Conference to draft a post-Soviet constitution. His policies came under increasing attack from his own vice president—former Afghan War veteran Colonel Alexander Rutskoi—and the speaker of the Congress of People's Deputies, Ruslan Khasbulatov. On September 21, Yeltsin threw down the gauntlet and issued a decree dissolving the legislature. In retaliation the Congress declared Yeltsin unfit to govern and appointed Rutskoi as president. Meanwhile, the rebels were arming themselves inside the parliament building. Unable to reach a compromise with the parliament, Yeltsin ordered the military to begin an assault on the rebellious deputies, including the shelling of the parliament building on October 3, 1993. This was the first—and only-- serious outbreak of violence in the capital since the Soviet collapse. At least 147 people died in the assault.

The United States backed Yeltsin in his struggle with the Congress of People's Deputies. As the standoff continued in the streets of Moscow, Clinton told reporters that it was clear that Yeltsin had "bent over backwards" not to use force. Clinton called the Russian leader with a message of support once the rebels had surrendered.[22] European leaders similarly supported Yeltsin. For many reform-minded Russians, the events of October 1993 represented a sobering watershed in the brief history of postcommunist Russia. "We had no alternative but to back Yeltsin," said Thomas Pickering, then U.S. ambassador to Russia, "This was the unfinished business of the August 1991 coup and the parliament had exceeded its bounds in many radical revisions of the constitution against Yeltsin."[23] Liberal Russian critics did not see it that way. The shelling of the parliament, writes Lilia Shevtsova, "destroyed the taboo against the use of force by the government. Neither Gorbachev nor the instigators of the 1991 coup attempt had dared to bring about such a fierce confrontation for fear of its unpredictable and irremediable consequences."[24]

Two months later, there came another shock—the first post-Soviet election of the Duma—when a virtually unknown far-right politician, Vladimir Zhirinovsky, and his woefully misnamed Liberal Democratic Party garnered 23 percent of the vote (to the Communists' 12.4 percent). It was, said Secretary of State Warren Christopher, a "wake-up call," highlighting the risks and reality of Yeltsin's Russia. The economy had recovered somewhat since the Soviet collapse, but for the majority of Russian citizens, the economic and social situation was very difficult.

Yeltsin's group of young reformers led by Anatoly Chubais had introduced a voucher privatization scheme, in a bid to prevent a return to communism, whereby workers were given vouchers in the enterprises in which they worked and were encouraged to sell them for cash. This scheme had enabled a relatively few beneficiaries to embark on the road to riches but had not brought a higher living standard to the majority of the Russian people. The 1994 Russian military incursion into Chechnya—the north Caucasus republic that had declared its independence from Moscow—and the constant struggles between the Kremlin and the Duma intensified opposition to Yeltsin and his advisors. The shocks were not over. In the 1995 Duma elections, the communists doubled their support, garnering 22 percent of the vote and the LDP received 11 percent.

Yeltsin was now facing challenges on the left and the right. As his physical condition—a result of a variety of maladies, including alcoholism and heart problems—deteriorated in 1995, the Clinton administration faced the prospect that the 1996 presidential election might do what had seemed unthinkable—return the Communist Party under Gennady Zyuganov to power. Yeltsin's poll numbers were in the single digits and the situation appeared perilous. In response, the United States led the move to secure a $10.2 billion loan from the IMF to the Russian Federation, to bolster the economy and support the Yeltsin government. As Clinton told Talbott, "I want this guy to win so bad it hurts."[25]

Yeltsin had other ardent supporters, namely the winners from privatization—Russia's new multimillionaires and natural resource billionaires, collectively known as the oligarchs. In February 1996, a group of the wealthiest oligarchs met on the sidelines of the World Economic Forum in the Alpine ski resort at Davos. They had just heard the communist leader Zyuganov tell those assembled in Davos that he was a "man of peace" who would not undertake wholesale renationalization of property were he to win. They saw with alarm how the Western media and entrepreneurs were fawning over him. They recognized that a return to power of the communists would not only turn the clock back but would also be disastrous for them—it could lead to expropriation, imprisonment, or worse—and they had to ensure that Yeltsin won. Otherwise they could lose everything.

Although several of them had previously clashed in their business dealings, they decided to band together for their own survival. Burying the hatchet, the two most powerful—Boris Berezovsky and Vladimir Gusinsky—devised a scheme for ensuring that Yeltsin won the election. The so-called Davos Pact—which eventually included the top oligarchs—involved raising money to finance Yeltsin's election campaign. The oligarchs also agreed to extend the loans-for-shares scheme by which Russian business provided substantial amounts of money to the Kremlin in return for the acquisition at bargain-basement prices of key strategic economic assets in the energy and minerals fields. The Russian government still owned these assets, and once they were sold, they created a new class of billionaires.[26] The Kremlin used the money for direct campaign expenses and for social spending, particularly paying pensions and wages that were in arrears. The Clinton administration was subsequently criticized for supporting a nontransparent, lucrative scheme that enhanced the economic and political power of the oligarchs and fostered the development of corruption in Russia. Yet administration officials were not party to these negotiations. Nevertheless, Talbott says, "We were enablers. We should have tried harder, working with Yeltsin and his key advisors to try find some way to get him re-elected without giving the oligarchs free rein over the economy."[27] The loans-for-shares project was designed in Russia and unique to Russia's particular situation, where the state still controlled the commanding heights of Russia's strategic assets and where the outside world had only a limited view into the inner workings of the opaque political system.

During the campaign, unbeknownst to most Washington officials, a team of American consultants connected with Dick Morris, a political consultant who was working in the White House on Clinton's election campaign, was brought to Moscow to advise the Yeltsin team—primarily his daughter and chief advisor Tatiana Dyachenko—on how to win an election campaign.[28] In 1996, after persistent rumors that he was being urged to cancel the elections, Yeltsin campaigned aggressively on the advice of his American consultants. He went from a single-digit popularity rating to winning the presidential election in the second round against Zyuganov. He did this partly by co-opting one of his rivals, General Alexander Lebed, and partly because, in the end, Russian citizens appear to have believed that Yeltsin represented the lesser of two evils. There is considerable debate about whether this was indeed a free and fair election, but the Clinton administration collectively heaved a sigh of relief when he was declared the victor—despite the fact that he had suffered a serious heart attack in between the two election rounds.

But the cost to the president had been high. Although they kept it quiet, the fact was that after 1996, Yeltsin never really recovered physically, and his rule became more erratic and controversial domestically. By 1997 the economy had recovered, but then in 1998 the full force of the Asian financial crisis had a devastatingly contagious effect on what had appeared to be Russia's postelection "economic miracle." The ruble collapsed in August 1998, causing great economic hardship for struggling Russians, many of whom lost all their savings. They remember the 1990s as a time of great hardship.

WASHINGTON'S RUSSIAN INTERLOCUTORS

The new Russian leadership faced a major foreign policy challenge—defining Russia's postcommunist identity and interests and devising effective means of successfully pursuing them. But what precisely were those interests? The Yeltsin administration never succeeded in creating a consensus on national identity or national interests, and it vacillated between cooperation and confrontation with the West. Initially it looked as if cooperation would prevail. Clinton administration officials believed that Yeltsin made most foreign policy decisions himself. *Tsarstvuiu* (I reign supreme) was the verb he liked to use.[29] Yeltsin's first foreign minister, Andrei Kozyrev, was a forty-one-year-old ex-Soviet diplomat. He articulated his views early on: "Our choice is . . . to progress according to generally accepted rules. They were invented by the West, and I'm a Westernizer in this respect—the West is rich and we need to be friends with it—It's the club of first-rate states Russia must rightfully belong to."[30] Kozyrev was pragmatic and understood that Russia's interests lay in integrating itself into Euro-Atlantic institutions. His deputy, Yuri Mamedov, was "a solid interlocutor" for American officials.[31] Yet Kozyrev soon came under attack from more traditional officials and pundits who accused him of not standing up for Russia's interests against the West.

In 1993 Richard Nixon, who had negotiated with Soviet leader Leonid Brezhnev, visited Russia and asked Kozyrev if he could explain what the new Russia's interests were. Kozyrev replied that "one of the problems of the Soviet Union was that we were too focused on national interests. Now we think more about universal human values." But he had a question for the former president: "If you have any ideas about how we might go about defining our national interests, I would be very grateful." He did not quite receive the answer he expected. Nixon replied, "When I was Vice-President and then President, I wanted everyone to know that I was a 'son of a bitch' and I would fight for American interests with all my strength."[32]

As the decade wore on, more and more Russians would accuse the Yeltsin administration of not acting enough like "sons of bitches" and acquiescing to an agenda set by the West, one that did not reflect Russia's national interests. Above all, Russians in their weakened state sought respect from the United States. Many Russians defined the national interest in a negative way. They may not have known what they wanted, but they knew what they did not want, and that included being treated as the United States' junior partner. "The United States treated Russia like a colony, not as an equal," is the bitter assessment of an advisor to the Foreign Ministry.[33] The list of complaints about American policies in the 1990s includes NATO expansion, having to cooperate with NATO in the Balkan wars, and Western criticism of the war in Chechnya. After the Soviet collapse, Russian officials were acutely conscious of the humiliation of being relegated to the role of economic supplicant. The Clinton administration argued that it tried to conduct its policy toward Russia with sufficient sensitivity to Russia's difficulty in adjusting to its reduced international status. Others disagree. Former ambassador Jack Matlock argues that Washington was unwilling to put itself in Moscow's shoes and craft policies that treated Russia with greater empathy.[34] Alexander Voloshin, former head of Yeltsin's presidential administration, agrees: "The United States is very egotistical and not ready to understand other countries' interests."[35]

Rising domestic criticism of Russia's relationship with the United States eventually led Yeltsin to relieve the pro-Western Kozyrev of his duties at the end of 1995. Bowing to the more nationalistic mood, he appointed Evgeny Primakov as foreign minister. Primakov had a much firmer base in the Soviet/Russian foreign policy establishment than did his predecessor. He had been a journalist, head of the Academy of Science's main international relations institute, IMEMO, and, most recently head of the SVR—the foreign intelligence service. An Arabist and expert on the Middle East, his personal relationship with Saddam Hussein and attempts to prevent the first Gulf War had not endeared him to the United States. Primakov represented the new foreign policy consensus within Russia. Well connected to intelligence and security circles, he deemphasized Russia's desire to be integrated with the West. Instead, he articulated a new "Eurasian vocation" for his country. Russia, according to this vision, is both a European and an Asian country, and its national interest lies in charting a unique course between those two worlds. Primakov advocated a multipolar world, where Russia, India, and China should band together to counterbalance American hegemony. "Russia should base its foreign policy on the premise that there are no permanent enemies, but there are always national interests," he wrote, adding that Russia must be viewed as a partner, not a client of the West.[36]

Primakov's advocacy of a selective, pragmatic, and "equal" partnership with the West and the need to pay more attention to Russia's "near abroad" reflected growing irritation with the West's approach. Strobe Talbott describes Primakov's strategy "to play a weak hand well" and believed that, just because he had a more hard-line reputation than his predecessor, he might be better able to negotiate agreements with the United States.[37] After Primakov's brief elevation to prime minister in 1998, the career diplomat Igor Ivanov took over as foreign minister.

Yeltsin was not the only leader who had to contend with domestic opposition. As soon as the Republicans won a majority in the U.S. Congress in 1994, the Clinton administration's policies toward Russia came under increasing scrutiny, especially from those members of Congress who retained a lasting mistrust of Moscow from the Cold War days. For them, Russian actions in Bosnia, Iran, Chechnya, and Kosovo raised serious questions about the wisdom of the new Washington-Moscow rapprochement. Perhaps the most graphic example of congressional reticence toward normalizing relations with Russia was the persistence of the Jackson-Vanik amendment.

Originally passed in 1974 as an amendment to a U.S.-Soviet trade agreement that was never implemented, Jackson-Vanik tied the granting of most-favored-nation status (MFN) for the Soviet Union to its policies on Jewish emigration. Thus, at the time of the Soviet collapse, the United States did not have normal trading relations with Russia, and Congress had to pass annual waivers for MFN to be applied to Russia. Even though Gorbachev had liberalized Jewish emigration, and over a million Jews emigrated to Israel and the United States after 1992, the U.S. Congress refused to graduate Russia permanently from the Jackson-Vanik strictures. Ukraine and other post-Soviet countries eventually had the restrictions lifted, but the symbolic act of repealing the legislation to "reward" Russia proved too controversial. Russian leaders beginning with Yeltsin found it humiliating that Russia was still subject to annual congressional review as if both countries remained in a Cold War time warp. Jackson-Vanik would not be finally repealed until the end of 2012—twenty-one years after the Soviet collapse.

In a situation of considerable uncertainty about how to chart a new relationship with Russia, the Clinton administration began to put in place the building blocks for constructing institutions that would promote bilateral relations. This reset was designed to be all-encompassing and both to promote domestic change and to re-create the U.S.-Russian relationship. Because Yeltsin's Russia was weak and only just beginning to define its new role, the United States was largely responsible for setting the agenda for the relationship and putting into place mechanisms for engagement. For many Russians, this asymmetry in power was a bitter pill to swallow.

CREATING THE BILATERAL POLICY FRAMEWORK

The Nuclear Legacy

The most important achievement of the Clinton administration's Russia policy was to complete the work begun by George H. W. Bush in denuclearizing Ukraine, Kazakhstan, and Belarus. In an example of bipartisanship, George H. W. Bush's national security advisor General

Brent Scowcroft insisted that the Bush team cooperate as closely as possible with the incoming Clinton team to ensure continuity in the nonproliferation programs.[38] Although much of the groundwork for this had been done before Clinton's election, the agreements remained to be signed and ratified. Talbott created a Strategic Stability Group within the new Gore-Chernomyrdin Binational Commission, which he cochaired with Deputy Foreign Minister Yuri Mamedov. In many ways, their relationship mirrored that of Clinton and Yeltsin, albeit with less volatility—but their personal contacts and commitment largely drove the relationship and determined the success or failure of U.S.-Russian security negotiations.

The main problem for the Clinton administration lay not in Russia but in Ukraine. It had not escaped the Ukrainian leadership's' notice that, as long as Ukraine was in possession of nuclear warheads, it received a great deal of attention from the United States. These warheads were the major form of leverage Ukraine had as it struggled to become a functioning independent state. After a considerable amount of negotiating and arm twisting, President Clinton flew to Kyiv in January 1994, met Ukrainian president Leonid Kravchuk, and flew with him to Moscow. President Yeltsin met them the next day, and the three signed the Tripartite Accord, committing Ukraine to eliminate all the nuclear weapons located on its territory. The Ukrainian Rada then ratified the START I treaty. The transfer of these warheads to Russia would be completed in 1996. At that Moscow meeting, Yeltsin and Kravchuk appeared to be reluctant signatories for their respective countries— Ukraine because it had to give up its weapons and Russia because it had to deal with Ukraine as an independent state—but Clinton was anything but reluctant. He was wearing a button that read "carpe diem."[39]

The Clinton administration also focused on strengthening the Nunn-Lugar Cooperative Threat Reduction Program that played such a crucial role in securing Russian nuclear materials. Congressional Republicans questioned why the United States was paying the Russians for doing what was in their interest to do anyway, suggesting that American financial support enabled them to spend more money on strengthening their own military. The answer was that this was decidedly in the U.S. interest.

Nevertheless, the program continued, and the Clinton administration focused on other nonproliferation issues. Highly enriched uranium (HEU) was a major concern. "We needed to give the Russians a commercial stake—something that did not smack of patronizing assistance," recalled Daniel Poneman, who worked on nuclear issues in the White House.[40] At the April 1993 Vancouver summit, the United States and Russia signed an agreement. The highly enriched uranium extracted from Russian nuclear weapons would be converted to low-enriched uranium for use in commercial power plants. National security director Rose Gottemoeller recalls that "1993–1994 was the Wild West in Russia. There were no rules or regulations. Times were desperate and the situation was very fluid."[41] Money was short, and there were many potential buyers of both nuclear material and know-how from unemployed Russian nuclear scientists. In response, officials focused on strengthening relations between American and Russians laboratories and nuclear scientists. This cooperation between professionals began to create a group of government and nongovernment stakeholders whose joint work would anchor the nuclear relationship for the next two decades.[42]

The administration was, however, unable to make much headway on further arms control, largely because domestic Russian politics and Russia's increasing opposition to other American policies stymied further negotiations. In January 1996, the U.S. Senate ratified the START II treaty that President George H. W. Bush had submitted to the Senate just before he left office in January 1993. START II would have eliminated two-thirds of the Russian and American nuclear arsenals, and in 1997 Clinton and Yeltsin had agreed on deeper cuts. However, the Russian Duma never ratified START II, leaving it to subsequent administrations to tackle the enduring Cold War strategic nuclear arms legacy. As Secretary of Defense William Perry explained, START II "was a casualty of NATO expansion."[43] It was also a casualty of the domestic struggle between the Kremlin and the Duma.

Nothing, however, was more controversial than missile defense. Since the 1960s, the United States had focused on offense over defense in its nuclear posture. But Washington's interest in defensive systems was growing. Ronald Reagan's Strategic Defense Initiative—designed to intercept an incoming nuclear missile before it could strike—had caused great concern in Moscow because the Soviets did not have the technology to compete with such a system. The proposed National Missile Defense (NMD) system that the Clinton administration was discussing contravened the U.S.-Soviet 1972 Anti-Ballistic Missile (ABM) Treaty, signed by Nixon and Brezhnev, which limited both sides to only two defensive systems around their main cities. The Russians were adamant that the ABM Treaty was a fundamental cornerstone of the U.S.-Russian nuclear relationship. The administration, seeking a cooperative approach to missile defense, began to focus on the construction of a regional theater missile defense (TMD) that could shoot down shorter-range missiles but not long-range Russian missiles. It hoped that this would be a more productive approach. The Clinton administration was interested in developing a TMD system that would have enabled Washington to keep the ABM Treaty in place.

However, Republican members of Congress were adamant about the necessity to construct the more robust missile defense system targeting long-range missiles. For the Kremlin, strategic arms control and the ABM Treaty were among the few areas where Russia and the United States remained equals and where Russia was still a superpower. Any move to alter that equilibrium exacerbated Moscow's complaints that Washington was ignoring its interests and trying to weaken it. And the Kremlin began to express concerns that a missile defense system allegedly designed to counter rogue states could also threaten Russia's own deterrent. Clinton administration officials differ in their interpretations of why it was impossible to reach agreement on missile defense. Ambassador Thomas Pickering regrets that U.S. officials never sat down with their Russian counterparts to engage in a broad-range discussion of how both sides viewed their respective security interests, making missile defense part of a larger discussion. Strobe Talbott's executive assistant Eric Edelman, by contrast, argues that the Russians never had any interest in reaching such an accommodation.[44]

The Iranian Nuclear Program

Russia's support for Iran's nuclear program also became a source of friction between the Clinton and Yeltsin administrations. However, one can understand the full dimensions of the Iranian issue only by placing it in its broader postwar context. The legacy of Soviet-Iranian ties was mixed. During the Second World War, British and Soviet troops occupied Iran. In what became the first Cold War crisis, the Soviets resisted withdrawing from the northern part of Iran, which shared a border with the Soviet republic of Azerbaijan. They only withdrew under pressure from the United Nations. Thereafter, Moscow was critical of Shah Mohammed Reza Pahlavi's regime and supportive of the Tudeh communist party, but nevertheless developed a profitable economic relationship with the country. It was always mindful of the geographic proximity of Iran—a country in which millions of ethnic Azeris lived—to the Azeri Soviet Socialist Republic and of the fact that both Persian and Azeri Muslims share the Shia faith.

The U.S. relationship with Iran was also complicated. In 1953, the United States and Britain collaborated with the Iranian opposition to remove Prime Minister Mohammed Mosaddeq, whom they believed to be pro-Soviet, and they helped restore to power the shah. The United States assisted Iran in developing limited nuclear power under the "atoms for peace" program. This was launched in 1953 by the administration of Dwight Eisenhower and envisaged the spread of civilian nuclear power around the globe. At that point, there was limited appreciation of the fact that atoms for peace could, under the right circumstances, become atoms for war, as became clear when India announced its first successful nuclear test in 1974. In 1975 German and French companies signed an agreement to help Iran construct a nuclear power plant at Bushehr in the south of Iran.

In 1979 the U.S.-backed shah was overthrown by fundamentalist Islamic clerics and their supporters. Branding the United States as the "Great Satan," they invaded the U.S. Embassy, holding its diplomats hostage for 444 days. From that time on, the U.S.-Iranian relationship was one of hostility, and diplomatic relations were never restored. The French and German companies pulled out of their nuclear contracts, and the Soviet Union began negotiations to assume the contracts.

During the Iranian Revolution, some Soviet diplomats were kidnapped, but after 1979 the Soviet-Iranian relationship remained generally cooperative (Russia was just the "Little Satan"). Gradually, Soviet-Iranian relations began to improve, particularly after the Soviets withdrew from Afghanistan in 1989, with the focus largely on arms sales and energy ties. In 1989 the Iranian president visited Moscow and signed agreements totaling $1 billion, mostly for weapons. The USSR and Iran also signed a cooperation agreement on peaceful utilization of "nuclear materials and related equipment."[45]

After the Soviet collapse, Iran was careful in its dealings with post-communist Russia. Separatists in Chechnya were demanding independence, and the whole of Russia's North Caucasus was restive. Despite its official goal of exporting radical Islam, Iran opted not to aid Muslim insurgents in Chechnya, thereby supporting Russia's territorial integrity. Russia was well aware that Iran could cause problems in its own Muslim area and viewed its relationship with Tehran as a form of insurance against Iranian interference in its domestic affairs. Tehran also cooperated with Moscow to end the civil war in Tajikistan, whose population is largely Shia. In the 1990s Iran worked with Russia to support Afghan forces in the Northern Alliance that opposed the Taliban. Thus, there were pressing domestic and regional political concerns that argued for cooperative relations with Iran.[46]

Russia's nuclear relationship with Iran increasingly became an issue of contention with the United States. During a period of economic crisis in August 1992, Russia signed an agreement with Iran to construct the nuclear power plant at Bushehr. Work began in 1994. However, by 1999 Iran threatened to withhold further nuclear contracts from Russia for failing to complete Bushehr on time.[47]

As Washington saw it, Iran is a country with considerable indigenous oil and gas resources—hence the belief from the outset that the mullahs' desire for a nuclear power plant was a ruse to acquire and master nuclear technology that could eventually enable Iran to develop its own nuclear weapons. Moreover, the conduct of Russian advisors in Iran also raised red flags for the Clinton administration. Experts now agree that during the 1990s Russian entities—whether state-sponsored or no—were involved in a variety of ways in Iran's nuclear development. Moreover, the Clinton administration had evidence that Russian universities were training Iranian missile scientists.[48]

The Iranian nuclear question involved the most sensitive issues of the relationship between the Russian government and nontransparent entities that represented the emergence of the new Russian system in which commercial interests were intimately connected to individuals from the former security services. Talbott describes the new Russian Ministry of Atomic Energy as "a rich, powerful remnant of the Soviet military-industrial complex," one where, the United States feared, there would be few inhibitions against the sale of lucrative high technology to states or groups whose intentions were malevolent.[49] The Clinton administration suspected that successive ministers of atomic energy ignored whatever directions the Kremlin sought to give them and continued to sell Iran a variety of items, including gas centrifuges that could be used to produce weapons-grade uranium.[50] In 1995, Prime Minister Viktor Chernomyrdin, in a confidential letter to Gore, committed Russia to limit its cooperation with Iran to completing the first reactor unit of the Bushehr plant, supplying fuel for it, and training Iranian specialists to operate the plant.[51]

The Iran problem highlighted a basic fact of life: Russia, however weak it was, could still thwart Western efforts to prevent Iran from acquiring a nuclear weapons capability that could threaten regional security. As U.S.-Russian negotiations over Iran dragged on, American officials and experts sought to understand the motivations behind Russia's policies, and the relationship between the actions of the Russian government and those of nonstate entities that were engaged in developing Iran's civilian nuclear program. The Iran issue raised fundamental questions about who was in control in Yeltsin's Russia and whether the Kremlin was truly unaware of the activities of gray entities involved with Iran. Some questioned whether it was really possible to work with Russia on nonproliferation.

Moreover, Iran was also a U.S. domestic issue, a prime example of how Congress could potentially jettison the results of years of hard negotiating work with sometimes recalcitrant Russian officials. The Republican-dominated Congress sought to impose tough sanctions on Russia. It had become increasingly concerned that Russian entities were equipping Iran to build nuclear weapons that it might then use against Israel, whose right to exist it denied. Not only was Israel putting pressure on the United States to stop Iran from acquiring nuclear weapons, but Arab states in the region were equally concerned about Iranian ambitions.

Throughout the 1990s, Russian officials would reiterate the mantra that Iran had done nothing to violate agreements it had signed with the International Atomic Energy Agency (IAEA) and that it only desired to acquire a civilian nuclear power capability. Whenever Clinton administration officials, including the president himself, presented evidence to Russian officials that Russian nuclear missile technology was being transferred to Iran in defiance of agreements that Russia itself had made, the response ranged from evasion to denial. Occasionally, Yeltsin would promise that this would not happen again, but according to U.S. information it always did.[52] The Kremlin's response was that Russia had as much right to export its military technology as did the United States, which was also a major arms exporter. Moreover, as the prospect of NATO enlargement grew, so did the Russian complaints that the new Central European members' arms markets, traditionally Russian clients, would be barred to them. Criticizing U.S. double standards, they would point to Russia's political and economic ties to Iran and intimate that the United States was seeking to deny them their legitimate right to trade with Iran and sell it technology while America exported similar technologies to other countries.

But the biggest issue between the United States and Russia would be over Europe and the strategic order that would fill the void left by the end of the Cold War era when U.S. and Soviet troops had eyed each other over the Fulda Gap that divided East and West Germany.

Chapter Two
Rethinking Euro-Atlantic Security

Where does Russia belong? As the largest country on earth, two-thirds of which is geographically in Asia, Russia views itself as both a European and an Asian country. Yet culturally Russians are Europeans, and Asians do not regard Russians as Asian. Nevertheless, Russia's self-concept as a uniquely Eurasian country has created a permanent ambivalence about its place in Europe. For two centuries Russians have argued about whether they should follow the West or create their own, unique civilization that is neither Western nor Eastern and follows its own rules. Russia is both a part of Europe and apart from Europe, and Russians have always been reluctant Europeans.[1] Whereas Russian leaders have been attracted to Europe as an economic model and since Peter the Great have sought to emulate Western technological achievements, they have generally been antagonistic toward the West's political system. The values associated with the European Enlightenment—individual rights, rule of law, due process, property rights—have been espoused only by small groups of the liberal intelligentsia, be it in tsarist, Soviet, or post-Soviet times. This ambivalence about Western values has had a major impact on Russia's relations with European and Euro-Atlantic structures.

Russia's place in Europe became one of the most neuralgic issues in Moscow's ties with the West. After the demise of the USSR and the dissolution of the Warsaw Pact, the United States and its allies faced the question of how to construct a postcommunist security architecture in Europe. NATO—which now included a united Germany—emerged intact from the Cold War, while the Warsaw Pact collapsed, and countries to Germany's east were rebuilding their military capabilities without membership in any alliance. There were voices in the United States, Western Europe, and Russia that questioned why NATO should continue to exist, given that the Soviet enemy was gone. Instead, they championed the Conference on Security and Cooperation in Europe (CSCE), an organization created in 1975 that included all of Europe and North America, as an alternative that could create more cooperative and inclusive security structures.

After the Soviet collapse, a small group of Russian liberal reformers around Yeltsin—encouraged by their American and European interlocutors—believed that Russia's major goal should be to "integrate with the West," which, for them, meant joining Western economic and security institutions. The idea was to create a group of Russian stakeholders who would be interested in supporting a more rules-based, consensual international order. The Clinton administration offered Russia G-7 membership and a special relationship with NATO. It also began the process of negotiating Russia's admission to the World Trade Organization. Europe accepted Russia into the Council of Europe—an organization dedicated to promoting human rights—despite qualms about the Chechen War. The European Union (EU) signed a partnership and cooperation agreement with Russia in 1994.

Throughout the 1990s, therefore, Russia had limited relations with the key European and Euro-Atlantic institutions, partly because full membership in these clubs was not on offer, but largely because Russians themselves, as one Clinton official put it, were "lousy joiners." Their ambivalence about being full participants in institutions whose rules they would have to abide by without being in a position to determine them was, for many Russians, unacceptable. The key point was that "integration" meant accepting an agenda created by the West. For those who argue that the mistake was not to offer Russia full EU or NATO membership, there is little evidence that, at that stage, Russia would have been willing or able to begin the complicated membership process had either of these institutions offered it—or accept the rules that they represented. Russia remained a "candidate member" in Euro-Atlantic structures.

What did the West promise Gorbachev at the time of German unification? This question has riled relations for more than twenty years, reinvigorated as more archival material has become available. Some Western participants in the German unification process insist that the United States promised Gorbachev that NATO would not enlarge after Germany was unified and accuse the West of reneging on commitments it made to the USSR.[2] Many Russian officials and experts, including Mikhail Gorbachev himself, subscribe to this view. "According to the Two-Plus-Four Agreements under which Germany was unified," he has said, "the United States, Germany, Britain and France promised us that they would not expand NATO east of Germany."[3] Yet a careful reading of the agreements that were signed in 1990 when a united Germany joined NATO reveals that NATO enlargement was not explicitly addressed. Gorbachev and his advisors may have with hindsight believed that promises had been made by the Americans. But the historical record shows that no explicit commitments about NATO not enlarging were made—simply because this issue was not on the table.[4] Secretary of State James Baker had told Gorbachev in February 1990 (before Germany was unified) that NATO's jurisdiction would not shift eastward from its present position, but he was referring to NATO's jurisdiction over the territory of the GDR, not to NATO's possible enlargement.[5] In other words, Baker was talking about not stationing NATO troops on the territory of the former East Germany after 1990, not about anything else.

Nevertheless, the ambiguity about what guarantees the West gave the USSR as the Cold War ended came to haunt the Clinton administration as it faced the question of how the post–Cold War world should be organized and into what Euro-Atlantic security structures former communist states should be integrated. Many Americans and Europeans view NATO enlargement as one of the Clinton administration's great successes; others in the United States, Europe, and Russia view it as a major mistake that poisoned relations with Russia.[6]

To understand the lasting significance of this debate, it is important to return to the years immediately following the Soviet collapse and to understand how NATO members and aspirants viewed the question of where the ex-communist countries belonged. It was not self-evident at the time of the Soviet collapse that Central and Eastern Europe would accomplish the successful transition to democracy and free markets. The economic transition required major sacrifices from the people, and in the aftermath of communism's collapse, nativist, nationalist parties formed alongside democratic, Western-leaning ones. The ghosts of its interwar authoritarian past continued to haunt the newly liberated *Mittleleuropa*. The breakup of Yugoslavia and its rapid descent into civil war and ethnic cleansing exemplified the worst of what could go wrong once the strictures of communism vanished. There were plenty of ethnic and border disputes in Central and Eastern Europe that had been suppressed under Soviet domination only to reemerge in the early 1990s.

American and Western European officials feared that the success of the largely peaceful collapse of communism could be threatened by unforeseen developments in Central and Eastern Europe. As German defense minister Volker Ruehe said in a 1993 speech, "Without democracy, stability and free market economy, this geographic part of Europe will remain vulnerable to the old problems of conflicting historical resentments, ambitions and territorial and ethnic disputes—*We cannot save reform in Russia by placing reform in Central and East-Central Europe at risk.*"[7] European Community membership would have been the best guarantor of democratic stability and good governance in these countries; but the road to membership was long and involved massive economic restructuring for which Russia was hardly prepared and a complex process of accession to tens of thousands of pages of the *acquis communautaire*. Joining NATO was a much faster—and simpler—process.

Central European countries had advocated their "return to Europe" after the collapse of communism, and President Bush, in a landmark 1989 speech in Mainz, had championed a "Europe whole and free."[8] But what did these words really mean? The United States and its allies confronted two seemingly contradictory goals—the first was to integrate Central Europe into Western security structures, thereby enhancing Euro-Atlantic stability and security and ensuring that communism was not replaced by nativist nationalism. The second was to reassure Russia that it too had a role to play in this new Euro-Atlantic security architecture and that it should also have a stake in a stable Europe. American officials repeatedly tried to convince their Russian counterparts that it was much better for Russia to have prosperous, stable, democratic neighbors in NATO than to have them adrift and unstable.

The Russians responded skeptically to the Clinton administration's reassurance that this was a "win-win" proposition. For Moscow, this was a zero-sum world, and the enlargement of NATO was ipso facto a threat to Russia, irrespective of the fact that NATO frequently reiterated that Russia was no longer its enemy. Added to this was the undeniable difference between rhetoric and reality. Officials would stress that the inclusion of Central European countries in NATO was in no way directed against Russia But it was clear that the subtext of NATO enlargement, at least for Poland, Hungary, and the Czech Republic, was the Article Five collective security guarantees that NATO membership would give them as an insurance against a possibly resurgent Russia.[9] Indeed, in his private conversations with Clinton, Yeltsin said that although he himself understood that NATO did not plan to attack Russia from bases in Poland, "a lot of people who live in the western part of Russia and listen to [communist leader] Zyuganov do."[10]

In January 1994, NATO had unveiled its Partnership for Peace (PfP) Program, which was offered to all former Warsaw Pact members and the CIS countries. Russia's reaction to this offer of a partnership with NATO with no promise of membership was lukewarm, because each country could sign its own bilateral agreement with NATO—as Ukraine did in 1994—and Russia's status would be no different from that of its former satellite states. Some officials from both the Bush and Clinton administrations believe that much more could have been done with the PfP program before rushing to enlarge NATO. When Chairman of the Joint Chiefs of Staff General John Shalikhashvili presented the PfP plan to Yeltsin, the Russian president asked whether PfP meant "*Partnertsvo*" or "*chlenstvo*." In other words, did PfP mean that the participant states would move to "membership" or was it indeed a "partnership." He was assured that it meant partnership for all participating states, with no implication of membership. Yet barely had PfP begun when the enlargement process began. "We reneged on our part of the deal," says one official. PfP was a flexible program, and it could have been used to involve Russia more effectively.[11]

The story of the politics of the American decision to enlarge NATO is a complex one.[12] Barely had the PfP program been introduced than the debate about NATO enlargement began. Clinton had been influenced by the arguments of key Central European leaders—especially Czech president Vaclav Havel and Polish president Lech Walesa—made at the time of the opening of the Holocaust Memorial Museum in Washington, D.C. If the world wanted to avoid another European catastrophe, they said, it should integrate Central Europe into Western structures, insisting as a prerequisite that these countries renounce irredentist territorial claims on each other and promote ethnic reconciliation.

Brent Scowcroft believes that the Clinton administration was so focused on Europe that it failed to pay enough attention to Russia's concerns about NATO enlargement. "The Clinton administration should have talked to Russia first, before it agreed to expand NATO."[13] But Clinton and his key advisors thought that it was possible both to enlarge NATO and to keep Russia inside the tent by offering it incentives such as G-7 membership and its own special treaty with NATO—the NATO-Russian Permanent Joint Council (PJC). According to Secretary of State Madeleine Albright, "We certainly worked hard at treating Russia with respect" in crafting a NATO-Russia relationship in which Moscow would have a stake.[14] The Russian government eventually, but reluctantly, signed on. Part of the issue with NATO was devising a framework for NATO-Russia relations that gave Russia a unique and distinctive role.

The PJC gave Russia a voice—but not a veto—in NATO deliberations and envisaged future areas of cooperation, such as crisis management, preventative diplomacy, joint operations, peace-keeping, arms control, nonproliferation, and disaster response. Regular meetings from the ambassador level down were held. Yet Russians who served at NATO found out that this was not a career-enhancing experience. Indeed, the PJC achieved very modest results. Moreover, weeks after the PJC program was put in place, NATO announced, to Russia's chagrin, that it would admit Poland, Hungary, and the Czech Republic as full members in 1999. Russian officials point out that they were not consulted over this decision. "Our conversations with Warren Christopher," writes Primakov, "left no doubts that they decided not to pay any attention to us as far as NATO enlargement was concerned."[15] According to Anatoly Chubais, then Yeltsin's chief of staff, "The United States had a unique chance to include Russia in European security structures, but it lost that chance by enlarging NATO."[16]

Russia's rhetoric and actions embodied its fundamentally contradictory attitude toward NATO: on the one hand, NATO was viewed as an adversary that threatened Russia's security, and on the other, it was an organization with which Russia now enjoyed a unique relationship. This dualistic view of NATO represented a continuing ambiguity for those within the Russian political and security establishment, some of whom understood the advantages of cooperating with NATO but many of whom continued to view the alliance in Cold War terms.

THE BALKANS

The worst crisis in the U.S.-Russian relationship erupted at the end of the Clinton administration, the result of the violent disintegration of Yugoslavia. The Yugoslav breakdown had provided some opportunities for U.S.-Russian cooperation in Bosnia but also pitted the two countries against each other over Kosovo. After the constituent republics of Yugolslavia declared their independence, Serbian strongman Slobodan Milošević supported the Bosnian Serbs, who had unleashed an ethnic war against Bosnia's Muslim population, including the massacre of eight thousand Muslim men and boys at Srebrenica in 1995. United Nations forces were unable to halt the ethnic cleansing by Serbs against Bosniak Muslims. The United States- led NATO intervention in 1995 eventually ended the conflict through the Dayton Accords at the end of 1995. In 1999 NATO once again intervened, this time to halt the bloodshed in Kosovo, a majority Muslim region that was part of Serbia but which wanted to secede from Belgrade. The wars in Bosnia and Kosovo highlighted Russia's deep ambivalence about whether it wanted to be a partner to the West or whether it insisted on a role in the Balkan conflicts that would thwart NATO's attempts to bring peace to the region.

Throughout the 1990s, Russian political and military figures would invoke Russia's historic alliance with Serbia based on common Orthodox religious and cultural links. Yeltsin supported UN and NATO policies in the Balkans only with extreme reluctance, repeatedly pointing out to Clinton that this support for actions against Milošević came at great domestic cost to his administration and to him personally. Even more moderate, Western-leaning Russian officials were wary of taking on Milošević, for fear that this would embolden the anti-Yeltsin forces in Russia. Clinton himself was concerned that, if the United States leaned too heavily on Russia to combat the Serbs, support for Yeltsin's reform efforts would be undermined.[17] Since the military campaign against the Bosnian Serbs was launched at the same time as was the debate about NATO enlargement, and NATO conducted the bombing campaign against the Serbs, this issue became particularly divisive. Richard Holbrooke, architect of the Dayton Accords, wrote that "what (Russia) wanted most was to restore a sense, however symbolic, that they still mattered in the world. Behind our efforts to include Russia in the Bosnian negotiating process lay a fundamental belief—that it was essential to find the proper place for Russia in Europe's security structure, something it had not been part of since 1914."[18]

The contrast between Moscow's actions in the Bosnian and Kosovo wars illustrates how far the domestic situation had changed in Russia by the end of Yeltsin's tenure. In both cases, NATO worked hard to secure Russian support in prosecuting the war. In both cases, military action was directed against Serbian forces and in support of beleaguered Muslims. In both cases, NATO, and particularly the United States, set the agenda, and Russia had to respond to it. Yet cooperation over Bosnia worked much better, perhaps because at that point, despite Yeltsin's erratic health, his colleagues—and particularly his foreign minister, Andrei Kozyrev—were willing to go along because they prized cooperation with the United States. Yet, after listening to why Russia should take military action against the Serbs, Kozyrev told Talbott that "it's bad enough you people tell us what you're going to do whether we like it or not. Don't add insult to injury by telling us that it's *in our interests* to obey your orders."[19] The United States included Russia in the Contact Group, founded in 1994, that met regularly to devise strategy for dealing with Milošević. As Holbrooke later recounted, "We felt that, despite occasional mischief-making, Moscow would be easier to deal with if we gave it a place as a co-equal with the E.U. and the United States."[20] Even before the Dayton negotiations, the United States and its allies had discussed with Russia an unprecedented plan—that, when the war was over, Russian troops would serve under an American commander in the Implementation Force (IFOR) in Bosnia, since the Russians refused to serve under a NATO commander. Despite initial Russian objections, IFOR, according to its participants, worked well, and Russian officers cooperated with their American colleagues. Bosnia, from the point of view of U.S.-Russian relations, was a hard-earned success, where Russia eventually became part of the solution instead of part of the problem.

In the second half of the 1990s, NATO began the enlargement process, Russia suffered an economic meltdown, Kozyrev was replaced by the more nationalistic Primakov, and Yeltsin's government became increasingly unstable as he changed prime ministers every few months. The ailing Yeltsin was under mounting pressure to stand up to the Americans. In his memoirs, Yeltsin suggests that Clinton, to distract from his domestic political battles, approved bombing Belgrade in March 1999 as a means of stopping the bloodshed in Kosovo. Yelstin's opponents were warning him that, if NATO could bomb Belgrade, "Today Yugoslavia, tomorrow Russia!" "Wasn't it obvious," Yeltsin asks, "that each missile directed against Yugoslavia was an indirect strike against Russia?"[21]

Igor Ivanov, who succeeded Primakov as foreign minister in 1998, insists that it would have been possible to find a political solution to the Kosovo situation. At issue was the right of the Muslim Kosovars, living in Orthodox Serbia, to declare their independence from Serbia and form their own state. "Yugoslavia was not a threat to regional stability," Ivanov argues, "and the United States' real motive was to impose its will through NATO bypassing the United Nations. This is when the United States laid the foundation of a unipolar world." What Ivanov terms "Madeleine's deal," after U.S. secretary of state Madeleine Albright, had an adverse impact on Russia's domestic situation.[22]

Disagreements over the war in Kosovo represented the lowest point in U.S.-Russian relations since the collapse of the USSR. In March 1999 Primakov was on his way to Washington. But when he heard that NATO had begun to bomb Serbia, he turned the plane around in mid-air and returned to Moscow. As the bombing campaign continued, the U.S. Embassy in Moscow was the site of the largest anti-American demonstrations since the end of the Cold War. Russian liberals warned that NATO's actions would further diminish the prospects of reform and stoke the fires of nationalism and reaction. Even after Victor Chernomyrdin joined the Finnish president Ahtisaari in brokering a cease-fire, it was clear that the top Russian military brass was chafing under the constraints of its civilian bosses.

Finally, at the end of the war, Russia and the United States almost came to direct physical blows in 1999 when Russian troops rushed to the airport in Pristina, Kosovo's capital, before NATO troops had entered Kosovo—directly contravening the terms of the cease-fire—in an attempt to establish control over the area.[23] The supreme allied commander in Europe, General Wesley Clark, was in favor of directly confronting the Russian soldiers at the airport, but British general Michael Jackson, who was in charge of NATO forces on the ground, informed his American colleague that he was "not starting World War Three for you," and the crisis was defused. The Russian soldiers who "dashed" to Pristina apparently disobeyed not only their political leaders but also their military superiors, but that is not how Yeltsin recounts it. Claiming that he decided to give the order for Russian troops to enter Kosovo before NATO troops did, he recalls, "This last gesture was a sign of our moral victory in the face of the enormous NATO military, all of Europe, and the whole world."[24]

Russia's actions during the Kosovo War revealed the depth of bitterness against and continuing desire to thwart NATO and the United States, and also Moscow's indifference to the fate of those Muslim groups that had been ethnically cleansed by Serbia. The PJC had been of little use in crisis management, and Russia broke off relations with NATO after the bombing began. Above all, it appeared to be more important for Russia to oppose what NATO was doing than to help solve a major humanitarian crisis in Europe. Although the Clinton administration tried hard to work with Russia to resolve the Kosovo problem, Moscow was reluctant to take any ownership of the solution.

EXIT YELTSIN: CLINTON, PUTIN, AND THE NEGLECTED ISSUE OF TERRORISM

It would be the last time that Yeltsin and Clinton would meet officially, and it was also the most difficult—and the shortest—summit. The meeting took place in Istanbul at the November 1999 summit of the Organization for Security and Cooperation in Europe (CSCE had been renamed OSCE). By that time Yeltsin had chosen a new prime minister—his fifth in just over a year—a little-known official from St. Petersburg named Vladimir Putin. Putin had launched the second Chechen War in October 1999, in response the invasion of neighboring Dagestan by Chechen-led militants and to a series of apartment bombings in Russia. The Clinton administration was under increasing pressure to condemn Russian military actions.

Yeltsin addressed the Istanbul conference first. This was a very different Boris Yeltsin. He attacked the West for its "sermonizing" and adding that the American-led "aggression against Yugoslavia deprived Clinton of the right to lecture Russia on how it should deal with terrorists within its own borders." In his memoirs, Yeltsin congratulates himself for giving such a tough speech that the OSCE did not condemn Russia for its actions in Chechnya, which it originally planned to do.[25] Clinton, in response, threw away his prepared speech and declared that Russia's use of brute force in Chechnya was unworthy of Yeltsin's own legacy. He praised Yeltsin for all his achievements in helping Russia to embark on its road to democracy and emphasized that, if Russia wanted to continue on that path with Western help, it should reconsider its actions in this war.[26] Some minutes into the speech, Yeltsin demonstratively threw off his earphones and almost staged a walk-out. When the two men met alone, Clinton put his feet up on the table. "Is your leg hurting you?" asked Yeltsin. Shortly thereafter, following a tirade from Yeltsin, Clinton left the room.[27] Once they were the younger and older brothers. Now they appeared to be antagonists. The Bill and Boris show was over.

The Istanbul summit crystallized the tensions and opposing narratives between Russia and the West that had been building for some time. Russian and American views of what constituted a terrorist threat increasingly diverged in the 1990s. Chechnya was the most contested issue. After the August coup in 1991, the Chechen government had declared its secession from the USSR. For three years, Chechnya had enjoyed de facto independence from Moscow, but in December 1994 Russian troops had marched into Chechnya to bring it back into the fold. Clinton on several occasions said that Moscow's move to reintegrate Chechnya was similar to President Lincoln's actions to keep the United States together during the U.S. Civil War.[28] Nevertheless, as the war dragged on and reports of atrocities on both sides filtered out, the United States became more critical, often referring to the Chechen rebels as separatists, as opposed to their Russian designation as terrorists. The first Chechen War ended with a truce in 1996, and Chechnya once again was de facto independent. However, violence continued to plague the region, and the launching of the second Chechen War in 1999 led to stronger U.S. condemnation of Russian actions. Russia reiterated that the West was guilty of pursuing double standards in its criticisms of Russia's Chechnya policy, while it supported the Muslim Kosovar Albanians, who themselves used what Russia termed terrorist methods.

Then, a month after Istanbul, came a dramatic surprise. Yeltsin, in failing health, went on television to announce that was retiring immediately, three months early, on December 31, 1999. He named Vladimir Putin as his successor. He congratulated himself on facilitating the first peaceful and voluntary transition of power in Russia. Clinton's first meeting with Putin had occurred some months earlier. "Putin presented a stark contrast to Yeltsin," writes Clinton, adding, "I came away from the meeting believing Yeltsin had picked a successor who had the skills and capacity for hard work necessary to manage Russia's turbulent political and economic life."[29]

Putin concluded early on that Clinton was a lame duck and conveyed the impression of disinterest in injecting new vigor into the U.S.-Russian relationship. Issues that had been contentious for the past decade continued to fester—Chechnya, the Balkans, NATO, Iran—and now missile defense, to which the U.S. administration committed itself during its last year in office, largely under congressional pressure, and to which the Russians took great exception. When Putin and Clinton met in Moscow in June 2000, Putin asked Clinton whether Russia could join NATO. Clinton said he would support it.[30]

Yet there was one issue on which the United States and Russia, in retrospect, could have cooperated more—that of international terrorism associated with Islamic fundamentalism. When Clinton raised Chechnya, Putin responded that both the United States and Russia were threatened by international terrorism. But there was the rub. It was difficult for the United States to devise a productive means of dealing with Russia on terrorism while at the same time criticizing the war in Chechnya. Moreover, with all the distractions facing Clinton toward the end of his tenure—culminating in the move to impeach him—the administration failed to fully grasp and focus on the seriousness of the threat from Al Qaeda.

The fate of one of Al Qaeda's top commanders highlights the quandary in which the United States found itself. In 1996 Ayman Al-Zawahiri, the Egyptian-born Al Qaeda second-in-command—who became the leader of Al Qaeda after U.S. Special Forces killed Osama Bin Laden in 2011—traveled to the North Caucasus with some of his supporters, planning to go to Chechnya to aid the rebels fighting Moscow. They were arrested by the Russian authorities and jailed in Makhachkala, the capital of neighboring Dagestan, before they ever made it to Chechnya. After a few months they were released, because the Russians did not have enough evidence to further detain them, and the U.S. authorities appeared not to be concerned about them. Zawahiri traveled to Afghanistan to work with Osama Bin Laden in plotting the 9/11 attacks.

By the time that Clinton left office, the U.S.-Russian relationship had deteriorated considerably from its promising beginnings. Yet that high point was largely an American construct. The White House and the policymaking community saw the immediate post-Soviet years as ones when a more dynamic, healthier Yeltsin and his group of committed reformers enthusiastically threw themselves into the project for which the United States wanted to support them—the building of a market economy and a democracy, accompanied by a foreign policy that sought to integrate Russia into the West. For most Russians, by contrast, the early 1990s are remembered as a period of chaos, when a few oligarchs began to enrich themselves while most Russians, facing unemployment and unpaid pensions, lived in poverty and confronted the breakdown of a predictable social order. They also believe that Moscow allowed Washington to dictate a foreign policy that disrespected it and further emasculated Russia's role as a great power. What the United States viewed as greater pluralism, freedom of expression, and competitive elections, many Russians viewed as disorder and unpredictability and humiliation by the West.

During the two Clinton terms, the ability of the United States to influence the evolution of Russia's political system was far more circumscribed than the administration may have appreciated at the outset. Much of the U.S.-Russian relationship was built on the personal ties between Clinton and Yeltsin, which became the key to moving the relationship forward. Yet they also highlighted the lack of institutional links between the two countries. Despite American government and NGO assistance, and a series of competitive elections, the foundations for transparent democratic institutions were barely laid. Nor did Yeltsin dismantle the Soviet KGB apparatus—it merely was restructured. The way in which the succession was decided also showed that Russia was, at best, a "managed democracy," since Putin was handpicked by a small group of Yeltsin confidants behind closed doors—very much in traditional Russian and Soviet style. From a Russian point of view, what counted most was being treated as an equal by the United States. Thus, membership in institutions such as the G-8, the Contact Group, and (very reluctantly) the PJC was touted as a success for Russian diplomacy. American forays into the post-Soviet space, be they in terms of democracy assistance or energy development, were regarded with greater suspicion. During the Yelstin administration, Russia sometimes neglected its "near abroad," but it resented American incursions into its backyard. And American criticism of Russia's two Chechen wars and its human rights record was viewed as an infringement on Russian sovereignty and unacceptable interference in Russia's internal affairs. By the time Putin appeared, it was clear that things would change.

Yet few in the West anticipated how much Russia would revise its trajectory after the former deputy mayor of St. Petersburg and sometime KGB lieutenant colonel and operative in Dresden ascended to the Kremlin.

Chapter Three
Bush and Putin in the Age of Terror

Al Qaeda's attacks on America's financial center—New York's World Trade Center—and the Pentagon on September 11, 2001, changed forever the way that Americans thought about both their personal safety and their country's security. But what was a national tragedy of immense proportions in the United States was seen in Russia as an opportunity to mend relations with the United States. Indeed, the Kremlin took the initiative. After the 9/11 terrorist attacks, Putin offered Russia as a strategic partner in the war on terror. At that point he believed that Russia's future prosperity and status would be enhanced by greater economic integration with the West and cooperation with the United States. But the partnership forged in the shadow of a catastrophic attack on the United States soon began to unravel as Russian recriminations about unfulfilled expectations grew and American officials pushed back. Moreover, with the passage of time, Moscow needed Washington less, because rising oil prices had put Russia on a much firmer economic foundation. The Bush-Putin honeymoon was shorter than the Clinton-Yeltsin honeymoon. After it was over, the U.S.-Russian relationship returned to a more familiar pattern of a selective partnership characterized by incremental improvements on some issues and continued disagreements over the most difficult issues—arms control, missile defense, Iran, and the post-Soviet space. Americans may question Russia's interpretation of what happened after 9/11, but, in the perceptions of Putin and his colleagues, America's disregard of Russian interests remains a key driver of Russian policy.

THE NEW MAN IN THE KREMLIN

Who is Vladimir Putin, and what is his vision for Russia in the twenty-first century? George W. Bush confronted this question soon after he entered the White House, and it remained with him throughout his presidency. The initially cautious and somewhat reticent new president gradually evolved into a more assertive and outspoken, sometimes confrontational, leader. His Western interlocutors increasingly looked for clues from his past to enlighten them about his real intentions.

Putin's biography offers several explanations for the nature of his leadership and his ambivalence toward the United States. He had a hardscrabble childhood, growing up poor in a postwar Leningrad *kommunalka* (communal apartment) in a family that had lost a son during the siege of Leningrad. He was, like many Soviet citizens of his generation, a survivalist. Planning for worst-case scenarios and wariness about making irreversible commitments have influenced his worldview.[1] A love of Japanese martial arts helped him to escape his unpromising origins and instilled in him the discipline he needed to embark on his chosen career in the KGB. Though he never rose to the top of the KGB, he was sent to Dresden—the one major city in the GDR that did not receive West German television broadcasts—as a midlevel officer. During that time, as he has subsequently explained, his major task was twofold: "working with people and with large amounts of information."[2]

His five years in the GDR from 1985 to 1990 influenced his outlook in two major ways. He completely missed the perestroika period in the USSR, the intellectual questioning of the Soviet system and ferment of the Gorbachev years. He lived instead in one of the most orthodox Soviet bloc countries whose leadership rejected Gorbachev's reformist policies. Moreover, he experienced the collapse of the GDR in 1989 and Moscow's abandonment of its officials serving there in their hour of need. When an angry East German mob tried to burst into the head-quarters of the Stasi—the East German secret police—Putin had to dis-suade them from ransacking the place. He had been feeding KGB re-cords into the building's furnace and was worried that the crowd would "come for us too." When he called the nearby Soviet military base for backup, he was rebuffed, recalling later "nobody lifted as finger to pro-tect us."[3] This reinforced for Lieutenant Colonel Putin the importance of a having strong state that protected its people.[4]

In the autobiographical interview that was published at the begin-ning of his presidential tenure, he expressed regret that the GDR had not lasted longer and that the Soviets withdrew so precipitously from Germany. "I only regretted that the Soviet Union had lost its position in Europe, although intellectually I understood that a position based on walls and dividers cannot last. But I wanted something different to rise in its place. And nothing different was proposed. That's what hurt."[5] His five years in Dresden had made him the "German in the Kremlin" who felt a special affinity for the country.[6] Putin the KGB officer who lost his position because of the implosion of the once mighty Soviet state is an essential part of his political biography.

After a brief period of unemployment after the Soviet collapse, Putin joined his former law professor Anatoly Sobchak, the reformist mayor of St. Petersburg, soon rising to become deputy mayor. Putin may never have shared Sobchak's politically liberal views, but he was instrumental in implementing an economically liberal program and engaging West-ern companies that wanted to do business with the city. Putin proved himself to be a highly capable manager. He was very loyal to his boss, defying the law to spirit Sobchak out of Russia for medical treatment in France when he was threatened with criminal indictment. However, Sobchak's loss in a 1996 electoral campaign marred by dirty tricks had a profound influence on Putin, deepening his skepticism about the value of competitive elections. What use was an election if you could not guarantee the outcome—or if it could be stolen from you?[7]

American officials who met Putin during his tenure in Sobchak's office in St. Petersburg describe a rather quiet, self-effacing man who handled foreign business ties, accompanied visiting Westerners (includ-ing Al Gore and Henry Kissinger) around the city, and was an effective operator.[8] The American consul-general viewed Putin as a "law and order man. He was not corrupt, but he was a crime fighter."[9] Other officials describe him as "a good case officer who listened to you and made you feel important."[10] None of these officials who met him in the early 1990s imagined that he would rise to the pinnacle of Russian power. But Putin was able to use his years in St. Petersburg to cultivate a strong network of political and commercial ties that helped him come to power. After Sobchak's electoral loss in 1996, Putin's colleague and mentor Alexei Kudrin brought him to Moscow where he quickly rose through the ranks—beginning as deputy head of the Kremlin's property department and moving through other positions to become head of the FSB in 1998 and then prime minister in August 1999.

There were few clues about Putin's worldview before he became president. In his autobiographical book, *First Person,* when asked about Russia's world role, he answered, "Russia is a country of European culture, not NATO culture."[11] In his millennial statement, "Russia at the Turn of the Century," which was published as he took office, he argued that a strong state is part of Russia's history and that liberal, democratic values did not have deep roots in Russia. Russia was and will remain a great power and needs a strong state to guide it through its difficult transition. "A strong state for Russia is not an anomaly—but, on the contrary, a source of guarantee and order." He also supported Russia's further integration into global markets.[12] These writings reflect a cautious rejection of communist ideology and recognition that Russia should move toward a market economy. Putin saw as his primary mission the need to restore the viability of what he viewed as a disintegrating state after the disorder of the 1990s. He is a *Gosudarstvennik*, a statist, in the classic Russian tradition. That required the imposition of order and stability.[13] In his first few years in the Kremlin, many of Putin's key advisors were Yelstin holdovers—for instance, Presidential Chief of Staff Alexander Voloshin, Foreign Minister Igor Ivanov, and presidential national security advisors Sergei Ivanov and Sergei Prikhodko. It would take him some time to establish his own base of support and put his own cadres in power.

Putin had come into office determined to reverse the humiliating decade of the 1990s, guarantee Russia's territorial integrity and restore Russia's role as a great power—a *velikaia derzhava*—that could reclaim its rightful place in the world. This involved, among other things, reasserting influence in the post-Soviet space and reaffirming the importance in international decision making of the United Nations, particularly the Security Council. It also entailed preserving as much as possible of the Cold War–era bilateral arms control structures with the United States, because these guaranteed Russia's status as a major power. Despite his time in the KGB and his regret over the USSR's demise, Putin was a pragmatist, willing to engage with the United States on a transactional basis, recognizing the great asymmetry in American and Russian economic and military power. Moreover he realized that Russia's future international influence would depend on its economic health and that its modernization would require Western investment and trade; hence his stated commitment to integrate Russia with the West—at least on an economic basis.

Three months after becoming president in 2000, Putin met World Bank president James Wolfensohn. Putin conveyed the impression that he was an economic modernizer who intended to rein in Russia's sprawling oligarchic culture and bring Russia more fully into the global economy. Putin told Wolfensohn that he wanted to modernize his country, pursue economic reforms, and reduce corruption. In these early days, the outside world was generally relieved to deal with a new younger, sober Russian leader who, they believed, would bring much-needed stability to Russia after a decade of disorder.

Yet underlying Putin's appreciation of the need to work with the West were more skeptical and deep-seated beliefs, a combination of prerevolutionary and Soviet views. This worldview has been described as "a Hobbesian understanding of the world as an essentially hostile and 'anarchic' place; the fear of encirclement by outside forces; and a strategic culture dominated by the geopolitical triad of zero-sum calculus, the balance of power and spheres of influence."[14] Russia's 2000 official Foreign Policy Doctrine embodied this outlook. It committed Russia to seek to achieve a "multipolar system of international relations," asserted that Russia was pursuing an independent, pragmatic foreign policy, called for the upgrading of the UN Security Council, insisted that the ABM Treaty must be retained, and recognized the need to create a "positive perception of Russia abroad."[15] The challenge for Putin's Russia was to reconcile this wary view of the world with the practical need to cooperate with the West if Russia wanted to restore its international influence.

ENTER GEORGE BUSH:
THE 2000 ELECTORAL CAMPAIGN

Although they came from very different backgrounds, Vladimir Putin and George Bush were both "accidental" presidents, inasmuch as neither of them had aspired to high political office in their earlier careers. Putin's rise from political obscurity was a result of both good luck and hard work—he happened to show up in St. Petersburg when Sobchak was looking for someone to manage the mayor's office's economic contacts, but he also earned the respect and trust of those whom he met in St. Petersburg, who then brought him to Moscow after Sobchak's defeat. His ascent to the presidency was engineered through the intervention of the Yeltsin "family" (both biological and political) after complex behind-the-scenes negotiations and a promise of immunity for the Yeltsin family, which Putin honored.[16]

Bush, by contrast, was born into politics. He came from a patrician political family, but he spent the first forty years of his life in a variety of pursuits that did not include seeking high political office; with one exception.[17] He had run unsuccessfully for Congress in 1978 and had been an owner of the Texas Rangers baseball team. He eventually overcame his reluctance to run for office and became governor of Texas in 1994. Bush's controversial and closely contested 2000 election victory raised questions about the legitimacy of his claim to the presidency. The Florida election debacle—in which thousands of ballots had to be recounted because they had not been properly tallied—certainly elicited derisive comments from Russian commentators, who questioned how the United States could criticize Russia's democratic credentials when there were clearly major flaws in America's own electoral system. Like Putin, who moved cautiously in his first year in office, George W. Bush was a largely unknown quantity as far as foreign policy was concerned. He had been governor of Texas but had little international experience and had hardly been out of the country.

Candidate Bush's ideas about Russia were significantly formed by his chief advisor on Russia, Condoleezza Rice, who had served as his father's Soviet expert on the NSC. Her views, in turn, had been influenced by her professor and PhD advisor at the University of Denver, Josef Korbel, the Czech émigré who first aroused her interest in things Soviet and also happened to be the father of Madeleine Albright, Clinton's secretary of state.[18] When Rice heard Korbel speak to her class on Stalin, she "fell in love" with the subject, and became intrigued by the "Byzantine nature of Soviet politics and by power: how it operates. How it's used."[19] She wrote her PhD on the Czech military. When she was working for George H. W. Bush, he told Gorbachev "She tells me everything I need to know about the Soviet Union." To which Gorbachev replied, "I certainly hope she knows a lot."[20]

Indeed, the second major influence on Rice's ideas about Russia was her time in the Bush administration when she dealt with German unification and the collapse of the Soviet Union. It was during this period that she won the trust of President Bush and National Security Advisor General Brent Scowcroft. She also had that run-in with Boris Yeltsin during his September 1989 visit to the White House. This reinforced her skeptical view of Yelstin, which led her to criticize the Clinton administration's wholehearted support of Yeltsin.[21]

A decade later, George W. Bush relied on Rice to help form his views of foreign policy during the campaign. When Rice first interviewed with candidate Bush, he told her, "I don't have any idea about foreign affairs."[22] The Bush campaign's most articulate statement on Russia came in Rice's 2000 *Foreign Affairs* article, "Promoting the National Interest." Advocating "a disciplined and consistent foreign policy that separates the important from the trivial," she stressed the universality of American values, cautioned against using the military unless it was absolutely necessary, and advocated a comprehensive relationship with Russia. Russia was a much freer country than during the Soviet times and had many of the attributes of a great power, she wrote, but its economic weakness and lack of a new national identity "threaten to overwhelm it." The Clinton administration erred by supporting Yeltsin, whose "agenda became the American agenda." It was time to move to a new agenda—away from the Cold War arms control regime and toward a recognition that "Russia is a great power, and that we will always have interests that conflict as well as coincide."[23]

During his campaign, Bush echoed these views. In a speech at the Reagan Library in California he stressed that Russia was a great power and should be treated as such, but reiterated his commitment to deploying missile defense systems and eschewing Cold War arms control treaties. The United States should support democracy in Russia, he said, but it could not support "a corrupt and favored elite." Moreover, although he pledged to cooperate with Russia on combating terrorism, he declared "that is impossible unless Russia operates with civilized self-restraint."[24]

A few months later, Bush discussed the possibility of cutting off IMF funding for Russia because of its conduct in Chechnya, adding, "This guy, Putin—has come to power as a result of Chechnya—the real fundamental question for Russia—is what will Russia look like—will she be a market economy, or will she be one of those economies where a favored few elites are able to put money in their pockets?"[25] During the first presidential debate, asked what he would do if Serbia strongman Slobodan Milošević refused to leave power, Bush replied that the Russians "have sway in that part of the world" and should persuade him to go. When asked a similar question in the vice-presidential debate, Dick Cheney was more explicit. Cooperation with Russia to oust Milošević, he said, was "an opportunity for the United States to test President Putin—to find out if he is committed to democracy (and) willing to support freedom and democracy in Eastern Europe." During the second presidential debate, Bush repeated his criticisms that the IMF, during the Clinton administration, had dispensed too much money to Russia without enough oversight over what happened to it, adding, "the only people who are going to reform Russia are Russians. They are going to have to make the decisions themselves."[26]

During the campaign, Condoleezza Rice argued that relations with Russia should be normalized after the Clinton administration's overemphasis on personal ties between the leaders. Russia, she implied, would be downgraded in U.S. priorities. The Bush camp signaled that it considered nuclear arms control treaties to be relics of the Cold War era, which the United States no longer needed, even if Russia had not recognized this reality. The dismissive attitude toward arms control was a source of anxiety for Russia, because its nuclear arsenal was the basis of its remaining great-power status and arms control treaties were one on the few areas where Russia and the United States were still equals. On inaugural night, Rice sent a message to Putin meant to reassure him, promising "We will be great friends."[27]

One Bush official who had decades of experience with the Soviet Union and Russia was Donald Rumsfeld, defense secretary for President Ford, who was to reprise the role in 2001. In the 1990s Rumsfeld had been a member of the RAND U.S.-Russia Business Forum, a group of high-level Russian and American business leaders that met twice a year. From his discussions with his Russian counterparts, he concluded that Russian leaders were considering two different ways to reclaim their status as a great power—either consorting with what the United States would term "rogue" regimes and pressuring neighbors or choosing economic integration with the West. In 2001, recognizing that it had been only a decade since the collapse of the USSR, Rumsfeld supported engagement with Russia: "I wanted Russia to join the circle of advanced, prosperous societies and would have been pleased to see the country grow in strength as a friend or even a partner of the West. Accordingly I thought the best path for the United States was to avoid hectoring Russia on imperfect democratic practices, but rather to encourage it along a path toward freer economic and political systems."[28]

During the 2000 electoral campaign, congressional Republicans attacked candidate Al Gore for what they considered the Clinton administration's flawed Russia policies. They published a polemical indictment of the Clinton administration's policies toward Russia, from which candidate Bush drew many of his arguments. The title made clear what their view was: *Russia's Road to Corruption: How the Clinton Administration Exported Government Instead of Free Enterprise and Failed the Russian People.* The report pictured Vice President Gore and Prime Minister Victor Chernomyrdin on its cover. The Report argued that the Clinton policy was flawed from the start, that it conducted Russia policy "in an elite and uniquely insular policy-making group without accountability to the normal checks and balances within the executive branch." It had particularly harsh words for the Gore-Chernomyrdin Commission, and for the vice president who, it said, rejected CIA reports of how corrupt Chernomyrdin and his colleagues were. It blamed the United States for pursuing policies that led to Russia's 1998 economic crash and for turning Russians against America, where they had been well disposed to the United States in the early 1990s. Nevertheless, despite the fact that the U.S.-Russian relationship was "in tatters," a "bright Russian future" was still possible, provided there was "a clear articulation of American interests, values and policies." The president should take charge of Russia policy himself and recognize that "a stable, secure, democratic and prosperous Russia is a vital American interest."[29]

As Bush was about to take office, the U.S. National Intelligence Council, which coordinates the work of America's intelligence agencies, highlighted the asymmetries between Russia and the United States in its 2000 report *Global Trends, 2015*. Moscow, it claimed, would in the next fifteen years be greatly challenged to adjust its expectations for world leadership to its dramatically reduced resources. "The stakes for both Europe and the United States will be high, although neither will have the ability to determine the outcome for Russia in 2015."[30]

"LET'S GET DOWN TO BUSINESS"

The new U.S.-Russian relationship did not begin auspiciously. Barely had Secretary of State General Colin Powell moved into his office in the State Department than two related spy scandals threatened to derail bilateral ties. According to Powell, "The Russians ignored our gentleman's agreement about spies. They kept expanding their activities."[31] The Russian ambassador to Washington, Yuri Ushakov, recalls that his first meeting with Colin Powell did not go well. He had gone to the State Department to congratulate the new secretary of state on his appointment only to be informed that Russian diplomats were going to be expelled for activities incompatible with their diplomatic status. After a few general pleasantries, Ushakov was ushered out.[32] Powell then called Foreign Minister Igor Ivanov to break the news. "We have a small problem," said Powell, "Let's get one thing out of the way. We will expel 50 diplomats and we expect you to do that too." Ivanov agreed, adding, "now let's get down to business."[33] Both sides expelled fifty-three diplomats, the largest such expulsion since the Reagan administration expelled eighty Soviet spies in 1986. Powell and Ivanov met shortly thereafter in Egypt and, having disposed of the spy issue, proceded to have a productive meeting.[34]

Another spy scandal was much more damaging—and dangerous. Barely a month into the Bush presidency, FBI agent Robert Hanssen was arrested and charged with spying for the Soviet Union and then Russia, earning a reported $1.4 million for selling secrets over a twenty-two-year period. Hanssen had arguably compromised U.S. national security as much as had Aldrich Ames, the CIA agent who was arrested in 1994 for espionage activities that spanned the Cold War period and continued in post-Soviet Russia. Hanssen's arrest was a reminder that, despite the collapse of the USSR, Russia continued to engage in aggressive espionage activities in the United States. The Russian press largely depicted Hanssen as a hero. According to one Russian commentary echoed in numerous other publications, "We should give Soviet Intelligence its due: to plant two such moles as Ames and Hanssen: that is excellent professional work."[35]

The Bush administration undertook an interagency review of Russia policy when it came into office. It revisited the issue of where Russia belonged by reexamining its place in the State Department bureaucracy. Clinton had created the Office of the Newly Independent State (S/NIS), whose first head was Strobe Talbott. In 2001 Congress inserted itself in this debate. Jesse Helms, the conservative chairman of the Senate Foreign Relations Committee, was determined to downgrade Russia's status by abolishing S/NIS. The Bush administration decided that Russia no longer deserved its own bureau, and despite vigorous resistance from officials who dealt with Russia, all of the post-Soviet states were folded into the Bureau of European and Eurasian Affairs, which now included fifty-four countries.[36] This was, according to Talbott, "a strategic demotion of Russia itself." Nevertheless, Elizabeth Jones, the new assistant secretary for European affairs, spent a disproportionate amount of time dealing with Russia because of its importance to the rest of NATO and the European Union.[37] In another break with the Clinton administration, the Gore-Chernomyrdin Bilateral

Commission was abolished, thus removing a network of contacts from what remained a bilateral relationship with few stakeholders.

During the first six months of the Bush presidency the United States appeared to have downgraded the U.S.-Russian relationship on various fronts from arms control to Russia's war in Chechnya. In his first address to a joint session of Congress, Bush announced, "to protect our own people, our allies and friends, we must develop and we must deploy effective missile defenses. And as we transform our military, we can discard Cold War relics and reduce our own nuclear forces to reflect today's needs."[38] In a rebuff to Moscow's depiction of Chechen separatists as Islamic terrorists, a senior State Department official met at a local university with Ilyas Akhmadov, the Chechen foreign minister in exile who subsequently received political asylum in the United States, much to Russia's irritation. Officials accused Russia of contributing to proliferation and questioned the value of the Clinton-era assistance programs, including the Nunn-Lugar program which they argued, was essentially subsidizing the Russian military.

Nevertheless, the administration continued to press on with the bilateral agenda in preparation for the first Bush-Putin summit in Slovenia, one of the Yugoslav successor states that had not experienced ethnic violence. The administration's top priority was securing Russian assent to U.S. withdrawal from the ABM Treaty in order to enable the American missile defense program to proceed. For Putin, the meeting was a chance to move beyond the Clinton-Yeltsin relationship that symbolized Russia's weakness and promote the U.S.-Russian relationship on the basis of greater equality.

THE FIRST PRESIDENTIAL ENCOUNTER

Bush and Putin met for the first time in an ornate sixteenth-century castle in Brdo, Slovenia, on July 16, 2001. "My goal at the summit had been to cut through the tension and forge a connection with Putin," writes Bush. "I placed a high priority on personal diplomacy."[39] The summit came at the tail end of a trying first trip to Europe for an American president with limited experience in foreign policy whose attempts at forging good personal ties with leaders such as German chancellor Gerhard Schroder had proved to be difficult. The European commentariat was skeptical and even condescending toward Bush (the German magazine *Der Spiegel* pictured him on its cover as a gun-toting cowboy), and his first meeting with his European allies were strained.

By contrast, the Russian leader was far less judgmental of the new American president. Putin no doubt realized that after Bush's less-than-enthusiastic European reception, it would be advisable to treat the new president with respect. To Bush, Putin seemed tense at the outset. He began reading from note cards about the Soviet-era debt. After a few minutes, Bush interrupted his presentation with a question: "Is it true your mother gave you a cross that you had blessed in Jerusalem?" This apparently broke the ice, Putin put down his note cards and told the story about how a fire had burned down his dacha but the cross had survived the blaze and had special religious meaning for him.[40] The two presidents went on to discuss a wide range of subjects, including religion.[41] Putin pointedly warned Bush about the dangers of Islamic fundamentalist-bred terrorism emanating from Russia's southern rim, a danger that he believed the United States did not take seriously enough. He was—prophetically—particularly vehement about Pakistan and Prime Minister Pervez Musharraf's regime's support of the Taliban and Al Qaeda. Putin told Bush that the go-to person in Moscow should be Defense Minister Sergei Ivanov, and Ivanov became National Security Advisor Condoleezza Rice's main interlocutor. According to several Bush administration officials, Rice seemed to work well with Ivanov.[42] There was, according to their advisors, good personal chemistry at the meeting. Indeed, the close personal relationship between the two presidents lasted well into the second Bush and Putin terms.[43]

Their joint press conference after the summit began in an unremarkable way. President Bush spoke about the importance of "building a constructive, respectful relationship with Russia." Putin rejoined, "We are counting on a pragmatic relationship between Russia and the United States." The two leaders discussed the importance of Russia's joining the WTO and their differences over missile defense and NATO enlargement. Putin raised an issue that he would continue to mention throughout his presidency, namely that, as early as 1954, the USSR had sent a note to NATO countries announcing its intention to participate in NATO. He complained that the human rights of ethnic Russians living in the Baltic states were being violated. Bush described Putin as "an honest, straightforward man who loves his country. He loves his family. We share a lot of values. I view him as a remarkable leader."

And then came the fateful phrase that was to haunt Bush for the rest of his presidency. In response to a question about whether he could trust Putin, Bush said "I looked the man in the eye. I found him very straightforward and trustworthy—I was able to get a sense of his soul."[44] Condoleezza Rice, listening nearby, visibly tightened at these words. "This is going to be a problem," she murmured.[45] "In the years ahead," Bush later regretfully wrote, "Putin would give me reason to revise my opinion."[46]

Rice laments that Bush had not rehearsed how to answer a question about trust: "We were never able to escape the perception that the President had naively trusted Putin and then been betrayed."[47] Colin Powell was less diplomatic. "I looked into his eyes and I saw KBG," he quipped later.[48] Putin's comments on Bush were less fulsome, but nevertheless the first presidential encounter was deemed a success by both sides.[49] Some Bush-era officials are less charitable: "Bush was played by Putin," said one, echoing the sentiments of the more skeptical group.[50]

Shortly thereafter, Bush gave an assessment of Putin that revealed his understanding of where the Russian leader stood: "I found a man who realizes his future lies with the West, not the East, that we share common security concerns, particularly Islamic fundamentalism, that he understands missiles could affect him just as much as us." Then Bush, with a clear diagnosis, went to the heart of the matter. "On the other hand, he doesn't want to be diminished by America."[51]

TERROR STRIKES—AND PUTIN PROPOSES AN ANTITERRORIST ALLIANCE

On September 9, 2001, Putin called Bush with an urgent message: Ahmed Shah Massoud, leader of the Afghan anti-Taliban Northern Alliance, which was supported by Moscow, had been assassinated in his compound by two Arab suicide bombers posing as journalists. Russian intelligence authorities concluded that Massoud's assassination presaged the beginning of a broader terrorist campaign. Putin warned Bush about the wider implications of this act: "I told him I had a foreboding that something was about to happen, something long in preparation."[52] Indeed, the Russian leadership, with its long and bitter experiences in Afghanistan, understood the dynamics of the ongoing strife in Afghanistan better than did the United States. Putin was convinced that Islamic extremists in Afghanistan were supporting Chechen fighters. He had warned Bush in Slovenia about the dangers of terrorism emanating from the "arc of instability," the unstable areas south of the Russian Federation.

Afghanistan was a difficult issue for Washington and Moscow. After all, the United States had been instrumental in helping defeat the Soviet Union in Afghanistan, thereby contributing to a train of events that eventually led to the demise of the USSR. The day the last Soviet troops withdraw from Afghanistan in February 1989, the CIA station chief in Islamabad sent a two-word cable home: "WE WON."[53] U.S. support of the anti-Soviet Mujaheddin between 1980 and 1988 helped to end the Soviet occupation of Afghanistan. But American money and weapons—along with money and recruits from Middle Eastern countries—also helped to create what later became the Taliban and Al Qaeda, which were the offspring of the Mujaheddin. The United States, then, inadvertently became midwife to what evolved into the greatest threat to its own national security in the twenty-first century.

Much has been written about the failure of the Bush administration in its first nine months to understand the gravity of the danger from Al Qaeda, despite warnings from the U.S. Intelligence Community that Osama bin Laden was planning a terrorist attack and that planes might be used for such an attack.[54] Veteran Russian official Evgeny Primakov believed that, more than a decade after the Soviets were defeated, the United States failed to grasp the seriousness of the threat that the successors to the Mujaheddin now posed to the United States. "The United States," he added, had no well thought-out plan to fight terrorism."[55]

On the morning of September 11, two days after Putin's call to Bush, terrorists struck the United States, killing three thousand people and forever changing U.S. views of its own security and introducing an unprecedented sense of vulnerability in the American homeland. In the chaotic hours following the attack on the twin towers, Vladimir Putin was the first foreign leader to put in a call to Bush and express his sympathy and support. However, he could not reach Bush on Air Force One, so Rice took the call in the White House bunker. She warned Putin that the United States had gone to DEFCON 3, a high state of military alert. The next day, Putin called off a military exercise in the northern Pacific Ocean that might have distracted U.S. forces.

When the two presidents eventually spoke, Putin said, "Good will triumph over evil. I want you to know that in this struggle, we will stand together."[56] Indeed, the attack on the Twin Towers vindicated the warnings Putin had given the new U.S. president and placed Russia in a unique position to offer advice and assistance, given its intimate knowledge of Afghan politics, the Afghan terrain, the location of terrorist training camps, and its experience working with the Northern Alliance. At that moment Rice realized that the Cold War was really over.[57] The message from the Kremlin was a clear "America we are with you," even if the Russian media reactions varied from *Schadenfreude* that arrogant Americans had it coming to them to conspiracy theories that the attack had been engineered by the American "special services." But, most Russians now understood the answer to an eternal question: "Against whom shall we ally?" (*Protiv kogo druzhit' budem?*).[58]

The real question, however, was how Russia would support the United States as it retaliated. In order to strike back at the Taliban, which had harbored Al Qaeda for many years, the United States needed to secure supply routes to Afghanistan, and establishing military bases in Central Asia was the best way to accomplish this. But, since the Soviet collapse, Russia had resented the growing American presence in its backyard. U.S. interests in Central Asia were both energy- and security-related, and leaders such as Kazakhstan's Nursultan Nazarbayev, Kyrgyzstan's Askar Akayev, and Uzbekistan's Islom Karimov had become quite adept at balancing Russia and the United States as they consolidated their power and sought investment and trade. The U.S. war in Afghanistan presented Central Asian leaders with a unique opportunity to secure an American military presence and the economic benefits that accompanied bases. However, there was the issue of overflight rights over

Russia. Even though the Central Asian states were independent, Russia had the ability to block access to U.S. bases in its former republics.

The Russian leadership was deeply divided over whether to support the establishment of U.S. bases in Central Asia. Although later Primakov claimed that "Moscow took a very proactive stance supporting U.S. assistance in Central Asia," this was not true at the beginning.[59] Initially, Putin called Kyrgyz leader Askar Akayev, Kazakh leader Nazarbayev, and Uzbek leader Karimov to warn them against accepting U.S. bases, but they apparently pushed back. Defense Minister Sergei Ivanov, former KGB official and close Putin advisor, opposed the move. If the United States had bases in Central Asia, he later recalled, it would begin democracy promotion there, and that was not good for Russia.[60] Putin sent his national security advisor Vladimir Rushailo to Central Asia to try and dissuade the Tajik leader Emomaly Rakhmon from accepting a U.S. base.[61] However, it became clear that the Central Asian leaders would not fall in line. So Putin changed course.

On September 22, Putin convened a meeting of his advisors in his presidential dacha in Sochi on the Black Sea, and they thrashed out the issue of bases in Central Asia. He argued in favor of supporting the U.S. war effort and permitting the bases, because he wanted better relations with the United States.[62] Despite vigorous objections from some of his colleagues, he prevailed. Then he called Bush to let him know that Russia would not object to the establishment of U.S. military presence in Central Asia "as long as it has the objective of fighting the war on terror and is temporary."[63] Two days later, he summoned the leaders of the major political parties in the Duma to meet him in Moscow. Only two of them—liberals Grigory Yavlinsky and Boris Nemtsov—fully supported his decision on the Central Asia bases.[64] The rest objected but fell in line when it became apparent that Putin's mind was made up. For many, it came down to weighing the "head," which urged cooperation with the United States on pragmatic grounds, against the "stomach," which argued emotionally against it. Putin announced his decision to support the U.S. war effort in Afghanistan during a televised address to the Russian people, where he pledged the "active cooperation" of Russian intelligence services in intelligence gathering and exchange with their U.S. counterparts.[65] The Cold War did really appear to be over.

American officials then fanned out to Central Asia to negotiate basing rights with the leaders of Uzbekistan and Kyrgyzstan. U.S. defense secretary Donald Rumsfeld, arguing that these leaders "were not saints, but saints are in short supply in the world," worked out a deal with Uzbek strongman Karimov that U.S. special operations forces could use the air field at Karshi-Khanabad (K-2), located 120 miles from the Afghan border. Karimov complained about Russian pressure to coordinate basing decisions with them.[66] He also asked Undersecretary John Bolton, "If we give you a base, will you be here in ten years?"[67] Given Uzbekistan's human rights record, the U.S. base agreement offered Karimov a respite from the international criticism to which he had been subjected. The Kyrgyz base was established at the Manas airport. Russian commentators were quick to point to the economic benefits that the Kyrgyzstanis and Uzbeks gained from these bases, from fuel contracts to construction jobs. Some questioned how temporary these bases would be, suggesting that America had longer-term designs on Central Asia and that the Central Asian elites' economic interest in the bases would grow.[68]

THE CRAWFORD SUMMIT

The honeymoon in U.S.-Russian relations that followed Putin reaching out to Bush lasted from September 2001 to May 2002. While American and Russian officials spoke about their newfound partnership, Russia was sharing intelligence about Afghanistan with the United States, which, according the U.S. officials, was important during Operation Enduring Freedom, which ousted the Taliban from power. Included were data that helped U.S. forces find their way around Kabul and logistical information on the topography and caves in Afghanistan.[69] Rice, who had urged "normalizing" relations with Russia a mere year before, was enthusiastic: "Russia has been one of our best allies in terms of intelligence sharing, in terms of support for American operations that have taken place out of Central Asia—this has been an extremely important relationship to us, really one of our most, and it is confirmation that there is a new basis for cooperative security relationship with Russia."[70]

Putin's rhetoric and actions after 9/11 reinforced the impression that he had made a strategic commitment to working with the West. In a speech delivered in German to the Bundestag at the end of September, he reiterated that the Cold War was over, and Russia and the West should cooperate in fighting terror.[71] Shortly afterward, Russia announced that it had closed its Signals Intelligence site in Lourdes, Cuba. It had also closed its naval base in Cam Ranh Bay, Vietnam. The Cuban listening post had been an irritant in U.S.-Russian relations; although it was shut down largely because it had become uneconomic. Its closing, nevertheless, was viewed as a positive symbolic gesture.

Rumsfeld recounts a meeting with Putin in the fall of 2001 during which the Russian president spoke nonstop for ninety minutes: "He was, as usual, somewhat of an enigma. Though he denied us tangible assistance for the Afghan effort, he was generous with his advice—which Afghans we could trust, the motives of regional players—right down to military tactics."[72] Former CIA director George Tenet is more guarded in his assessment of Russia's contribution to fighting terrorism, noting that "their contribution was a disappointment—they were preoccupied with Chechnya and were not players in the global war against terrorism, certainly as we defined it." Tenet believes that Cold War habits were too deeply ingrained for broad-based intelligence cooperation: "In the final analysis, it was still a game of spy versus spy."[73] Tenet highlights the fact that Russia defined terrorism through a much narrower lens that did the United States, namely Islamic fundamentalism in the North Caucasus that threatened Russia itself. Inasmuch as there were Chechens fighting with Al Qaeda in Afghanistan or Al Qaeda operatives fighting in the North Caucasus, Moscow would acknowledge the global nature of the terrorist threat. But, from an American point of view, Russia did not face the same challenge from Al Qaeda and its affiliates as did the United States. Limited intelligence sharing during the three-month war in Afghanistan was productive. Beyond that, Russia's willingness to cooperate on counterterrorism was constrained. Moreover, the collaboration was selective and the provenance of some of its data was not transparent, raising issues about its reliability.[74]

But how, once the Taliban had been routed from Kabul, to sustain the momentum for a more productive relationship? Putin made his first official visit to the United States in November 2001. The two presidents met at the White House, Bush promised to "work with Congress to end the application of the Jackson-Vanik amendment to Russia."[75]

The high point of the Putin trip was his visit to Bush's ranch in Crawford, Texas. Initially, the Russians had balked at going to Texas, not understanding that it was a special honor to be asked to the president's private residence.[76] They insisted on an Oval Office meeting first. The Crawford visit was intended to emphasize the importance that Bush attached to a close personal relationship with his Russian counterpart. In a highly symbolic gesture, the former KGB agent attended Bush's morning intelligence briefing. At their press conference at Crawford High School, Bush reiterated his praise for Putin: "a new style of leader, a reformer, a man who loves his country as much as I love mine." Putin was complimentary if somewhat less enthusiastic, and had some words of caution on the Bush administration's pledge to emancipate the women of Afghanistan: "What we should avoid in the implementation of such programs, and as an end result of their implementation, is that a lady would turn into a man."[77]

The atmosphere that evening was relaxed when the eighteen Americans and twelve Russians sat around the campfire at Crawford. It was the first visit to an American ranch for all the Russian guests who expressed surprise that a U.S. president would choose such a modest home for his "dacha."[78] In his toast, Putin remarked on how fortunate everyone was to have President Bush in the White House. Later he asked Commerce Secretary Donald Evans, "How has America accomplished so much in two hundred years?" Evans responded, "It's our freedoms. You have to create an environment for competition. The American people are good people. They wake up every morning trying to do the right thing."[79] Later on the Russians were treated to a spirited round of square dancing by top U.S. officials.

Bush announced that the United States was going to reduce its nuclear arsenal to between 1,700 and 2,200 warheads over the next decade, and $3.5 billion of the Soviet debt was to be forgiven. But the warmth around the campfire would not last. The camaraderie masked the fact that there was little agreement on the most difficult issues that would continue to irritate the relationship for the rest of the Bush presidency: missile defense and the U.S. withdrawal from the ABM Treaty.

GREAT EXPECTATIONS

Because Putin is still leading Russia more than a decade after 9/11 and he continues to harbor resentments over what he depicts as broken U.S. promises, the debate about what happened after 9/11 continues to influence the U.S.-Russian relationship. When countries form partnerships forged out of exigencies such as the 9/11 attacks, the shelf life for these alliances is usually short because they have a specific and limited focus—defeating a common enemy. After all, the wartime U.S.-Soviet alliance—which the Russians invoked as a model for the post 9/11 partnership—was formed with one sole aim, defeating Hitler. Once Germany was on the way to defeat, the alliance began to fray as the victors disagreed about what would happen after Germany surrendered, and the Cold War began. Similarly, in 2001, the common goal was to defeat the Taliban. There was no discussion about what might happen afterward or indeed how the bilateral relationship might develop. And yet there were unspoken expectations that affected the relationship after the rout of the Taliban from Kabul. With hindsight, it is clear that U.S. and Russian expectations were mismatched.

In the decade since the terrorist attacks, Putin has on numerous occasions complained to visiting Americans that the United States failed to live up to the commitments that were implicit in the post-9/11 bargain. There is a general consensus, as one Russian put it, that "Putin was interested in an equal partnership of unequals."[80] In return for supporting the United States, Putin hoped that Russia would be accepted as part of the international entourage that decides everything. John Beyrle, former ambassador to Russia, agrees: "Russia was looking for respect and acknowledgment that Russia's voice mattered and that the United States would listen to Russia and act as if its opinions mattered."[81] Igor Ivanov emphasizes that Russia wanted a new partnership against new threats. "We wanted an anti-terrorist international coalition like the anti-Nazi coalition. This would be the basis for a new world order."[82]

Why did Putin initiate this third U.S.-Russian reset? It is important to examine his goals in 2001, since many Russian officials' subsequent public and private comments have focused on what they regard as broken U.S. promises. Yet these quid pro quos were never explicit, nor were they discussed when Putin launched his reset. Putin wanted to present Russia as an essential partner in what came to be known as the United States' Global War on Terror, thereby upgrading Russia's significance for Washington, and equating Russia's own struggle against North Caucasus Islamist opponents with the American struggle against Al Qaeda. According to Alexander Voloshin, Putin believed that, if Bush understood Russia's own terrorist problem, this would improve relations.[83] Beyond that, Putin entertained hopes that supporting the United States would restore to Russia some of its erstwhile status.

Putin may have also expected that he could secure U.S. recognition of what he defined as Russia's vital interests. These included appreciating the importance of bilateral arms control arrangements and recognizing that the post-Soviet space was Russia's rightful sphere of influence. Putin expected that counterterrorist cooperation would bring Russia rewards that extended beyond Afghanistan, making up for ten years of the West's relegating Russia to a second-rate status and imposing a U.S.-led agenda on Moscow. Putin was more than well aware of the decade-long and ultimately unsuccessful Soviet occupation of Afghanistan. Even though he must have appreciated how difficult it would be for the United States to win in Afghanistan, he somehow believed (and Bush initially promised him) that U.S. bases in Central Asia would be temporary and would close once military operations had ceased. He expected—correctly—that in supporting the U.S. war on terror, the United States would cease criticizing Russia's conduct in Chechnya and would instead equate Chechen fighters with other Islamic terrorists. Events would subsequently underline that conclusion.

On the night of October 22, 2002, 850 spectators were sitting in Moscow's Dubrovka Theater enjoying a performance of the musical *Nord-Ost*. Suddenly a group of Chechen terrorists seized the theater midway through the performance, taking the audience—many families with small children—hostage. They demanded an end to the second Chechen War and independence for Chechnya. For two and a half days, the terrified audience sat in the theater as fruitless negotiations with the terrorists dragged on. Eventually the Russian authorities pumped the anesthetic fentanyl into the theater, and the terrorists were incapacitated and killed. The siege was over. However, there were no preparations for dealing with the hostages who had also been knocked out by the fentanyl. Eventually 130 people died as a result of inhaling a substance about which no information had been given and for which the authorities had provided no antidote. Bush blamed the civilian deaths squarely on the Chechens.

What concrete expectations did the United States have from this partnership with Russia? Bush administration officials agree that they sought no quid pro quos. The main task was to secure Russian cooperation for Operation Enduring Freedom, which involved securing Russian assent to continued operations in Central Asia and sharing Russian intelligence on the Taliban. Russia supported the U.S. view that it was entirely appropriate to use military force to defeat terrorism—indeed, the U.S. concept was used to justify Russia's own campaign in Chechnya.[84]

The Bush administration believed that, in routing the Taliban, America was "cleaning up Russia's back yard," enhancing Russia security by eliminating the terrorist cells emanating from Afghanistan that threatened Russia's southern neighbors and its own North Caucasus. The assumption was that Russia would acknowledge that the U.S. campaign was in Moscow's interest. The White House did not expect gratitude—a commodity that is usually in short supply in international politics—but it assumed that there would be recognition of the U.S. role in enhancing security in Russia's neighborhood. Beyond that, Washington was willing to adopt a virtual vow of silence about Russia's domestic situation, from the Chechen War to the limitations on media freedom and the selective assault on oligarchs who did not swear fealty to Putin. In short, the Bush administration's initial post 9/11 relationship with Russia focused on Realpolitik. In return for Russia's support, the United States was willing to facilitate Putin's primary stated goal—economic modernization and integration into the global economy—by offering accelerated WTO membership negotiations, graduation from Jackson-Vanik, and other economic incentives. A high-level energy dialogue group was formed to promote joint energy projects and to explore closer economic cooperation. In return, U.S. officials expected that Russia would come to accept the premise that Cold War–era arms control negotiations were obsolete and would eventually modify its views on missile defense.

It took ten weeks to oust the Taliban from power. After that, the United States and Russia turned to the other pressing issues facing them. The inbox that Bush and Putin inherited from their predecessors necessitated negotiations on issues over which there had been continuing disagreements over the past decade, namely missile defense, NATO enlargement, and Russia's relationship with Iran.

EXITING THE ABM TREATY

The Bush administration came into office determined to jettison Cold War–era arms control agreements. Candidate Bush and his advisors had argued throughout the electoral campaign that it was imperative for the United States to deploy a missile defense system to counter nuclear threats from rogue states (the "Axis of Evil" Bush described in his January 2002 State of the Union address) and nonstate actors that might seek to acquire and launch nuclear weapons. Whereas the Clinton administration had sought ways of reconciling missile defense with maintaining the 1972 Anti-Ballistic Missile Treaty, the Bush administration had made it clear from the outset that the ABM Treaty was an unnecessary impediment to the United States deploying missile defense components to fend off a potential attack from Iran or North Korea.

Russian objections to missile defense stemmed from the Kremlin's opposition to abandoning the thirty-year-old arms control regime that had been the cornerstone of U.S.-Soviet relations and which enabled Russia to interact as an equal with the United States in its otherwise greatly weakened state. Moreover, there was, from the beginning, a Russian suspicion about the intended target of the missile defense installations.[85] Were they really aimed at Iran and North Korea? Or was the ultimate aim of missile defense deployments to target and challenge the viability of Russia's own nuclear arsenal?

In December 2001, the Bush administration announced its withdrawal from the ABM Treaty. John Bolton, under secretary of state for arms control and international security, who had the missile defense portfolio, was exultant: "With President Bush's announcement of the U.S. withdrawal from the ABM Treaty on December 13, a dangerous relic of the Cold War was officially put to rest."[86] Defense Minister Sergei Ivanov, by contrast, meeting with Secretary Rumsfeld—who had a few months earlier called Russia "an active proliferator" of weapons technology to Iran and North Korea—said "this unilateral decision of the United States was not a surprise for us. We still believe it was a mistake."[87]

Putin's reaction to the ABM withdrawal was muted. In his official response, he reiterated his view that the decision was mistaken but committed Russia to continued cooperation with the United States. In an interview on the day of the announcement, he conceded that the United States had the legal right to withdraw from the ABM Treaty and that he would not use this decision to stoke "anti-American hysteria." He also admitted that Bush had been straightforward about his intentions from the beginning and had not deceived him.[88] For his part, Bush talked about a "new strategic partnership" with Russia. In his 2002 State of the Union address, he spoke of new alignments: "In this moment of opportunity, a common danger is eroding old rivalries. America is working with Russia and China and India in ways we never have before to achieve peace and prosperity."[89]

Despite the appearance of equanimity about the ABM withdrawal, the Russian side objected to this unilateral act. It was the first signal, coming a mere three months after 9/11, that the Bush administration would push ahead with its new strategic concept irrespective of Moscow's views. Fearing that the White House would jettison the other pillar of arms control—the START treaty—Putin had told Bush at the Shanghai APEC conference in October 2001, "I need a treaty." So Bush, rejecting the advice of the extreme arms control skeptics in his administration, agreed to a new treaty.[90] "I believe we must have something that lasts beyond our presidencies. The strategic relationship with Russia is something that's important for the next ten years," he said, adding, "Putin is at huge risk, and he needs to fight off his troglodytes."[91]

The next chapter in the Bush administration's move toward down-grading arms control with Russia was the Strategic Offensive Reductions Treaty (SORT) or Moscow Treaty, signed during Bush's first visit to Moscow in May 2002. It was a vehicle for the United States to offer serious reductions in nuclear weapons while avoiding what it considered the excessive regulations of the previous SALT and START agreements. The treaty itself is minimalist (a "haiku," according to some U.S. critics), three-page document committing both parties to reduce the aggregate number of deployed strategic nuclear warheads to between 1,700 and 2,200 by December 31, 2012.[92] This number was three times lower than the limits for warheads established by START I. SORT represented the largest proposed reduction in strategic nuclear weapons ever codified in an international agreement, yet it did not obligate either side to destroy these weapons. They could be stored and redeployed, if necessary. SORT also lacked the verification mechanisms that START had embodied.[93] According to Primakov, "Russia signed the treaty primarily to end the cycle of *unilateral* decision making by the United States in matters of security."[94]

Yet the Moscow Treaty also represented the high point of the third reset. Bush and Putin announced that this was the dawn of a new strategic partnership, one that would involve broad-based cooperation on a range of global political and economic issues.[95] At this point Putin's broader goals of securing recognition by cooperating with the United States overrode Russian irritation about the downgrading of arms control. The Bush administration believed that the Russians would swallow their disappointment and accept the new agenda outlined in the Moscow summit documents. In reality, this new agenda—nonproliferation, missile defense, counterterrorism, Russia's WTO accession—was the 1990s agenda refashioned to highlight Russia's new post-9/11 orientation. After initially announcing that it would cut funding for the Nunn-Lugar program, the Bush administration reversed itself and requested extra funding. Moreover, despite the Bush administration's excoriation of the Gore-Chernomyrdin commission, the United States and Russia established a bilateral Russian-American Consultative Group on Strategic Stability, comprising the two countries' foreign and defense ministers, which had its first meeting in September 2002 and covered a range of issues form North Korea to Iraq, Afghanistan, and further arms control issues. Nevertheless, the issue of Euro-Atlantic security architecture continued to present major challenges.

NATO'S "BIG BANG"

Shortly after he entered the Kremlin, Putin, like Yeltsin before him, suggested the possibility of Russia's joining NATO. In addition to raising the issue with Bill Clinton, he asked NATO secretary-general George Robertson and German chancellor Gerhard Schroeder when Russia could join. Robertson told him Russia would have to apply.[96] In a July 2001 press conference, Putin said that one option for the alliance was "to include Russia in NATO. This also creates a single area of defense security." Senior Russian officials believe that Putin was serious about exploring NATO membership—even if he was unsure about whether Russia would indeed join.

These ideas resonated with some incoming Bush administration officials. During the review of Russia policy at the beginning of the Bush administration, the State Department's Office of Policy Planning sent a memo to Secretary Powell suggesting that NATO had always been a protean organization and that the NATO of the twenty-first century could find a place for Russia. It suggested issuing an invitation for Russia to join NATO—including a road map of how negotiations should proceed—as part of the discussions on further NATO enlargement, rather than continuing to enlarge NATO and exclude Russia. It concluded, "It is in our long-term interest to have Russia as a partner, not a spoiler."[97] Richard Haass, director of Policy Planning, was strongly supportive: "Having Russia inside NATO was a big idea. NATO had become a set of discretionary relations and having Russia close to NATO is not inconsistent with what NATO has become." The memo never made it past Powell's desk. In retrospect, says Haass, "We neglected the Aretha Franklin principle with Russia—we did not give them enough respect."[98]

A few months later, former secretary of state James Baker wrote an article advocating that Russia be offered the prospect of NATO membership, reminding his audience that NATO is "a coalition of former adversaries—one sad lesson of the twentieth century is that refusing to form alliances with defeated adversaries is more dangerous than forming such alliances."[99] Having helped negotiate the end of the Cold War, Baker spoke with special authority. But there was as little interest in the Bush administration as there had been in the Clinton administration in seriously offering Russia the prospect of NATO membership. Russia's size—and the fact that it shares a border with China—and anticipated demands for a unique role in NATO acted as a deterrent. Or perhaps it also reflected officials' lack of imagination and reluctance to think creatively about what would admittedly have been a major challenge.

Because NATO membership was not in the cards, the administration looked for ways in which Russia and NATO could interact more productively. When the NATO-Russian Permanent Joint Council was established in 1997, the United States and its allies hoped that it would go some way toward lessening Russia's antipathy toward the organization and provide a venue where common issues of European security could be discussed. But the results were rather meager. Russian officials retained their visceral distrust of NATO, which they viewed as a U.S.-dominated organization inimical to Russia's geostrategic interests. After 9/11 the United States and its allies sought ways of upgrading the NATO-Russian relationship in the hopes that this might enhance cooperation. The result was the establishment of the NATO-Russia Council (NRC) at the NATO Rome summit in May 2002. Welcoming the new council, NATO secretary-general Lord Robertson said the PJC was "simply not enough now" and a "new qualitatively better relationship was needed." Whereas the PJC had operated in a "19 + 1" format, with Russia meeting with NATO after NATO had taken its decisions on issues of mutual interest, the NATO-Russia Council was designed to operate on the basis of 20. That meant that Russia could make its views known before NATO had taken a collective decision and NATO would supposedly take them into account. However, the Russians continued to suspect that the NRC still operated on the basis of 19 + 1 on all major decisions. In reality, the NATO-Russian Council represented an upgrade of the PJC inasmuch as it was to operate by consensus but was to cover all of the same areas as had the PJC—counterterrorism, crisis management, nonproliferation, arms control, theater missile defense, search and rescue at sea, military-to-military cooperation, civil emergencies, and new threats. The rhetoric of the NATO leaders at the Rome summit—including that of President Putin—was enthusiastic, with much talk of new beginnings.[100]

At the same time that the Bush administration was seeking to upgrade the NATO-Russia relationship, it was also committed to something that would undermine the U.S-Russian relationship—the next stage of NATO enlargement. NATO had created the membership action plan (MAP) process, which established benchmarks for aspirant countries to achieve that would make them eligible for membership. The question was whether the three Baltic states—Estonia, Latvia, and Lithuania—should be admitted. This would establish the precedent of admitting countries that had formerly been part of the USSR, a particularly sensitive issue for Moscow. Although there were skeptics within the executive branch who questioned how much Poland, the Czech Republic, and Hungary had contributed to NATO since they joined in 1999, the prevailing consensus was that it was prudent to enlarge NATO to include more countries in the second round. The U.S. Senate had strong bipartisan support for NATO enlargement to include all three Baltic states. The momentum could not be stopped. NATO enlargement, it was argued, was necessary to complete the post-1989 vision of a "Europe whole and free." U.S. officials repeated that Russia could have no veto over NATO's plans and stressed that "NATO enlargement threatens no-one."[101]

There was disagreement among the NATO allies over who should join and also opposition from Russia. According to Primakov, "Russia remains staunchly opposed to NATO expansion, since it brings a military alliance right up to our borders for no real purpose."[102]

In the run-up to NATO's 2002 enlargement decision, the United States was the leading advocate of a robust enlargement. Germany and France were more cautious, concerned about what the Russian reaction might be. Britain, too, was cautious, favoring a smaller number of countries. The Nordic states and new Central European members were the most enthusiastic supporters of Baltic membership and the southern states focused on the need to strengthen the southern flank. There were three options—take some, take all of the seven aspirants, or take none, although the last was not a viable option.[103] In the end, the alliance adopted the "Big Bang" plan, offering invitations to the three Baltic states—Estonia, Latvia, and Lithuania—and to Central European states Bulgaria Romania, Slovakia, and Slovenia to join in 2004. The communiqué welcomed "the significant achievements of the NATO-Russia Council and expressed NATO's determination "to intensify and broaden our cooperation with Russia."[104] The official Russian reaction was restrained. However, this belied deeper Russian resentments that, once again, the United States had ignored Russia's interests.

By the end of 2002, Russia had to live with three Bush administration initiatives which it had previously opposed—the U.S. unilateral withdrawal from the ABM Treaty; the SORT treaty, which deemphasized strategic arms control; and NATO enlargement to include the three Baltic states. Bush administration officials dealt with Russian objections by arguing that Russia's concerns about NATO enlargement and future missile defense were groundless because neither was directed against Russia. American officials believed that, in private, men like Sergei Ivanov, Igor Ivanov, and even Putin himself understood this. Nevertheless, the Kremlin remained highly ambivalent about U.S. policy, and Russians began to question what Russia had indeed gained from supporting the U.S. war in Afghanistan.

Other bilateral problems remained. Washington continued to criticize Moscow's ongoing nuclear assistance to Iran, particularly after Putin withdrew Russia from the previous Gore-Chernomyrdin agreement on Bushehr. In July 2002, Russia signed a deal to build five more civilian nuclear reactors in Iran over the next decade in addition to Bushehr, much to the displeasure of U.S. officials.[105] For Russia, this would bring in billions of dollars in exports. Putin invited Kim Jong Il, North Korea's reclusive leader, a major proliferator and part of Bush's Axis of Evil, to visit Russia. Positive rhetoric and more intense bilateral engagement could only go so far in overcoming significant differences of interest born of the asymmetries in power between the two countries and Russia's difficult domestic transformation.

PUTIN'S "VERTICAL OF POWER"

While candidate Bush had criticized Russia's domestic situation and the war in Chechnya and committed himself to supporting human rights and democracy, after 9/11 he rarely mentioned Russia's internal politics and repeatedly called Putin a reformer and a patriot. Nevertheless, administration officials were divided between those who focused more on interests and those more concerned with values. And Russia's domestic evolution certainly gave people cause for concern. Within his first two years in office, Putin had exiled oligarchs Boris Berezovsky (who had helped bring him to power) and Vladimir Gusinsky and, by taking over their media empires, gave the state much greater control over the flow of information. The Kursk disaster, during which Putin failed to return from vacation and deal with the sinking of the submarine in which 118 sailors lost their lives, elicited strong media criticism. This apparently convinced him that it was time to limit freedom of expression.[106] Putin began to recentralize political power by appointing seven super governors who were directly responsible to him. He was determined to restore order and statehood to Russia. The "vertical of power" was designed to give him unparalleled control at the top of the political pyramid.

Putin's most dramatic move to take charge had already occurred in 2000 when he summoned Russia's richest oligarchs to an ornate blue room in the Kremlin. "You had control over the political system," he told them. "If you don't like what I am doing, you only have yourselves to blame." From now on, he warned them, if they wanted to keep their assets, most of which were acquired through the nontransparent schemes of the 1990s, they would have to eschew politics. "You stay out of politics and I will not revise the results of privatization."[107] Seeking to strengthen his legitimacy, Putin revived symbols from the Soviet era, including restoring the melody of the old Soviet national anthem, albeit with new lyrics, a move publicly opposed by Yeltsin. By early 2001, he had consolidated most of the levers of power in his hands and had neutralized the most influential Yeltsin holdovers. He brought to Moscow his own supporters from St. Petersburg, many of whom came from the security services. Known as the Siloviki (Securocrats), they began to dominate all branches of government and parts of the private sector and also to accumulate their own assets, some of which they took from the exiled oligarchs.[108] In the name of rescuing Russia from the chaos and poverty of the 1990s, he began to rein in the regions, and he controlled the flow of information to the Russian people, appealing to traditional Russian values of *derzhavnost'* (a sense of "great power," where a strong ruler can project authority and influence abroad).

ON THE EVE OF THE IRAQ WAR

By 2002, it became clear that there were serious divergences among officials in the Bush administration about how Washington should deal with Moscow. At least three groups that cut across several government agencies espoused different views. The first group included the arms control skeptics, the ideological opponents of the ABM Treaty who were in the State Department, the Pentagon, and the Office of the Vice President. They believed that America should take advantage of Russia's weakness ("a second-rate trouble-maker with useless nukes" in the words of one of them) and forge ahead with diluting the Cold War–era arms control treaties. They were largely indifferent to Russia's domestic developments. The second group consisted of Department of State, National Security Council, and Department of Commerce career officials and political appointees, moderate pragmatists who were committed to improving relations with Russia. They believed in the importance of engaging Russia on a broad range of political and economic fronts and in treating Russia diplomatically, with respect. Rice, who shared many of these views, believed that it was time to engage Russia as if the Cold War was really over, but she was criticized by colleagues in other agencies who did not share her convictions.

A senior State Department moderate describes a dysfunctional interagency process on Russia where ideological divisions led to guerrilla warfare over whose competing memo went to the president, leading that particular official to question whether the United States actually had two governments in power in Washington. To some extent, the differences were between ideologues and pragmatists.

But there was a third group in the Bush administration, the neoconservatives who focused on Russia's internal development and believed that President Bush needed to criticize Russia publicly on Chechnya and human rights. But the neoconservative voices did not assert themselves forcefully during the period when the exigencies of the Afghan War were uppermost.

As for Russia's America policy, Putin's decision-making processes remained a subject of intense speculation in both Russia and the United States. It was assumed that there were both ideologues and pragmatists in Moscow and that some officials in the Defense and Foreign Ministries were more skeptical about Putin's turn to the West and his support for the United States than those in the Kremlin. However, it was less clear whom he consulted before making decisions. There may not have been a consensus in Russia on America policy, but apparently there was only one "decider," as Bush was to term his own role. That decider—Vladimir Putin—was able to prevail over his critics, who continued to nurture their resentments about America's treatment of Russia.

At the end of Bush's second year in office, Putin still believed that he would get results from his reset. The U.S.-Russian relationship appeared to be strong, despite the fissures beneath the surface. Expectations for a qualitatively new, improved relationship had been raised by both sides. The main driver of this new partnership was the personal relationship between Putin and Bush, ties that were mirrored in frequent contacts between the foreign and defense ministers. The Russian side appeared to have bought in to Rice's argument that the Cold War was over and that the U.S.-Russian relationship had entered a new phase. The Consultative Group on Strategic Stability and the U.S.-Russian Energy Dialogue were attempts to create a larger group of stakeholders to promote the relationship, going beyond antiterrorism cooperation to include discussions of the Arab-Israeli peace process, North Korea, missile defense, and further arms control issues.

Nevertheless, the third reset had its limits. Tensions remained over unresolved issues that increasingly came to dominate the Bush administration's foreign policy. But soon it became clear that there was a greater obstacle to the new U.S.-Russian partnership, one that would begin to unravel this reset: Moscow did not share America's dire views about one of the members of the "Axis of Evil"—Saddam Hussein's Iraq—and it certainly did not share America's views about what to do about him.

Chapter Four
The Iraq War

After 2002 the Putin reset all but disappeared. U.S.-Russian relations began to fray as two issues became particularly contentious: the use of military force to effect regime change and the legitimacy of undertaking military intervention without United Nations sanction. U.S.-Russian disagreements over these issues would lead to an increasingly polarized relationship. Moscow insisted on the principle of sovereignty and non-intervention in other countries' internal affairs, while Washington justified the use of military force to unseat a regime that it viewed as a threat to world security. The core of these divergences involved the issue of regime change in the greater Middle East and, by implication, elsewhere.

These disagreements were evident in the Russian reaction to what became the leitmotif of George W. Bush's presidency, namely the Freedom Agenda. Bush articulated these ideas in his second inaugural in January 2005, although his administration had pursued this agenda well before the speech.: "The best hope for peace in our world is the expansion of freedom in all the world—so it is the policy of the United States to seek and support the growth of democratic movements and institutions in every nation and culture, with the ultimate goal of ending tyranny in our world."[1] The Freedom Agenda was a new expression of the Clinton-era liberal internationalist view that democracies do not go to war with each other and that the United States had a duty to promote democracy around the world. Bush wrote about the "transformative power of freedom—in places like Eastern Europe," adding "I viewed NATO expansion as a powerful tool to advance the freedom agenda." He admitted that "Russia stands out as a disappointment in the freedom agenda."[2] Rice describes the Freedom Agenda as "a long-term strategic shift in the way we defined our interests" and "a redefinition of what constituted realism."[3] Moscow, however, did not view this doctrine as a new form of realism. Rather, the Freedom Agenda, by committing the United States to support democratic movements around the globe—especially in Russia's backyard—was anathema to the Kremlin's definition of its interests.

Russia presented itself to the world as a status quo power, whereas it viewed the United States as a revisionist power. The Cold War tables had completely been turned. Gone was the Soviet commitment to global regime change. Soviet foreign policy had been stripped of its international communist mission and deideologized under Gorbachev. Now, in contrast to America, Russia advocated noninterference in other countries' internal affairs. It was Washington, not Moscow, that wanted to remake the world in its image. The Bush administration became increasingly irritated by Moscow's ongoing relationship with three regimes that the U.S. president had singled out during his 2002 State of the Union address—Iran, Iraq, and North Korea. "States like these, and their terrorist allies," he said, "constitute an axis of evil, arming to threaten the peace of the world."[4] Putin and his advisors in turn were irked by what they viewed as a reckless American discussion about overthrowing regimes it found distasteful, thereby threatening regional security. Both the Clinton and Bush administrations puzzled as to why Russia was adamantly against U.S. proposals about how to deal with brutal dictatorial regimes that had aspirations to develop WMD and supported terrorist networks

The Kremlin's view was different. Washington, in its view, was pressuring Russia to stop doing business with countries the U.S. characterized as "rogue states" but where Russia had some political influence and strong economic relations, from arms sales to oil deals, whereas the United States' economic interest in these countries was minimal. Given Russia's difficult economic situation, this was a direct threat to Moscow's interests, especially since U.S. energy companies would supposedly gain a great deal from the overthrow of the Iranian or Iraqi regimes—although that was not the way it turned out. Moreover, Russian officials privately observed that both Russia and the United States supported "their" dictators—Saddam versus U.S. ally Hosni Mubarak of Egypt—and accused the United States of hypocrisy, a charge that grew as the Freedom Agenda spread. Finally, the Bush administration's unilateral policies threatened to further devalue the one international organization in which Russia and the United States exercised equal weight—the United Nations Security Council.

PUTIN'S MANAGED DEMOCRACY

Despite the Bush administration's post-9/11 decision to eschew criticism of internal developments in Russia, Putin's domestic policies began to have an adverse impact on the bilateral relationship. The Russian president continued to consolidate the system of Putinism, known by some as "managed democracy." In this system, elections were too important to be left to chance—a lesson Putin had learned after Mayor Anatoly Sobchak's defeat in St. Petersburg—so uncertainty about electoral results had to be removed. During his first term, Putin set about ensuring that there would be no effective opposition to his rule. By February 2004, just before his own reelection, he dismissed his entire cabinet—including the Yesltin holdover, Prime Minister Mikhail Kasyanov—and appointed Mikhail Fradkov, a former foreign trade minister with an intelligence background, as the new prime minister. In this increasingly centralized and hybrid authoritarian system, any meaningful opposition was greatly weakened. Moreover, despite his rhetorical commitment to modernizing Russia, Putin's economic reforms petered out after a couple of years.

The most dramatic example of Putin's consolidation of power was his relationship with the Yeltsin-era oligarchs. In July 2000, as already noted, Putin had met with the richest magnates and told them that they could keep their assets as long as they stayed out of politics. Most of them complied, particularly after he exiled oligarchs Boris Berezovsky and Vladimir Gusinsky and had their media holdings taken over by Kremlin-connected companies. But Mikhail Khodorkovsky, Russia's richest man and the CEO of the Yukos oil company, did not, going so far in 2003 as to publicly accuse Putin of tolerating corruption during a gathering of businessmen that was filmed.[5] Putin, alluding to the assets that Khodorkovsky had acquired for a song in the 1990s, replied, "And the question is, how did you obtain them?" acidly adding, "I'm returning the hockey puck to you."[6]

In October 2003, Khodorkovsky was arrested on embezzlement and tax evasion charges. He had not heeded Putin's admonitions and had not eschewed politics, pouring money into influencing Duma votes, challenging Putin himself, and seeking to sell Yukos to a U.S. company—and he brushed off offers to emigrate. Khodorkovsky's arrest was a stark warning to oligarchs who sought to use their wealth to influence the political system against Putin's wishes. In the December 2003 Duma elections, the ruling United Russia party won the majority of seats, followed by the communists and LDP. Yabloko, the main liberal opposition party, failed to cross the 5 percent threshold. It was during the ensuing presidential election campaign that Putin declared that the collapse of the USSR was "a national tragedy on an enormous scale." In March 2004 Putin won 71 percent of the votes in the presidential election.

In September 2004, thirty-two Chechen and Ingush terrorists seized an elementary school in Beslan, North Ossetia, and held children, their parents, and teachers hostage on the first day of school, demanding an end to the war in Chechnya, as had the Chechen hostage-takers two years earlier in the Dubrovka Theater. There were 1,100 hostages held during a three-day siege. In the end, Russian troops stormed the school, but not before 331 people had perished, 186 of them children.[7] Immediately after the end of the siege, Putin blamed outside forces who "want to tear off a large piece of Russia" for instigating the hostage taking and excoriated Western news media for referring to North Caucasian "separatists" instead of "terrorists."[8]

Beslan occurred during the first meeting of the Valdai International Discussion Club, a project of the state-run RIA Novosti news agency, which had invited a group of international Russia experts to meet with the president. Over the course of an intense three-hour meeting, two days after the hostage crisis had ended, Putin criticized the West's double standards on the terrorism question. When asked why Russia had not sought a negotiated settlement with Chechen rebels, he responded, "Why don't you negotiate with bin Laden?"[9] In fact, the Bush administration expressed its solidarity with Russia during and after the siege. When President Bush visited the Russian Embassy to sign the condolence book, he blamed North Caucasus terrorists for the attacks.[10] In remarks to the UN General Assembly, he pointed out that "the terrorist massacre of schoolchildren in Beslan" underscored the need for global action to combat terrorism.[11]

After the Beslan tragedy, Putin tightened his hold over the country by eliminating regional centers of power. He abolished the direct election of governors for Russia's eighty-nine federal units and also abolished single-mandate party lists.[12] Henceforth the Kremlin would nominate all the regional leaders. In the name of fighting terrorism, he also tightened the state's control over the electronic media. Vladislav Surkov, deputy head of the Presidential Administration, known as Putin's "gray cardinal," although he was quite young for a gray cardinal, created Nashi, a pro-Putin youth movement, to fight opposition youth groups. Putin's actions to consolidate power in the wake of Beslan initially elicited a limited response from Washington.

A Bush-Putin meeting in Bratislava in February 2005 highlighted how much the U.S.-Russian relationship had changed since the 2002 Moscow summit. National Security Advisor Stephen Hadley describes it as a "low point."[13] President Bush made a speech lauding his Freedom Agenda, but Putin parried back, saying that Russia's democracy was no different from that of the United States. He likened the firing by CBS of news anchor Dan Rather for misrepresenting Bush's National Guard record to the firing of Russian journalists whose political views did not meet with the Kremlin's approval.[14] The parrying continued.[15] Later on that year, at a meeting in Santiago, Chile, Putin lectured Bush on Russia's unique history, explaining that Russia needed to have "a style of government that was consistent with Russian history."[16]

The U.S. Congress, however, was of a different mind. Throughout the Bush administration, Congress acted as a brake on pursuing any reset with Russia. Following Khodorkovsky's arrest, Republican senator John McCain and Democratic representative Tom Lantos denounced Russia as a "despotic regime" and called for its expulsion from the G-8. Freedom House, a Washington-based NGO that promotes freedom and human rights around the globe, downgraded Russia to "not free" for the first time since 1989. Investigative journalists and critics of the regime began to disappear. For instance, Paul Khlebnikov, the American editor of the Russian edition of *Forbes* magazine, who was investigating organized crime, was assassinated and his case never solved. Yuri Shchekochikin, a pioneering investigative reporter, fell ill, eventually succumbing to what some claim was a rare poison.[17] The Duma passed a law curtailing the activities of Western NGOs by imposing harsh registration procedures on new and existing organizations. Putin's national security advisor Sergei Prikhodko summed up the Kremlin's dim view of U.S. policies: "The U.S. kept lecturing us on democracy. Did we have to listen to them like a preaching messiah?"[18]

THE ROAD TO WAR

In the aftermath of the 1991 Gulf War, Moscow and Washington had continued to deal with their disagreement over Iraq within the framework of the United Nations Security Council. In 1997, when Iraq began to challenge the UN inspection system designed to prevent Saddam from acquiring or retaining WMD, the five permanent members of the Security Council began to disagree more openly over how to handle Saddam. Russia argued that Iraq had gone far to meet its disarmament obligations and, together with China and France, abstained over resolutions intended to impose a more robust inspections regime. After Saddam threw out weapons inspectors in 1998, the Clinton administration launched Operation Desert Fox, a bombing campaign designed to degrade Saddam's weapons program. Yeltsin denounced the action and recalled his ambassador to Washington. Moscow's motivations after 1998 were twofold: to constrain U.S. actions and preserve Russia's authority by insisting that Iraq be dealt with within the Security Council framework, thereby retaining its influence in the greater

Middle East. Russia was Iraq's largest trade partner in 2003. Moreover, by 2003, Iraq's debt to Russia—mostly for arms sales—was estimated to be in the vicinity of $8 billion, which reinforced Russia's desire to prevent regime change if it wanted to recoup its money[19]

The Bush administration came into office determined to deal decisively with Saddam Hussein and complete the unfinished business of the 1991 Gulf War. After ousting Saddam from Kuwait in 1991, George H. W. Bush had made the decision to halt Operation Desert Storm's advance ninety miles outside Baghdad, without destroying Saddam's Republican Guard—a decision that his son and his principal advisors were intent on revising. Although UN Resolution 687 required Saddam to give up his extensive WMD program after 1991, he increasingly resisted the UN weapons inspection team and diverted nearly $2 billion from the UN oil-for-food humanitarian aid program to enrich himself and his supporters. UN sanctions and the imposition of a no-fly zone did not seem to have much of an impact on his aggressive policies. The Iraqi dictator was considered a major threat to regional and U.S. interests because of his pursuit of WMD programs and support for state-sponsored terrorism.[20]

Much has been written about how and why the Bush administration launched the Iraq War. There was no unanimity within the government. Some of his top officials had come into office determined to remove Saddam by force. Others favored trying diplomacy and more robust sanctions. The terrorist attacks of 9/11 added a new dimension to this debate: the Bush administration asserted that there were connections between Iraqi intelligence agents and Al Qaeda. In the minds of Bush and his advisors, Saddam's support of terrorist groups was part of the growing post- 9/11 global terrorist threat, even though the evidence of direct contacts between Iraq and Al Qaeda was hotly disputed.[21] Moreover, some U.S. officials were highly skeptical about the United Nations, regarding it as a corrupt, inefficient bureaucracy with an anti-American agenda that pandered to some of the world's worst regimes.[22] According to Rumsfeld, "By the end of 2002, the United Nations had reached a new low," electing Libya to chair the Commission on Human Rights and Iraq to chair the UN Disarmament Commission.[23] Nevertheless, Bush concluded that it was preferable to have the UN legitimize any military action that was taken. The absence of UN endorsement of the Kosovo campaign had angered the Russians, and the prospect of a Russian veto over action in Iraq influenced Bush's thinking. On September 12 he addressed the UN General Assembly, urging it to act more decisively against Saddam's Iraq. On November 8, the UN Security Council passed Resolution 1441, condemning Iraq's weapons programs, demanding that Iraq re-admit weapons inspectors, and threatening "serious consequences" if it failed to comply.

From November 8, 2002 to March 19, 2003, the Bush administration sought to secure support for an attack against Iraq both from Russia and from America's key European allies. After all, in 1991 George H. W. Bush had managed to assemble a coalition of thirty-four countries to support Operation Desert Storm, including the Soviet Union. Could this kind of coalition—which in 1991 had UN backing—not be reassembled? Bush initially believed that German chancellor Gerhard Schroder would support him but, during the 2002 German election campaign, Schroeder used the issue to bolster his support and heavily criticized American talk of using force in Iraq. His justice minister, Herta Daeubler-Gmelin, went much further, claiming that Bush was seeking to divert attention from America's domestic problems by focusing on a foreign enemy, adding, "Hitler also did that." Needless to say, this infuriated Bush, and his relationship with Schroeder never recovered. After the November UN vote, Schroeder made it clear that Berlin would vote against military action were Iraq not to comply with Resolution 1441, and Germany took up a rotating seat on the Security Council in January 2003.

The other major holdout was France, a permanent member of the Security Council. French president Jacques Chirac also opposed military action, bluntly telling Bush, "We are both moral men. But in this case, we see morality differently."[24] On January 22, Schroeder and Chirac announced that they would oppose ousting Saddam by force. Defense Secretary Rumsfeld's acid response characterized Germany and France as "old Europe," as opposed to "new Europe"—the new Central European members of NATO—who, said Rumsfeld, understood what tyranny was and who supported the United States.[25] "Cool down," responded German foreign minister Joschka Fischer, "We are good friends and allies."[26] Thus the intra-alliance battle lines were drawn. Ten East European nations pledged their support for U.S. plans to oust Saddam. In the lead-up to the Iraq War, Washington focused much more effort on securing French and German support than on getting Russia's endorsement.[27]

Was Russia with "old" or "new" Europe? Russia wanted to support the West, but which West? The Bush administration seemed to assume that, given the post 9/11 partnership with Russia, it could count on Moscow's support as it had on Soviet backing in 1991, and it made little attempt to seek Russian assent. Strikingly, no high-level official went to Moscow to argue the case for war.[28] In contrast, France and Germany assiduously courted Russia, realizing that its role on the Security Council would be key in determining whether there would be a UN-sanctioned war. On February 5, Powell, in a lengthy address to the Security Council, made the case for military action, detailing the biological, chemical, and nuclear weapons programs in Iraq. He repeated the allegation that Iraq had ties to Al Qaeda.[29] Powell was clear: "The facts and Iraq's behavior show that Saddam Hussein and his regime are concealing their efforts to produce more weapons of mass destruction." He subsequently admitted that he had harbored doubts about the accuracy of the information he had been given.[30]

Immediately after the Powell speech, Putin flew to Berlin to consult with Schroeder and then to Paris, at Jacques Chirac's invitation. Chirac literally rolled out the red carpet for Putin, personally going to the airport to meet him. Russian media deemed the Paris welcome even warmer than that in Berlin, and one progovernment newspaper announced that "Putin and Chirac have spoken out against America."[31] Whereas Putin had been contemplating following the Chinese position of quietly declining to support the United States, Germany and France spared no effort in winning him over to their position.[32] Sensing that Putin might be wavering, Schroeder flew to Moscow at the end of February to persuade Putin not to support a second Security Council resolution authorizing force. At this point, Bush was calling Putin to make his case, promising incentives such as adding certain Chechen groups to the list of international terrorist organizations.

At the eleventh hour, Presidential Administration head Alexander Voloshin—one of the few remaining supporters of closer Russian ties with the West in the Kremlin—came to Washington hoping to broker a deal. He met with all the U.S. key officials. He concluded that Washington mistakenly believed that Russia's only interest in Iraq was material. Hence, in addition to being offered government briefings on the U.S. evidence about Saddam Hussein's WMD program, U.S. officials raised the issue of material compensation for Russia's potential economic losses from the war. What the Bush administration failed to understand was that, given Russia's own domestic problems with radical Islamic terrorism, there was great concern in Moscow that an invasion of Iraq would have adverse repercussions in Russia's neighborhood, destabilizing its southern neighbors and the North Caucasus. Voloshin was unable to get his deal.[33] Nor could his colleague Evgeny Primakov. On February 22, 2003, Putin dispatched Primakov (who had known Saddam since 1969) to Baghdad to implore Hussein to step back and comply with UN demands so as to avoid a war that he could not possibly win.But it was to no avail.[34]

On March 5, the Schroder-Chirac-Putin "coalition of the unwilling," announced its opposition to another UN resolution authorizing force. "Chirac and Schroeder turned against us," said a senior State Department official; "they recruited Putin and asked him to unite against us."[35] The day the war began, Putin denounced the military campaign as illegal and unnecessary, claiming that, in invading Iraq, the United States and its allies had replaced international law by the "law of the fist."[36] Russia had made common cause with old Europe.

Why was the Bush administration unable to persuade Russia to support Operation Iraqi Freedom? In his memoirs, Bush has a straightforward answer: "Vladimir Putin didn't consider Saddam a threat. It seemed to me that part of the reason was Putin didn't want to jeopardize Russia's lucrative oil contracts."[37] Rice also believed that the Russian opposition was straightforward and had to do with economic interests.[38] Putin told senior U.S. officials that he was concerned that oil prices would fall precipitously if there was a war.[39]

The real story is more complex and includes other important elements: Russia's anger at the lack of consultation and Washington's dismissive attitude toward the United Nations. Moscow had supported the first Gulf War after Primakov made three trips to Baghdad on Gorbachev's behalf to try to persuade Saddam to withdraw from Kuwait. Prior to and during the Gulf War, the Bush administration consulted intensively with Gorbachev, Shevardnadze, and other officials. According to Richard Haass, who worked on the NSC under Bush 41 and was the Director of the State Department's Office of Policy Planning under Bush 43, "Bush 41 understood the need to treat the Soviet Union with respect." In his opinion, this contrasts to the less solicitous attitude of the Bush 43 administration toward dealing with Russia over Iraq.[40]

Some observers believed that the Russian unwillingness to hold Saddam to his UNSC obligations to disarm had more sinister motives. Bush administration officials suspected that, for some time, Russian firms had been delivering global positioning system jamming equipment, antitank missiles, and night-vision binoculars to the Iraqi armed forces, equipment that was subsequently used to fight coalition forces in Iraq.[41] These allegations raised serious issues with which the Clinton administration had also grappled. In the 1990s various legal and semi-legal commercial and scientific entities, with or without the knowledge of government officials, had been involved in a variety of illegal activities with "rogue" states that involved the transfer of military know-how and hardware to countries like Iraq and Iran. Given the chaotic state of the Russian body politic in the 1990s, it was possible for individuals and entities to moonlight in such deals without the knowledge of the leadership itself. But the opacity of the system raised suspicions about who was in charge and whether top officials turned a blind eye to the activities of these entities. It was rumored that Vladimir Zhirinovsky, the flamboyant LDPR leader, and colleagues of his had been advising Iraqi security organs for some years. During the Iraq War, it appeared that Saddam's advisors included former Soviet officials who could have been free-lancing. Putin denied these allegations and, indeed, just before the war, Putin prevailed on a delegation of Russian businessmen and politicians not to visit Baghdad, much to their displeasure.[42]

Putin faced a tough choice in the run-up the Iraq War. He theoretically had three options: support the United States, support France and Germany, or follow China and remain uninvolved. With both the United States and the combination of Germany and France wooing

Russia, it was a period of maximum leverage. Given Russia's own war in Chechnya and its general outlook on the world, the principle of using military force to deal with threats was not in question. But Putin faced domestic constraints, particularly concerns about how Russia's assent to a U.S.-led war in Iraq might adversely impact on Russia's own Muslim regions. Moreover, much of the Russian elite believed that Russia had not received anything for its support of the United States post 9/11. In January 2003, 52 percent of Russians were against a possible U.S.-British operation in Iraq and a mere 3 percent supported it.[43] With the exception of a few liberals such as Yabloko's Grigory Yavlinsky and oil billionaire Mikhail Khodorkovsky, both of whom urged him to support the United States, there were few voices in Moscow that favored military action. Putin did not want to have to accept U.S. unilateralism and the prospect of the overthrow of a long-term Russian client. America was once again about to expose the impotence of the United Nations and downplay Russia's international role.

Putin's advisors—particularly Evgeny Primakov—realized that the war in Iraq would be long and bloody. "I was constantly called a 'friend of Saddam Hussein,'" Primakov writes, "especially after my three visits to Baghdad in 1991."[44] With the United States embroiled in a protracted war in Iraq, Primakov remarked that it was unfortunate that no one in the United States asked the opinion of someone with his knowledge of Iraq about what the outcome might be because he could have predicted how difficult the conflict would be. (It is highly unlikely that anyone in the Bush administration would indeed have solicited Primakov's advice—he was not exactly a popular figure in Washington.)

Putin's conduct in the run-up to the war indicated that he was cautious about breaking with the United States and that the assiduous courtship by Schroeder and Chirac was an important factor in cementing his decision to oppose the war. He hoped that, by joining France and Germany, Russia would gain concrete benefits, including closer ties with the EU, easier visa regimes, and assistance in modernizing the Russian economy. Perhaps if the Bush administration had courted Russia as vigorously as did the Germans and French, it could have secured the Kremlin's assent in the campaign, but it is unlikely. Given Russia's economic interests in Iraq, its role as Iraq's primary great-power interlocutor, its focus on the UN as a vehicle for its great-power ambitions, and its visceral distaste of American-style regime change aimed at toppling authoritarian rulers and its skepticism about the outcome, there were few benefits to be gained from voting with the United States to authorize war.

Underlying this calculation was continuing resentment about U.S. disregard for Russia, which had begun under Yeltsin, but erupted in the wake of the Iraq War. "What sort of allies are we?" asked a frustrated Alexander Voloshin two months after Saddam's fall; "Russia undertook lots of steps for the USA. We closed our radar stations in Cuba, offered intelligence and communications with the Northern Alliance to help bring victory in Afghanistan. What was the response? The USA tried to push Russia out of Afghanistan and oust members of the Karzai government who supported us. It has fought against Russia's interests in the CIS, encouraging Radio Liberty to broadcast in Ukrainian. It is really aimed at weakening Russia's position. Jackson-Vanik has not been rescinded twelve years after the collapse of the USSR. It's a political signal that we are not good partners. We are glad-handing and there are no real, tangible steps being taken toward us."[45]

If Putin had initially believed that joining the "Axis of Opposition" would lead to a more robust troika partnership, he was soon to realize that there was less to this coalition of the unwilling that met the eye. The attempt to benefit from a divided West and play the United States and Europe off against each other yielded limited results. Weeks after the war began, the three leaders met in St. Petersburg to urge that the United Nations be given a leading role in the governance of postwar Iraq. Putin stressed the importance of respecting international law and criticized the United States for failing to find any WMD in Iraq. Admitting that the world was better off without Saddam Hussein, he criticized the war: "We have always said the regime of Saddam Hussein does not correspond to democracy and human rights—but you cannot solve such problems with military means."[46] Powell countered the troika's suggestions for postconflict Iraq, stressing that the U.S.-led coalition, and not the United Nations, would have the leading role there. The three leaders subsequently met at the UN General Assembly in September to discuss a new UN resolution on Iraq, as well as other issues, emphasizing that their partnership was based on more than opposition to the Iraq

War.[47] The following year they met in Sochi, but by then the focus on Iraq was gone, the discussion topics broader, and the three leaders had moved on to other issues.[48] The Franco-German-Russian entente had evaporated; but that was partly because Putin, despite his opposition to the war, did not want to jeopardize entirely the U.S.-Russian partnership that he had championed in 2001.

Shortly after the war began, Putin called Bush and said, "This is going to be awfully difficult for you. I feel bad for you." Bush later recalled, "It was a genuine call. It wasn't a told-you-so. It was a friendship call. And I appreciated it—that's the only one I got along those lines, by the way."[49] In fact the United States had given Russia advice on how to evacuate its Baghdad embassy after the war began.[50] After the war was over, Bush was concerned to repair relations with Russia. Rice agreed, articulating her views in what she believed was a private quip that leaked to the press: "Punish France, forgive Russia and ignore Germany." Rice went to Moscow weeks after the war was over to talk about mending bilateral relations and had a productive meeting with Putin: she noted that "our personal chemistry was good." Putin asked that the United States take Russia's economic interests into account as it rebuilt Iraq.[51]

U.S. officials would privately say that they had lower expectations of Russia than they did of France or Germany, which were, after all, NATO allies. While Putin harshly criticized U.S. actions, the U.S. side responded with restraint. Bush came to St. Petersburg in late May to attend the lavish celebrations for its three-hundredth anniversary at the height of the White nights season. As confirmation of Rice's remarks, he did not meet with Chirac, who also attended the celebrations. Citing scheduling problems, Chirac diplomatically flew out as Bush arrived.[52] Bush's demeanor toward Schroeder was frosty. The quick collapse of Saddam's regime and the speedy military victory bolstered Washington confidence about the decision to go to war and its consequences. Earlier, he had privately said, "I think Gerhard knows he made a mistake."[53]

Bush positively beamed as he watched the fireworks and ballet in the dazzling summer palace outside St. Petersburg built by Peter the Great. Clapping Putin on the back, he spoke about "my good friend Vladimir," inviting him to Camp David in the fall. "We will show the world that friends can disagree, move beyond disagreement, and work in a very constructive way to maintain peace." The Duma finally ratified the 2002 SORT treaty, and the two leaders signed the instruments of ratification. Later on, at Camp David, Bush all but endorsed Putin's reelection with words that surprised some of his advisors" "I respect President Putin's vision for Russia: a country at peace within its borders, with its neighbors, a country in which democracy and freedom and rule of law survive."[54]

By the fall of 2003, therefore, the U.S.-Russian relationship seemed to have returned to its prewar equilibrium. However, that equilibrium also exposed the limits of the post-9/11 partnership. Beyond the positive rhetoric, the relationship lacked substance. While Russians questioned whether the Putin administration had benefited concretely from its support for the war on terror, and complained about perceived slights, the U.S. side noted that Russia had not delivered on its promises about proliferation of WMD to outlaw states. U.S. officials were disinclined to believe that Russia should benefit economically or that it should be treated as a great power, given its weakened situation. As one Russian critic wrote, "The Russian-American partnership was turning into a façade created by the powerful and efficient diplomatic and political machines in both countries, convenient for both sides, but neither side would ever admit that they were largely pretending to be partners."[55]

Events in Russia's backyard were soon to test that partnership even further.

Chapter Five
The Color Revolutions

In 2003 and 2004, developments in Russia's neighborhood revealed how divisive the Freedom Agenda had become. A new issue inflamed U.S.-Russian relations—Washington's role in supporting "color revolutions" in Russia's backyard. The post-Soviet space had evolved into a battleground between the two countries.

Russia has only partly reconciled itself to the loss of its former Soviet republics and continues to believe that it is entitled to special relations with these countries. The United States, by contrast, has insisted that these are independent states and that they have the right to choose their own geopolitical orientation. It has never acknowledged publicly that Russia has any unique or special rights in the post-Soviet space and has rejected the legitimacy of the concept of spheres of influence in the area. These different views are apparent in a most fundamental way—the lack of a consensus on what to call these countries.

More than twenty years after the Soviet collapse, there is still no agreement on how to describe this area collectively. Russia, Ukraine, and Belarus formed the Commonwealth of Independent States on December 8, 1991, and by 1993 the CIS included all the former Soviet republics minus the Baltic states. Whereas many Russians initially described the CIS as an instrument for civilized divorce, it has endured.

Russians often refer to their neighbors as the "near abroad," implying that they do not regard these nations as truly foreign countries, unlike the "far abroad." They also use the phrase post-Soviet space, implying that what binds these countries is their common Soviet inheritance. The State Department, however, referred to these countries as Newly Independent States (NIS). More than two decades after the Soviet collapse, this became increasingly anachronistic. The preferred regional term in Washington is Eurasia, but, as Ukrainians will point out, they are Europeans, not Eurasians. The failure to come up with a new name for this region that is widely accepted symbolizes a far deeper problem, namely that Moscow sees Washington as a rival in its backyard, believing that the United States seeks to erode its influence there. Washington denies that the two countries are rivals in the area, but during the Bush administration this is in fact how many officials viewed the issue.

The mantra of both the Clinton and Bush administrations was that the Cold War was over and Russia should not view its relationship with the United States in zero-sum terms. Washington officials were fond of using phrases like "win-win situation" (a concept that translates poorly in the Russian language), but Moscow suspected that this was a cover for the reality of the United States competing with Russia for influence in the post-Soviet space, continuing to impose its global agenda on Russia, and treating it as a junior partner. Many Russian officials began to believe that the United States had no plans to leave Central Asia and was using the ongoing war in Afghanistan as an excuse to erode Russian influence in the region. These suspicions grew as regime change moved from the battlefields of Iraq to the streets of Tbilisi, Kyiv, and Bishkek.

Washington and Moscow also had to deal with what were called "frozen conflicts" in the region. These were all a result of the unraveling of the Soviet system that had created multinational union republics in which different ethnic groups were forced to coexist but nurtured resentments against each other—the Stalinist policy of divide and rule. As soon as the USSR collapsed, smaller ethnic groups in three new states sought independence from their new central governments. There were four unrecognized statelets, stemming from ethnic wars that had begun in the waning days of the USSR. The first was Nagorno-Karabakh, a region of Azerbaijan inhabited by a majority Armenian population, which declared its independence after a war with Azerbaijan, creating up to a million Azeri refugees. The second was Transnistria, a region that officially belonged to Moldova but where the Russophone population, supported by the Soviet-era Fourteenth Army, had declared independence and announced the creation of a state with its own currency and flag in 1992.

The other two frozen conflicts were the regions of Abkhazia and South Ossetia, formally part of Georgia, where the local population, supported by Russian troops, had declared its de facto independence from Tbilisi in the early 1990s. These unrecognized entities functioned quite successfully as mini-statelets.[1] However, the possibility of a recurrence of violence was always present. Moreover, three of these conflicts were in the South Caucasus, as a result of which Armenia and Azerbaijan remained in a state of war with each other and Georgia's territorial integrity was compromised. Although both the United States and Russia were involved in multinational negotiations to resolve these conflicts, Washington suspected that Moscow might not be interested in any definitive resolution because the process of negotiation reinforced Russia's continuing role in the area.

THE POST-SOVIET SYNDROME

Despite the post-Soviet states' attempts to create their own independent identities and competences, in reality there were continuing and strong connections between them. One of the most powerful legacies of seventy-four years of Soviet communism was the development of what might be called the "post-Soviet syndrome" in all of these countries, with the exception of the Baltic states, which rapidly joined the West. This syndrome exists on a continuum and is more pronounced in the Central Asian states, all of which soon became authoritarian states, and less so in some of the Western NIS, but all twelve countries share some features that differentiate them both from their Western and Eastern neighbors. Western-style democracy has barely begun to take root in any of them, unlike in Central Europe.

Post-Soviet political systems are run by a small group of political and/or family clans, where nominally competitive elections are, if fact, managed and the outcomes predetermined. Personal ties are much more important than institutions of governance, which are only partly developed. The rule of law is weak. There are few transparent succession mechanisms. The economy is controlled by a small elite with close ties to the political leadership, and together they control substantial assets. Corruption and nepotism are rife. Freedom of expression is curtailed. Electronic media are either state-controlled or run by magnates close to the political leadership. Commercial ties between Russian oligarchs and wealthy businessmen in the post-Soviet states reinforce the influence of Russia's ways of doing business on its neighbors. The ties that bind are often stronger than those that divide Russia and most of its neighbors. Under Putin, Russia has increasingly used its soft power—in the form of linguistic, educational, and cultural ties and Russian-language television—to retain its influence in its neighborhood.

A decade after the Soviet collapse, the populations in some of these countries—especially those with aspirations to move closer to Europe—began to challenge this syndrome. Exasperated by the arbitrariness and corruption of the system, and using the new technology provided by the Internet and text messaging, they began to interact with regime critics in their own countries and with democracy and human rights activists abroad. At the beginning of the twenty-first century, a new phenomenon appeared in the post-Soviet space, one that set off alarms in Russia—popular uprisings that came to be known as the color revolutions, what has been called a "brief, and optimistic, moment in post-Soviet but also American history."[2]

These revolutions shared common features. They occurred in response to elections—presidential or parliamentary—that were deemed fraudulent. The incumbent had limited public support, and the regime was either unwilling or unable to use a high level of force to suppress the revolt. Other features included a political opposition capable of organizing and uniting people; public and elite support for the opposition in key urban areas; and at least one major media outlet supporting the opposition, enabling it to air its point of view. Text messaging was used to circumvent the authorities' eavesdropping and rally activists to street gatherings. International NGOs with foreign funding were on hand to train and support opposition activists. In short, color revolutions succeeded because the incumbents were unable to use coercive means to crush them, in part because sections of the police and armed forces were alienated by the arbitrariness and corruption in the system, and partly because the new communications technology was able to evade surveillance.

Precisely because the political system in the post-Soviet states resembled that of Russia, the Kremlin felt threatened by these revolutions. Post-Soviet Russia viewed politics in the post-Soviet states as an extension of its own domestic politics. After all, if Ukrainians could take to the streets and overthrow their government, so could Russians. The fact that Western NGOs were actively promoting civil society and encouraging people to demand greater transparency and accountability in their societies made it easy for the Kremlin to portray these movements as yet another example of American attempts to weaken Russia's influence in its rightful sphere of influence.

Like its predecessor, the Bush administration was divided over how much its policy toward the post-Soviet states should take Russian concerns into account. The Office of Vice President Cheney advocated a tough policy toward Russia, generally supporting Russia's neighbors and expressing suspicion about Moscow's intentions. It viewed the post-Soviet space as a litmus test for the Freedom Agenda, particularly after it became clear that Iraq might not pass that test. Matthew Bryza, who covered the South Caucasus in the White House, articulated this view: "We needed to demand that Russia play by the same rules as everyone else—we should not treat them as special and give them a free pass."[3]

Thomas Graham, a key Russia expert in the administration, advocated a more realist and interest-based policy toward Russia, recognizing the necessity of taking Russian interests into consideration when crafting U.S. policy in the post-Soviet space. Graham was associate director of the State's Department's Office of Policy Planning until 2002 and then moved to the National Security Council, where he served as director and then senior director for Russia until 2007. During his time in the White House, he often disagreed with officials from Cheney's staff and later with the State Department's assistant secretary for Europe and Eurasia Daniel Fried and his deputy assistant secretary for Russia and the Western NIS David Kramer, both of whom believed that U.S. policy toward Russia's neighbors should not be influenced by Russian concerns. Graham believes that a key problem was that, while he was responsible for Russia on the NSC, there was no coordination with those on the NSC in charge of the other post-Soviet states. There was no discussion in the NSC about the impact of American actions in Georgia or Ukraine on U.S.-Russian relations. The Bush NSC, in his opinion, lacked a holistic and coherent policy toward the area.[4]

The divisions were not only between different branches of the executive but within them. In the Defense Department, the uniformed military, which regularly interacted with its Russian counterpart, tended to have a more sanguine view of cooperation with Russia than political appointees in the Office of the Secretary of Defense, although neither of these organizations is, of course, monolithic. Congress continued to look on Russia with suspicion, as was clear from the failure of either the Clinton or Bush administrations to persuade Congress to lift Jackson-Vanik restrictions.

Outside the government, a variety of NGOs and ethnic lobbies competed to influence administration policy and those who advocated tough policies toward Russia had considerable influence. Ukrainian-American groups advocating for large financial and political assistance to Kyiv also found a sympathetic ear in the OVP. The U.S.-Russia Business Council and the U.S. Chamber of Commerce, on the other hand, promoted more proactive commercial ties with Russia and repeal of Jackson-Vanik for Russia.

American-backed NGOs were active in some of Russia's neighboring states. George Soros's Open Society organization poured billions of dollars into democracy-promotion efforts in the post-Soviet space. Soros, a Democrat, became increasingly critical of the Bush administration's domestic and foreign policies; he said in 2003 "defeating George Bush is the central focus on my life."[5] But the Kremlin—perhaps because of the nature of the Russian system—failed to grasp the fact that he was an independent actor and conflated his organization's activities with those of the U.S. government. The National Democratic Institute, International Republican Institute, and National Endowment for Democracy received government funds and were also active in organizing political parties and civil society groups in the post-Soviet space. While each of these NGOs pursued its own individual agenda, the Kremlin eyed all of them and their funding with suspicion—and began to restrict their activities in Russia. It also believed that the U.S. government coordinated its policies with those of the NGOs, misunderstanding how the U.S. system operated and attributing a far greater coherence to U.S. policy than was the reality. These suspicions came to a head when the first colored domino began to fall in the Caucasus—in Georgia.

THE ROSE REVOLUTION

The Russian-Georgian relationship historically has been more fraught than Russia's ties with other parts of the tsarist empire and the USSR. Culturally, Russians feel that they have a special bond with Georgia. Russia's literary giants—Lermontov, Pushkin, and Tolstoy—all spent time in Georgia, and Georgians have traditionally admired Russian culture. Russian-Georgian relations stretched back to the first half of the eighteenth century, when Russia conquered the Georgian kingdom as the southernmost Orthodox outpost of an empire, competing with the Turks and Persians for influence in the region. After a brief period of independence between 1918 and 1921, Georgia was reincorporated into what became the USSR. As commissar of nationalities in the early 1920s, the former Georgian seminarian Josef Stalin presided over a multinational empire with at least one hundred different ethnic groups. He divided up the Soviet territory into a patchwork of union republics and autonomous regions based on ethnicity to ensure that different groups would be pitted against each other and to guarantee that no single ethnic group would become strong enough to resist Moscow's rule.

In 1936, when the three South Caucasus republics were given their new territorial boundaries, three regions within Georgia that were not ethnically Georgian were given special autonomous status: Abkhazia, Adjaria, and South Ossetia. Like many of these territorial arrangements in the USSR, they worked because were held together by coercion, but once the Soviet Union disappeared, so did the glue that bound them. Of course, some of the most prominent—and infamous—Soviet leaders were Georgian, beginning with Stalin, who ruled the USSR for a quarter of a century. His fellow Georgian Lavrenti Beria ran the NKVD (secret police) during its most notorious years. Later, Eduard Shevardnadze, who was Georgia's minister of internal affairs before he became Soviet foreign minister, presided with Mikhail Gorbachev over the dismantling of the Soviet empire. Thus, the relationship between Tbilisi and Moscow during the Soviet times was both intimate and conflicted. Some Russians felt a special attraction for this beautiful, exotic, Mediterranean-like region where they would vacation. Others resented the strong nationalistic feelings that united the Georgians. When the USSR collapsed, Russia reacted especially negatively to Georgia's determination to move out of its orbit. "We are upset because of Georgia's unsanctioned political choice to orient their policy toward the West," complained one senior Russian official.[6] A former U.S. ambassador put it more bluntly: "Russia-Georgia was like a bad divorce."[7] Georgian president Eduard Shevardnadze was a polarizing figure for the Russian leadership. He was seen as a crucial figure in the collapse of the USSR. Many in the Russian political establishment regarded him as a traitor.

As the USSR was falling apart, Georgia descended into chaos under its new leader Zviad Gamsakhurdia. South Ossetia and Abkhazia declared their independence from Georgia, and armed conflict between Tbilisi and the two regions erupted. When it was over, 230,000 Georgians had been ethnically cleansed from Abkhazia, and Russian peacekeeping troops remained in both Abkhazia and South Ossetia. Shevardnadze returned to Tbilisi from Moscow in 1992 and was elected president in 1995. He ran the state Soviet-style, fusing the ruling party with the executive branch.

From the beginning, his relationship with Moscow was difficult. As Soviet foreign minister, he had played a decisive role in the events that led to the collapse of the GDR when Putin was a beleaguered KGB officer in Dresden. On the one hand, he owed his continuing ability to stay in power to Russia; on the other hand, during a period when the Yeltsin government itself was disorganized, elements of the Russian military not fully under Moscow's control were assisting both Abkhaz and South Ossetian rebels, and there were several assassination attempts against Shevardnadze. Moscow became increasingly concerned that Georgia's Pankisi Gorge was becoming a haven for Chechen fighters and that Tbilisi was unable—or unwilling—to deal with them. Primakov charged that Georgia was using Chechen fighters in its struggle against the separatist regions, but tensions eased when Georgian special forces began to cooperate with the Russian special services by turning some Chechen fighters over to the Russians.[8] However, the respite was short-lived. Tbilisi's resistance to close ties with Russia and the growing activity of Western NGOs in Georgia meant that the stage was set for confrontation.

Georgia struggled to develop as a viable state. Georgian refugees from the breakaway regions had to be resettled. South Ossetia and Abkhazia were known as "frozen conflicts," but either of these territorial disputes could become unfrozen and armed hostility could erupt. Georgia's government exhibited many of the features of the post-Soviet syndrome. A younger, largely Western-educated generation of aspiring Georgian politicians became increasingly alienated from the Shevardnadze government. In the run-up to parliamentary elections in November 2003, these opposition groups became more vocal as they organized demonstrations and demanded change.

Because of its strategic location and Washington's close ties with Shevardnadze dating from the 1980s, Georgia was one of the world's largest per capita recipients of American democracy assistance and economic development aid in the 1990s, totaling nearly $1 billion during Shevardnadze's eleven years in office.[9] Washington had invested a considerable amount, both politically and economically, in Georgia, and the Bush administration became increasingly concerned about the brewing discontent as parliamentary elections approached in the summer of 2003. In July, Bush asked James Baker, former secretary of state—and the man who had successfully argued Bush's case in the disputed 2000 U.S. election—to go to Georgia and try and mediate between the opposing groups. Baker had a close relationship with Shevardnadze dating back to the George H. W. Bush era, when the two foreign ministers had negotiated the peaceful end of the Cold War. He brought his considerable powers of negotiation and persuasion to bear on the different parties, meeting with both Shevardnadze and the opposition, warning the latter not to hold massive street demonstrations.[10] He believed that he had secured agreement on what came to be known as the "Baker Plan" that was designed to reduce the chances of electoral fraud and to assure greater representation to opposition parties. After Baker left, however, the Georgian parliament, which was dominated by progovernment forces, approved rules for the composition of the Central Electoral Commission that ran counter to the stipulations in the Baker Plan by stacking the Commission with pro-Shevardnadze appointees.

The parliamentary elections took place on November 2, 2003. The OSCE's Office of Democratic Initiatives and Human Rights (ODIHR) and other international NGOs sent observers to the polling stations and to the vote counting locations. *Kmara* (Enough), the Georgian civil rights organization partly funded by Soros's Open Society Institute, worked with other NGOs to conduct parallel vote counts based on exit polling. The Central Election Committee declared that Shevardnadze's party had won a plurality of votes. The ODIHR declared that the elections fell short of internationally accepted democratic practices. Street demonstrations grew in size and intensity over the next three weeks. They were led by a trio of young, reformist politicians: Mikheil Saakashvili, Zurab Zhvania, and Nino Burjanadze.

Saakashvili, tall, charismatic, and eloquent in several languages, had studied at Columbia and George Washington Universities, held an American law degree, and had practiced law in the United States before returning to Georgia and joining Shevardnadze's party. He was elected to parliament in 1995 and became minister of justice. Zhvania and Burjanadze, like Saakashvili, were Western oriented and had also been members of Shevardnadze's party in the 1990s, but they had become disillusioned by the corruption and cronyism and had broken away to form their own parties. Shevardnadze and his supporters tried to ignore the mounting protests. On November 22 Shevardnadze arrived at the parliament intending to open the new session. As he tried to speak, Saakashvili and his supporters suddenly burst into the parliament carrying roses, disrupting the proceedings and shouting that Shevardnadze must go. Shevardnadze ordered the mobilization of the army to dispel the ten thousand protestors who had gathered in the central Rustaveli Square, but the troops refused to support him. Meanwhile, Rustavi-2, one of the two major television channels, switched sides and began to back the protestors, providing them with an outlet to broadcast their views. Alarmed at the turn of events, Russia dispatched foreign minister Igor Ivanov—himself half Georgian—to defuse the situation. He had close ties to Shevardnadze, who had been his boss in the USSR Foreign Ministry, and to opposition leader Zurab Zhvania.[11] Ivanov persuaded Shevardnadze to accept a compromise that was supposed to keep him in office.

But Shevardnadze reneged and was forced to resign.[12] After Shevardnadze left office, new presidential elections were arranged, and on January 4, 2004, Mikheil Saakashvili was elected president of Georgia with 94 percent of the popular vote. Thus, the first color revolution succeeded with a minimum of violence, sending a clear message to other post-Soviet states: young people were becoming increasingly disillusioned with corruption, falsified elections, and ways of doing business that were too reminiscent of the Soviet past. They could mobilize crowds, win the military over to their side, and force the incumbent and his cronies out of office.

Georgia became a major source of contention in the U.S.-Russian relationship for much of the Bush administration. For Washington, Saakashvili, Zhvania, and Burjanadze represented a promising, new generation of Georgians who sought integration with the West and were pro-American. Moreover, Georgia was an important country in counterterrorism operations after 9/11—both as a net contributor and as a weak link—because of its location in a strategic and dangerous part of the world. The South Caucasus provided U.S. access to Central Asia and Afghanistan and overflight rights over the area enabled America to project power into the main theater of the Global War on Terror. Moreover, around seven hundred Chechen fighters had been using Georgia's Pankisi Gorge as a base from which to wage their war against Russia.[13] The Bush administration had begun a program to train the Georgian armed forces to deal more effectively with Chechen fighters. Known as the Georgia Train and Equip Program (GTEP), it was the first partnership of its kind in counterterrorist operations. Rice describes the U.S. program designed to train Georgian military forces in counterterrorism as at attempt to show the Russians that Georgia could be an asset in the war on terrorism.

But Georgia was also strategically significant for Washington in terms of energy security. It was the critical transit country for transporting Caspian oil and gas to the world market, and the Baku-Tbilisi-Ceyhan (BTC) oil pipeline ran across its territory. This project, initially conceived under the Clinton administration and completed during the Bush years, transported Caspian oil to the Mediterranean without traversing Russian territory, thereby diversifying energy supplies, a key goal of U.S. policy.

Russia's stakes in Georgia were very different. Moscow sought to block Tbilisi's westward orientation. Despite Russia's concern about Chechen fighters in the Pankisi Gorge, Evgeny Primakov made it clear that Moscow did not want U.S. troops in Georgia, even if they were training Georgia troops in counterterrorist tactics.[14] Defense Minister Sergei Ivanov denigrated the Georgian effort and threatened to send Russian troops into the Pankisi Gorge to take care of the terrorists.[15] Moreover, Russia opposed the BTC oil pipeline. Because the pipeline's clear aim was to bypass Russia and transport oil to the Mediterranean, Moscow viewed it as part of the U.S. strategy to lessen Russia's influence in its backyard and Europe.

Saakashvili has been described by a Clinton administration official who became his vocal advocate as "Flamboyant, brash—a swashbuckling figure in a region that had produced a disproportionate share of bigger-than-life personalities."[16] He saw himself as the heir of David the Builder, the legendary Georgian King whose statue stands in the center of Tbilisi and who defeated separatist forces to unite Georgia. Saakashvili sought to integrate Georgia into the West and professed his commitment to democracy. At his inauguration, the European Union flag was raised over the Georgian parliament building and Beethoven's *Ode to Joy*, the EU anthem, was sung right after the Georgian national anthem, much to Russia's consternation. When Colin Powell accompanied the newly inaugurated president into City Hall, it was festooned with Georgian and American flags. Powell himself was struck by the contrast between two groups of Georgian troops at the festivities—those that were Soviet-trained did the goose-step, those that were American-trained marched like Americans.[17] Yet despite Saakashvili's unabashedly pro-American stance, the Bush administration was cautious at the beginning. Richard Miles, the U.S. ambassador, was a seasoned career diplomat who had previously served in Moscow, among his many assignments, and he enjoyed good relations with Shevardnadze. He was wary of Saakashvili, whom he regarded as a nationalist who was needlessly provocative toward Russia and who constantly dealt with U.S. officials over Miles's head.[18]

As soon as Saakashvili had been elected president, he went out of his way to court the United States, and he was enthusiastically embraced by much of the Bush administration as a prime example of the success of the Freedom Agenda. At a time when the United States was the focus of international condemnation for its invasion of Iraq, Georgia supported the United States, eventually sending troops to fight alongside Coalition forces in Iraq and Afghanistan. Saakashvili and his young cabinet members came to Washington early in 2004 and, during an intense few days, impressed their audiences with their talk of reform and democracy. Saakashvili's agenda dovetailed perfectly with the Bush administration's agenda, and he soon developed a network of enthusiastic supporters in the executive branch and on Capitol Hill.[19]

Despite Russia's suspicions about Saakashvili, Putin's initial reaction to the Rose Revolution was cautious. Saakashvili came into office vowing to improve relations with Russia. Putin may have initially hoped to work out a deal with the new Georgian president that would enable Russia to maintain its influence in Tbilisi. Although the first Saakashvili-Putin meeting appeared to go well, it soon transpired that Saakashvili was unwilling to show the Russian president the respect that he believed he deserved.[20] The relationship soon soured, as it became evident that Saakashvili's main goal was to reincorporate the separatist regions into Georgia and to bring Georgia into Euro-Atlantic structures. Shortly after becoming president, he achieved the first of his goals by reincorporating the separatist region Adjaria into Georgia. In this case, the reincorporation was effected with speed and no violence and with assistance from Igor Ivanov. But Russia made it clear that it would not broker such an arrangement for Abkhazia or South Ossetia. As Putin told the Valdai Club in September 2004, just as Georgia had wanted to leave the USSR, so Abkhazia and South Ossetia understandably wanted to leave Georgia.[21]

As Saakashvili became increasingly outspoken about Georgia's aspirations to join the West, Russian reactions to the Rose Revolution became more pronounced. Conspiracy theories abounded, and these were echoed by Western critics of the Bush administration. The Rose Revolution, in this view, had little to do with democracy and freedom but was an example of American and European NGOs' financing regime change that would turn Georgia against Russia and give the West access to Russia's backyard. The United States was alleged to have spent millions of dollars to bring Saakashvili to power. George Soros and the CIA were cast as co-conspirators—albeit as unlikely a cast of co-conspirators as one could find.[22] By the fall of 2004, it was clear to Moscow that the relationship it had enjoyed with Shevardnadze—however difficult—would not be replicated under Saakashvili, whom it viewed as increasingly anti-Russian. A progovernment Russian website posed the critical question: "Who's Next?"[23] As the Ukrainian presidential elections loomed closer, the answer appeared to be Kyiv.

THE ORANGE REVOLUTION

Ukraine became a major source of contention between Washington and Moscow during the Bush administration, second only to Georgia in terms of its ability to ignite tensions and to highlight how differently both capitals viewed the world. For the Kremlin, the stakes in Ukraine were higher than those in Georgia—Ukraine's population was ten times larger than Georgia's, 80 percent of Russia's gas exports to Europe pass through Ukraine, the Black Sea Fleet is headquartered in Crimea, which is on Ukrainian territory, and roughly one-sixth of the country's population is ethnically Russian. Ukraine emerged as a key Russian foreign policy priority from the moment that Presidents Yeltsin and Kravchuk signed the agreement dissolving the USSR. Although Yeltsin needed to destroy the Soviet Union in order to oust Gorbachev, he and his colleagues did not think through the longer-term implications of the breakup. The loss of Ukraine was a major blow to Russia. Moreover, many Russians simply do not regard Ukraine as a foreign country.

The roots of Russia's tangled relations with Ukraine stretch back for centuries. Russian and Ukrainians have long clashed over their respective national identities. The Russian-Ukrainian argument harks back to the authorship of an 1187 epic narrative poem and continues through to 1654, when part of Ukraine united with Russia. From Moscow's point of view, the Russian state was born in Kyiv and the Ukrainians are not a separate ethnic group, but "Little Russians," descendants of the same ancient East Slavic tribes. Ukrainians have begged to differ.[24] After the eighteenth-century partitions of Poland, the western half of Ukraine was incorporated into the Austro-Hungarian Empire, and its population spoke Ukrainian. The eastern part was absorbed into the Russian Empire and became Russophone. In 1918 the western part of Ukraine became the eastern half of the newly independent Polish state. But in 1939 it was occupied by the USSR as part of the Nazi-Soviet pact after the outbreak of war.

The current borders of Ukraine date back to 1945, when, as a result of the Tehran and Yalta conferences, Poland moved West and the USSR gained what had been the eastern part of Poland, which was incorporated into the Ukrainian Soviet Socialist Republic.[25] Before 1991, Ukraine had experienced two brief periods of independence, 1648–1654 and 1917–1921. During the Soviet era, Ukrainians were disproportionately prominent in the officer corps and were largely integrated into the Soviet elite. Given the cultural and historical divide between eastern Ukraine—which had long been Russified—and western Ukraine—which joined the Ukrainian Soviet Socialist Republic only in 1945—Ukraine achieved independence without having resolved issues of identity, language, and its relations with Russia.

Beginning with the Clinton administration, Washington sought to bolster Ukrainian independence. Influenced by the activities of an effective Ukrainian-American diaspora, the government had poured money into Ukraine, making it the third largest recipient of U.S. aid after Israel and Egypt. Yet U.S. officials also became increasingly aware that Ukraine was developing an acute case of the post-Soviet syndrome, with groups of corrupt and criminally connected oligarchs tied to the political elite, operating in a nontransparent and largely nondemocratic political system. Under President Leonid Kuchma, the situation deteriorated. In

2000 the decapitated body of muckraking journalist Hihory Gongadze was found, and there was evidence that his murder had been ordered by those close to the president. Young people became increasingly critical of their government and restive about the lack of political competition. As Kuchma's term in office was coming to an end, popular marches demanding "Ukraine without Kuchma" increased, and the competition to succeed him intensified. His chosen successor—even though Kuchma was not that enthusiastic—was Viktor Yanukovych, a former prime minister favored by Moscow who had served time in jail for robbery as a young man and was backed by the Donetsk clan of oligarchs, whose base was in Russophone eastern Ukraine. Arrayed against him were two opposition figures—Yulia Tymoshenko, a successful businesswoman (known by some as "the gas princess"), and Viktor Yushchenko, former Central Bank governor and former prime minister, who was popular in Washington and whose American wife had worked in the Reagan White House. Their base of support was in western and central Ukraine and they were westward leaning and more critical of Russia.[26]

Moscow was determined not to be taken by surprise, as it had been in Georgia, and it adopted a proactive strategy toward the Ukrainian elections. After Kuchma designated Yanukovych as his successor in July 2004, the Kremlin pursued a two-pronged policy: it dispatched its best public relations experts to Ukraine to campaign for Yanukovych and offered a series of political and economic concessions to convince the Ukrainian public of the importance of cooperation with Russia. The Russian "political technologists"—Gleb Pavlovsky, Sergei Markov, and Vyacheslav Nikonov—pursed an aggressive strategy that had worked in Russia, namely focusing all the media on certain limited subjects and depicting the opposition as unpatriotic and in the pay of the West.[27] Markov acknowledged that he had been working for the Kremlin and the head of the Presidential Administration, Dmitry Medvedev.[28] What Russia failed to realize was that transferring Russian electoral strategies in a "managed democracy" to a different political environment did not necessarily work.

In May 2004, Condoleezza Rice visited Putin in his presidential dacha outside Moscow and was introduced to Victor Yanukovych, whom Putin praised, making it clear that Washington should understand that this was Russia's candidate for president.[29] Putin made seven trips to Ukraine during the election campaign and endorsed Yanukovych. The Kremlin would leave no stone unturned to try and guarantee its preferred outcome—as it had successfully done for Putin's own March 2004 reelection in Russia. But the Kremlin also hedged its bets, reaching out to the Yushchenko camp by holding a series of back-channel meetings with his advisor Oleh Rybachuk, seeking to ascertain what Yushchenko might do were he elected.[30]

Washington was also involved in the Ukrainian campaign, urging Kyiv to hold a clean election and supporting groups that favored greater transparency. European and American NGOs, in cooperation with Georgian, Serbian, and other civil society groups, trained Ukrainian groups in tactics such as election monitoring and parallel vote counting, as they had in Georgia. Although the United States expressed no explicit preference for a candidate, Yushchenko was popular in Washington from his days as chairman of the Central Bank. But Washington stressed procedures, not personalities. A string of prominent Americans—including George H. W. Bush, Madeleine Albright, Zbigniew Brzezinski, and Richard Holbrooke—all visited Kyiv in 2004 with the same message: the Ukrainian authorities must ensure that the election was free, fair, and transparent. It was a test case for political transformation in the post-Soviet space. The Soros foundation in Ukraine contributed $1.3 million to Ukrainian NGOs, and USAID contributed $1.4 million for election-related activities, including training the Central Elections Commission, as it had in Georgia.[31] However, American public relations firms were also working for the Yanukovych campaign.

The battle lines were drawn as the election approached. On September 5 Yushchenko had dinner with officials from the security services. After dinner, he was suddenly stricken with a mysterious illness. While the Russian media attributed his illness it to "bad sushi," his Austrian doctors—aided by American physicians, who were given blood samples to test—identified the source as dioxin, a lethal poison that could have killed him. Experts also identified its provenance: it was a pure form produced only in a few Soviet-era laboratories with highly restricted access, raising serious issues about who had ordered the poisoning.[32] As the election approached, Yushchenko's disfigured face became a symbol of the significant stakes and hostile tactics involved in the electoral campaign.

The first round of elections was inconclusive. The second round was planned for November 21. In the interim, Putin personally campaigned for Yanukovych, while Yushchenko supporters stepped up street demonstrations. On November 22, Putin congratulated Yanukovych on winning of the second round before the results were in, and on November 24 the Central Election Commission announced that he had indeed won. Since all of the exit polls and parallel vote counts by NGOs indicated that the victor was Yushchenko, not Yanukovych, the opposition was mobilized. In the days following November 24, thousands gathered in the snow-covered central Maidan Square, eventually reaching one million, and there, in subzero temperatures they camped out, demanding that the election be rerun. TV 5, owned by an ally of Yushchenko, broadcast their demands. Protestors blockaded the main government buildings, effectively shutting down the government for weeks.

The situation appeared to be stalemated. But at a key moment, Washington acted. Secretary of State Colin Powell announced that the United States could not stand by, saying that "we cannot accept the Ukraine election result as legitimate."[33] Europe was initially divided. "New Europe," led by Poland's president Alexander Kwasniewski and Lithuanian president Valdis Adamkus, was highly critical of the vote, whereas "old Europe" was more wary of challenging a Russian-backed outcome. Nevertheless, as the protests grew, Kwasniewski and Adamkus were joined by a reluctant EU high representative Javier Solana, as well as Russian Duma Speaker Boris Gryzlov, in talks with the contending parties.[34] During the tense standoff, there were concerns in Washington that the Russian military might intervene on the side of the Yanukovych forces. Even though some in Moscow may have favored that outcome, Russia refrained from military intervention, and Yanukovych himself realized that many of the Ukrainian troops were more sympathetic to the Maidan crowd than they were to him. Powell also prevailed on Kuchma not to send his Interior Ministry troops to disperse the crowds.[35]

European mediation efforts led to an unexpected result: the Ukrainian Supreme Court declared the elections null and void. The second round was rerun on December 26. This time Yushchenko was declared the winner with 51.99 percent compared to Yanukovych's 44.2 percent. On January 23, 2005, Victor Yushchenko was sworn in as president of Ukraine. Russia's preelection strategy had failed, and a pro-Western candidate had won. Through careful Western mediation, a free and fair second round of elections had occurred. In January 2005, it appeared that Ukraine had rejected the post-Soviet syndrome and had embarked on a course toward greater transparency, freedom, and democracy—another victory for the Freedom Agenda.

Although the U.S. government and private organizations had put money into Ukraine seeking a more transparent election process, the U.S. government was caught off guard by the Orange Revolution. Few experts or officials believed that the entrenched elites could be brought down by a group of committed opposition protestors. The main message from U.S. officials—after Powell and his advisors made the crucial decision not to accept the election results—was the need for dialogue and compromise among the parties. The focus was not on who would be president, but how he would be elected. Nevertheless, there was a sense of amazement and satisfaction when Yushchenko was inaugurated and a belief that things might really change. In April 2005 he visited Washington. When he spoke to Congress, he received a standing ovation.

Moscow, needless to say, was equally caught off guard by the Orange Revolution. Because Putin had invested considerable capital in backing Yanukovych, it was a personal challenge to him. The Orange Revolution sent an alarming message about the possibility that, if regime change could come to Russia's biggest neighbor, it could come to Russia.[36] A consensus emerged in Russia that the West—and especially the United States—had engineered the entire revolution to ensure that its candidate came to power.[37] For example, Sergei Markov told an international audience in May 2005, "The CIA paid every demonstrator on the Maidan $10 a day to protest."[38] It was much easier to believe in a Washington-engineered conspiracy than to admit that Russia had backed the losing side. Yet Stanislav Belkovsky, another well-connected Russian commentator, presented a more sophisticated view: admitting that Washington had been careful not to back one side over the other, he argued that the United States had shown its hand only once it became clear that Yanukovych had no legitimacy after the election: "In that sense, America's tactics were much more skilled and competent than Russia's, which counted on the completely baseless illusions of Viktor Yanukovych's victory until the very last moment."[39]

The most important lesson that the Kremlin took away from the Orange Revolution was the need to ensure that nothing similar would ever happen in Russia—hence the focus on creating pro-Kremlin youth groups and minimizing the impact of Western NGOs. But there was also a foreign policy lesson. Russian officials suspected that America was trying to pry Ukraine away from Russia's faltering embrace. From Moscow's point of view, the Orange Revolution highlighted the reality that Russia would increasingly have to compete with the United States for influence in its own neighborhood. It was, indeed, a zero-sum game for both countries. For all of Washington's official rhetoric denying that it engaged in zero-sum thinking, Bush administration officials—especially in the Office of the Vice President—increasingly viewed Ukraine and the rest of the post-Soviet space as a litmus test for Bush's Freedom Agenda and as an area of competition with Russia.

THEN IT WAS TULIPS

A month after Yushchenko was inaugurated as president, Kyrgyzstan became the next—and more unlikely—candidate for a color revolution. This time, however, the United States and Russia were not arrayed on different sides of the political spectrum, and thus the Tulip Revolution did not cause major disagreements between them.

Central Asia had developed unevenly since the collapse of the USSR. Located in a difficult but strategic neighborhood, with important natural resources, the region was of major interest to both Moscow and Washington. Whereas all five Central Asian states were authoritarian countries led by groups of clans, Kyrgyzstan was the most pluralistic, largely because governing the multiethnic country, with a significant Uzbek population, entailed negotiations between opposing clans in the north and south and in the volatile Fergana Valley.[40] Kyrgyzstan had been ruled by Askar Akayev, a former physicist, since its independence, but the country had become increasingly authoritarian and corrupt, with his sons and daughter controlling the country's most lucrative assets.[41] His poor handling of a public protest in 2002 and rumors that he sought to have a pocket parliament elected in 2005—one that would change the constitution and allow him to run for president again—led to increasing doubts about whether he would voluntarily give up power at the end of his term. These fears increased when leading opposition figures, such as former ambassador to the United States Roza Otunbaeva, were barred from running, with her seat going to Akayev's daughter Bermet.

After two rounds of what was seen as fraudulent parliamentary elections in February and March 2005, mass protests began in the capital Bishkek, in the southern city of Jalal-Abad, and in Osh in the Fergana Valley. Government buildings were occupied, police used force against the protestors, and there was widespread looting in Bishkek. Protests spread around the country. Unlike in Georgia or Ukraine, there was no obvious leader, and the opposition was divided along ethnic lines. Moreover, there was widespread violence and chaos in the capital. Eventually, Akayev and his family fled to Russia via Kazakhstan. New presidential elections were held, and former prime minister Kurmanbek Bakiyev won by a landslide. He remained president until 2010—when he was ousted in another mini-revolution. As in Ukraine and Georgia, one faction of a divided elite had taken over from another.[42]

The Bush administration's interest in Kyrgyzstan stemmed primarily from its importance as a military base for operations in Afghanistan. The U.S. base at Manas airport outside Bishkek had been established in 2001 and was a vital part of the transport system in the ongoing war in Afghanistan. It was generally popular within the country because it offered employment opportunities. The United States paid $50 million per year for the use of the facility. Condoleezza Rice termed the base "a front line in the war on terrorism," and the Bush administration was initially concerned about whether the Tulip Revolution would jeopardize its presence in Kyrgyzstan. But it soon became clear that the new leadership was as interested in lucrative base contracts as had been its predecessor.

Kyrgyzstan also appeared to validate the Freedom Agenda. Unlike in Georgia and Ukraine, however, there was no clearly pro-Western opposition leader and little anticipation that Bakiyev would implement a reform agenda. Thus, the military stakes in Kyrgyzstan were high, but the Tulip Revolution was not viewed as a contest between the Russian and Western way of doing business, as were the Rose and Orange revolutions.

Moscow's interest in Kyrgyzstan was of a different order of magnitude from its stakes in Georgia or Ukraine. Russia had established a military base at Kant, in southern Kyrgyzstan, in 2003 and planned for this to be permanent. Since Bakiyev stressed the need for close relations with Russia, Akayev's ouster was not viewed as an anti-Russian move, according to Russian officials. The government-owned RIA Novosti news agency argued that "the West's hand" was not evident in Bishkek, as it had been in Tbilisi or Kyiv and that Rice and Lavrov could "find a common language" on events there.[43] Thus, the Kyrgyz events did not become a major source of tension between Washington and Moscow. The same could not be said of events that same year in Uzbekistan.

NO COLOR REVOLUTION: ANDIJON AND THE LOSS OF KARSHI-KHANABAD

Since independence, Uzbek leader Islam Karimov had sought to maximize his independence and room for maneuver by balancing his relations with Washington and Moscow and keeping a distance from both. His main concern after 9/11 had revolved around how long the United States would retain its military base in Uzbekistan and was concerned about a premature U.S. withdrawal. He had irked Moscow by joining GUUAM (Georgia-Ukraine-Uzbekistan-Azerbaijan-Moldova), the one multilateral organization in the post-Soviet space that excluded Russia. However, he was irritated by the United States' criticism of his human rights record. Constantly suspicious that radical Islamist groups would seek to bring down his government with their own version of regime change, he branded all critics as dangerous opponents.

The Bush administration's involvement in Uzbekistan highlighted the dilemma of reconciling contradictory domestic and foreign policy priorities after 9/11 and the disagreements within the government over how to handle Tashkent. As Rumsfeld wrote, "By his own admission,

President Islam Karimov was not an American-style democrat—there were few if any in the region—but he had shown no hostility toward U.S. interests."[44] Rumsfeld had personally negotiated the establishment of the U.S. military base in Karshi-Khanabad (K-2) in October 2001, and the Department of Defense regarded the base as an important element in the global war on terror. Moreover, Uzbekistan apparently participated in the Bush administration's "Extraordinary Rendition Program" that housed suspected terrorists in undisclosed prisons.[45] Uzbekistan had a poor human rights record, which affected the State Department's attitude toward the relationship. Under the terms of the 1992 Congressional Freedom Support Act, the allocation of assistance to the post-Soviet states was contingent on their conforming to certain human rights standards. Uzbekistan received funding from this program, and the secretary of state had to certify annually that Uzbekistan was making progress toward democracy. In 2002 the State Department had sent a split memo to Powell evaluating Uzbekistan's progress. The European Bureau certified Uzbekistan, but the Bureau of Democracy, Labor and Human Rights demurred. Powell chose to certify Uzbekistan, but Karimov nevertheless complained about this slight.[46]

Uzbekistan faced serious problems from Islamic extremists, including the Islamic Movement of Uzbekistan (IMU). In 2000 the Clinton administration, after Uzbek lobbying, placed the IMU on the list of international terrorist organizations. However, there was more disagreement within the United States about whether other Islamist groups should be branded as terrorists, or whether Karimov wanted to label them terrorists because they opposed his regime. The status of Hizb ut-Tahrir (HT) was particularly controversial. An Islamist group based in London, HT claimed to favor the peaceful establishment of a Caliphate over the entire Islamic world, but the Uzbek government—and some Western experts—considered it to be a terrorist organization.[47] Russia was concerned about Islamic extremism in Uzbekistan—and its potential spread to the North Caucasus—and supported Karimov's repressive policies. Moscow had also become increasingly wary of the U.S. presence in the country and of U.S. democracy-promotion efforts which, it believed could stimulate the growth of fundamentalism. By early 2005, the Uzbek-U.S. relationship had been jolted by tensions over basing arrangements, fee structures, and continued criticism of the human rights situation. Russia, after the Tulip Revolution, was seeking to shore up its influence in the region.

The U.S.-Uzbek relationship was derailed by the Andijon crisis, which led to the closing of the U.S. K-2 base. In June 2004, Uzbek police had jailed twenty-three businessmen in Andijon, a city in Eastern Uzbekistan, who were charged with "extremism, fundamentalism and separatism." The men all belonged to an Islamist organization called Akramiya—which supported charitable works and employment opportunities in the region. The accused denied the charges. In 2005 their trial began, and the verdict was due on May 12. In the lead-up to the verdict, a crowd gathered outside the courthouse. On the night of May 12–13, a group of armed men broke into the prison, freed the prisoners, and then proceeded to the regional administration building, where they took senior officials hostage and tried to seize the headquarters of the National Security Service. Thousands of demonstrators filled the main square, and Karimov flew in to assess the situation. Twenty-four hours later, many of the protestors were dead, killed by government troops. Estimates of how many died ranged from three hundred—the official Uzbek figure—to fifteen hundred, a figure given by a Security Services official who fled to the West.

Years after the Andijon uprising, there is no agreement on the facts, and interpretations of the events remain contested. The controversy over Andijon involves both how one views the businessmen and their followers and how one assesses the government response. In his memoirs, Rumsfeld asserts that the businessmen were part of an Islamic extremist group. Video footage taken by Akramiya suggests that the protestors were armed. Human Rights Watch and other NGOs, however, disagree, claiming that the businessmen were not fundamentalists but were peaceful Islamists and that government forces had used excessive, indiscriminate force against civilians.

Two weeks after Andijon, Senators John McCain and Lindsay Graham traveled to Tashkent, condemned the Karimov regime for shooting its people, and called on the U.S. government to withhold the next installment of its basing fees to the Uzbeks. The Uzbek government refused to agree to an international commission of inquiry into the massacre, as the United States and EU proposed. Russia and the Shanghai Cooperation Organization—an alliance of Russia, China, and the Central Asian States—backed Karimov on this issue. The EU imposed an arms embargo on Uzbekistan, and mutual recriminations between Tashkent and Western capitals escalated. In July 2005 the Uzbek government informed Washington that the United States was no longer welcome to use its K-2 base. In November, Russia and Uzbekistan signed a Treaty of Friendship. Both Washington and Moscow viewed the Andijon events and their aftermath as a reversal of fortune for U.S. interests in Central Asia and a net gain for the Kremlin.

Andijon revealed divisions within the Bush administration about how far to push the Freedom Agenda and how to prioritize competing interests in Central Asia.[48] Should security interests trump concerns about internal developments? How important was the commitment to human rights, and should that take precedence over counterterrorism and security concerns, including support for U.S. troops in combat? To what extent should Russia's interests influence U.S. policy? Rumsfeld, expressing the opinion of many in the Department of Defense, is unambiguous: "Human rights," he argues "had become a sizable global industry." Admitting that the Uzbek government did not help its case by refusing to provide information about what had really happened in Andijon, he advocated quiet diplomacy with Tashkent that avoided public berating. Emphasizing the paramount importance of maintaining a good relationship with Karimov because of the war in Afghanistan, he argued with Rice and her Deputy Nicholas Burns. They stated, "We made a clear choice, and that was to stand on the side of human rights." The State Department publicly berated the Uzbeks for their conduct. Rumsfeld called Rice and asked her to "back off" from her criticism of Karimov. She demurred, explaining, "The President obviously wanted to keep the military base, but he didn't tell me to tone it down, so I didn't."[49] After the ejection from K-2, Rumsfeld wrote to National Security Advisor Steven Hadley: "We are getting run out of Central Asia by the Russians. They are doing a considerably better job at bullying those countries (than) the U.S. is doing to counter their bullying."[50]

Russia's stakes in Uzbekistan were of a different order of magnitude from those in Georgia, Ukraine, or Kyrgyzstan, and the Kremlin reaction to Andijon and to the U.S. ejection from K-2 was relatively muted. Russia's involvement in Uzbekistan had been more circumscribed because of Karimov's desire to limit his dependence on any single power, so Andijon and its aftermath were an unexpected boon. With the exception of independent human rights organization Memorial, the Russian media supported the theory that the people who had incited the violence were Islamic extremists. Only fringe media made an explicit connection between George Soros, the CIA, and Akramiya. The Russian government officially endorsed the actions that Karimov had taken against the protestors.

Putin met with Karimov in June and broached the idea of a Friendship Treaty. Uzbekistan subsequently left GUUAM and rejoined the Russian-led Collective Security Treaty Organization—only to leave it again in 2012. Thus, Russia was able to use Andijon and its aftermath to rebuff the Freedom Agenda and send a message to the other rulers in post-Soviet space: we will not interfere in your domestic affairs, unlike the United States; we will help you maintain order in your countries, and our aid is not contingent on your domestic behavior. Criticizing those in the West who "hide behind some demagogic rhetoric about freedom of expression," Putin said over dinner in September 2005, "We are not against changes in the former Soviet Union. But we are afraid that those changes will be chaotic. Otherwise there will be banana republics where he who shouts loudest wins, and that would be very dangerous."[51]

COLOR REVOLUTIONS IN PERSPECTIVE

In the initial aftermath of the color revolutions, the Bush administration felt that events in Georgia, Ukraine, and Kyrgyzstan had supported U.S. interests in the post-Soviet space. As Rumsfeld wrote, "So-called color revolutions brought reform-minded, pro-Western leaders to power in Ukraine, Georgia and Kyrgyzstan. These democratic changes demonstrated the practical and moral value of President Bush's efforts to spread freedom."[52] In May 2005, Bush visited Moscow to commemorate the sixtieth anniversary of the end of World War II. He met with a cool reception, given the growing tensions between the United States and Russia. Then he traveled to Georgia, where thousands of enthusiastic fans came out to greet him in Tbilisi—in sharp contrast to his treatment in Moscow. A central street in Tbilisi was named after him. Here was proof that his Freedom Agenda had been vindicated. Shortly thereafter, he described his feelings: "It was a fantastic honor to stand side-by-side with a true lover of freedom, Saakashvili. It was an unbelievable experience to stand in Freedom Square to celebrate the peaceful revolution that took place 18 months ago."[53]

Within a few years, it became clear that the color revolutions were not all that they appeared to be. "The Color Revolutions," writes one American expert, "were not the paradigm-shifting events they seemed to be at first. Instead they turned out to be further chapters in the post-Communist evolution of Georgia, Ukraine and Kyrgyzstan whose overall impact was, in general, significantly less than first thought and, indeed, hoped."[54] In the summer of 2005, however, U.S. enthusiasm was as strong as were Russian suspicions about American intentions in the post-Soviet space. The U.S.-Russian relationship had deteriorated from its high point in the summer of 2002. The United States remained frustrated by Russia's continuing assistance to Iran's nuclear program and by its support for antidemocratic forces in the post-Soviet space. But Russia was only one of several major foreign policy concerns, with Iraq, Iran, and Afghanistan preoccupying the administration a great deal more than Russia. The United States occupied a higher place in Putin's priorities, which was a constant source of irritation in Moscow. Washington had the unique ability to confer legitimacy, prestige, and status on the Putin government. By the same token, it had the ability to block Russian political and economic ambitions and to challenge its influence in its neighborhood.

From Russia's point of view, America's refusal to recognize a Russian sphere of influence in the post-Soviet space, the continuing U.S. military presence at Manas, the refusal to take into account Russia's interests in Iraq or Iran, and Russia's continued inability to join the WTO or secure the lifting of Jackson-Vanik—all these contributed to growing frustration about unmet expectations. In September 2004, Putin had all but endorsed "my friend George" for a second term. A few years later, they were barely on speaking terms.

Figure 1.

Mikhail Gorbachev calls George H. W. Bush on December 25, 1991, to say that he is resigning and the Soviet Union is no more. As for the future, he hopes the Russian people "will live in a prosperous, democratic society."

Figure 2.

George H. W. Bush and the new Russian leader, Boris Yeltsin, tour Camp David in February 1992. Yeltsin refers to his first U.S.-Russia summit as his "big exam."

Figure 3.

At Vancouver, April 1993, Yeltsin meets Bill Clinton, who judges that "Russia was lucky to have him at the helm."

Figure 4.

Clinton plays a saxophone just given to him by Yeltsin, who describes him as "powerful, energetic, and handsome."

Figure 5.

Boris Yeltsin dances his way to victory during his uphill 1996 Presidential campaign. Bill Clinton declares, "I want this guy to win so bad it hurts." Shortly after, Yeltsin suffers a heart attack.

Figure 6.

Coal miners stage a sit-in in Red Square during Russia's August 1998 financial meltdown. The United States is blamed for offering Russia bad economic advice.

Figure 7.

"I looked the man in the eye," said George Bush of his first meeting with Russia's new president Vladimir Putin in Slovenia in July 2001. "I found him very straightforward and trustworthy—I was able to get a sense of his soul." Bush later wrote "In the years ahead, Putin would give me reason to revise my opinion."

Figure 8.

"The Axis of the Unwilling." French president Jacques Chirac, Vladimir Putin, and German chancellor Gerhard Schroeder unite in early 2003 to oppose the United States' invasion of Iraq.

Figure 9.

Ukraine's Orange Revolution is victorious in November 2004. Yulia Tymoshenko and Viktor Yushchenko, backed by the United States and the European Union, overturn the results of a flawed election that would have brought Moscow's candidate Viktor Yanukovych to power.

Figure 10.

George W. Bush and Georgian President Mikheil Saakashvili and their wives in Freedom Square in Tbilisi in May 2005. Bush described the Georgian President as "a true lover of freedom."

Figure 11.

German chancellor Angela Merkel argues in April 2008 with Secretary of State Condoleezza Rice and George W. Bush against near-term NATO membership for Ukraine and Georgia. Rice later calls the exchanges "one of the most pointed and contentious debates with our allies that I've ever experienced."

Figure 12.

Russian tanks rolled across Georgia in August 2008 in response to Georgian shelling of the South Ossetian capital. The short war was a major setback for U.S-Russian relations.

Figure 13.

"Lenin" and "Stalin," taking a break from posing with tourists in Red Square, buy hamburgers at a McDonalds in Moscow. Whatever the ups-and-downs in U.S.-Russian political relations, the growing consumer market attracts U.S. business.

Figure 14.

Igor Sechin, former Russian deputy prime minister and now CEO of Rosneft, the largest listed oil company in the world, signs newly installed oil pipeline.

Figure 15.

In March 2009, Russian foreign minister Sergei Lavrov and U.S. secretary of state Hillary Clinton pressed the "reset" button to symbolize a new start in the U.S.-Russian relationship. But "reset" was mistranslated in Russian as "overload," which some thought was prophetic.

Figure 16.

"The Cheeseburger Summit." Demonstrating the "reset" in 2010, President Barack Obama and Russian president Dmitry Medvedev enjoyed a meal at Ray's Hell Burgers in suburban Virginia. Within a couple of years Medvedev had moved out of the Kremlin, Ray's Hell Burgers had closed, and the reset was over.

Figure 17.

Ten Russian "sleeper spies" are expelled from the United States in June 2010. The most glamorous, Anna Chapman, is featured on the left. When the spies returned to Russia, Putin sang patriotic songs with them. Chapman took up modeling, and she launched her own weekly television show.

Figure 18.

"Crooks and Thieves—Give Back the Elections." Tens of thousands of protestors challenged the results of the December 2011 parliamentary elections. Putin blamed the United States for financing the protestors, warning "they want to show us they can rock the boat."

Figure 19.

Putin rides his Harley-Davidson to victory in the run-up to the 2012 Presidential election.

Figure 20.

A Russian nuclear ice-breaker cuts through the Arctic. The Arctic represents a potential new frontier for future U.S.-Russian cooperation.

Figure 21. Reset on ice? Obama and Putin meet at the 2013 G-8 summit in Northern Ireland amidst mounting disagreements over a range of issues. Shortly thereafter, Russia would grant NSA-leaker Edward Snowden political asylum, leading Obama to cancel his September summit with Putin.

Chapter Six
The Munich Speech

As far back as November 2003, Bush and British prime minister Tony Blair had had a conversation in which they talked about Vladimir Putin. The Russian president, they agreed, was turning out to be very different from what they had initially hoped for and it would be prudent to approach him with greater wariness.[1] By the beginning of 2006, that had turned into a wholesale reappraisal of the U.S. relationship with Russia. The ejection from Uzbekistan and continuing Russian criticism of U.S. policies in Ukraine and Georgia reinforced the White House's conviction that the areas of bilateral cooperation were narrowing. As Bush's second national security advisor Stephen Hadley put it, "US-Russia relations were foundering in the near abroad."[2]

Growing tensions in U.S.-Russian relations manifested themselves at a time when America's international standing was on the decline. Far from a "mission accomplished" in Iraq, a civil war was raging with an increasingly violent insurgency, and Iran appeared to be a major benefactor of the U.S. invasion. In Afghanistan, the Taliban was back, conducting its own insurgency, supported by elements in Pakistan. Anti-American sentiment was on the rise and many of America's traditional European allies continued to distance themselves from Washington, even if the "newer" Europeans remained supportive. Administration officials questioned where Russia fit into U.S. foreign policy. Afghanistan, Iraq, and Iran were at the top of U.S. priorities—and these were all areas where Russia was at odds with U.S. policy. Russia was no longer an antagonist, but it had not become an ally. Two main questions stood out: How much should the United States emphasize its Freedom Agenda in relations with Moscow? Should it focus on common interests, irrespective of what was happening inside the country?

A reassessment was also going on in Moscow. While Washington appeared to be floundering, Russia for the first time in fifteen years began to project the image of a rising power. There had been tangible improvements in the Russian people's lives. Oil revenues were growing, and increased revenues meant that pensions were paid. Benefiting from rising oil prices, growing financial reserves and a prudent macroeconomic and fiscal policy, Russia was experiencing high growth rates, earning its sobriquet as a BRIC, a major emerging market, allied with China, India and Brazil. In recognition of Russia's increasing international status, Germany had ceded its 2006 chairmanship of the G-8 to Russia, a country that had barely qualified for membership a decade before. Recognizing its growing clout as an energy producer, Moscow began to question where the United States fit into its own priorities. America still had one trump card—to acknowledge Russia's status as a great power in a way that no other country could. Bilateral U.S.-Russian negotiations on key issues—Iran, Afghanistan, Iraq, missile defense, and NATO-Russia relations—continued. Since the United States' response to his 2001 reset had disappointed him, Putin turned to Europe, China, and the other BRICs as alternative partners to the United States. The Moscow-Washington relationship had become more brittle. Channels of communication—particularly those that were out of public sight and had never been extensive at the best of times—had narrowed, and acrimonious public megaphone diplomacy was on the rise.

In this increasingly charged atmosphere, the National Security Council's senior director for Russia, Thomas Graham, was one of the few remaining advocates in Bush's second term of working more closely with Russia and focusing on pragmatic engagement. He argued that Washington had to deal with the semidemocratic Russia that existed, not with a hypothetical democratic Russia that was unlikely to emerge for some time, and that public criticism of Russia was counterproductive when the United States needed Russia's cooperation on issues such as Iran and Afghanistan. He had tried through multiple channels to promote ties with Russia, including initiating a dialogue on the post-Soviet space with his counterpart Oleg Chernov from the Russian Security Council. He believed that Bush himself supported these efforts and wanted to promote better U.S.-Russian ties.[3] Both Hadley and Rice were supportive of these moves. Graham left the National Security Council early in 2007 and was replaced as senior director for Russia by Mary Warlick, a career State Department officer. She continued to pursue engagement with Russia on a variety of issues.

However, proponents of a more pragmatic, interest-based policy toward Russia were gradually eclipsed by those promoting a "values-centered" policy that took an increasingly dim view of Putin's Russia and its policies toward its neighbors. They were concentrated in the Office of the Vice President, which adopted a much more skeptical—even hostile—attitude toward Russia, as Vice President Cheney's memoirs attest. They cautioned against the pursuit of engagement with Russia and urged closer U.S. ties to Ukraine and Georgia as a means of diminishing Russian influence in its neighborhood. Some viewed Yushchenko and Saakashvili as democratic leaders bravely fighting an imperial Russia, although Bush himself remained cautious about both Saakashvili and Yushchenko.[4] Bush liked listening to his advisors' opposing views and usually sided with those who favored more pragmatic engagement with Russia.[5] The U.S. Congress also subscribed to the darker view of Russia, as did various lobbying groups that had the ear of the OVP and the Congress.[6]

Overall, Russia policy remained fragmented, with no integrated policy toward Eurasia as a whole. In February 2006 the State Department's Office of Central Asian Affairs was moved from the European Bureau to the newly created Bureau of South and Central Asian Affairs. The political message behind this reorganization was that Central Asia had more in common with countries in South Asia such as India or Bangladesh than with other post-Soviet states. This was at best aspirational, and a rather questionable—even bizarre—view of reality and it made policy even more uncoordinated. The interagency process on Russia/Eurasia was becoming dysfunctional. In addition to policy disagreements among different players, structural problems resulted because there were few mechanisms for those dealing with Russia to coordinate with those dealing with the post-Soviet space.[7] This became evident when Cheney threw down the gauntlet.

"COMRADE WOLF"

Cheney's advisors believed that public criticism of Russia was not only appropriate but necessary for consistency, given the administration's focus on the Freedom Agenda as the centerpiece of its foreign policy. Since Putin's measures restricting freedom of expression and electoral choice went against everything that Bush had articulated in his 2005 State of the Union speech, the administration felt that it could not ignore what was happening in Russia. Moreover, Russia's cutoff of gas to Ukraine on New Year's Day 2006—which for several days deprived parts of Europe of heat in subzero temperatures—reinforced the specter of an aggressive Russia.

Cheney's increasingly negative view of Putin was confirmed by his experience in Poland in January 2006, when he led the U.S. delegation to Krakow to commemorate the sixtieth anniversary of the liberation of the Auschwitz-Birkenau death camp. Putin was scheduled to attend the meeting, but, in what was interpreted as a deliberate slight to the Polish president Aleksander Kwasniewski and Ukrainian president Viktor Yushchenko—whose election Kwasniewski had helped negotiate during the Orange Revolution—Putin kept delaying his departure from Moscow and failed to show up when it was his turn to speak. When he finally arrived, he interrupted the ongoing proceedings in an abrupt way and gave his speech. "Watching his behavior that day," wrote Cheney afterward, "reminds me why Russia's leaders are still so disliked by their neighbors and why we were right to expand NATO and offer membership to former Soviet client states like Poland and Romania."[8]

A few months later, in May 2006, Cheney was a lead speaker at the Vilnius Conference in Lithuania, which brought together heads of state from the Baltic and Black Sea regions to discuss common interests, particularly how to promote democracy in the region. He lauded the

Baltic and Central European states for their firm embrace of democracy. He praised Georgia and Ukraine for their advances toward democracy. Then he launched into the most controversial part of his speech—on Russia:

> America and all of Europe also want to see Russia in the category of healthy, vibrant democracies. Yet in Russia today, opponents of reform are seeking to reverse the gains of the last decade. . . . No legitimate interest is served when oil and gas become tools of intimidation or blackmail, either by supply manipulation or by attempts to monopolize transportation. And no-one can justify actions that undermine the territorial integrity of a neighbor, or interfere with democratic movements.

Although he added, "None of us believes that Russia is fated to become an enemy," he had, in no uncertain terms, announced that, as far as he was concerned, the post-2001 talk of partnership was a thing of the past.[9] Moreover, he had delivered these criticisms in, of all places, Vilnius, the capital of Lithuania, whose membership in NATO and the EU was viewed with great displeasure in Moscow.

Cheney's speech roused considerable controversy, not only because of its content and place of delivery but because it was bookended by two other high-level visits that once again raised the issue of double standards in U.S. policy toward Eurasia and the credibility of the Freedom Agenda.[10] Shortly before the speech, Azeri president Ilham Aliyev visited Washington. He spoke at the Council on Foreign Relations and met with President Bush in the Oval Office. Bush described Azerbaijan as "a modern Muslim country that is able to provide for its citizens, that understands that democracy is the wave of the future."[11] Azerbaijan's significance for the United States was considerable. It is a secular Muslim state, as well as an important country for U.S. energy and security interests, and it sits strategically between Russia and Iran—which has a substantial Azeri population. As a neighbor of Iran, it occupies a critical position. It was an active partner in the Caspian Guard program—part of the U.S. antiterrorist program—providing logistical support for U.S. operations in Afghanistan. It is a major oil producer and the starting point for the Baku-Tbilisi-Ceyhan oil pipeline. Thus, one could manifestly justify close cooperation with Azerbaijan from the point of view of U.S. national security interests. However, Aliyev had succeeded his father Heydar in a dynastic transition, and the presidential election was deemed to have had major irregularities by both the OSCE and the U.S. Department of State.

After his Vilnius speech, Vice President Cheney took off for Kazakhstan, another key player for U.S. energy and security interests, whose leader, Nursultan Nazarbayev—party chief in the last days of the USSR—had also recently been reelected for the third time; he won with 91 percent of the vote, in an election whose democratic deficits had been criticized in the West. Kazakhstan's large energy resources, its strategic location between China and Russia (it shares the world's longest border—seven thousand kilometers—with Russia), and its cooperation in counter-terrorism operations also qualified it for special U.S. attention. When asked in the capital Astana about his view of Kazakhstan's internal developments, the vice president replied, "I have previously expressed my admiration for what has transpired here in Kazakhstan over the past fifteen years, both in terms of economic development as well as political development."[12]

The Bush administration sought to encourage these oil-rich, strategically located, secular Muslim states to continue their successful balancing of relations with Russia and the United States (and, in Kazakhstan's case, China) and to maintain their cooperation with U.S. energy diversification projects and with the U.S. counterterrorism campaign. Russia appealed to these countries by supporting the political status quo, warning them that the United States and its NGOs were cooking up color revolutions. Thus, it was rational, from an American point of view, to downplay criticism of their political systems in the context of broader U.S.- interests. The problem with this approach, however, was that it fed into Russian charges of double standards and U.S. hypocrisy, and Moscow's claims that it was no different from Washington in seeking a sphere of influence. The Kremlin pointed out that the White House invoked the Freedom Agenda only vis-à-vis Russia, and not when it was praising Azerbaijan or Kazakhstan. The bureaucratic dysfunction in Washington exacerbated this problem. Since those U.S. officials working on Cheney's Vilnius speech did not coordinate with those working on the Kazakh trip, there was no integrated view of the impact of one part of the Cheney trip on the other.[13]

The White House also underestimated the impact that the Cheney's speech would have in Russia.[14] The Russian reaction was swift and scathing. Duma member Andrei Kokoshin declared that there were exceptionally high rates of corruption and shady business deals in Georgia and Ukraine, two states praised by Cheney.[15] Some Russians likened this to Winston Churchill's 1946 speech in Fulton, Missouri pronouncing the existence of an "iron curtain," which is generally viewed as the first acknowledgment of the Cold War. But Foreign Minister Lavrov refused to characterize it as a new Cold War declaration. Still, he said that the Vilnius democracy meeting was part of a grouping whose agenda was, as he ominously put it, "directed against someone."[16] Many Russian commentators challenged the notion that either Georgia or Ukraine, let alone Azerbaijan or Kazakhstan, could be held up as a model for democracy or transparency.

For most Russians who paid attention to these issues, the United States was involved in old-fashioned geopolitical competition with Russia in the post-Soviet space and was using the Freedom Agenda rhetoric as part of its Realpolitik strategy. The Russian leadership did not for a moment believe that Bush and his colleagues really cared about democracy, and they held up the example of Iraq—now said by the White House to be on its way to democracy—as a particular example to criticize. Nevertheless, they were highly irritated by Cheney's criticisms. As Putin told a gathering of Russian lawmakers a few days later, "As the saying goes, Comrade Wolf knows whom to eat, it eats without listening, and it clearly is not going to listen to anyone."[17]

"SOVEREIGN DEMOCRACY"

The next Russian move was to make official what Putin had reiterated to Bush on several occasions—that Russia had its own unique history and its own definition of democracy that was different from Western concepts but equally valid. The spokesman was Vladislav Surkov, Putin's enigmatic deputy chief of staff, the young "gray cardinal" who had once worked for the imprisoned oil tycoon Khodorkovsky. Surkov was tasked with managing the United Russia party and its youth wing, Nashi, which was his brainchild. Surkov's reputation had suffered after the Orange Revolution, and he needed to burnish his credentials.[18] Early in 2006, Surkov had surfaced the term "sovereign democracy" in a speech to United Russia members, but he articulated the concept explicitly in an article published later on that year. Sovereign democracy, is a "form of political life where the political powers, their authorities and decisions are decided and controlled by a diverse Russian nation for the purpose of reaching material welfare, freedom and fairness by all citizens, social groups and nationalities and by the people that formed it."[19] In other words, neither the United States nor another country had any business telling Russia what democracy was, and Russia's political system met the needs and expectations of its population.

Sovereign Democracy was not only conceived as a rebuff to the Freedom Agenda and a counterideology to Western democracy promotion. It was the essence of what was emerging as a major element of Russia's soft power project—to challenge the universality of the Euro-Atlantic historical experience and claim that Russia's political system, derived from its unique history, was as legitimate as that of the United States or Europe. As the Russian phrase goes, *"Nashe Ne Khuzhe"* (Ours is no worse than yours). Or, as Surkov said at a news conference held before the G-8 summit, "They tell us about democracy while thinking about our hydrocarbons."[20] At the G-8, Putin added, "We would not like to have the kind of democracy they have in Iraq." To which Bush replied, "Russia has democracy Russian-style, and I understand that it does not exactly resemble American democracy."[21] A year later, Bush was more explicit: "In terms of whether or not it's possible to reprogram the kind of basic Russian DNA, which is a centralized authority, that's hard to do."[22]

Sovereign democracy became the mantra of the Russian political class. Yet Putin himself gave mixed signals about the term. He told the Valdai group in 2007, "I think that sovereign democracy is a debatable term. It creates some kind of confusion. Sovereignty is something that refers to the quality of our relations with the outside world, while democracy refers to our inner state, the inner substance of society."

In a revealing phrase, he made clear that sovereignty, not democracy, was the operative concept. "Frankly speaking," he said, "there are not so many countries in the world today that have the good fortune to say they are sovereign. You can count them on your fingers. China, India, Russia and a few other countries. All other countries are to a large extent dependent on each other or on bloc leaders. This is not a very pleasing situation, but it is my deep conviction that this is the reality today."[23] In other words, only large countries not involved in entangling alliances are truly sovereign which, of course, excludes the United States.

Russia's rising international status was on display when it hosted the 2006 G-8 summit—a coming-out party of sorts—in Putin's hometown of St. Petersburg. Putin intended to showcase that Russia was "back" after more than a decade of weakness.[24] Russia spared no effort to impress the other G-8 members, organizing the meeting in the baroque Konstantin palace and dazzling visitors with St. Petersburg's summer beauty during White Nights, as it had the year before with the tricentennnial celebrations.[25] Bush met privately with Putin and subsequently had a meeting with human rights activists, informing Putin beforehand about the meeting so as not to show disrespect to the Russian leader.[26] Whereas some members of the U.S. Congress—notably Senator John McCain—had advocated expelling Russia from the G-8, the meeting focused on a variety of global challenges, from "hard" military and security issues such as North Korea and the situation in the Middle East and energy security, to "soft" questions of narcotics trafficking and education. The U.S.-Russian rhetoric was generally cordial. Participants agreed that Russia should be admitted to the WTO "as soon as possible." Some Russians questioned what the point of this "elite" G-8 club was, but most Russians realized that the G-8 was proof that Russia was now respected as a global player that had returned to the world stage.

After the G-8 summit, the Russians put out feelers to the Bush administration for another Putin-Bush meeting. The White House proposed that Bush stop over in Moscow to refuel on his way to the November 2006 APEC summit in Hanoi. The meeting at Vnukovo airport was brief. The Russian side had an extensive agenda, but Bush was preoccupied with the situation in Iraq and was not focused on Putin's topics of nonproliferation and the WTO. National Security Senior Director for Russia Tom Graham believes that, because the White House's focus was elsewhere, the United States missed several opportunities to engage Moscow more productively.[27] Former Russian ambassador to the United States Yuri Ushakov agrees. For their part, the Russian side complained that Bush was often disengaged in meetings and that, while Putin would have liked to have had longer sessions that delved into substance, the U.S. president insisted on keeping to a strict schedule and limiting discussions to more general topics.[28]

THE DOMESTIC POLITICS OF SUCCESSION

U.S.-Russian relations were, of course, also affected by domestic politics in both countries. As Putin's second term neared its completion, bilateral ties were increasingly influenced by maneuvering over succession and the uncertainty about how the Kremlin would handle the second transfer of power in Russia's postcommunist history. The Russian constitution stipulated that Putin must leave office, although he was not prevented from running for a subsequent term later on. In its thousand-year history, Russia has had a complex succession system. Under the tsars, sons and daughters usually inherited the throne from their fathers (or, occasionally, mothers) unless court intrigues and assassinations changed the succession line. In the Soviet era, five leaders died in office, one—Khrushchev—was removed by his colleagues in a palace coup and one—Gorbachev—quit because his country disappeared. The hope had been that a post-Soviet Russia would finally institutionalize a transparent succession process. Putin, although formally elected by the people, had been preselected by the Yeltsin "family" in a nontransparent process with a guaranteed victory in the polls.

In Putin's second term, the Kremlin was sufficiently alarmed by the color revolutions that it focused on ensuring that no popular unrest could threaten its grip on the country. Against a background of a stronger "vertical of power" that manifested increasingly less tolerance for criticism, the process of succession was unfolding. Restrictions on media freedom and on the operation of foreign NGOs continued apace. Government critics were barred from appearing on state television and opposition figures were harassed.

In 2006 two assassinations captured international attention and provoked greater questioning of where Russia was heading. On October 7, 2006, pioneering and influential opposition journalist and human rights advocate Anna Politkovskaya, a trenchant critic of Russia's policies in the North Caucasus, was gunned down as she entered her apartment building laden with groceries after a shopping trip. The assassin was clearly a professional killer. She had already endured serious harassment, including poisoning on a plane as she made her way to Beslan to cover the 2004 school seizure. She had been particularly critical of Ramzan Kadyrov's brutal rule in Chechnya. Ramzan, who had just turned thirty, was the Kremlin's strongman in Grozny, imposing order on the war-torn republic through the use of his own militias, and he had a particularly virulent hatred for Politkovskaya. While her many Russian and foreign admirers expressed outrage at her murder, Putin at first said nothing. Then, a few days later, he implied that one of his opponents had her killed to make him look bad, and then he let the world know what he thought of Politkovskaya: "She had minimal influence on political life in Russia. This murder does more to harm Russia and Chechnya than any of her publications."[29]

A more spectacular assassination with international repercussions was that of Alexander Litvinenko, a former FSB officer who worked for the exiled Boris Berezovsky and had been granted political asylum in London. Litvinenko was investigating, among other things, Politkovskaya's murder. On November 1, 2006, he met with a former KGB official Andrei Lugovoi and another Russian at London's Millennium Hotel restaurant. Shortly thereafter he fell ill with a mysterious illness and deteriorated rapidly until he died three weeks later. His supporters released a haunting photograph of him on his deathbed. At the last moment, doctors in London diagnosed him with poisoning by polonium-210, a powerful radioactive substance produced almost exclusively in one Russian laboratory. It turned out that the plane on which his Russian interlocutors had flown had strong traces of polonium and that radioactivity was also detected in the London restaurant. Litvinenko's murder was an act of nuclear terrorism by foreign agents on British soil. The British security services concluded that Litvinenko's death was a "state-sponsored assassination orchestrated by Russian Security services."[30] The Russian intention had been to conceal the poison, so that no one would know what had killed him, but the assassins mishandled the polonium. Nevertheless, the murder sent a strong message to Russians inside and outside Russia who might be contemplating opposing the Putin regime. Russia refused to extradite the main suspect, Lugovoi, and secured him a seat in the Duma, where he enjoyed immunity from prosecution. On his deathbed, Litvinenko had accused Putin of ordering his murder, but the Kremlin's response was that enemies of the regime—namely, those associated with Boris Berezovsky (for whom Litvinenko had worked)—had ordered the murder to make Putin look bad.[31]

Against this background of tighter government controls and harassment of opponents several presidential candidates emerged—Defense Minister Sergei Ivanov, Russian Railways chief Vladimir Yakunin, and Presidential Administration head Dmitry Medvedev. Of the three, the most likely initially appeared to be Sergei Ivanov, former KGB general (as opposed to Putin's lieutenant-colonel), who had been stationed in Europe, spoke fluent English—which he claimed he had learned from listening to Beatles records--, and was well versed in security issues. Rice recalls that she made her prediction about his future in 2005 during the sixtieth-anniversary celebrations of the end of World War II, as he stood saluting the Russian troops in Red Square. *"Putin will never let him become President,"* I thought. *"He will not want a strong successor and rival in the Kremlin when he finally moves on."*[32]

Since Putin had created a new political system after he ascended to the Kremlin, it was difficult to believe that he could leave power and that the system could continue as it was. The elite had important interests to protect, and Putin was their guarantor. Hence there was speculation that he would change the constitution and remain in the Kremlin. He repeatedly denied this, telling the Valdai Club in 2007, "I am very concerned that today in Russia so much depends on only one person. And I want to change this. I am not planning to disappear altogether. I am not planning to emigrate, to take up residence in another country. I love my country. I'm Russian—my goal is to ensure that power in Russia remains stable. And I have every reason to believe that it will."[33]

By the fall of 2007, the guessing game grew more intense. In the December Duma elections, the ruling United Russia party officially secured 64.3 percent of the vote, although OSCE and Council of Europe election monitors declared the elections not fair and falling short of generally accepted democratic norms. Shortly thereafter, Putin surprised his fellow citizens and the outside world by announcing that Dmitry Medvedev would run for president, and he, Putin, would become the prime minister. Russia would now have a "tandem" government. It was an unexpected and clever move. Putin had not violated the constitution and yet was able to remain in power.

PUTIN'S BROADSIDE

While the succession was still being negotiated and a few months after the G-8 summit in February 2007, Putin removed the gloves, directly attacking the United States for what he described as its unilateral and reckless attitude toward the world. He did so by attending his first Munich Security Conference, a gathering of Euro-Atlantic defense ministers, officials and experts focusing on the world's most pressing security issues. Putin's speech was eagerly anticipated. It would be his reply to "Comrade Wolf," Dick Cheney—but it was much more than that.

Putin began his speech by warning his audience that his remarks might be "unduly polemical." The speech certainly brought all the Russian criticisms together. He began by lambasting the idea of unipolarity, in which "there is one master, one sovereign. And at the end of the day this is pernicious not only for all those within the system, but also for the sovereign itself because it destroys itself from within. And this certainly has nothing to do with democracy—we are constantly being taught about democracy. But for some reason those who teach us do not want to learn themselves." Putin went on to name names: "Today we are witnessing an almost uncontained hyper use of force—military force—in international relations, force that is plunging the world into an abyss of permanent conflicts. One state and, of course, first and foremost the United States, has overstepped its national borders in every way." The solution was to return to multilateral diplomacy under the guidance of the United Nations and to eschew the use of military force. Putin also stressed that, with the rise of the BRICs, the future undoubtedly lay with multipolarity, not with unipolarity.[34]

The U.S. delegation—which included Senators John McCain, Joseph Lieberman, and Lindsay Graham—was stunned by this public polemic, and the audience's applause was restrained. Czech foreign minister Karel Schwarzenberg's response was pointed: "We must thank President Putin—who has not only shown concern about the publicity for this conference, but has clearly and convincingly demonstrated why NATO had to enlarge."[35] Nevertheless, audience reaction reminded both Russia and the United States that some Europeans shared Putin's criticisms of U.S. unipolarity.

Defense Secretary Robert Gates, seeking to defuse tensions, gave the official U.S. response the next day. After the Republican losses in the 2006 congressional elections Gates, the former director of Central Intelligence and a student of Russian history, had left his position as president of Texas A&M University to replace the outspoken Donald Rumsfeld. Gates was pragmatic, low-key, and disinclined to engage in public polemics. Acknowledging that he, like Mr. Putin, was a former spy, he announced that he had been to "re-education camp" during his four-year stint as president of Texas A&M. Emphasizing that "one Cold War was quite enough," he said he would soon travel to Russia because, as he put it, "Russia is a partner in our endeavors." He did, however, specifically question Russia's support for Iran's nuclear program.[36] The White House reaction was also measured. Spokesman Tony Snow described Russia as "a valued ally."[37] Almost a year after Cheney's confrontational Vilnius speech, the Bush administration, facing increasing problems in Iraq and Afghanistan, had clearly decided to downplay the reaction to the Munich speech and instead focus on issues where it needed Russian cooperation—Iran, Missile Defense, and Kosovo. Moreover, some analyzed the speech not only in foreign policy terms but also in its domestic aspects—Putin was in his last year as president and, given the great uncertainties about succession, raising the specter of an external enemy could be a useful tool as the elections approached.[38]

The Munich speech ushered in a new phase in Russia's relations with the West, one in which an energy-rich Russia had served notice that it would no longer accept an agenda that had been scripted in Washington. Although Putin had expressed all of these sentiments before, this was the first time that he had integrated them into a structured broadside at a prestigious international gathering.[39] Just to drive home that point, a few months later during the commemorations of the sixty-second anniversary of the end of World War II, Putin likened American foreign policy to that of the Third Reich.[40] This new truculent assertiveness apparently earned him the distinction of being named *Time Magazine*'s Person of the Year in 2007. "A Tsar Is Born," declared the lead article, "He stands, above all, for stability—stability before freedom, stability before choice, stability in a country that has hardly seen it for a hundred years."[41]

One of Russia's most astute foreign policy observers, Dmitri Trenin, provided the context for the Munich speech. Russia, he said, had left the West: "Until recently, Russia saw itself as a Pluto in the Western solar system, very far from the center but still fundamentally part of it. Now it has left that orbit entirely: Russia's leaders have given up on becoming part of the West and have started creating their own Moscow-centered system" He concluded, "The West needs to calm down and take Russia for what it is: a major outside player that is neither an eternal foe nor an automatic friend."[42]

Was the Bush administration prepared to deal with this more assertive Russia and reconsider the question of its legitimate interests? Iran soon reemerged as a key issue for Washington and Moscow as they moved in different orbits. It was part of the U.S. presidential inbox that constantly caused tensions with Moscow and could not easily be "reset."

IRAN

Despite the administration's long-held conviction that Tehran was intent on acquiring a nuclear weapons capability, Iran had cooperated with the United States in the early stages of the Afghan war, providing intelligence about the Taliban, which it regarded as a threat.[43] By 2004, Iran's clout in its neighborhood was on the rise. Teheran's archenemy Saddam Hussein, was gone, as was the Taliban regime. Indeed, Iran was a major—and unanticipated—beneficiary from the U.S. policy of regime change, as it could now assert its influence with the majority Iraqi Shiite population in Bagdhad, which had been persecuted under Saddam.

In May 2004 a reformist group in the Iranian government communicated a proposal for normalizing relations with the United States via the Swiss government. This "grand bargain" would have involved Iran addressing a host of U.S. concerns—from proliferation to terrorism to the Arab-Israeli problem, in return for Washington recognizing what Tehran defined as Iran's legitimate security interests and lifting economic sanctions.[44] In the end, nothing came of this proposal after the election of Mahmoud Ahmadinejad in 2005. There was a debate within the U.S. administration about whether and how to engage Tehran—which, after all, had been defined as part of the "Axis of Evil"—and this led to differing prescriptions about how to deal with Russia on the issue. In 2007 the National Intelligence Council published a National Intelligence Estimate on Iran, whose declassified Key Judgments concluded that Iran had halted its nuclear weapons program in 2003 under former President Khatami, a judgment—challenged by some within the Bush administration—that appeared to vindicate Russian arguments about Iran's peaceful nuclear programs.[45]

Russia's goals vis-à-vis Iran were multiple and, like those of the United States, not always consistent. In 2000 Putin—claiming that the United States had violated its promises—had abrogated the 1995 Gore-Chernomyrdin secret agreement whereby Russia had promised to cease supplying conventional weapons to Iran. In early 2001, Iranian president Khatami visited Moscow to discuss military and technical cooperation.[46] Moreover, shortly after President Bush denounced the "Axis of Evil," Defense Minister Sergei Ivanov confirmed that Russia indeed intended to continue military and technical cooperation with Iran.[47] Russian arms deliveries to Iran increased, as did the variety of weapons, leading some in the United States to call Russia "Iran's nuclear godfather."[48] Russia also began discussions of the sale of S-300 surface-to-air missiles, which Israel viewed as a direct threat to its national security.[49] A contract to deliver S-300s to Iran was signed in late 2007.[50]

As Putin admitted in his Munich speech, Russia had concerns about Iran's longer-term nuclear ambitions. According to John Bolton,

Alexander Rumyantsev, then minister of Atomic Energy, believed that Iran was developing a nuclear weapons capability, and he sought to slow down the completion of the Bushehr nuclear power plant. But this view was not widely shared in Moscow, and most Russian officials believed that they could handle the Iranians. They also figured that Iran was more of a problem for the United States than for Russia.[51] Russia did not want Iran to acquire a nuclear weapons capability. However, it also wanted to limit the U.S. role and military presence in the region and retain its own influence. Russia had a considerable economic stake in Iran, valued in the billions of dollars, which it wanted to preserve, and it viewed U.S. attempts to impose sanctions as a direct assault on its commercial ties.

Russia also had domestic reasons for approaching Iran with caution. It wanted to contain the spread of imported Islamic fundamentalism to its Muslim population and believed that engaging Iran was an important element in its own efforts to combat domestic extremism. It also worried that any Western military conflict with Iran could further inflame the North Caucasus.

A key development in Russia's relations with the Islamic world was its accession to the Organization of the Islamic Conference (OIC) organization as an observer nation with a Muslim minority population, enabling it to argue that it could act as a mediator between Iran and the West. Moreover, the Shanghai Cooperation Organization in 2006 granted Iran observer status in an organization that brought Russia, China, and Central Asia together. Moscow argued consistently against isolating Tehran. However, as evidence surfaced in 2002 of Iran's secret uranium enrichment facility at Natanz, it became increasingly difficult to brush aside questions about Iran's long-term intentions. Despite professions of a "strategic partnership" between the two countries, Tehran and Moscow had their own tensions. They could not agree on the issue of Caspian Sea demarcation, which hindered the exploitation of energy resources.[52] Iran was highly critical of Russian support of U.S. and UN policies designed to limit its nuclear activities. Nevertheless, Russia also recognized that the Iranian nuclear program was an issue where the West had to acknowledge its influence—hence its limited interest in resolving the situation. At least that was how it was seen in Washington.[53]

"Most Russians were not interested in helping us on Iran," according to Bolton.[54]

For the period of the two Bush administrations, Russia consistently argued that there was no evidence that Iran had violated its commitments to the IAEA, that Iran was interested only in developing nuclear energy for peaceful purposes, and that Russian involvement in Iran's nuclear energy program did not present any security threat. In 2005 Russia introduced additional safeguards at the Bushehr plant and announced that it had agreed on a spent-fuel take-back agreement with Iran.[55] Nevertheless, evidence began to grow of Tehran's less peaceful nuclear intentions after Iran withdrew from an earlier agreement with the IAEA and resumed enrichment activities at Natanz and also failed to implement its promises to send spent fuel to Russia.

Between 2005 and 2008, Moscow pursued a complex strategy of softening United Nations resolutions condemning Iran and eventually supporting them. In an October 2005 press conference, Lavrov insisted that the IAEA inspectors in Iran could take care of the issue, while Rice argued in favor of referring Iran to the United Nations Security Council.[56] A few months later Russia proposed that Iran suspend its uranium enrichment activities at Natanz but still be permitted "limited research activities" in uranium enrichment. But the United States rejected any proposal that did not ban all domestic nuclear enrichment.[57] Moreover, Russia opposed any new sanctions against Iran.[58]

Eventually, after a series of tough three-way negotiations involving the United States, the EU3 (represented by the United Kingdom, France, and Germany) and Russia, three Security Council resolutions were passed. Resolution 1737, passed in December 2006, called on Iran to suspend all of its uranium enrichment-related and reprocessing activities, and until it did so, sanctions were imposed to block the import or export of sensitive nuclear material and freeze the assets of persons or entities involved in sensitive nuclear activities. Resolution 1747, passed on March 24, 2007, criticized Iran for failing to comply with Resolution 1737 and put tighter sanctions on Iran. Resolution 1803, passed on March 3, 2008, further chiding Iran for failing to comply with the previous two resolutions, reaffirmed the sanctions unless Iran ceased its enrichment activities.[59]

Between these resolutions there was a brief period in which it appeared that Russia and the United States might cooperate more effectively on Iran. In September 2007 Rice broached with Lavrov the possibility of the United States, which had no presence on the ground in Iran, opening an interest section in Tehran, similar to that which exists in Havana. It would take care of the interests of U.S. citizens visiting Iran. Lavrov responded positively, and Putin agreed to raise the issues with the Ayatollah Khamenei at a Caspian summit in October. However, the Iranians never took up the issue, and according to Rice, "By the end of October 2007, the Russians' attitude toward the Iranians had soured significantly."[60]

Thus, toward the end of the Bush administration, Russia and the United States had reached a modus vivendi on Iran: Russia supported UN sanctions—albeit considerably weaker than those that Washington or Brussels favored—but Russia also continued with the construction of Bushehr and conveyed to Tehran that Russian protection against tougher Western sanctions was necessary and not to be taken for granted. Russia's stance continued to perplex American officials. As John Bolton told the Russians, "Iran is more dangerous for Russia than it is for America."[61] Russia was indeed concerned about Tehran's long-term ambitions but appeared to believe that Iran's timetable for acquiring a nuclear weapons capability was considerably longer than the estimates of the United States—or Israel. And inextricably linked to the Iran nuclear question, of course, was the vexed issue of missile defense.

MISSILE DEFENSE

U.S.-Russian discussions on missile defense had been ongoing since the 2001 Crawford summit. Although the United States repeatedly assured the Russians that MD was directed against Iran, and not against them, Russian officials remained skeptical. Even though some were willing to admit that the initial system as conceived in Washington could not threaten Russia's nuclear deterrent, they argued that there was no guarantee that the system would not eventually develop into a much larger network of U.S. missile defenses, which could compromise Russia's second-strike capability. Part of the problem centered on whether to focus on intentions or capabilities. Missile defense, in the U.S. view, was a system that could protect countries from a possible nuclear attack from Iran or North Korea. The U.S. interest was not to counter Russia's huge strategic and tactical nuclear arsenal. But, from Moscow's vantage point, what mattered were capabilities. Once the U.S. deployed interceptors that were in striking distance of Russian territory, there was no long-term guarantee about how they might be used.

Washington's decision to deploy parts of the system in two of Moscow's erstwhile Warsaw Pact partners intensified Russian suspicions. In 2004 Bush approved sites in Poland and the Czech Republic for MD components. Stephen Rademaker, assistant secretary of state for International Security and Nonproliferation, flew to Russia and briefed his counterparts, explaining to them that it was much easier to shoot down Russian missiles from Alaska than it was from Poland. But they did not buy that argument. "The real problem is that we were creating a U.S. footprint in the former Warsaw Pact countries," said Rademaker. Eric Edelman, undersecretary of defense for policy, agreed: "It was about geography, not physics."[62]

The United States began formal negotiation in July 2007 to deploy radars in the Czech Republic and interceptors in Poland. Washington also announced agreements with new NATO allies Bulgaria and Romania to open military bases there. Bush administration officials privately expressed frustration about Russia's position on missile defense, arguing that the Russian side knew perfectly well that missile defense was not directed against Russia and could in no way threaten its nuclear deterrent. But that missed the point. Not only was the system going to be deployed on Russia's border, but the two designated European participants were countries with whom Russia had a long and sometimes turbulent relationship. The Czechs and Poles wanted the missile defense sites because they were a physical manifestation of U.S. support, with all that conveyed. As former Warsaw Pact members, their support of America's project was particularly galling for Moscow. The political symbolism of missile defense deployments in Central Europe undoubtedly influenced the combative Putin narrative on display at Munich.

As the Bush administration moved to implement its program, the Kremlin announced its own undefined plans to counter U.S. missile defense deployments. Putin's press spokesman Dimtry Peskov said, "We feel ourselves deceived. Potentially we will have to create alternatives to this but with low cost and higher efficiency." General Vladimir Belous added, "The geography of the deployment doesn't give any doubt the main targets are Russian and Chinese nuclear forces. The U.S. bases represent a real threat to our strategic nuclear forces."[63] Defense Minister Sergei Ivanov brushed aside talk of possible U.S.-Russian cooperation on missile defense: "We believe this system—strategic missile defense—is, to put it mildly, of a somewhat fanciful nature."[64] During Rice's first visit to Moscow after Putin's Munich speech, she tried to sound upbeat, announcing that the revived 2+2 mechanism, bringing together the Russian and American ministers of defense and foreign affairs would improve both consultation and cooperation on a range of security-related issues, including missile defense.[65]

The Russians resorted to a familiar tactic of trying to divide Europe and the United States on the issues of missile defense. Only this time it was more difficult, since Europe itself was split over the issue. Poland, the Czech Republic, and other "new" European states were largely in favor of the project, while Germany and other parts of "old" European were wary of antagonizing Russia and skeptical about the efficacy of the entire scheme. At a NATO-Russia Council meeting in April 2007, Lavrov lobbied hard against missile defense. Using vaguely threatening words in the closed-door meetings, he raised the specter of Russian countermeasures. These actions were counterproductive, bringing old and new Europe together and evoking a united European response that supported missile defense. Moreover, Lavrov's attempts to lobby for a formal cooperation agreement between NATO and the Russian-dominated Collective Security Treaty Organization (CSTO) were rebuffed.[66]

In December 2007 Putin launched another salvo against missile defense, announcing that Russia had suspended its participation in the Treaty on Conventional Forces in Europe (CFE), which, since 1990, had placed limits on the number of troops and military hardware that thirty countries could deploy in Europe. In so doing, an important measure of confidence building was forfeited, since CFE involved regular on-site inspections.[67] Moscow had long resisted complying with CFE's provisions, claiming that they unfairly penalized Russia, but Putin explicitly linked Russia's withdrawal to U.S. missile defense deployments.[68]

To try and clear the air after the Munich speech, Bush invited Putin in July 2007 to an informal "lobster" summit at Walker's Point, a small peninsula jutting out into the Atlantic Ocean, his family's compound in Kennebunkport, Maine. Father George H. W. Bush played host, and the three presidents enjoyed speedboat riding, fishing, and other recreational activities to defuse tensions (Putin caught the only fish). Russians generally viewed the elder Bush favorably, since he was associated with ending the Cold War in a manner that was respectful of Russia and its leaders.

In Maine, Putin elaborated on a proposal he had made at the 2007 G-8 meeting in Heiligendamm, Germany: America should use Azerbaijan's Gabala radar station where the United States and Russia could jointly monitor possible missile activity from Azerbaijan's neighbor, Iran. Russia had leased the radar station until 2012, and it was unclear whether Baku would renew the lease (it did not). The Gabala proposal was a shrewd move: it offered a way for the United States and Russia to cooperate on missile defense. From the Russian point of view, it eliminated the need for deployments in the Czech Republic, although U.S. technical experts rejected that argument. Russia also argued that it made much more sense to deploy radars in Azerbaijan if the target was indeed Iran, as the United States insisted. Indeed, Iran wasted no time in criticizing the proposal. As an additional incentive, Putin proposed that the United States and Russia could cooperate on a joint early-warning system based at Armavir in southern Russia.[69] Bush replied that that he found the proposal innovative and strategic but added that the Czech Republic and Poland needed to be part of the system. Sergei Ivanov, now first deputy prime minister, responded that, if the United States did not accept Putin's compromise proposal, Moscow would conclude that missile defense was indeed aimed at Russia and would react accordingly.[70]

Rice believes that there was a miscommunication between Bush and Putin over whether Gabala was an alternative or an addition to the sites in Poland and the Czech Republic but concludes that "George W. Bush and Vladimir Putin did have good chemistry, and on this occasion it helped calm the waters—temporarily—of our increasingly choppy relationship."[71] In remarks to reporters, Bush said that he believed that Putin always spoke the truth with him: "Do I trust him? Of course!"[72]

U.S.-Russian negotiations on Gabala and a possible joint radar site in Armavir continued intermittently over the next year but were inconclusive. Eric Edelman, who was part of a U.S. delegation that went to inspect the Gabala radar site, was unimpressed: the station was dilapidated, and it was clear that Russia was hoping to use U.S. technology to upgrade the facility. Moreover, Gabala had failed to detect several tests of Iranian missiles next door.[73] The U.S. team concluded that the Russian offer could help monitor the threat of an Iranian missile attack but could not defend against it.[74] Russian officials express resentment that Putin's initiatives were not taken seriously enough. Former Russian ambassador to the United States Yuri Ushakov argues that Putin made a "bold proposal" at Kennebunkport, which was never taken up by the U.S. side.

Missile Defense was center stage at the last Bush-Putin formal summit at Putin's presidential dacha in Sochi on the Black Sea in April 2008. Both sides affirmed that they were interested in a missile defense system "in which Russia and the United States and Europe will participate as equal partners." To mollify the Russians, the U.S. side proposed that Russian military personnel be stationed as observers in the planned missile defense sites—an idea that, to say the least, lacked appeal in Poland and the Czech Republic. Nevertheless, in their joint press conference, Putin reiterated, "Our fundamental attitude to the American plans has not changed." Bush administration officials privately expressed frustration that, after years of negotiations with Russia, and countless proposals designed to assuage Russian concerns and offer cooperative solutions, Washington and Moscow were no nearer to reaching a compromise than they had been in Crawford, Texas, more than six years earlier.[75] In the spring of 2008, with oil prices at an all-time high and Russia's currency reserves standing at $450 billion, there was little incentive for Moscow to reach a deal on missile defense, particularly since Washington would not back down on the question of basing elements of the system in the Czech Republic and Poland.

But missile defense was not the only contentious issue between Washington and Moscow. The territorial integrity of the new states that had emerged out of the upheavals in Eastern Europe and the collapse of the Soviet Union put new strains on the U.S-Russian relationship. In particular, the status of Kosovo and its ramifications for Russia's neighborhood had moved to the front burner in the relationship.

Chapter Seven

From Kosovo to Georgia:
Things Fall Apart

Disagreements over the Balkans were a constant undercurrent in the U.S.-Russian relationship almost from the moment that the USSR collapsed. Moscow's claim to be the protector of the Orthodox Serbs against the Muslims and Catholics in Yugoslavia provided a powerful narrative for a Kremlin that was intent on holding on to as much of its traditional spheres of influence as possible. Yeltsin's Russia had been a reluctant partner in the NATO-led Bosnia campaign and the subsequent postwar peace-keeping force. Yet the Contact Group, where the United States, Russia, and key European countries met to discuss how to deal with the conflict, had worked. Indeed, Russian troops had served under an American commander, contributing 1,200 of the 20,000 peacekeepers in the NATO-led Stabilization Force.[1] The Kosovo campaign in 1999 had been much more contentious, and the Russian dash to Pristina had almost brought the two sides into direct conflict. Now that Putin was president and Russia had recovered from the doldrums of the late 1990s, the Kremlin's stance became more uncompromising. It was intent on undermining any Western attempts to grant Kosovo independence.

Many Russians—including critics of the Kremlin—view Kosovo as the critical factor that decisively ended the both the Clinton and Putin resets. They consider the Kremlin's role in 1999, particularly Viktor

Chernomyrdin's role in negotiating Serbia's capitulation, as one of the darkest chapters in Yeltsin's foreign policy. Even though Russian troops participated in the Kosovo Stabilization Force after the war was over, officers who served in the Balkans did not find this a career-enhancing move when they returned to Moscow, and in 2003 Defense Minister Sergei Ivanov withdrew Russian forces from KFOR.[2] For the Kremlin, the fact that NATO was operating without a UN mandate (because Russia would have vetoed it) outside NATO's traditional area of operation and in an area with which Russia believed it had special interests was particularly galling. From NATO's point of view, Russia's seeming indifference to the plight of Kosovars who were ethnically cleansed by the Serbs raised questions about the extent to which Russia and the West indeed shared values. But Kosovo also raised other grating issues for Russia: If the breakaway province could be granted independence, why not Chechnya and other separatist regions? If NATO was now active in Kosovo, who was to tell where it might next intervene without a UN mandate?

After the end of the war, Kosovo (which has a population of less than 2 million people) was administered by a UN Interim Administration Mission (UNMIK). The Kosovo Liberation Army, which had fought the war, was demobilized, and the rudiments of a system of administration were created. Yet in 2004 there was renewed ethnic violence between Serbs and Kosovars. By 2005, the Contact Group began to debate Kosovo's future status. Most agreed that the current situation was untenable, and Finnish diplomat Martti Ahtisaari, who had negotiated the 1999 cease-fire with Viktor Chernomyrdin, was chosen for the unenviable task of developing a comprehensive proposal for Kosovo's future status. Rice describes her arguments with Lavrov about Kosovo's status as one of the most contentious U.S.-Russian problems that was "a harbinger of what was to come: an increasingly difficult relationship with the Kremlin—until the end of the Bush years."[3]

Between 2006 and 2008, Moscow blocked UN decision making on Kosovo, claiming that Ahtisaari failed to take into account Serb objections or Russia's concerns about the implications of Kosovo's independence for other unrecognized states. Yet the Western negotiating side, which included veteran American ambassador Frank Wisner, came to the conclusion after months of hard negotiations that granting independence to Kosovo was the only possible solution to years of conflict. There was great concern that, if Kosovo were not granted independence, violence between Serbs and Kosovars would once again erupt. The Serb and Kosovar positions were too far apart and their mutual history too bloody for any compromise solution. But Bush administration officials did not unanimously support this position. The lack of a coordinated policy was once again evident—officials who worked on the Balkans did not communicate regularly with those who worked on Russia and thus did not fully take into account what Russia's response might be.[4] At the 2007 G-8 Summit, Putin had repeated previous assertions that universal principles should be applied to the right of self-determination "be it in the Balkans or the post-Soviet Caucasus—I see no difference between (Kosovo) and post-Soviet separatist states."[5] (He did not, however, mention Chechnya in this connection.)

After Russia refused to support the Ahtisaari Plan and with no mutually acceptable UN-backed solution in sight, Kosovo unilaterally declared its independence from Serbia in February 2008. The United States and twenty-two of the twenty-seven EU states, and many others around the world, recognized Kosovo's independence. They explicitly said that the situation in Kosovo was sui generis and did not constitute a precedent. Nevertheless, Russia, Serbia, Spain, Slovakia, Greece, Cyprus, and Romania did not recognize Kosovo's independence, largely because all of these countries faced their own separatist challenges. Russia deemed Kosovo's declaration illegitimate under international law, and Lavrov forcefully warned that it would endanger international stability.[6]

Putin was more blunt: "This is a harmful and dangerous precedent—the Kosovo precedent is a terrible precedent—you can't observe one set of rules for Kosovo and another for Abkhazia and South Ossetia."[7] Serbia then requested that the International Court of Justice issue an advisory opinion on the legality of Kosovo's declaration of independence. It released its findings two years later in 2010—Kosovo's declaration did not violate principles of international law. Right after Kosovo's declaration, the Russian Duma and Council of Federation released a statement saying that, if Kosovo could declare its independence, so could Abkhazia and South Ossetia. Russia's obstructionist position on Kosovo was, from the Bush administration's point of view, part of a larger problem.

Moscow appeared to be blocking most of what Washington sought to achieve in Europe. Of course, the Russian claim that Washington was rewarding a group that contained extremist elements—the Kosovo Liberation Army—was in part borne out when some KLA officials, including a prime minister, were indicted by the International Criminal Tribunal for the former Yugoslavia for War Crimes.

The United States and its European allies were frustrated that Russia objected to Western suggestions but never produced any alternative proposals to Kosovo's independence other than its continued status as a province of Serbia. Perhaps there were no viable alternatives, and no middle ground between the U.S. and EU position and that of Russia was possible. Under Secretary of State Nicholas Burns declared, "I do not see any kind of crisis with Russia over this. I expect Russia to be supportive of stability in this region." But there was concern about Russia's warnings that what was legitimate for Kosovo was equally legitimate for Georgia's separatist regions.[8]

The last Bush-Putin summit took place in Sochi in April 2008, after Dmitry Medvedev's election as president. It was a far cry from the initial summit in Ljubljana when Bush had looked into Putin's eyes. This time, the two leaders sought to salvage what was possible from the troubled U.S.-Russian relationship. Rice describes the Sochi summit as "a bit anticlimactic." Bush and Putin covered the range of contentious and less contentious issues and signed their valedictory agreement, the U.S.-Russia Strategic Framework Declaration.

The basic elements of the Sochi declaration had been written earlier, for the Moscow summit in 2002, but they were resuscitated for the April 2008 meeting.[9] Rice argues that, although this declaration was less momentous that the 1972 U.S.-Soviet agreement on Basic Principles, it was a framework document that focused on the cooperative side of the relationship.[10] The declaration was divided into four sections: Promoting Security, Preventing the Spread of Weapons of Mass Destruction, Combating Global Terrorism, and Strategic Economic Cooperation. It laid out a detailed road map for cooperation on these issues, while acknowledging disagreements over missile defense and other questions. The document is a comprehensive road map for an improved relationship, and the Obama administration subsequently followed many of its prescriptions. Indeed, Bush and Putin agreed to begin negotiations on a treaty to replace the START treaty, which the Obama administration took up as soon as it came into office. The problem was that Sochi came too late to achieve anything in a situation of presidential transitions and growing tensions over Georgia.[11]

During their joint press conference, Putin praised Bush for his "honesty and openness" while reiterating that Russia's attitudes toward missile defense had not changed. Bush described his "remarkable relationship with Putin" and reiterated that missile defense was not aimed at Russia. He praised Putin for sharing intelligence on terrorism and for his "leadership on Iran." He promised to engage Congress to abolish Jackson-Vanik: "I think it's time to get rid of Jackson-Vanik."[12]

At Sochi, Bush also met with Medvedev, who would take office a month later. Rice writes that she "doubted he'd be powerful enough to challenge his political sponsor. The President-in-waiting didn't seem particularly confident, and he was determined to avoid substantive issues." But she believed that, inasmuch as he came from a different generation and not from a KGB background, he could, if left to his own devices, alter Russia's path.[13] Bush had the impression that Medvedev was an intelligent and forward looking, albeit rather reticent man.[14] He took a liking to Medvedev but wrote, "The big question, of course, was whether he would actually run the country."[15]

At Sochi, Bush declared that "the Cold War is over." Nevertheless, its historical legacy remained inescapable.

NATO—AGAIN

The apparent rapport at Sochi between the Russian and American leaders masked a growing gulf between Washington and Moscow over how to balance Russia's interests in the post-Soviet space with those of its neighbors. Bush visited Sochi right after the Bucharest NATO summit, where U.S.-Russian and U.S.-European tensions were on full display. The core question at Bucharest was whether NATO should offer a membership action plan (MAP) to Ukraine and Georgia. A MAP was not an offer of membership, but it was a road map that stipulated what a country had to do in order to be eligible for membership, and countries that had in the past been awarded MAPs had eventually joined NATO.

Russia's relationship with NATO remained problematic. The creation of the NATO-Russia Council in 2002 had been intended to establish a forum where Russia could feel that NATO treated it more as an equal than had been the case in the PJC, but six years later the NRC's accomplishments were modest. "The Council had made little progress," writes Rice, "because the Kremlin never fully embraced it."[16] Victoria Nuland, U.S. ambassador to NATO, argues that practical cooperation on a number of issues worked well, but dialogue in the NRC was always difficult.[17] At the same time that NATO sought to improve ties with Russia, the issue of further enlargement to the post-Soviet states was on the table. From Moscow's point of view, enlargement to the Baltic states had been hard enough to swallow. The prospect of NATO offering membership to Ukraine and Georgia was absolutely unacceptable.

Ukraine and Georgia had both requested a MAP, but the administration had delayed action on MAPs for two reasons: divisions within the administration and divisions within the alliance. Decisions on NATO membership involved two basic questions: What does the applicant bring to the alliance, and what does the alliance bring to the aspirant? The Georgia question was complicated by Saakashvili's declaration of a state of emergency in November 2007, after government forces had clashed violently with opposition protestors, and outside observers criticized the Georgian government for excessive use of force.

Both Rice and Gates had their doubts about the advisability of a MAP for Georgia at this juncture.[18] National Security Advisor Hadley was in favor, as was NATO ambassador Nuland. In the months preceding the summit, three "deep dives"—where government analysts briefed the president and members of the cabinet—were held on the MAP question.[19] The vice president's office was particularly critical of those analysts who called into question whether either Ukraine or Georgia was ready for MAPs and what it would bring to the alliance.[20] The president was indeed the "chief decider" on this issue, and he believed that granting MAPs to Ukraine and Georgia was part of the Freedom Agenda. He also hoped that the prospect of one day joining NATO would serve as an incentive for Ukraine and Georgia to push forward with democratic reforms. Rice describes how, at the NSC meeting that was to take up the issue, she herself was unsure how to proceed since she had assumed that the issue would be taken up after Bush left office. But both Yushchenko and Saakashvili were pleading their case in Washington. The president came down firmly on the side of granting both countries MAPs. Rice realized, "*I have to deliver this. This is going to be really hard.*"[21]

The next problem was securing allied consent. The White House had underestimated the European opposition to granting MAPs to Georgia and Ukraine. Putin had told Rice and Gates that bringing Georgia into NATO was a "red line," and the message had also been conveyed to the Europeans. The vehement Russian reaction to the MAP issue had found a receptive ear in the capitals of many "old" European countries, especially in Berlin.[22]

In the latter part of the Bush administration, Russia had increasingly become an issue of transatlantic contention. Europe had a far larger stake in relations with Russia than did the United States. Russia is a major energy supplier to Europe, providing nations such as Finland and the Baltic states with 100 percent of their natural gas and significant amounts of their oil. It is also a leading trading partner for Europe, and hundreds of thousands of jobs in both old and new Europe were dependent on contracts with Russia. More than half a million Russian citizens live and work in Britain, France, Germany, and Spain. Russia is Europe's large and sometimes awkward neighbor, but it is a neighbor with whom Europe has to live and with whom engagement is a necessity, not a choice.[23]

As the EU's most powerful member, Germany was the key country in the debate over MAPs. Germany was Russia's number one European interlocutor and advocate, largely in recognition of the peaceful way in which Germany had been unified.[24] Angela Merkel, the East German pastor's daughter, had initially taken a more critical view of Russia than had her predecessor Gerhard Schroeder. Nevertheless, as time wore on she realized that, given Germany's extensive economic interests in Russia and the unique historical relationship between the two countries, she needed to emphasize continuity in German policy. Although Berlin had criticized some of Moscow's actions both at home and abroad, many Germans—both inside and outside the government—believed that Russia under Putin was developing in the right direction and that it would eventually evolve into a more modern society. The fact that Germany and Russia shared a history of having to overcome a totalitarian legacy influenced Berlin to judge Moscow through a different lens from that of Washington. Berlin had a more realistic timetable for the pace of change in Russia than did many in Washington. A senior German official summed up the difference by describing America as suffering from "empathy deficit disorder" in its dealing with Russia.[25]

Bush liked and respected Merkel. However, they disagreed on the MAP question. Germany's attitude toward the issue was a product both of the desire not to alienate Moscow and also of serious doubts about whether either Ukraine or Georgia was ready for a MAP. After the initial euphoria of the color revolutions, both countries had sunk back into internal squabbling and had squandered much of the initial political capital they had earned with their own populations and in Europe. In Ukraine, President Viktor Yushchenko and Prime Minister Yulia Timoshenko spent more time fighting with each other than introducing needed political and economic reforms.

In Georgia, Saakashvili appeared to have little tolerance for opposition. He evidently also did not understand the need to cultivate good relations with Merkel. Their first meeting has been described as "a disaster," with Saakashvili dismissive of Merkel's offer to help Georgia introduce the rule of law by providing German judges to train Georgian lawyers.[26] Merkel also insisted that no country could join NATO if it had unresolved territorial issues.[27] The more evident Merkel's doubts about MAP became, the more intemperate Saakashvili's language about her. At a German Marshall Fund Bucharest conference the day before the NATO summit, Saakashvili accused Germany of appeasing Russia, betraying Georgia, and acting as a "Trojan horse" for Moscow. This kind of rhetoric did not advance Georgia's case for a MAP.[28] Nor did it bolster Merkel's confidence in Saakashvili.

Poland and other new NATO members saw the MAP issue as a crucial litmus test that would decide NATO's future direction. Would NATO stand up to Russia and admit more former Soviet states? Or was the enlargement that had integrated Central Europe into the West largely over, implying a tacit recognition of a Russian sphere of influence? In the weeks leading up to the summit, there was intense consultation between Hadley and his German counterpart Christof Heusgen to try and find a compromise.[29] So great were the divisions among NATO allies that the delegations left for Bucharest not knowing what the outcome would be.

The Bucharest summit was one of NATO's most dramatic ever. On the first evening, separate dinners were held for heads of state and for foreign ministers where MAPs were the main subject. Rice describes "one of the most pointed and contentious debates with our allies that I'd ever experienced." The German foreign minister Frank-Walter Steinmeier argued that the Ukrainian government was too weak to warrant a MAP and that Georgia's frozen conflicts precluded granting Tbilisi a MAP. A Central European minister countered that West Germany was a frozen conflict during the Cold War (because of a divided Berlin and Germany's limited sovereignty), and yet Germany had become a NATO member in 1954 without an army. Polish foreign minister Radek Sikorski accused Germany of being more worried about Moscow than about its allies. The dinner ended inconclusively, and Steinmeier was quite shaken by the criticism he had heard.[30]

The North Atlantic Council was to meet the next morning at nine o'clock. In a rare late-night session, President Bush and his advisors tried to hammer out compromise language that would satisfy both the proponents and opponents of MAP. Until the last moment, it was unclear what would happen. Then Merkel finally ended the deadlock by brokering an eleventh-hour compromise. The next morning the brightly clad Merkel and Rice stood up in front of "all the men in grey hair and suits."[31] The declaration read, "We agreed today that Georgia and Ukraine will become members of NATO."[32] There was no MAP. Still, this was the first time that NATO had explicitly said that a country would join NATO. But what did that sentence really mean?

Vladimir Putin arrived later that day for a NATO-Russia Council meeting. It was the first time that a Russian president had ever attended a NATO summit (Yeltsin had demurred in 1997 because of the prospect of the first wave of enlargement). Although MAPs had not been granted, the Russians were very unhappy with language saying that one day these countries would join NATO. In his speech, Putin recited his litany of complaints about the West's treatment of Russia, and particularly the threat that NATO expansion to Ukraine and Georgia posed for Russian security.[33] He reserved special criticism for Ukraine. "George," he said to Bush, "You have to understand that Ukraine is not even a country. Part of its territory is in Eastern Europe and the greater part was given to us."[34] Nevertheless, he did sign a transit agreement permitting NATO supplies for Afghanistan to pass through Russian territory via the Northern Distribution Network.[35]

After the summit was over, the controversy over its implications for European security began. This was not the result that either Georgia or Ukraine had wanted. Saakashvili, putting on a brave face, claimed that the outcome was positive because Georgia was guaranteed to join NATO.[36] But the real issue was whether the failure to grant a MAP to Georgia was an invitation to Saakashvili to try and resolve the territorial Abkhazia and South Ossetia issue by force as quickly as possible in order to qualify for a MAP. Or was it an invitation to Russia to ensure that Georgia would never join NATO by dismantling its territorial integrity? Four months later, the unintended consequences of one of NATO's most contentious summit in its six decades of existence were on graphic display in the streets of Tskhinvali, the capital of the tiny breakaway enclave of South Ossetia.

THE GUNS AND TANKS OF AUGUST 2008

Relations between Saakashvili and Putin had quickly deteriorated after the Rose Revolution, as the Georgian president made clear his intention to reintegrate South Ossetia and Abkhazia, as well as his desire for Georgia to join NATO and the EU. When President Bush visited Tbilisi in May 2005 he proclaimed, "I am proud to stand beside a President who has shown such spirit, determination and leadership in the cause of freedom—Georgia is today both sovereign and free, a beacon of liberty for this region and the world."[37] What was not made public, however, is that on this occasion, as on subsequent ones, Bush explicitly warned Saakashvili not to let the Russians provoke him and not to use force to take back the regions, making it clear that the United States would not come to Georgia's rescue if it did.[38]

Russian Federation | Georgia | De facto independent state on Georgian territory

Map 2.

Georgia and Russia's North Caucasus.

Moscow was irritated at Bush's praise for Saakashvili and at the contingent of Georgian troops fighting in Iraq and Afghanistan.[39] In 2006, Georgia's public expulsion of four Russian spies (ignoring the customary practice of settling such matters out of the public eye) led the Russians to boycott Georgian wine and mineral water, to rising anti-Georgian rhetoric in Russia, and to expulsions of migrant Georgian workers from Russia. The Russians understood Saakashvili's mercurial temperament, as well as how to provoke him, circulating stories that he was mentally unbalanced. Meanwhile, Moscow increased the distribution of Russian passports to people living in Abkhazia and South Ossetia. The mutual rhetorical invective was matched by a steady military buildup on both sides.

As tensions between Russia and Georgia escalated, both sides began to hold a series of military exercises that extended to July 2008. The United States, through the Train and Equip Program, had one hundred military advisors in Georgia, both to train Georgians to fight terrorists and to ensure they were fit for combat in Iraq and Afghanistan. In mid-July 2008, a U.S.-led military exercise took place outside Tbilisi involving seventeen hundred troops from Georgia, the United States, Armenia, Azerbaijan, and Ukraine. At the same time, Russian troops carried out a large-scale military exercise in the North Caucasus military district on the Georgian border.

Russian rhetoric linking Kosovo's independence to South Ossetia's and Abkhazia's right to secede from Georgia became more strident in the lead-up to the war. Russia was also increasing the number of peace-keeping troops it had in South Ossetia. Saakashvili had significantly raised defense spending after he came to power and had purchased weapons from a number of countries. On April 20, a Russian MIG-29 fighter shot down an Israeli-built Georgian unmanned aerial vehicle (UAV) that was conducting surveillance over Abkhazia, and Moscow threatened to "act through military means" if Tbilisi made a military move against Abkhazia.[40] In the weeks preceding the outbreak of war, the Georgians were convinced that Abkhazia, rather than South Ossetia, was the most dangerous flash point.

During the weeks, leading up to the war, Russian officials began to demand that Georgia sign a no-use-of-force pledge as a prerequisite to deescalating the crisis.[41] Secretary of State Rice and German foreign minister Steinmeier developed a plan that would involve both sides agreeing not to use force, and Rice went to Tbilisi on July 10 to obtain Saakashvili's agreement. "He's proud and can be impulsive," she wrote, "and we all worried that he might allow Moscow to provoke him and use force." He refused to sign on. Rice left him with the following blunt warning: "Mr. President, whatever you do, don't let the Russians provoke you—No one will come to your aid and you will lose."[42]

Bush administration officials repeatedly sent the same message to Saakashvili: we support Georgia's Euro-Atlantic aspirations, but we do not support the use of force to restore Georgia's territorial integrity. Yet there were some Americans—both inside and outside the administration—who admired Saakashvili and conveyed a different impression, encouraging Saakashvili to stand up to Russian pressures and emphasizing U.S. support for him. The real question is one of perception and misperception. What did Saakashvili hear when he listened to the different American representatives? Did he understand that the Bush administration would not support him in a war against Russia? Ronald Asmus, another strong Saakashvili supporter, argued that the Bush administration failed to pursue an effective prevention strategy:

"What was unfortunately missing—was a clear and unequivocal message to Moscow that any moves against Georgia would have real consequences in Russia's relations with the United States."[43]

Mutual provocations had been going on for months. Then, on the night on August 7, 2008, a "massive Georgian artillery attack" was launched against the South Ossetian capital of Tskhinvali that killed Ossetes and Russian peace-keepers who were protecting them.[44] The next day, Russian troops marched into Georgia through the 2.3 mile Roki tunnel connecting North and South Ossetia. The fighting quickly spread to other parts of the country. Over the next five days, a total of forty thousand Russians troops entered Georgia. At the same time, Georgia was subject to a massive, coordinated cyber attack that disabled all the major government sites and financial institutions and hindered the conduct of military operations. Despite the ramshackle conditions of some of their equipment (they lacked global positioning equipment) and primitive communications (officers used cell phones to communicate with their men), the Russians overwhelmed the much smaller Georgian army. At one point it looked as if they might take the capital Tbilisi and overthrow Saakashvili. On August 12, with 850 dead or wounded and more than 100,000 refugees, a cease-fire was declared.[45] On August 16, Saakashvili appeared on television disoriented, chewing on his tie.[46] On August 25, Russia recognized the independence of South Ossetia and Abkhazia. Two "frozen conflicts" were no longer frozen. The five-day war was over, and Georgia and the separatist enclaves had suffered many casualties, with homes and infrastructure destroyed. Moscow had given its answer to the United States' and Europe's offer of Euro-Atlantic integration to Russia's neighbors.

Georgian officials explained their actions on the night of August 7–8 as a defensive move against a Russian invasion that was already underway. Russians describe this as Georgian aggression and genocide against South Ossetians. Rice described Russian attacks as "premeditated," and a report by the independent institute U.S. Cyber Consequences Unit concluded that the cyber attacks were carried out by Russian civilians who had advance notice of Russian military intentions and were tipped off about the timing of their operations.[47]

In September 2009 the European Union issued a three-volume fifteen-hundred-page report, *Independent International Fact-Finding Mission on the Conflict in Georgia*. It apportioned blame for the conflict equally to both sides. It remains the most authoritative source on the conflict, although both the Georgians and Russians reject parts of its findings. However, both also argue that it vindicates their claim that the other side was the aggressor.[48] The report stressed that the shelling of Tskhinvali on the night of August 7 was the "culminating point of a long period of increasing tensions, provocations, and incidents. Indeed, the conflict has deep roots in the history of the region."[49] It accused Russia of using disproportionate force in response to Georgia's shelling of Tskhinvali.

During the short war, American and Russian troops came closer to facing each other on opposite sides of an armed conflict than at any time during the Cold War. American troops were in Georgia, training soldiers who were going to Iraq and Afghanistan. This sobering fact was fully appreciated only after the war was over, but the conflict revealed both the limits of the post-Soviet U.S.-Russian rapprochement and the constraints on the United States' ability to project its power and influence into Russia's neighborhood.

U.S.-Russian communications during the war illustrated how much the relationship had deteriorated. The war broke out on the eve of the Beijing Olympic Games, and President Bush first called President Medvedev, as protocol demanded, asking him to deescalate immediately. Medvedev responded that Saakashvili was like Saddam Hussein and had unleashed an unprovoked, barbarian attack. Bush then spoke by phone to a shaken Saakashvili and reassured him of U.S. support. At the opening ceremonies for the Beijing Olympics, Bush was seated in the same row as Putin. Despite the heightened tensions as a result of the war, they asked the person seated between them to change seats so that they could have a conversation.[50] Putin called Saakashvili a war criminal. Bush told Putin: "I've been warning you Saakashvili is hot-blooded." "I'm hot-blooded too," Putin retorted. Bush stared back at him. "No Vladimir," he said. "You're cold-blooded."[51]

When the war broke out, the U.S.-Russian military dialogue—which had survived the ups and downs of the relationship—proved invaluable. Hadley asked Admiral Mike Mullen, chairman of the Joint Chiefs of

Staff, to contact his Russian counterpart, General Nikolai Makarov. During the war, the Mullen-Makarov channel was the only working, high-level U.S.-Russian channel of communication, since Lavrov refused to talk to Rice for the first few days. They had seven conversations, and in one of them Mullen asked for Russian assistance in not hindering the return of Georgian troops from Iraq—which Makarov gave.[52]

By this time France had taken over the presidency of the European Union, and President Nicolas Sarkozy was eager to assume the mantle of peacemaker. Given the strained relationship between Washington and Moscow, it was prudent to pass the responsibility for ending the conflict to the French, but some in Washington bristled at the idea that the United States was now on the sidelines in this conflict.

Sarkozy's conversation with Putin when he went to negotiate the cease-fire was instructive. He had first met with Medvedev, who, it was clear, was not equipped to discuss the cease-fire, so Putin joined the talks. According to the French press, "Putin said: 'I want to hang Saakashvili by the balls.' 'Hang him?' a startled Sarkozy interjected. 'Why not?' Putin replied. 'The Americans hanged Saddam Hussein.' 'But do you want to end up like Bush?' asked Sarkozy. Putin paused and said: 'Ah there you have a point.'"[53]

The day before the cease-fire came into effect Rice and Lavrov had a key conversation. Inter alia, Lavrov demanded that one of Russia's conditions was that Saakashvili had to go. Rice retorted that the American and Russian foreign ministers do not have conversations about overthrowing a democratically elected president. Much to Lavrov's dismay, she then proceeded to communicate his demands to U.S. allies who then discussed it at a UN Security Council meeting.[54]

The next day, at a White House principals' meeting, members of both Hadley's and Cheney's staff raised the issue of a limited military response in support of Georgia. Hadley asked, "Are we prepared to go to war with Russia over Georgia?" He went round the table and all the principals agreed that the military option did not make sense. "I wanted to make people show their cards about a possible military response," said Hadley. "As National Security Advisor I had to make sure that the full range of options was discussed." In 2009, at a lunch with Russian ambassador Sergei Kislyak, the Russian asked, "Did you really discuss sending U.S. troops to Georgia?" He was shocked when Hadley replied in the affirmative.[55]

When the war was over, Rice went to Tbilisi and held a joint press conference with Saakashvili. She asked him to thank the Europeans and Americans for standing with him but not to say anything about Russia. Needless to say, he did not respect her wishes and described the Russians as barbarians. Still worse, he accused the Europeans of being appeasers, mentioning Munich in his tirade. Rice was furious and departed immediately. She saw Lavrov on the sidelines of the United Nations General Assembly in September 2008. The meeting was frosty. "It was," said Rice, "a rather bitter end to what had been a hopeful start for U.S.-Russian relations at that first meeting in Slovenia." In a valedictory speech at the German Marshall Fund, she criticized Russia for its aggression in Georgia and its domestic crackdown but exhorted her successor to continue the engagement with Russian civil society.[56]

The Georgia War also added to the tensions with some of America's European allies. "New Europe" felt that Tbilisi had been abandoned by both old Europe and the United States. It believed that if Georgia had been granted a MAP at Bucharest, the Russians would not have invaded. French officials claimed that the United States was "out of the game." According to Foreign Minister Bernard Kouchner, "The Americans were nowhere—they were sending navy ships to the Black Sea, but so what? So we had to stop the Red Army ourselves."[57] As soon as the war began, the war of words between the United States and Russia heated up. U.S. media in the days and weeks following the war were almost uniformly hostile to Russia, and many outlets featured daily press conferences with Saakashvili. Anti-Russian sentiment was on the rise. After a few months, the narrative began to shift in the West, and a more critical view of Georgia's role in the conflict emerged. But the Georgia war was caught up in the presidential campaign. Senator John McCain, a staunch supporter of Georgia, accused his opponent Senator Barack Obama of being "soft" on Russia. The Russian media from the beginning was uniformly hostile to both Georgia and the United States.[58] Both Putin and Medvedev insinuated that Washington had planned and orchestrated the war.[59]

Medvedev told the Valdai gathering in 2008 that Georgia launched the war "after serious preparation and with the moral, material and military support of another country, a big country claiming the right to set the rules of the world order."[60] Deputy Chief of the General Staff of the Russian Armed Forces Anatoly Nogovitsyn gave a detailed military briefing to the group designed to give irrefutable proof of Georgian aggression. State-controlled television in the fall of 2008 likened Saakashvili to Hitler, and students at the prestigious Moscow State Institute of International Relations (MGIMO) collected supplies for the "survivors of genocide."[61] Unlike in the United States, the official and unofficial Russian story has not really changed. Even more liberal Russians were critical of Georgia's actions, and there has been no revisionist history of the war. And some of Putin's European allies, such as former German chancellor Gerhard Schroeder, have endorsed the Russian view.[62]

After the war was over, the Bush administration took an unprecedented step in the post-Soviet era. It cut off all official U.S.-Russian contacts above the level of deputy assistant secretary. "The Russians needed to understand that they could not get away with something like invading Georgia," says Hadley.[63] This meant that it was practically impossible to accomplish anything as the new U.S. ambassador, John Beyrle took up his post. The West refused to recognize Abkhazia and South Ossetia, as did every post-Soviet state and China. The only other countries and entities to recognize the separatist enclaves were Nicaragua, Venezuela, and Hamas; they were followed later on by the tiny Pacific islands of Nauru, Vanuatu, and Tuvalu (in the latter three cases in return for financial incentives).

The cease-fire held, even though it turned out that the hastily negotiated agreement did not have a text on which all sides agreed. The Russian version of what had been agreed on was different from the French one. Moreover, Sarkozy inexplicably went into the negotiations without an actual map of the region, much to the consternation of the U.S. side.[64] Talks between Georgia, Russia, and other parties continued in a desultory way after the war in Geneva. While no one in the West recognized the two entities, they also realized that Georgia's territorial integrity had been irrevocably compromised.

No side emerged unscathed from the war. Georgia was judged to have recklessly initiated the conflict; Russia had used disproportionate force in response; the Europeans had largely been absent until Sarkozy was galvanized into action after the fact; and the United States, while it had verbally supported Georgia's territorial integrity, had not been able to prevent its ally from launching an attack and had backed away after hostilities started. There were no winners in this war. Nevertheless, the Russians had drawn a red line, one that was clearly understood by the West. The states of the South Caucasus drew their own lessons from the war, which reminded them, in case it had slipped their mind, of where they were located and which country in the region possessed the preeminent force. Whatever Bush might say about his Freedom Agenda, it appeared that Euro-Atlantic integration would stop at the borders of the old Soviet Union.

The 2008 Russia-Georgia War of August 2008 destroyed what remained of the Putin-Bush reset and left ties between Washington and Moscow at their lowest level since the Soviet collapse. It also led to a rupture of official ties between Moscow and Tbilisi, ensuring that Georgia remained one of the most contentious issues between Washington and Moscow. We may not know the full story of the origins of the war for a long time, and both sides continue to offer starkly different narratives of how it began. But the conflict reverberated in the U.S.-European-Russian relationship long after the cease-fire. The war was a major shock for the Europeans, who had hoped that the Yugoslav conflict would be the last in their backyard. It also highlighted the transatlantic differences over how to deal with Russia and Georgia that had been on display at Bucharest.

In November 2008, with the U.S. election over, Bush went to one more summit, the Lima meeting of the Asia-Pacific Economic group. His valedictory comment on the U.S.-Russian relationship was sober: "We've had our agreements. We've had our disagreements. I've tried to work hard to make it a cordial relationship so when we need to work together we can, and when we disagree we are able to do it in a way that is respectful to our two nations."[65]

The Bush administration's Russia policy had descended from the optimistic partnership of the post-9/11 reset to the wreckage of the Georgia War. America's attempts to project influence into Russia's neighborhood had their limits, and the next U.S. administration would soon digest that lesson as it embarked on its own reset with Russia.

Chapter Eight
Economics and Energy:
The Stakeholder Challenge

For the past two decades, each U.S. administration has fashioned its own distinctive political relationship with Russia. But the economic relationship has not been as dependent on which party or president is in office. Indeed, every U.S. administration since the Soviet collapse has promoted economic relations between the United States and Russia—and each has puzzled over why it has been such a challenge to enhance commerical and energy ties. The Russians have also consistently argued that there is considerable untapped potential in the economic relationship.

This chapter discusses the development of commercial ties since 1991, situating them within the broader evolution of the Russian economy and of Russia's rise as an energy superpower. The Clinton, Bush, and Obama administrations all supported the promotion of commercial relations, irrespective of the political climate. Putin has also consistently sought to enlarge U.S.-Russian economic relations and attract U.S. investment. While Moscow has been preoccupied with restoring Russia's role as a great power and ensuring that its interests are respected, the American and Russian private sectors have operated under different rules of the game unburdened by Cold War legacies.

Once Russia abandoned state-run socialism, there seemed to be great potential for deeper, more extensive and very different commercial ties between the United States and Russia. However, although some American firms and investors have done very well in the Russian market, as have Russians in the U.S. market, the bilateral economic relationship remains modest compared to the size of the markets in both countries and the potential for expanding commercial ties. The net result is that, so far, neither country has developed a sizable group of stakeholders who can credibly convey to their respective political leaderships that, if political relations deteriorate, there will be serious consequences for the economy. This chapter examines the trade, investment, and energy aspects of the bilateral relationship and seeks to answer the question of what promotes or limits economic ties and what the consequences have been.

In the years after Putin came to power, Russia experienced an economic resurgence, fueled by high oil prices and effective macroeconomic and fiscal policies. As the first decade of the twenty-first century wore on, the United States found itself dealing with two different Russias, the political and the economic. The political Russia pursued a more assertive foreign policy while it shaped its sovereign democracy at home. The economically rising Russia added a new, more complex dimension to the U.S.-Russian relationship. On one hand, members of the private sectors in both countries, including the new class of young Russian entrepreneurs, interacted with each other as they pursued global business opportunities, generally free of Cold War stereotypes. Russia's energy endowment and the need for investment seemed to offer opportunities for collaboration. But Russia's increasing global energy clout and the exercise of that clout sometimes exacerbated foreign policy conflicts with the U.S. government.

For two decades, Russian and American business elites have expressed the same sentiment: while the bilateral economic relationship has great potential, it has barely begun to fulfill its promise. In 2012, trade with Russia accounted for less than 1 percent of total U.S. trade. Compared to China, with whom the United States had a robust and growing economic relationship, Russia would seem to be an economic afterthought—at least in macro terms. U.S.-China trade in 2012 totaled $555 billion, U.S.-Russian trade was only $41 billion.[1] That was partly a function of Russia's economic realities. Whereas China exports a wide range of manufactured goods that U.S. consumers are eager to purchase and is a manufacturing base for global companies, there is little U.S. demand for Russia's two major exports—energy and military hardware. The U.S. companies that have done best in Russia are those involved in the consumer market and investment goods, such as Ford, General Motors, and Proctor & Gamble, as well as financial investors. But the overall total remains modest and is a long way from achieving the much larger, multifaceted dimensions of Europe's economic ties to Russia. Europe and Russia, of course, are neighbors and the complementarity between them—Russian energy exports in return for European manufactured imports—ensures a strong economic relationship.

Two factors have, from the U.S. point of view, acted as a barrier to closer economic ties. The first is the difficulty of doing business in Russia, with rules of the game that can change unpredictably and a weak rule of law to redress grievances, particularly on the issue of sanctity of contracts. In 2012 Russia was rated 79 out of 82 countries on its policy toward foreign investment and 120 out of 183 economies in terms of business regulation.[2] Putin told the Valdai Club in 2012 that he is committed to a substantial improvement of these ratings.[3] The second is Russia's energy relations with its neighbors and with Europe, which have raised questions about its use of economic levers for political means.

The U.S. private sector sees Russia as an emerging market that shares characteristics with several other countries at a similar stage of economic development around the world where corruption, weak rule of law, and state dominance in various strategic sectors are the norm.[4] But Russia also has a growing middle class with rising purchasing power, eager to buy Western goods. As the Russian economy grew, so did the opportunity to make significant amounts of money on the Russian stock market and in the consumer sector. Thus, U.S. companies have a longer-term, more comparative—and hence more upbeat—view of Russia and the commercial opportunities it offers than do many foreign policy experts whose interaction with the private sector is often limited. This accounts for the strikingly different views of Russia that one could read in American business as opposed to scholarly and policy publications.[5]

RUSSIA INC.

When American firms entered the Russian market, they encountered an opaque system of networks unique to post-Soviet Russia. Under Putin, the system became both more consolidated and more opaque than under Yeltsin, particularly on the key question about how decisions are made. Countless analysts—both inside and outside the government—have sought to penetrate the "black box" that is the Kremlin and its associated structures. The current system seems to some a twenty-first-century version of the traditional tsarist Russian patrimonial state. The traditional Russian state's features were described by Harvard historian Edward Keenan in a 1986 article, "Moscovite Political Folkways," five years before the collapse of the USSR.[6] In this system, the rulers controlled state resources and secured the loyalty of their subjects by distributing assets to them.

One of the legacies of this traditional system that makes it challenging for any U.S. administration is that formal institutions in Moscow have never explained how Russia is ruled, and nontransparent informal mechanisms remain the key to understanding the system. These relationships are difficult for an outsider to identify and understand. They can also complicate operating in the Russian environment, as some business people have discovered. Some call the Putin system "Russia Inc." arguing that Putin is the CEO of the Russian "Corporation."[7] In this system, political and economic elites are symbiotically connected. The informal structures of Russia Inc. operate as a conglomerate similar to those of a corporation. The Kremlin functions as the headquarters of the "corporation."[8] The top officials who manage the affairs of state also largely manage and control the state's major economic assets—all the more so with the expansion of state control of the overall economy. In this system, it is sometimes difficult to differentiate between what is political and what is commercial, especially in in state-dominated companies that collect rents of various kinds, including energy revenues. As one Russian observer put it, "Russia is run by the people who own it."[9]

In his first years in power, Putin dismantled much of the Yeltsin oligarch clan, either taming them or sending them into exile, where they became bitter Putin critics. Indeed, the man who played a crucial role in his selection was the oligarch Boris Berezovsky, who died in 2013 in exile in the United Kingdom. Putin inherited the system of oligarchic capitalism tied to political power, but he also changed the system. The turning point came with the October 2003 arrest of Mikhail Khodorkovsky. After that, a new group of oligarchs was created, many of whom come from the security services, and all of whom owe their wealth and status to Putin. Under Putin the state launched the systematic recapture of the commanding heights of the economy, most graphically illustrated by the imprisonment of Khodorkovsky and the takeover over his oil company Yukos—by state-owned Rosneft.

In the current hybrid Russian system—part petro-state, part heavy-industry, part high-tech economy—the political and commercial elites are focused on preserving their influence and their assets.[10] Transparency International rates Russia 143 out of 180 countries in the world on its corruption perceptions index, below Eritrea and Sierra Leone.[11] Despite Medvedev's commitment to tackling corruption, very little was accomplished during his presidency, and corruption remains a key characteristic of modern Russia, a fact that Putin himself acknowledged in his January 2012 article.[12] Crony capitalism is the hallmark of the system.[13] It is this opaque and often unpredictable system, where the state controls the commanding heights of the economy, that creates significant deterrents for the U.S. private sector to enter the Russian market—although many nevertheless do.

Russia Inc. has influenced Russian economic relations with the United States in a variety of ways. For Western energy companies, negotiating deals has been difficult because the stakes are high and top Russian officials are involved. The British super major BP had a particularly challenging experience when its joint venture with the Russian company TNK ran afoul of battles between different groups of oligarchs and Rosneft chairman Igor Sechin.[14] But American and European energy companies have also had to deal with unanticipated changes in the rules of the game, particularly when tax, environmental regulations, and other concerns have been used to oust them from projects whose agreements were already signed.

THE RUSSIAN ECONOMY, 2000–2013

A fundamental factor has been the improvement in the Russian economic situation since 2000. When Putin came to power, Russia was just beginning to recover from the crash of 1998. Between 1999 and 2008, Russia was one of the fastest-growing economies in the world. GDP grew by 7 percent per annum, the stock market increased twentyfold, and poverty rates fell from 30 percent of the population in 1998 to 14 percent in 2007. Real wages rose by 140 percent. In 2001 Goldman Sachs coined the term BRIC (Brazil, Russia, India, and China) to describe what it viewed as the most dynamic emerging markets, predicting in 2003 that in less than forty years they could overtake the G-7 countries.[15]

Russia's impressive economic growth was, to significant degree, a result of steadily rising oil prices and a doubling of oil output. In that sense, Putin was much luckier than either Gorbachev or Yeltsin, who had to contend with collapsing oil prices that devastated government revenues. But Russia's growth was also a product of skillful economic policies. Finance Minister Alexei Kudrin, a colleague of Putin's from his St. Petersburg days and the man responsible for bringing him to Moscow, was the architect of these conservative fiscal practices. Kudrin was determined to ensure that Russia would never again find itself in the situation of extreme vulnerability that had shaken the country in 1998. His policies involved paying back Russia's $130 billion sovereign debt to the IMF by January 2005—three and a half years early—and building up reserves from rising oil prices to create stabilization funds on the Norwegian model. By 2008, Russia had $600 billion in currency reserves and had the third largest currency and gold reserves in the world.[16]

Putin also presided over economic reforms during his first term: rationalizing the chaotic taxation system; introducing a flat income tax rate of 13 percent; implementing judicial reforms that enabled businesses to operate in a more predictable environment; adopting a land code that legalized private ownership of agricultural land; and devising a simpler, more effective customs system. Reforms slowed down after Khodorkovsky's arrest and stopped after 2005, partly because of popular opposition to pension reform that brought discontented senior citizens into the streets.

In 1997 Russia had established the St. Petersburg International Economic Forum, which began as a modest affair. By 2008 it had developed into Russia's answer to Davos, a packed three-day conference in the Lenexpo Center overlooking the city, with lavish receptions in the city's most prized venues and festive boat rides down the Neva River during White Nights. Top officials from the United States, Europe, Eurasia, and Asia were in attendance, with significant business representation from Europe and the United States. The June 2008 St. Petersburg Economic Forum was held during the height of Russia's economic self-confidence before the crisis had hit Russia. Newly inaugurated President Medvedev proposed that Moscow should become a global financial center and touted Russia's success and its attractiveness for foreign investors, suggesting that other countries should better manage their own economies.[17] Russia seemed resilient. A few weeks after Medvedev's speech, oil prices reached $147.27 a barrel. But then the full fury of the global financial crisis hit with the September 2008 collapse of the investment bank Lehman Brothers. The panicked world economy seemed to be on the edge of another Great Depression. Russia was not immune.

Indeed, Russia was very badly affected by the 2008 global financial crisis. Oil prices fell to $35 per barrel in six months, the stock market suffered a 75 percent fall in value over the same period, and its hard currency reserve fell from $600 billion to less than $400 billion. Growth rates fell from 7 percent to 2–3 percent in one year.[18] Unemployment rose to 9 percent, threatening some of the social stability on which the Putin administration's legitimacy was based. After all, the implicit bargain that Putin had established was that Russians would accept a much stronger and more assertive state in return for the government providing greater prosperity and predictability.

Before 2008, Russian leaders had not grasped how integrated the new, capitalist Russia had become with the global economy. The crisis changed that view. As Medvedev said in 2010, "The beginning of the crisis in our own country was a surprise because the extent to which it fell was more than I could have expected."[19] Putin acknowledged that

Russia was affected by the crisis because it had become globally integrated, which is what Russia had fought for.[20] Whereas in foreign policy Putin could blame the United States for trying to undermine Russia, it was more difficult to accuse one country of causing the financial crisis. Nevertheless, Putin blamed "parasitic" Western countries—and specifically the American subprime mortgage industry—for the financial crisis.[21] "Everything that is happening in the economic and financial sphere has started in the United States."[22] He also suggested that the dollar should no longer be the main reserve currency, but that the ruble should become one. "The existing financial system has failed," he told the 2009 World Economic Forum delegates in Davos, adding that it had "seriously affected" the Russian economy. "The crisis has made the problems we had more evident. They concern the excessive emphasis on raw materials in exports and the economy in general and a weak financial market."[23]

When oil prices collapsed in 2008 as a result of the global financial crisis, Russia was confronted with the downside of its failure to diversify its economy and continued dependence on oil and gas. In the words of two economists, Russia was "addicted to resource rents." "Addiction," they wrote, "refers to a specific form of inefficient allocation of rents in the economy, as the backward production structure which Russia inherited from the Soviet Union demands a huge share of the rents at any time." However, they also argued that it was quite rational for Russia to be dependent on oil and gas, given its resource endowments, and uneconomical to suggest that it should diversify its economy away from this energy focus.[24]

In contrast to 2008, the 2009 St. Petersburg Economic Forum was a much more modest affair—with no lavish parties—and the tone more realistic, reflecting the shocks of the previous year.[25] By then, Russia had responded quickly and effectively to the financial crisis, and in the medium-term it weathered the crisis better than many other countries and was in a much better position to survive the storm than it had been a decade earlier in 1998.[26] Since Putin and Kudrin came to power they had worked to ensure that Russia would never repeat the 1998 crash. The day after Lehman Brothers went bankrupt on September 15, 2008, Putin's economic team gathered to work out an emergency plan to stave off the bankruptcy of their own businesses. Aleksei Kudrin, who was subsequently named "Finance Minister of the Year" by *Euromoney* magazine, proposed a plan to provide lines of credit from the Central Bank to keep the economy afloat.[27] Russia used the large currency reserves in the sovereign wealth funds to pour money into the economy in order to mitigate the worst aspects of the crisis. Liquidity injection prevented a collapse of the banking system, and those banks that did fail were dealt with in an orderly fashion. There were no major nationalizations of private companies. Nor were there major bailouts of oligarchs.

There were, however, a few spectacular televised moments when Putin upbraided oligarchs for their conduct. The most graphic was in June 2009, when Putin decided to make an example of a man who had been one his favorite oligarchs, the aluminum magnate Oleg Deripaska. He summoned Deripaska to a beleaguered provincial town called Pikalyovo, where workers were striking over 41 million rubles of unpaid wages at three factories, one of which Deripaska owned. Calling the factory owners "cockroaches," Putin threw his pen at Deripaska, telling him he had to sign a paper promising to pay back wages owed to his five hundred striking workers.[28] Deripaska glumly signed the paper. The workers applauded. The Russian government spent about $11 billion in refinancing failing firms.[29]

The global financial crisis also provided Russia with the opportunity to play a more prominent role in the international economy via the multilateral mechanism of the G-20 which, for a time, to some of its participants, seemed destined to become the board of directors of the world economy. Russia viewed the rise of the G-20 as a vindication of its claim that new global economic structures were replacing the smaller clubs previously dominated by the West. The shift to the G-20 also seemed to underscore the growing importance of the BRICs. Moreover, the longer the world economy continued to face serious problems, the greater was the reinforcement of the Russian narrative about the negative effects of profligate U.S. policies on Russia's domestic economic situation. Russia's higher profile was on display when Medvedev appointed Alexander Voloshin, former head of the Presidential Administration under Yeltsin and Putin, to coordinate the plan to turn Moscow into a new global financial center with the intent of rivaling New York, Frankfurt, and London. Despite the plan, that ambition remains an aspirational goal.

U.S. BUSINESS IN RUSSIA

American investors had entered the Russian market even before the Soviet collapse. The prospect of the limitless pent-up demand of millions of citizens deprived of consumer goods for seven decades was very tempting. The natural resource sector initially seemed to be open for business and certainly in need of foreign investment and technology. Yet Russia soon became known as the "Wild East," with rapid, nontransparent privatization, and mafia-like structures proliferating in a largely unregulated economy. Texas native Robert Strauss, who became the last U.S. ambassador to the USSR and the first to Russia, and subsequently the first chairman of the U.S.-Russia Business Council, said that Russia reminded him in some ways of the Texas of the 1920s in which he had grown up—poor but with great prospects. That is, there were attractive opportunities for young entrepreneurs who were up for the ride wanting to make a fortune—and willing to take the risks.

Some Americans who showed up in Russia participated in the first wave of privatizations, buying and selling privatization vouchers and participating in the stock market boom of the 1990s.[30] Real estate was another profitable sector. But that also carried its dangers. Paul Tatum, part owner with a Chechen partner of Moscow's first Western-style hotel, the Radisson Slavanskaya, was gunned down in a metro station in 1996 in a contract killing after disputes with his partner. Investors who believed they had signed contracts with Russian partners subsequently discovered after handing over their money that their investments were not protected, and their Russian partner had absconded with their money. Others established successful businesses only to have them taken away—sometimes at gunpoint—by Russian partners with no compensation. Nevertheless, the enormous opportunities offered by a market of 143 million people no longer shackled by socialism continued to attract the U.S. private sector.

In a pioneering study of the Soviet economic system published in 1957, Joseph Berliner outlined the key to success in the centrally planned economy: *znakomstvo i svyazy*—knowing the right people and having the right connections.[31] This remains true for Americans operating in the Russian economy today. The most successful American entrepreneurs were those who worked systematically to understand the rules of the game, developed the right personal connections, and identified sectors that were open to foreign participation. Drew Guff of Siguler Guff is a prime example of an American entrepreneur who understood the rules and did well in Russia. In the early 1990s, Guff, a Russian-speaking Harvard graduate, worked for the investment bank Paine Webber, and his firm began a joint venture with an oil-trading firm partly owned by the Russian Orthodox Church. Their connections with then Patriarch Aleksei II extended to the highest levels of the Russian government, and in 1994 Guff agreed with Prime Minister Victor Chernomyrdin to launch the first private equity fund in Russia, a private-public partnership with the Russian government as an anchor investor. He launched Russian MTV in September 1998, a month after the collapse of the ruble. Subsequently, one of Guff and Siguler's portfolio companies became involved in running the Internet cloud in Russia. They were able to launch this venture because Medvedev and his colleagues are "part of the IT generation" and accept the need for greater Western involvement in this sector.[32]

The reforms undertaken by Putin in his first term were welcomed by foreign businessmen, for whom the prospect of greater stability offset less appealing parts of the system. U.S. business generally credits Putin for improving the business climate for foreign investors. After Putin entered the Kremlin, there were some reforms in business law, and foreign investments were more protected. As one American investor said, "There was no rule of law in this country in the '90s. [Putin] has brought the rule of law to Russia—foreign businesses feel more comfortable in Russia now."[33] Under Putin, American business has successfully expanded its operations in the Russian market. For instance, the Boeing Company has a $10 billion business there. "Boeing has a simple vision in Russia," explained Thomas Pickering, former under secretary of state and ambassador to Russia and subsequently senior vice president for international relations at Boeing, "We need titanium for our planes and Russia has it. It works because of our mutual dependence."[34] Boeing also employs highly trained engineers and software developers in Russia as part of its global supply chain. Russian engineers helped design the Boeing Dreamliner 787 plane.

Russia also seems poised to overtake Germany as the largest automobile market in Europe. The Ford Motor Company and General Motors have plants in several Russian cities. General Motors alone intends to invest $1 billion in Russia over five years. "I would put Russia in the same category as China," the head of GM's international operations said at a groundbreaking ceremony in St. Petersburg.[35] Russians have enjoyed McDonald's hamburgers and both Pepsi and Coca-Cola for more than two decades. Russia is Pepsi's second largest market after the United States.

Investment also became a two-way street. As Russia's economy recovered, Russian investment in the United States, which started out modestly in the 1990s, increased. The most visible investors included the steel magnate Alexei Mordashov, whose Severstal steel company purchased ailing steel mills in the industrial heart of the United States, enabling them to operate in difficult economic times. LUKOIL one of Russia's largest private oil companies, purchased three thousand gas stations from Getty Oil and Mobil and began selling its branded gasoline to Americans. Billionaire Mikhail Prokhorov, who unsuccessfully ran for president of Russia in 2012, purchased the New York Nets. And Facebook founder Mark Zuckerberg sold a 2 percent stake in his venture to Russian billionaires Yuri Milner and Alisher Usmanov in 2009. Given the Putin administration's suspicion of social networks, this was a noteworthy Russian investment. Two years later, in December 2011, Facebook was used to mobilize more than thirty thousand demonstrators in Moscow to protest the results of the December Duma elections.

During the Medvedev presidency, with its rhetorical emphasis on modernization and innovation, the Kremlin was successful in attracting interest from Silicon Valley. Medvedev announced the creation of an "innovation village" at Skolkovo, outside Moscow, which was intended to be a Russian version of Silicon Valley. Viktor Vekselberg, a leading oligarch, was asked to organize the Russian side of the project for the innovation city. The Massachusetts Institute of Technology signed on to be a research partner. Major American corporations such as Microsoft and Cisco invested in the project. Anatoly Chubais, the author of Russia's privatization policies of the 1990s, who in 2008 became head of RosNano, Russia's high-tech state corporation, reached out to Russian émigrés and their children in major American research universities to join in the Skolkovo project.

However, there was a fundamental asymmetry in the approach. The American high-tech sector was created by private entrepreneurs making their own, autonomous investment decisions. Hewlett Packard, Apple, Google all began in garages. Many successful American innovators succeeded only after several failed ventures. Can one replicate that experience in Russia? The idea that one could "create" an innovation city from the top down, without the possibility of failure, defied the conventional understanding of innovation, which is a bottom-up concept. Moreover, three years into the project, it became clouded with charges of corruption.[36]

Moreover, the Russian market still has many restrictions. Around 2004, a debate began about what constituted "strategic sectors" of the Russian economy that required greater state control. Eventually the state reclaimed many strategic sectors and expanded them, deterring foreigners from investing in them. In 2008 Russia passed a law restricting foreign investment in forty-two strategic sectors, including space, aviation, nuclear energy, telecoms, media, and natural monopolies. Private foreign companies looking to purchase a 50 percent stake or greater in a company in one of these sectors would be required to receive government approval first.[37] This legislation, plus a subsoil law restricting foreign investment in the energy sector, restricted the activities of U.S. companies. However, in fairness, one should remember that the Unites States had also introduced legislation in 1975 to oversee foreign investments in U.S. strategic sectors and created the interagency Committee on Foreign Investments in the United States (CFIUS) to vet proposed investments. Russians complained about this legislation, but in fact no proposed Russian investment was denied for national security reasons.

THE ENERGY SUPERPOWER

Nowhere can the Russian ambivalence about foreign investment be seen more clearly than in the energy sector. Russia vies with Saudi Arabia as the world's largest producer of oil, and it has the world's largest conventional gas reserves. Russia therefore offers a major complement to Middle Eastern oil and gas. Moreover, both Russia and the United States must deal with the common challenges of global climate change. Yet politics has inevitably intruded and energy became a contentious issue in U.S.-Russian relations for three reasons: the Putin administration's reluctance to give foreign companies access to its resources; Russian gas cutoffs to Ukraine in 2006 and 2009, which affected the United States' European allies in the depths of winter; and Moscow's opposition to U.S.-backed oil and gas pipelines that bypass Russia and transport Caspian hydrocarbons—whose transit to Europe Russia sought to monopolize—westward. Behind these issues lies a larger issue: the substantial role of Russian natural gas in Europe and the political implications of this reality. Indeed, Russia's international energy policy has two main objectives: influence and profit.

Russia's dependence on oil to fuel its economic growth and the centrality of oil in Russian politics are relatively new phenomena, because the USSR's reliance on oil was not as central for the Soviet leadership as is Russia's today.[38] Russia's global importance as an energy provider is undisputed. In 2011 it accounted for 18.5 percent of the world's gas production and 12.8 percent of the world's oil production. It possesses 5 percent of proven global oil reserves, 21 percent of global conventional natural gas reserves, and 18 percent of known coal reserves.[39] It is the world's leading pipeline gas supplier and a top oil exporter. More than 90 percent of its energy exports go to Europe.[40] Putin has repeatedly emphasized that Russia's definition of energy security differs from that of the United States and Europe. While the West focuses on security of supply and diversification of suppliers, Russia emphasizes the need for what it calls "security of demand" via long-term gas contracts and also for control of transit routes and the purchase of Eurasian and European downstream gas assets.[41] In this sense, gas, not oil, is the real issue between Russia and Europe and the real American concern.

Putin developed his keen interest in the role of the state in Russia's energy sector after he returned from Dresden to St. Petersburg in 1990. His ideas about Russia's natural resources and the role of the state were foreshadowed in the candidate's thesis that he defended at the St. Petersburg Mining Institute and Technical University in 1997 and in a subsequent published article. After his boss, Mayor Anatoly Sobchak, lost his reelection in 1996, Putin, between jobs, apparently had time to study at the institute. The dissertation, "Strategic Planning for Rehabilitation of the Mineral Resources Base of the Region during the Formation of Market Relations (St. Petersburg and Leningrad Oblasts)," examined the role of strategic planning in the exploitation of raw material resources in the St. Petersburg region.[42] In an article published in 1999 when Putin was already in Moscow, he called for the government to reassert control over the country's natural resources. Russia's oil and gas reserves were key to economic recovery, to the "entry of Russia into the world economy," and to restoring Russia's status as a great economic power. Given their strategic importance, these resources had to be under the aegis, if not the total control, of the state.[43] This would guarantee Russia better chances for economic revival. By the time he became president, therefore, Putin clearly believed that energy resources were fundamental to Russia recovery and role in the world. As Russia's most strategic asset, they should be under state control.

At one of the Valdai meetings, the author asked President Putin whether Russia was an energy superpower, to which he replied:

> This whole idea of power, superpower, why should we keep using it now? If you've noticed, I have never referred to Russia as an energy superpower. But we do have greater possibilities than almost any other country in the world. This is an obvious fact. Everyone should understand that these are, above all, our national resources, and should not start looking at them as their own.

After reiterating that he did not like Cold War terminology, Putin went on to describe Russia's extensive energy ties with the post-Soviet space, Europe, and Asia, exhibiting an impressive familiarity with the details of oil and gas deals. He implied that Russia did not need much from the West because, as an energy superpower, it could set its own agenda.[44] In subsequent Valdai meetings, Putin returned to these themes. He admonished the EU for restricting the range of activities in which Gazprom could engage in Europe and reminded the group that Russia had other alternatives for its vast and desirable energy resources—namely, exporting them to Asia instead of Europe. At one, he expressed strong environmental views, criticizing those European countries such as Poland that wanted to develop shale gas and warning of the ecological perils of hydraulic fracking. He went so far as to draw a diagram of how fracking works on his dinner napkin, which he held up for his guests to see. The message was clear—Europe should continue to purchase natural gas from Gazprom and not embark on a perilous shale experiment.[45]

Indeed, Gazprom's role has been an issue of contention in both U.S.-Russian and EU-Russian relations. The behemoth Gazprom was founded in 1989 as the successor to the Soviet Ministry of Gas Industry, and future prime minister Viktor Chernomyrdin became its CEO and president. In the 1990s it was partially privatized, but the state remained the majority shareholder. Until Putin came to power, Gazprom operated largely independently of state oversight, and under its CEO Rem Vyakhirev (Chernomyrdin remained president) large fortunes were made by its officials in a variety of opaque ways.[46] When Putin came to power, he decided that the state needed to rein in Gazprom. Chernomyrdin was sent to Kyiv as Russian ambassador, Vyakhirev was fired, and they were replaced by Dmitry Medvedev as Gazprom chairman and Alexei Miller as CEO. Gazprom was designated as a "national champion" with very close ties to the Kremlin. It is 50.1 percent owned by the state, and the taxes it pays constitute about 15 percent of the total government budget. It produces 80 percent of Russia's total natural gas output and has a monopoly over gas transportation within Russia and over all gas exports.[47] Gazprom is also an important player in the media business. It took over the NTV channel, after Putin forced its previous owner Vladimir Gusinsky to flee the country, ensuring that it would be strictly proregime. Gazprom also owns *Kommersant*, one of the leading daily newspapers, which also used to reflect a more independent voice.

During one Valdai meeting, participants were taken to Gazprom headquarters to witness for themselves in living color the nature of the energy superpower. The control room at Gazprom's gleaming Moscow headquarters contains a vast screen with a mazelike map of all of Gazprom's interconnected pipeline routes stretching from the Pacific to the Atlantic and from the Arctic to the Caspian and Black Seas. The map highlights how much gas Gazprom delivers to Europe. Each pipeline route lights up to show how the gas flows and warning lights flash to indicate problems on any line. Those lights also reminded the participants that, with the flick of a switch, Gazprom can shut off the gas tap to any of its customers. In the nerve center of the world's largest company, Gazprom's top officials spared no details to emphasize how critical the company is to Europe's and Eurasia's gas supplies—and to the world's energy future. "What's good for Gazprom," said deputy chairman Alexander Medvedev, "is good for the world."[48]

RUSSIAN ENERGY AND THE BUSH ADMINISTRATION

In view of the central importance of energy throughout the world and especially in Russia, it is no surprise that energy has been at the center of U.S.-Russian relations. The U.S.-Russian energy relationship has three major components: the U.S. private sector's involvement in Russian oil and gas development; the U.S. government's attempts to cooperate with Russia on a variety of energy projects; and U.S. efforts to encourage the diversification of pipeline routes that transport Eurasian energy to Europe, reducing Russia's pipeline monopoly. The latter goal has led to conflicts with Russia, while the former two have promoted a more cooperative relationship. The Russian energy sector remains attractive for U.S. business because of Russia's vast resources. U.S. companies have the advanced technology that Russia needs and the experience of executing complex megaprojects. For their part, American companies need access to major new oil resources.

During the Bush administration, Russian gas supplies to Europe became an issue of contention, but it was by no means the first time this had happened. Indeed, Russia's role as an energy provider to Europe has periodically caused major strains in relations between Washington and Moscow and between the United States and its European allies going back to the height of the Cold War. In the early 1960s during the Kennedy administration, the United States unsuccessfully tried to prevent the construction of the *Druzhba* ("Friendship") oil pipeline from the USSR to Eastern Europe by forbidding its ally West Germany from selling the USSR the pipe for the pipeline. That effort failed.

The next U.S. attempt to restrict Soviet energy exports to its allies came after the first Soviet natural gas began to flow to Western Europe in 1970. Washington was concerned that the Kremlin would use Europe's dependence on Soviet gas for political leverage. During the Reagan administration in the early 1980s, Washington tried to prevent its allies from selling the USSR equipment for the construction of gas pipelines from West Siberia, only to have Reagan's great anti-Soviet ally British prime minister Margaret Thatcher personally travel to Scotland to show her solidarity with the British company exporting the equipment.[49] With 20 percent unemployment in the region where the equipment was produced, she was determined not to give in to American demands. She also took the embargo personally: "We feel particularly wounded by a friend," she remarked, referring to Reagan.[50] In fact, the United States has never succeeded in limiting Europe's dependence on Russian gas because, quite simply, the geography and economics of global energy supplies make Europe a natural and economic market for Russian energy, and gas is part of Europe's own energy diversification strategy.

During the entire Cold War period, the USSR was a reliable energy supplier to Western Europe—although not always to its fraternal allies in Eastern Europe, with whom energy was at times used as a political lever.[51] Before and after the collapse of the Soviet Union, the United States was often much more concerned about Europe's dependence on Russian energy than was the majority of Moscow's customers in Europe.

Russian energy policy became a particularly acrimonious issue in U.S.-Russian relations when Gazprom turned off the gas tap to Ukraine on a chilly New Year's morning in 2006. The dramatic shutdown of gas supplies, which affected not only Ukraine but Europe—80 percent of Russia's gas supplies to Europe passed through Ukraine at the time—was the culmination of a post–Orange Revolution conflict between Moscow and Kyiv. But Russian-Ukrainian gas relations were far more complicated than an "us-versus them" model. Much of the "Russian" gas exported to Ukraine was in fact Central Asian gas from Turkmenistan, which Gazprom purchased and whose sale to Ukraine was handled by an opaque middleman company, RosUkrEnergo (RUE), a joint Russian-Ukrainian project. Although the ownership and operation of RUE were carefully hidden, it was clear that both the Russian and Ukrainian owners profited from this trade, irrespective of the political configuration.[52]

As the rhetorical animosity between Putin and Yushchenko grew in 2005, Gazprom was engaged in a tough negotiation with Ukraine over the price it was to pay for Russian gas. Since the collapse of the USSR, Russia had continued to charge much less to its immediate neighbors than to Europe. With Yushchenko in power, the paradigm had changed. As Putin told the Valdai group, if Ukraine wanted to join the West and turn its back on Russia, there was no reason why Russia should continue to subsidize its energy. Ukraine was paying as little as $50 per 1,000 cubic meter for Russian gas, while Europe paid roughly three times more. As the December 31 deadline for renewing the gas contract approached, Ukraine refused to budge, leading to the January 1 cutoff. The question that was on everyone's minds—given the symbiotic relationship between the Kremlin and Gazprom—did Gazprom or Putin shut off the gas? Was this a political or an economic move? It was, of course, both. In the autumn of 2005, Ukraine dragged out negotiations on completing a new gas contract. Moscow was furious about Ukraine's Orange Revolution and seeking to influence the upcoming March Rada (parliamentary) elections. When it publicly announced the gas cutoff on a cold New Year's morning without informing its customers in Western Europe, this created the impression of political bullying, whereas there was also commercial justification for what it did. As former foreign minister Igor Ivanov put it, "Our energy problems with Europe are purely economic. It has nothing to do with European security."[53]

But the Kremlin miscalculated. Whereas Ukraine made sure that it had enough gas by siphoning off supplies destined for Europe—thereby imposing gas shortages on some European consumers—the Europeans blamed Russia, rather than Ukraine, for their shortages. The gas cutoff came the same day that Russia assumed the chairmanship of the G-8 and Germany the EU presidency. Angela Merkel rebuked Putin for not consulting Europe before the gas was cut off. Gas supplies resumed a couple of days later. The State Department initially reacted by calling on both sides to resume negotiations. By March, Dick Cheney in his Vilnius speech was accusing Russia of using energy as a form of political blackmail.

History repeated itself three years later, when Gazprom, after failing to reach agreement with Ukraine over gas prices, once again shut off the gas tap on January 1, 2009. But this time both Ukraine and Europe were better prepared, and the disruption, for the most part, was barely noticed.[54] Even after the more pro-Russian Viktor Yanukovych came to power in 2010, the pricing issue and pipeline ownership structure in the Russian-Ukrainian gas relationship remained contentious, indicating that geopolitics was only part of the reason for these disputes.

Russian energy supplies also became an issue of transatlantic dispute, as they had twenty-five years previously. "New Europe" was much more dependent on Russian gas and more concerned about the political use of Russia energy than was "Old Europe," whose experiences with Russian gas supplies and the politics around them had a more positive history. Gas, not oil, was the problem. The customer at the end of the gas pipeline can import gas from only one provider, in this case Gazprom. It cannot substitute another country's gas in the event of a supply interruption. The main issue for Washington was whether consciousness of dependence of Russian energy would affect political decision making in European capitals—especially Berlin—and possibly prevent European governments from adopting firmer policies toward Russia, should the need arise. The debate—including some of the rhetoric emanating from the U.S. Congress—was reminiscent of that during the Cold War.

Of particular concern to the Bush administration was the Nord Stream pipeline designed to transport Russian gas to Germany under the Baltic Sea, thus bypassing Ukraine and Poland and enabling Russia to reduce supplies and transit fees to countries with whom it had difficult relations. Nord Stream was controversial because Chancellor Gerhard Schroeder negotiated the agreement with Putin shortly before he was defeated by Angela Merkel in 2005, only to assume the position of chairman of the Advisory Board of Nord Stream after he left office. There were also environmental concerns about building the world's longest underwater pipeline. Poland's defense minister Radoslav Sikorski described the planned pipeline as a new version of the 1939 Molotov-Ribbentrop pact—a German-Russian condominium that was against Poland's interests—a somewhat hyperbolic expression of traditional Central European fears. Nevertheless, Nord Stream was also an example of greater diversification of gas supplies. Eventually, the objections to the project among Germany's EU allies were overcome, and the pipeline began operating in 2011.

The Bush administration's questions about Europe's energy dependence on Russia downplayed the fact that the Russian-European energy relationship is one of interdependence. It is an asymmetrical interdependence, where Europe could be more vulnerable to Russian supply disruptions than Russia would be to loss of European revenues. Russia depends on its European customers for energy revenues and on the CIS transit states for their continued cooperation in the transport of Central Asian and Russian gas. Russia and Europe are dependent on each other and will remain so for the foreseeable future. Indeed, after the 2011 Fukushima nuclear power accident in Japan, Germany announced that it was immediately phasing out its own nuclear power program, and this could increase its reliance on Russian gas.[55] The perception until 2008 for the Bush administration's Russia skeptics was that a prosperous and assertive Russia enjoying high energy prices could credibly interrupt supplies to Europe for a time without suffering economically. Needless to say, German and other European officials did not appreciate lectures from U.S. officials about their dangerous dependence on Russia.[56] And certainly European leaders asked why Washington was seeking to interfere in their dealings with their largest neighbor—one endowed with large resources and a large market for their goods.

American concerns about Russian gas exports to Europe became less pressing after Bush left office. The major energy story since 2008 in the United States has been the production of unconventional gas from shale rock formations. Shale gas has risen from 2 to 44 percent of U.S. production and the United States will begin to export liquefied natural gas later in the decade. International LNG capacity that had been built to export to the United States is now instead dispatching supplies to Europe, because the United States does not need them, thereby reducing Europe's demand for Russian gas.[57] Moreover, the United States is likely to become an LNG exporter to Europe, creating further competition for Gazprom. Gazprom was sufficiently concerned about the potential of the "shale gale" to reduce European purchases of its gas that, at the 2010 St. Petersburg Economic Forum, CEO Alexei Miller graphically warned about the environmental dangers of shale gas.[58] In short, Europe was looking at a future where there were potentially several alternatives to Gazprom including shale gas resources in Poland and Ukraine.

THE CASPIAN DERBY: HAPPINESS IS MULTIPLE PIPELINES

Caspian energy also became a problematic issue in U.S.-Russian relations. Both the Clinton and Bush administrations sought to enhance global energy security by supporting new export routes for Caspian oil and gas destined for Europe that bypassed Russia, diminishing its role as the dominant export outlets for the region's energy production. After the breakup of the Soviet Union, the Caspian Sea basin was colorfully described as the site of the "new Great Game." But whereas Rudyard Kipling's great game focused on the geopolitics of Russian-British rivalry in Afghanistan, the new game was more complex, geo-economic as well as geopolitical, a competition for lucrative resources as well as influence. There were now five Caspian littoral states—Russia, Azerbaijan, Turkmenistan, Kazakhstan, and Iran—where prior to 1991 there had been only two. And the stakes for the newly independent states were high, as it became apparent that the Capsian Sea was likely to hold abundant reserves of hydrocarbons, perhaps on a scale comparable to the North Sea. The challenge for U.S. policy was to help the new states to develop economically while establishing their autonomy. From the beginning, Russia claimed that the United States had no basis for being involved in the Caspian. The U.S. position was that as long as at least two littoral states were in agreement about projects, they did not need Russian approval. From the beginning, therefore, the United States and Russia had a fundamental disagreement on the legal status of the Caspian.[59]

Russia had a difficult time coming to terms with this new reality. A Russian energy minister in the 1990s, when asked about Caspian oil, pounded his fist on the table, saying *"Eto nasha neft"* (This is our oil).[60] But beginning in the early 1990s, Washington consistently supported the construction of oil and gas pipelines to connect the Caspian directly to the Mediterranean by way of Turkey and Georgia, thus bypassing Russia—and incidentally Iran. The State Department appointed its first special envoy for Eurasian gas, Ambassador Richard Morningstar, in 1995. He served in this role in the Clinton and then again in the Obama administration until he was appointed as ambassador to Azerbaijan in 2012. Russia viewed U.S. attempts to construct alternative gas pipelines as part of Washington's broader strategy of diminishing Moscow's influence in its neighborhood. Indeed, when Morningstar first met Igor Ivanov in 1998, Ivanov said of him with a somewhat jocular edge, "We know who he is and we don't like what he is doing."[61]

Washington found ready allies in the international oil companies, and the two sides worked closely together throughout this period. Their most notable success was the construction of the Baku-Tbilisi-Ceyhan (BTC) oil pipeline. Negotiations for the BTC project between the U.S. government, oil companies, Azerbaijan, and its neighbors were long and difficult. In the end, the pipeline route that was chosen was one of the longest pipelines in the world, traversing difficult mountainous terrain, and it was also very expensive. Russia objected to BTC, but the international players were determined. As Madeleine Albright said: "We don't want to wake up in ten years from now and have all of us ask ourselves why in the world we made a mistake and didn't build that pipeline," she said.[62] After years of tough negotiation and considerable U.S. encouragement, Azerbaijan, Georgia, and Turkey signed an agreement for a pipeline that would transport oil from Baku's Sangachal terminal on the Caspian Sea via Georgia to Turkey and then on to Ceyhan on Turkey's southern coast. The 1,099-mile long BTC pipeline took four years to build and cost $4 billion. Twenty-seven lending institutions were involved with fifteen hundred pages of formal documents.[63] The pipeline delivered its first oil in 2006. BP had a 30 percent share in the project, and ConocoPhillips, Amerada Hess, Lukoil, and Unocal each had smaller shares. A parallel pipeline, the South Caucasus Pipeline, was subsequently built alongside the BTC line, carrying gas from Azerbaijan's Shah Deniz field to Turkey.

The Russian reaction to the BTC project was, as expected, negative. It was, commentators said, a "political project," a U.S.-backed enterprise that was uneconomical and carried security risks because it passed through territory in Georgia and Azerbaijan that was the site of ethnic disputes. Washington was seen as the major force behind the project.[64] Nevertheless, once the pipeline was finished, the Russians did not interfere with its operation, then or later. During the 2008 Russia-Georgia War the pipeline was left undisturbed, even though parts of it were located in battle sites.

After BTC, the next episode in the evolving great gas game was competition over a southern route for Caspian gas to Europe. The United States and its European allies began to pursue various options during the Bush administration, the most ambitious of which was the Nabucco pipeline (named after the Verdi opera, which those who conceived the idea had watched together one evening in Vienna while discussing the project), which was to carry gas from Turkey to the Balkans and then to Southern Europe. The main question was what gas would be available to fill the pipeline.[65] The initial idea was to source the gas from Turkmenistan, but, as time went on, the discovery of major gas resources in Azerbaijan made the latter a more attractive option (although over time other sources have been discussed as well, including from Iraqi Kurdistan).

Whereas Gerhard Schroeder was the main spokesman for Nordstream, his former foreign minister Joschka Fischer became the spokesman for Nabucco.[66] Discussions continued for years, but there were questions about whether the project was commercially viable, and it was unclear whether it would be built. Determined not to see a repeat of BTC, Russia countered with its own proposed pipeline for a southern corridor, South Stream, which would be another way of bypassing Ukraine. Gazprom signed the Italian ENI, the German company

Wintershall, and the French EDF on as its main partners. But this pipeline, too, ran into obstacles, and it was unclear when it would be built.[67] Ironically, a major obstacle for both was Turkmenistan, which increasingly looked East. In 2009 a gas pipeline from Turkmenistan to China began operating, with commitments to construct more lines. Europeans remained wary of increasing their dependence on Russian gas via South Stream. As a senior EU official said, "We don't want these energy projects going over Putin's desk."[68] As for he Obama administration, Ambassador Morningstar explained, "We don't see this as a zero-sum game, but they do."[69] In 2013 Azerbaijan chose to participate in the Trans-Adriatic pipeline transporting gas to Italy.

U.S. ENERGY COMPANIES IN RUSSIA

The private-sector experience in the Russian energy sector has been mixed. Many of the large U.S. oil companies began investing in Russian energy projects in the early 1990s and remained there, despite all the difficulties they encountered. There were two main challenges. The first was to persuade the Russians of the need for a major Western presence in their oil sector. The second was to find mutually acceptable legal vehicles to balance risk and reward for those willing to take the plunge. In the end, the first challenge was the more fundamantal one and explains why the total share of U.S. companies in Russian oil production is only about 5%. Exxon and Conoco were initially willing to take the risk. The Yeltsin government agreed to offer production sharing agreements (PSAs) to several companies. This allowed a company to recoup all of its costs before it had to share its profits with the state. Exxon was given a 30 percent share in a consortium for the development of resources on the island of Sakhalin, known as Sakhalin 1 (as opposed to Sakhalin 2, where Shell was later penalized by overzealous Russian environmental officials). Exxon had several partners in this venture, including Rosneft, which was largely state-owned. Conoco later on purchased 20 percent of the privately owned Lukoil, after Putin had given his assent to the project, but it later on sold its share and left Russia.

Once Putin came to power, and given his strong views on the importance of energy resources being under the aegis of the state, it became clear that no major energy deal with a foreign company could be signed without his blessing. The Khodorkovsky affair highlighted these new rules. Khodorkovsky had violated the pact that the oligarchs had made with Putin when he came into office by challenging him politically. He had bought enough votes in the Duma to defeat a Kremlin-sponsored bill to increase taxes on oil companies. It was rumored that he harbored ambitions to replace Putin and become the president of Russia or prime minister in a new parliamentary republic. .[70] Khodorkovsky also broke another rule. He began discussing with both ExxonMobil and Chevron about selling them a controlling interest in Yukos. Exxon's CEO Lee Raymond met with Putin in September 2003 and had the impression that Putin would not object to the deal.[71] As events a few weeks later demonstrated, this was a mistaken impression.

On October 25, 2003, while Khodorkovsky's plane was refueling in Novosibirsk, armed FSB agents stormed the plane in the dark, led Khodorkovsky away in handcuffs and put him in jail, where he has remained ever since. After Khodorkovsky's arrest, Rosneft acquired Yukos's main assets in an opaque transaction in the provincial city of Tver.[72] A little less than a year after Yukos was broken up, Putin called Donald Evans, a close friend of President Bush, who had been his Secretary of Commerce from 2001 to 2005, and offered him the position of chairman of Rosneft. Evans turned down the job, but the offer highlighted several aspects of the U.S.-Russian relationship. Clearly, Putin believed that the Yukos affair had had a minimal effect on the U.S.-Russian relationship. Indeed, the Yukos affair did not have a major impact on U.S.-Russian relations.[73] While Khodorkovsky had his supporters—and an active public relations effort—in the United States, especially in the U.S. Congress, many in the U.S. private sector who had dealt with him regarded him as a tough businessman and did not jump to defend him after his arrest.

Putin did agree to several Western partnerships with a Russian oil companies. The first was the BP/TNK merger. The deal, signed in 2003 with Prime Minister Tony Blair and President Putin looking on, created TNK-BP in which both sides had a 50 percent stake. Subsequently, Putin said that this had been a mistake, and that fifty-fifty deals did not work. The new company brought significant profits to both sides but was from the beginning plagued by problems between the Russian and BP partners. The Russian side was led by oligarchs Mikhail Fridman, Viktor Vekselberg, and German Khan (the fourth partner, Len Blavatnik, had emigrated decades earlier to the United States). Eventually, after a series of clashes, TNK-BP's American CEO Robert Dudley was force to flee the country in 2008 for an "undisclosed location." Nevertheless, on January 14, 2011, Dudley, now BP CEO, appeared with Prime Minister Putin and Deputy Prime Minister Sechin in front of a blazing fire and Christmas tree to announce that BP and Rosneft had agreed to set up a joint venture to develop Russian Arctic shelf energy. The deal apparently had Putin's blessing. However, the Russian partners in the TNK venture challenged the deal, arguing that BP was legally obligated to give them the right of first refusal for any project that developed energy resources in Russia.[74]

Rosneft then turned to other potential partners. On April 16, 2012, with Vladimir Putin and Igor Sechin looking on, Exxon Mobil CEO Rex Tillerson and Rosneft CEO Eduard Khudaynatov signed a $3.2 billion deal in Moscow for joint exploration of the Arctic.[75] As part of the deal, Rosneft will acquire a 30 percent interest in onshore and offshore Exxon Mobil projects in the United States and Canada.[76] Exxon will also help Rosneft develop tight oil in West Siberia. The day after the signing Igor Sechin, made his first trip to the United States to talk to shareholders.[77] The project, declared Mr. Sechin, overcame the "over-politicization" and "historic stereotypes that hampered" the U.S.-Russian relationship. He described the deal as "a really big window of opportunity."[78] Did this landmark energy agreement herald a new phase in U.S.-Russian relations? Given the complexity of the project, and the challenges of the Arctic, it will take some years to answer that question.

A decade after its creation, the TNK-BP joint venture came to an end. BP sold its share to Rosneft, acquiring as part of the deal just under 20 per cent of the Russian oil giant. Soon after, the Russian partners and TNK sold out their interest to Rosneft as well.

ENERGY COOPERATION IN THE PUBLIC SECTOR

U.S.-government-sponsored energy cooperation began under Bush but grew more important during the Obama administration. At the May

2002 Moscow summit, Bush and Putin announced the creation of a U.S.-Russian energy dialogue, designed to open new areas for joint projects. The first U.S.-Russia Commercial Energy Summit, which brought together senior government officials and corporate executives from seventy U.S. and Russian companies, was held at Rice University in Houston in October 2002 with both Khodorkovsky and LUKOIL CEO Vagif Alekperov as keynote speakers. It discussed, inter alia, U.S, investment in the Russian energy sector as well as future U.S. imports of Russian oil.[79] However, this U.S.-Russian energy dialogue achieved only modest results because of the difficulty of finding enough common projects, especially after the arrest of Khodorkovsky and the new emphasis on oil and gas as "strategic" sectors. Although the dialogue continued, U.S. companies found it challenging to agree to joint projects at a time when the Russian state was becoming a larger player in the energy sector. Commerce Secretary Evans was initially hopeful about the dialogue: "I felt as if we were making progress," he says, adding "but then oil prices took off and it started getting tough to get them to do the simple things they had to do."[80]

In 2009, the Obama administration formed an Energy Working Group under the rubric of the new Presidential Bilateral Commission, focusing not only on joint projects but also on issues such as energy efficiency, new technologies like clean coal and smart grids, climate change, and nuclear energy. "There has been a genuine convergence of interests," said Deputy Energy Secretary Daniel Poneman, "but it's a work in progress."[81]

The Arctic

On August 2, 2007, the Kremlin dispatched a nuclear-powered icebreaker and two submarines to plant the Russian flag on the floor for the North Pole's sea—an act made possible by the warming of the Arctic icecap, which has been melting for some time (summer ice cover, some experts said, could completely vanish in thirty years). Professor Artur Chilingarov, explorer and member of the Duma representing the ruling United Russia party, declared, after planting the Russian tricolor, "The Arctic is ours and we should manifest our presence."[82] A few days later, Russia ordered strategic bomber flights over the Arctic Ocean for the first time since the Cold War, prompting the Canadian foreign minster to retort "Look, this isn't the 15th century. You can't go around the world and plant flags and say 'We're claiming this territory.'" Would this be the next area for U.S.-Russian competition?

The potential stakes are high. According to the U.S. Geological Survey, the Arctic holds as much as one-quarter of the world's remaining undiscovered oil and gas deposits, as well as diamonds, gold, platinum, tin, manganese, nickel, and lead. If Arctic melting proceeds at its current pace, major parts of the Arctic ocean will be ice-free in a couple of decades, greatly facilitating seabed mineral resource extraction and opening up the northern sea route as an alternative route between the Atlantic and the Pacific. For the United States, Russia, and the other Arctic littoral states (Canada, Norway, and Denmark), the Arctic involves core national security issues: territorial control, access to energy resources, and accessible transportation. China is also presenting itself as an Arctic power. Russia's major Arctic policy objective so far has been to promote and protect its claims to continental shelf territories beyond the two-hundred-nautical mile economic exclusion zone provided by the UN Convention on the Law of the Sea, in order to exploit the natural resources located there. The majority of the Arctic's energy reserves, according to Moscow, lie within Russia's zone. The region already provides the Russian economy with 12 to 15 percent of its GDP.[83]

In 2009 Russia published a document that spells out its policy toward the Arctic. It highlights Russia's commitment to exploit the significant hydrocarbon reserves there and to develop the Northern Sea Route, a wholly integrated transportation system linking Europe and Asia. The document also discusses the necessity of maintaining a military presence there to ensure security in the region. Overall, the document is quite mild, and hard security issues receive relatively little attention. Russia's Arctic strategy highlights both the Kremlin's assertive attitude toward the region and also its willingness to cooperate with the other Arctic states in developing the area.[84] Russia continues to claim that the Arctic seabed's underwater ridges are an extension of Russia's own continental shelf, and the other Arctic nations dispute these exclusive territorial claims. Nevertheless, the United States and its partners, including Russia, are working together within the Arctic Council, founded in 1996, to promote greater cooperation in the area. Indeed, the Arctic is one of the areas where the United States and Russia—together with the other littoral states—have quietly been making progress on both commercial and geostrategic issues, perhaps because potential bilateral conflicts are diffused by shared and crosscutting interests among all of the member states.

Climate Change

Vladimir Putin has on several occasions remarked that global warming is good for Russia since it will cause the temperature to rise by two or three degrees in Siberia. Indeed Russia is likely both to benefit from and to be adversely affected by the impact of climate change. President Medvedev's remarks at the 2009 Copenhagen conference on climate change and his promise that Russia would cut emissions by 25 percent from 1990 levels through 2020 indicate that parts of the Russian leadership take climate change more seriously than previously. Is this an issue on which Russia and the United States might cooperate? After all, Russia is the third largest emitter of carbon dioxide after the United States and China, ahead of India.

Experts agree that there could be considerable variability in the impact of global warming on Russia—the largest country on earth with very varied climate and topography—but its long-term consequences could be quite serious.[85] On one hand, a warming climate will open up new areas for agricultural cultivation in northern Russia and will reduce and shorten the heating season, thereby reducing energy demand. On the other hand, the melting of the permafrost in Siberia will place extra strains on Russia's aging energy and transportation infrastructure. Given Russia's reliance on fossil fuel exports to sustain its economic growth, and the adverse impact of climate change on its energy sector, there are significant incentives for Moscow to join with the United States, China, and India to reduce carbon emissions.

As was clear at the Copenhagen Conference, Russia does not see itself as a leader in combating climate change, nor has it played a major role on the issue until now. Nevertheless, Medvedev promised that Russia is willing to support further global negotiations. In November 2009 Putin gave tentative backing to a Danish initiative on emissions that would replace the Kyoto Protocol, as long as it took

Russia's interests into account, particularly its huge CO_2-absorbing forests. Given Russia's stated commitment to cooperation, the Obama administration reached out to Russia to work on questions of emission reduction and carbon trading, issues for which major Russian enterprises—such as Rosneft—have expressed support. While Medvedev was president, the White House and the Kremlin agreed on the importance of tackling climate change issues, despite persistent skepticism about the urgency of this issue in some parts of the Russian political establishment. It is unclear how the Kremlin will deal with these issues. Climate change is a top priority for Washington, but the same cannot be said for Moscow.

Civilian Nuclear Energy

One area where the United States and Russia are discussing cooperation and where Russia has a comparative advantage is that of civilian nuclear energy. This is an industry in which Russia has a great deal of expertise, and one in which the United States has increasingly less as the previous cohort of engineers who built the United States' nuclear industry is retiring and is not being replaced by a younger generation. Washington and Moscow began talks on peaceful nuclear cooperation before the collapse of the USSR in 1991, when the subject of a 123 agreement was first discussed. (The section that regulates international cooperation in the U.S. Atomic Energy Act of 1954 is number 123, and the United States has 123 agreements with a variety of countries.) The discussions of the early 1990s foundered on the Iran issue. Washington made any commercial nuclear industry cooperation with Russia conditional on Moscow ceasing its nuclear cooperation with Iran. After the 1995 agreement for Russia to complete the Bushehr reactor, negotiations were suspended. In 2005, when the Bush administration recognized that the Bushehr reactor did not pose a proliferation threat, U.S.-Russian talks on civilian nuclear cooperation resumed. In May 2008, a U.S.-Russian agreement on Cooperation in the Field of Peaceful Use of Nuclear Energy was signed. However, it did not come into force because it required congressional review, and the Russia-Georgia War intervened. The Bush administration then withdrew the 123 agreement from congressional consideration.

The Obama administration resubmitted the agreement and it came into force in January 2011.[86] Although it will take time before opportunities under the 123 agreement can be fully fleshed out, it appeared that the most promising areas for US-Russian cooperation include joint development of advanced fuel cycle or innovative nuclear power reactor technology.[87] Deputy Secretary Daniel Poneman explained: "The 123 agreement is not a gift. It is in both countries' security interests. Both sides are committed to making it work. We have found that peaceful nuclear cooperation is not necessarily affected by the ups and downs in the bilateral political relationship."[88]

WTO AND THE END OF JACKSON-VANIK

Despite Russia's rise as a market economy and its integration into global markets, it remained outside the major global trading organization, the World Trade Organization, until August 2012. It took Russia eighteen years of laborious negotiations to get into the WTO, the longest negotiation in the WTO's history. The negotiations took so long because of domestic opposition within Russia on the part of those businesses and ministries that did not want to operate in the more competitive market that the WTO would bring.[89] Indeed, until the moment that the Duma ratified the final protocol there was fierce debate within Russia about the wisdom of joining. On May 31, 2012, eighty-one business leaders sent an appeal to Putin and Medvedev requesting a postponement of Russia's accession, claiming that it would hurt domestic manufacturers and lead to "massive" unemployment in manufacturing and agriculture.[90] Putin acknowledged that WTO is "a sensitive issue," adding that "I am very anxious about it too."[91]

Another obstacle was overcoming the objections of Georgia, which was already in the WTO, and which wanted to ensure that Russia would not supply weapons to South Ossetia and Abkhazia. Russia insisted that the United States should put pressure on its partner Georgia to lift its objections to Russian membership. After a hard-fought compromise, Swiss private contractors agreed to monitor the disputed border crossing points.[92]

Both Democratic and Republican administrations had agreed that, despite the lack of transparency in significant sectors of the Russian economy, it was preferable to have Russia as a member of a rules-based organization than to have it outside these structures. With Russia in the WTO, U.S.-Russian trade could double—even though that would still constitute only about 2 percent of total U.S. trade.

However, a major obstacle remained. The United States was the only country in the WTO that had failed to grant Russia permanent normal trading status (PNTR). The Jackson-Vanik amendment tying PNTR to the USSR's (and Russia's) record on emigration remained on the books. It was a complete anomaly. Initially passed in 1974 to tie Jewish emigration to U.S.-Soviet trade, it made no sense in 2012 when anyone was free to emigrate from Russia, Putin had made several state visits to Israel, there were daily flights between Moscow and Tel Aviv, and Russians and Israelis enjoyed visa-free travel (unlike Russians and Americans). Yet the U.S. Congress remained stubbornly opposed to removing a piece of legislation that, it believed, continued to give it leverage over Russia. During the first Bush administration, Congress came close to lifting Jackson-Vanik, but the Khodorkovsky case and Russian restrictions on the import of American pork and chickens intervened and scuttled the negotiations. There was a limit to how much political capital the White House was willing to expend to get Jackson-Vanik repealed.

In 2012, with Russia's WTO membership in sight, the administration began to lobby Congress to lift Jackson-Vanik. It was supported by groups representing U.S. business interests in Russia, such as the U.S.-Russia Business Council and the American Chamber of Commerce in Moscow. The main argument was that, once Russia was in the WTO, U.S. business would be at a disadvantage because the United States had not granted Russia PNTR. Russia would be more likely to take its business to countries that did not charge extra tariffs than to the United States, which did. That would cost the U.S. jobs that would go to Europe or Asia instead.[93]

This argument did not sway some members of Congress. House International Affairs Committee chair Ileana Ros-Lehtinen in July 2012 called the granting of PNTR a "gift" to Russia although in fact it would benefit U.S. exports and export-related jobs. But there was a new bipartisan twist—tying the granting of PNTR to legislation that would replace Jackson-Vanik. The House and Senate agreed that revoking of Jackson-Vanik had to be tied to the adoption of the Magnitsky Act (discussed in Chapter 10). The White House was reluctant to agree to this linkage. Nevertheless, it became clear that it would be impossible to revoke Jackson-Vanik without linkage between the two pieces of legislation. After a series of intense negotiations, the Magnitsky bill was passed in both Houses of Congress and Russia was granted PNTR.

It remains to be seen how Russia's entry into the WTO will affect U.S.-Russian relations, but the spat over PNTR in 2012 highlighted the continuing constraints on the bilateral economic relationship—and the limits of the fourth reset.

Chapter Nine

Reset or Overload?
The Obama Initiative

When Secretary of State Hillary Clinton held her first meeting with Foreign Minister Sergei Lavrov in Geneva in March 2009, she handed her Russian counterpart a small gift box. With reporters eagerly looking on, Lavrov unwrapped the gift and found inside a red button emblazoned with the English word "reset" and the Russian word *peregruzka*. Lavrov took one look at the button and, with a surprised look on his face, exclaimed, "You got it wrong."[1] He had been given a button with the Russian word for "overload." The Russian word for reset was *perezagruzka*, not *peregruzka*. Clinton brushed aside this embarrassing mistranslation with a joke, and they both bantered about the fact that the agenda was, indeed, overloaded.[2] The Russian newspaper *Kommersant*'s headline the next day read "Sergei Lavrov and Hillary Clinton push the wrong button."[3]

What did "reset" mean? This was both a literal and a philosophical question. Did it mean pressing the button and returning to the status quo ante? If so, which status quo? Reset encompasses all that came before; it is not a new slate. The metaphorical possibilities for interpreting reset were as extensive as were the policy implications. Several Russian commentators at the time argued that *peregruzka*—overload—was in fact a better translation of the nature and possibilities of the U.S.-Russian relationship than was *perezagruzka*.[4] In the end, the Russian government never took ownership of the reset, insisting always that it was an American, not a Russian initiative. As Deputy Foreign Minister Sergei Ryabkov pointed out, " 'Reset' as a term is not our style, not our language, not our word. We prefer to talk about continuing the positive trend of recent times."[5] By the time Medvedev left the Kremlin and Putin returned to the presidency, the original button seemed to have been more prescient than the correct translation. U.S.-Russian relations were indeed overburdened by a legacy of disagreements and mutual mistrust from both the Cold War and post–Cold War periods; yet, despite all that, the Obama administration in its first term did manage to press the button and improve both the atmospherics and the substance of the relationship.

Whereas the post-9/11 rapprochement was a Russian initiative, this fourth attempt at resetting post–Cold War U.S.-Russian relations originated in Washington. The Obama administration came into office when U.S.-Russian relations were in the doldrums, and it made improving ties with Moscow a foreign policy priority. From the Russian point of view, the Obama reset was an American course correction, an admission that the American side was responsible for the deterioration in bilateral ties. Reset involved the United States changing its policy toward Russia more than Russia changing its policy toward the United States, a fact that supporters and critics in both countries recognized. It was also facilitated by having new faces in the White House and in the Kremlin.

U.S. administration officials stressed that the reset had limited objectives, most of which were met, and that by 2012 it was no longer an appropriate term for U.S.-Russian relations.[6] Putin himself, in his marathon four and a half hour press conference in December 2012, claimed that the war in Iraq had spoiled the relationship and reiterated that reset was a term invented by Washington and that there was nothing in the bilateral relationship that needed resetting.[7] Like the Clinton and Bush administrations, the Obama White House was to find Russia a more challenging partner than it anticipated at the beginning of its second term.

THE 2008 PRESIDENTIAL CAMPAIGN
AND OBAMA'S ELECTION

The post-Georgia deep freeze in U.S.-Russian relations coincided with the most intense phase of the U.S. presidential campaign. As in previous presidential campaigns, Russia policy intruded into debates. Yet it was a tangential issue. In 2000, the Republicans had accused the Democrats of overpersonalizing relations with Yeltsin's Russia and failing the Russian people. In 2008, the Democrats charged the Bush administration with overpersonalizing relations with Putin's Russia and pursuing irresponsible policies that had brought the two sides dangerously close to confrontation in the Caucasus. Politicians and commentators argued about how to advance the relationship without compromising American values and interests. Republican candidate John McCain, who had a reputation as a harsh critic of Russia, tried to brand his opponent Barack Obama as inexperienced and naïve about Russia. Obama was rhetorically cautious about Russia during the campaign Once elected, the new president had to manage expectations about the relationship and convince a sometimes skeptical Congress—especially when the Republicans regained control of the House in 2010—that U.S.-Russian relations had indeed entered a more productive phase. Nearly two decades after the Soviet collapse, could this new administration reverse a decade of "cranky" relations and deliver concrete results?

Whereas John McCain had decades of experience in the world of international security and defense issues, Barack Obama's foreign policy experience was limited. Although he had chaired the Subcommittee on Europe in the U.S. Senate, he held only a few hearings, and his views on Russia were largely unknown. He had visited Russia once as a senator in August 2005 with Republican Richard Lugar, whom he had accompanied on a trip to Russia and Ukraine to discuss the implementation of the Nunn-Lugar Cooperative Threat Reduction programs to strengthen security at Russia's nuclear installations. They visited Saratov and Perm, where SS-24 and SS-25 ICBMs were being dismantled. For reasons that remain obscure, the senators' plane was held for several hours on the runway in Perm, Siberia, without explanation, and eventually released to allow them to fly to Moscow. Despite this unexpected detention, which Obama said was reminiscent of Cold War days, he came away convinced of the "seemingly irreversible process of economic, if not political, integration between East and West."[8]

During the first televised presidential debate, Obama sounded tough on Russia. The entire relationship had to be evaluated in the aftermath of the Georgia War, he argued. Russia, he said, "cannot be a 21st century superpower, or power, and act like a 20th-century dictatorship." He went on to say that the United States and Russia did have common interests, such as nonproliferation, and that the next president should not deal with Russia "based on staring into his eyes and seeing his soul" but based on the national security interests of the United States.[9] During the second debate, he reiterated many of these points, adding the "resurgence of Russia" was a central issue with which the United States would have to deal in the coming years and pledging both "moral support" and concrete assistance to Poland, Estonia, and Latvia—and especially Georgia—against Russian pressure.[10] Russian commentary on the debates reflected considerable skepticism about the differences between the two candidates' policies on Russia.[11]

Meanwhile, Obama had assembled an advisory team that was thinking about how to improve relations with Russia and redesign ties to be more coherent, broad-based, and productive.[12] Highly critical of Bush's failure to engage Russia seriously on nuclear issues, the group advocated a number of initiatives on nuclear weapons, including approaching missile defense "firmly, pragmatically and diplomatically," and enlisting Russian cooperation as the deployments went forward. Admitting that "the United States does not have enough leverage over Russia to influence internal change through coercive means," it recommended dual-track diplomacy, engaging Russia on issues of vital interest to the United States—particularly in the nuclear sphere—while continuing democracy-assistance programs. On Russia's relations with the former Soviet states, recommendations included promoting multiple pipeline routes through Eurasia and supporting democracy in Ukraine and Georgia. These ideas were part of a broader strategy of re-engaging America's allies and reaching out to great powers such as Russia to tackle global issues.[13]

During the election campaign, there was also a flurry of activity from task forces in the major U.S. think tanks, Republican and Democratic, many eager to offer advice to the incoming president on how to improve ties with Moscow—and what to do about Russia. Many of them made suggestions similar to those in think-tank reports during the 2000 election, but this time the deterioration in ties in the wake of the Georgia War added a sense of urgency. But it was two heavyweights with great authority who set the tone—former Secretaries of State Henry Kissinger and George Shultz. They criticized the lack of high-level contacts since the August war, urged a go-slow policy on further NATO expansion, and concluded that "isolating Russia is not a sustainable long-range policy."[14]

RESET AND THE TANDEM

The initial Russian reaction to Obama's election was, to put it mildly, odd. On the day after Obama's victory, President Medvedev gave his first annual address to the Russian Federal Assembly. He began by denouncing Georgian aggression, the presence of NATO naval vessels in the Black Sea, and U.S. missile defense plans. He ended by promising that Russia would deploy the Iskander missile system in Kaliningrad to neutralize the U.S. missile defense system, adding "we have no issue with the American people, we do not have inherent anti-Americanism."[15] He did not mention that the United States had just elected a new president. It was not an auspicious start to the relationship between the two new presidents. Ten days later Medvedev traveled to Washington to attend a G-20 summit on the global financial crisis. He took time off to address the Council on Foreign Relations in Washington, where Bill Clinton's secretary of state Madeleine Albright interviewed him. On this occasion, Medvedev sounded more conciliatory, welcoming Obama's election. A participant asked why he chose the day after the U.S. election to threaten to deploy new missiles. He had twice postponed his address to the parliament, he explained, and was hurried when he looked over the text. As for the date, "With all my respect to the United States, I absolutely forgot about the important political event that had taken place that day."[16]

The Obama administration turned its attention to Russia soon after taking office, establishing Russia as a priority for the first term. From the beginning the White House faced a challenge: how to deal with the tandem, this unique Russian power-sharing agreement. In January 2009 Medvedev had been in power a little over half a year. Whereas Putin was part of the transitional generation spanning both the Soviet and post-Soviet eras, Medvedev belonged to the post-Soviet generation. He was born in 1965 and, like Obama, had reached maturity in the waning days of the Cold War. While Putin was serving as a KGB agent in Dresden, Medvedev had been a student at Leningrad State University during the height of the perestroika era in the midst of student ferment. Unlike Putin, he came from a family of university professors that was comfortably off, and he had not served in the security services. He had met Putin in Mayor Sobchak's office in St. Petersburg in the early 1990s and had worked for him since then. He was a Putin man, albeit not a Silovik, but was intimately involved as a lawyer in Putin's economic activities in St. Petersburg. He had moved to Moscow in 1999 to work in the Presidential Administration, subsequently becoming head of the Presidential Administration as well as chairman of the Board of Directors of Gazprom.

As soon as Medvedev came into office, he tried to establish his own distinct persona. He stressed his commitment to eliminating what he called "legal nihilism" in Russia and to modernizing the country. His rhetoric on domestic problems was forward-looking and remained so throughout his four years in office. Medvedev appeared to have the foreign policy—particularly the U.S.—portfolio, whereas Putin dealt with economic issues. Obama, like other Western leaders, decided from the beginning to take Medvedev at his word and act as if he was the de facto as well as the de jure leader of Russia, who wanted to make Russia a more modern society based on the rule of law. The Obama administration decided to place its bets on Medvedev and focus on that half of the tandem, hoping that eventually Medvedev would be able to assert himself and take control. The buzzword among officials was "empowering" Medvedev, overestimating the influence that the United States could have on Russian domestic politics. Yuri Ushakov, Putin's foreign policy advisor, would criticize the Obama administration for not meeting more with Putin during his years as prime minister.[17] Although it might indeed have been a more prudent policy to deal with both members of the tandem, U.S. officials emphasize that they made several attempts to arrange meetings between President Obama and Prime Minister Putin, but that their efforts to do so were rebuffed.[18]

Senior U.S. officials emphasize that, from their point of view, the personal relationship between Obama and Medvedev was the key to the success of the reset. The two men were from the same generation, they had similar styles, and their personalities were compatible. They eschewed pomp and circumstance and found a productive way to do business with each other. Obama invested a great deal of time and effort in negotiating with Medvedev, and his personal intervention was decisive on several key issues, such as concluding the New START treaty. Even though it became clear that no major decision could be taken without Putin's assent, Medvedev was Obama's key interlocutor.

Vice President Joseph Biden announced the new U.S. policy at the annual gathering of top defense and foreign policy officials, the Munich Security Conference in February 2009. It was from that same podium that, two years earlier, Putin had blasted the United States; but in 2009 the tone was different. First, Sergei Ivanov, now deputy prime minster, made a less confrontational speech.[19] Next to take the podium was Biden, a Munich veteran. He laid out the Obama administration's commitment to eschew unilateralism and engage with the world. Then he came to Russia: "The last few years have seen a dangerous drift in relations between Russia and the members of our Alliance. It is time—to paraphrase President Obama—it's time to press the reset button and to revisit the many areas where we can and should be working together with Russia."[20] Ivanov declared the remarks "very positive" and the government-owned *Rossisskaia Gazeta* commented, "The Americans see an important partner in Russia. And they are ready to cooperate with us on many things, including contentious issues."[21] With a short phrase, the American vice president had changed the terms of the debate and offered to reengage Russia.

At the heart of the reset was prudent expectations management. In this sense, the Obama policy resembled that of George H. W. Bush more than that of either Clinton or George W. Bush. The Obama team recognized the perils of overpromising. From the outset, Obama, Biden, and other senior officials used moderate rhetoric and sought to create a set of achievable expectations. They committed themselves to listening to what they heard as Russian concerns and responded to Russian rhetorical provocations with restraint. Washington was more willing to engage with Russia on the basis of interest-based pragmatism than had been the case in the Clinton or Bush administrations. This was evident in two areas: the post-Soviet states and democracy promotion. After the debacle of the Georgia War, the Obama team was much more careful in what it said and did in Georgia and Ukraine, and remained largely silent on the issue of further NATO enlargement beyond general commitments to keep the process open.

Similarly, there was, for the first time in a few years, little public criticism of Russia's domestic political system and no linkage was made between foreign policy engagement and Russia's democratic deficits. The outlook was more transactional and pragmatic. The White House espoused a dual-track policy: government-to-government contacts should be reinforced by nongovernmental contacts, from NGOs to the private sector, thereby broadening the relationship.[22] Dual-track engagement meant that progress on foreign policy issues should not be explicitly linked to domestic issues. The United States had pursued a dual-track policy toward the USSR—after all, that was the essence of détente—as had the first Bush administration, but during the second Bush term linkage between domestic and foreign policy issues had reappeared. As Obama's officials were fond of saying, Russia should be part of the solution, not part of the problem, on issues of national security. The United States needed Russia's cooperation in several key areas: nuclear nonproliferation, Afghanistan, and Iran. The alternative was Russian obstruction of vital American national security interests, as had sometimes been the case since the Soviet collapse. There were fewer internal differences over Russia policy than there had been during the Bush administration.

LONDON AND MOSCOW, 2009

The reset was inaugurated when Obama and Medvedev met in London on April 1, 2009, ahead of a G-20 summit. Their first official meeting as presidents took place against the background of the global financial crisis. The meeting covered a wide range of issues from missile defense, arms control, Iran, and Afghanistan to global financial regulation. Obama was pleasantly surprised when "out of the blue" Medvedev suggested expanding the Northern Distribution Network for transporting American equipment to Afghanistan. They also discussed the future of the Manas air base in Kyrgyzstan.[23] Unlike the first Bush-Putin summit in Slovenia, this meeting produced no effusive rhetoric. Admitting that there were "real differences" between the two countries, Obama announced the beginning of "new progress" in U.S.-Russian relations and praised Medvedev for his contribution to that progress. The tone was cordial but restrained, in keeping with the intent of the reset.[24] On his official website, Medvedev announced his optimism about the relationship, remarking that there was more that united than divided the two countries.[25] In a speech at the London School of Economics, Medvedev declared that the Obama administration, unlike its predecessor, now listened to Russia's views.[26]

Obama's visit to Moscow three months later highlighted the potential and the limits of reset, given the complex and opaque politics of the tandem. His visit received very little play in the state-run electronic media. His most challenging meeting was a two-hour breakfast with Putin at the prime minister's Novo-Ogarevo residence. This was the only Obama-Putin meeting held during Putin's tenure as prime minister. A week before the meeting, Obama had said that Putin had "one foot in the old ways of doing business." In a prescient Freudian slip, he referred to him as president, instead of prime minister, before quickly correcting himself.[27]

Obama began the meeting by asking, "How did we get into this mess—this low point that U.S.-Russian relations have been in for the past years?"[28] Putin then delivered a ninety-minute monologue about everything that had gone wrong in the relationship, recounting the history of U.S.-Russian relations and the slights and broken promises from the George W. Bush administration. In Cold War speak, this was a "frank and businesslike meeting." Emerging from the breakfast, Obama said, "Putin is smart, tough, shrewd—he is very unsentimental, very pragmatic. He thinks in terms of what's good for Russia and will pursue Russia's interests aggressively."[29] At the 2009 Valdai meeting shortly thereafter, Putin was restrained in his remarks about Obama, saying his decision-making power was limited by Congress (a problem that Russian leaders did not face with the Duma). It would be possible to do business with America only after the U.S. president was able to obtain congressional support for his agenda and secure passage of health care reform. Nevertheless, Putin expressed "moderate optimism" about the relationship, saying that Russia wanted to do "constructive and reliable work" with the United States.[30]

By contrast, the more cordial Obama-Medvedev meeting in the Kremlin produced several agreements that were to define the agenda for the next three years. This signaled the end to the post–Georgia War freeze in relations. The presidents agreed to begin work on a follow-up to the START treaty, committing themselves to significant reductions in both delivery vehicles and warheads. They agreed to pursue a broader nuclear security agenda, including the opening of a joint early-warning center to share data on missile launchings. (Clinton and Yeltsin had announced the same agreement in 1998—as had Clinton and Putin in 2000 and Bush and Putin in 2007—but the center had never been built.) They signed an agreement to permit the transit of up to forty-five hundred flights of U.S. troops and lethal military equipment over Russian territory to Afghanistan every year. And they announced the creation of the U.S.-Russian Bilateral Presidential Commission, coordinated by Secretary Clinton and Foreign Minister Lavrov, to broaden and deepen the relationship. Acknowledging their differences over issues such as Georgia and missile defense, they agreed to work together to improve ties. When asked by a reporter who he thought was really in charge of Russia, Obama diplomatically sidestepped the question: "My understanding is that President Medvedev is the President, Prime Minister Putin is the Prime Minister, and they allocate power in accordance with Russia's form of government in the same way that we allocate power in the United States."[31] Sometime thereafter a senior State Department official privately summarized the administration's understanding, "Medvedev was in an impossible situation. He wanted to establish his own power base. But if he had done this it would have threatened Putin."[32]

While in Moscow, Obama sought to broaden the U.S.-Russian relationship by reaching out to the younger generation. He gave a speech at the New Economic School, an up-and-coming new university that emphasized economics and governance. Further defining the reset and its commitment to engage Russia in new, twenty-first-century issues, he exhorted the younger generation to become active in contributing to greater prosperity and better governance in their country.[33] It was not broadcast on any state media. He also attended a parallel civil society summit. Medvedev, who was also invited, opted not to attend, and potential Russian participants were discouraged by the Kremlin from attending. Obama's message to the civil society activists was clear: "Strong, vibrant nations include strong, vibrant civil societies." Evoking his experience as a community organizer in Chicago, he encouraged responsible civil activism.[34] More controversially, Obama had a private meeting with leading opposition figures. He wanted to make the point that a reset in government-to-government relations would not affect American support for democracy and human rights in Russia. His chief Russia advisor Michael McFaul, who had previously worked for the National Democratic Institute in Russia, sought to ensure that the reset in government-to-government relations was not viewed in Moscow or Washington as a return to pure Realpolitik. This was to prove to be a difficult balancing act—and a lasting challenge.

At the Moscow summit—Obama's only visit to Russia during his first term—the administration announced the establishment of the Bilateral Presidential Commission, an improved version of Gore-Chernomyrdin. After several years of tense relations, the White House felt some urgency to make progress in advancing its agenda. The advent of Medvedev and his criticism of Russian corruption and lawlessness opened up space for greater discussion of political and economic issues. Thus, Obama concentrated on his personal relationship with Medvedev, although aware that the complex decision-making process in Moscow raised question marks about how far the relationship could advance. The new U.S. president found himself in the same conundrum as his predecessors. Personal ties between the two leaders remained indispensable in moving the relationship forward, in the absence of other mechanisms. But the tandem meant that this was in reality a triangular relationship, albeit with one side of the triangle often out of view.[35]

Medvedev's views about the United States had sounded indistinguishable from those of Putin prior to Obama's election. However, in 2009 his rhetoric changed, and his comments about the United States and about President Obama grew more positive.[36] There were two reasons why Russia moderated its policies toward the United States in 2009–the change in American policy and the 2008 global financial crisis. Not only was Russia harder hit by the crisis than it had initially anticipated, but both the government and the business sector believed that Russia needed Western capital and know-how to help it deal with the crisis and its consequences.

DEALING WITH THE PRESIDENTIAL INBOX

New START

Nuclear nonproliferation and arms control—including a commitment to an ultimate "global zero"—were at the heart of Obama's foreign policy priorities. Signing another arms control treaty was also a priority for Moscow, partly because a reduction in nuclear weapons would free up economic resources to spend on other priorities. Equally important was the fact that negotiating an arms control agreement with the United States boosted Russia's international prestige and was one of the few areas in which the United States and Russia as the world's two nuclear superpowers dealt with each other as equals. Whereas the Bush administration had denigrated START-type agreements as a Cold War relic, the Obama administration embraced them. When Obama came into office, the 2002 SORT agreement regulating strategic nuclear weapons was due to expire in December 2012 and the 1991 START treaty in December 2009. In 2008, the Bush administration was unable to agree with Russia on terms for replacing START I.

Even though Moscow and Washington had achieved a consensus on the terms of the agreement and both sides recognized that a deal was in their mutual interest, the eight rounds of negotiations were especially challenging. Rose Gottemoeller, an experienced arms control official who had negotiated the denuclearization of Ukraine and Kazakhstan in the early 1990s, led the U.S. side, while Anatoly Antonov, another veteran negotiator, led the Russian side. Gottemoeller recalls that "there were times when I thought we would not make it."[37] While she negotiated the overall framework, Chairman of the Joint Chiefs of Staff Admiral Mike Mullen and his Russian counterpart General Nikolai

Makarov negotiated the technical details.[38] A major stumbling block was the Russian side's insistence on linking a new START agreement to the U.S. missile defense program. As the negotiations entered the home stretch in December 2009, Putin gave a tough speech in Vladivostok warning that if there were no constraints on the U.S. missile defense program, Russia would not sign the START agreement: "The problem," he said, "is that our American partners are building an antimissile shield and we are not building one"[39] (he failed to note that the Russians still have an ABM system around Moscow). In the end it took a tense ninety-minute phone call between Obama and Medvedev at the eleventh hour to hammer out the details and walk the Russian side back from linking START to missile defense.[40] "New START is often called the low-hanging fruit," explained a senior administration official, "but in reality we almost didn't get it done."[41] American officials understood that there was a disagreement between Putin and Medvedev on New START; yet they also believed that Putin in the end played a role in convincing skeptics in his Ministry of Defense to support the treaty.

New START was signed in Prague by the two presidents in April 2010. It was the biggest nuclear arms pact in a generation and was the first—and arguably the single-most important—achievement of the reset. Russian officials almost uniformly praised it. Medvedev said that "this treaty reflects the balance of both countries' interests," adding that U.S.-Russian relations were now "on a higher level."[42]

By the terms of the treaty, both sides agreed to limit themselves to no more than 1,550 deployed strategic warheads (down from the 2,200 previously allowed), no more than 700 deployed strategic delivery vehicles, and no more than 800 deployed and nondeployed launchers. The limits were to be implemented by February 2018. The treaty contained a set of verification measures including data exchange, notifications, and on-site inspections that would enable both sides to detect militarily significant violations in a timely manner.[43] New START offered significant security benefits for the United States. It ensured that Russia would limit its strategic nuclear forces, giving the United States greater leeway to decide how to develop and deploy its own nuclear deterrent going forward. The verification measures also added greater transparency to the relationship.

In the United States, New START encountered a difficult group of skeptics—members of the U.S. Congress. The congressional ratification process, which took place during 2010—a year of mid-term elections—became contentious. Some administration officials commented that they were not sure what was more difficult—negotiating with the Russians or with the Republicans in the U.S. Congress. In the end, the Senate added its own resolutions exhorting the administration to increase military spending so that the ongoing development of U.S. missile defense systems and nuclear weapons modernization would continue after the treaty came into force.[44]

Russian officials viewed New START as a vindication of their arguments about the importance of bilateral arms control treaties that the Bush administration had belittled. Despite their failure to link New START to missile defense, they believed it reinforced their claim to great-power status. Moreover, New START was economically advantageous because it would enable Russia to reduce its strategic nuclear arsenal while still maintaining a significant nuclear posture. The first achievement of the Obama reset was presented as a success for Russian diplomacy. As Deputy Foreign Minister Antonov put it, "This treaty is the 'gold standard' in resolving problems of strategic stability."[45]

Closely tied to these negotiations was the Obama administration's commitment to strengthen nuclear security by reducing and safeguarding nuclear materials and ensuring that they did not fall into the hands of rogue states or non-state actors. The Global Threat Reduction Initiative had been established in 2004 and in April 2010 Washington hosted a Nuclear Security summit under its auspices. Attended by twenty-nine countries, it focused on the need to reduce the dangers of nuclear terrorism. Washington and Moscow agreed to dispose of a combined sixty-eight metric tons of weapons-grade plutonium under an agreement that would eliminate enough material to produce seventeen thousand nuclear weapons. Other countries agreed to work with the International Atomic Energy Agency to dispose of highly enriched uranium from civilian nuclear plants.[46]

New START entered into force after both the Senate and Duma ratified it in 2011. It represented the completion of unfinished business, a coda to Cold War–era negotiations and concerns. It was likely to be the last comprehensive U.S.-Russian arms control agreement of its kind. It was, in retrospect, the most straightforward and easiest of the U.S.-Russian arms control negotiations and the one in which both sides shared a common vision and common interests.

Nevertheless, the Obama team determined that New START should be only the first step in a much more ambitious process of global denuclearization. In his 2013 State of the Union speech, Obama committed the United States to more arms control: "We will engage Russia to seek further reductions in our nuclear arsenals."[47] There were several agenda items. The first was to try to negotiate further reductions in deployed strategic warhead and delivery vehicles. While the U.S. side was willing to contemplate this, Russia was much more reluctant, given that its remaining nuclear arsenal could offset its weakness in conventional forces. Moreover, because of Russia's concerns about China's longer-term intentions, it was prudent to maintain a nuclear force capable of deterring future Chinese actions. Nuclear weapons were one of Moscow's few remaining great-power attributes, and it was unlikely to want to further reduce its nuclear weapons, particularly in the face of uncertainties about U.S. missile defense plans. Washington remained interested in negotiating reductions in tactical nuclear weapons, where the Russians have a numerical superiority, but which also, from Moscow's point of view, can offset strategic weapons deficits. Meanwhile, the most contentious issue remained missile defense.[48]

Missile Defense

During Bush's two terms as president, U.S. plans for missile defense—particularly the deployment of radars in the Czech Republic and ten interceptors in Poland—became one of the most difficult and corrosive problems in U.S.-Russian relations. The offer on the table—Putin's proposals for joint radar sites in Azerbaijan and southern Russia if the United States eschewed deployments in Central Europe and Bush's countersuggestion that Russian officials could be present at the sites in Poland and the Czech Republic—failed to resolve anything. Moscow continued to insist that missile defense was really aimed against Russia, not against Iran or North Korea, and that Washington's goal was to neutralize Russia's nuclear deterrent. After seeking to link missile defense to New START, Russia eventually accepted that the treaty would not limit missile defense, although it left open the possibility that, if missile defense deployments went ahead, Russia could withdraw from New START. Meanwhile, several of the United States' "old" European allies remained skeptical about the need for or feasibility of missile defense deployments, partly because they were concerned about Russia's negative reaction to the program.[49]

During his July 2009 summit in Moscow, Obama had promised Medvedev that the United States would review the missile defense plans that it had inherited from the Bush administration. The most pressing issues were the Polish and Czech deployments. Shortly after the Moscow summit, and alarmed about the implications of the U.S.-Russian reset for their own security, a group of distinguished former Central European leaders—including former Czech president Vaclav Havel, and former Polish presidents Alexander Kwasniewski and Lech Walesa—hit back. They wrote an open letter to the Obama administration expressing their concern that "Central and Eastern European countries are no longer at the heart of American foreign policy." They lamented the fact that the Atlantic alliance had stood by as Russia invaded Georgia and violated the principles of the Helsinki Final Act. Russia, they argued, "is back as a revisionist power pursuing a 19th-century agenda with 21st-century tactics and methods." They urged Obama not to abandon the missile defense installations without consulting Poland or the Czech Republic, warning that this would undermine U.S. credibility around the region.[50]

But six weeks later, the Obama administration did just that— modifying its program without consulting its Central European allies. Arguing that a new study indicated that the Iranian long-range missile program was progressing more slowly than previously thought and that medium-range missiles presented a greater danger, Obama announced that the United States had abandoned its plans to deploy radars in the Czech Republic and interceptors in Poland. He called the Polish and Czech leaders to inform them just before the public announcement was made. He said that the new U.S. program would involve a "phased, adaptive approach" and would amount to a "stronger, swifter and smarter" defense for Washington and its allies. This would involve a series of more flexible deployments in four phases up till 2020, beginning with deployments aboard ships, and moving on to land-based deployments.[51]

A Russian spokesman described the move as "obviously a positive sign for us." Needless to say, both the Czech and Polish governments expressed disappointment that, after all of the political capital they had expended selling the idea of deployments to their own populations, Washington had apparently abandoned the idea in face of Russian pressure. Republicans joined the chorus of criticism.[52] Although the White House vigorously denied this, it was hard not to conclude that the Central European deployments were subordinated to the U.S.-Russian reset. Nevertheless, many NATO countries welcomed the move, as did the NATO secretary-general. German Chancellor Merkel saw the decision as a chance for "intensified cooperation with Moscow on international issues."[53]

The next move was to broaden the plan to include NATO and then pursue a cooperative Missile Defense program by negotiating with Russia through the NATO-Russia Council mechanism as well as through the bilateral U.S.-Russia negotiations. The U.S. side pressed hard to come to an agreement, despite recurrent Russian objections. According to Ivo Daalder, U.S. ambassador to NATO, "the second half of 2010 was the most hopeful period" and there was optimism that an agreement was feasible.[54] In November 2010, Medvedev attended the Lisbon NATO summit for a NATO-Russian Council meeting, the third since its founding in 2002 and the first since the Russia-Georgia War. The council agreed to undertake a joint ballistic missile defense threat assessment and to resume theater missile defense cooperation.[55]

Although the Obama administration's phased adaptive approach had somewhat assuaged Russian concerns about U.S. deployments in Central Europe, the new plan allowed for stationing more advanced interceptor missiles in Poland as early as 2018 should Iran's missile capabilities continue to improve. Russia was most concerned with phases 3 and especially 4 of the new U.S. plans, which some officials saw as a potential threat to Russia's own nuclear deterrent.[56] There were inconclusive discussions about how to create a joint Russian-NATO system. Increasingly, Russian officials from Foreign Minister Lavrov to the confrontational NATO ambassador Dimity Rogozin took up the refrain of the past twenty years: missile defense was not really aimed at Iran or North Korea. The true target, they said, was Russia. The phased adaptive approach did not address the question of U.S. intentions, only its capabilities. And, they claimed, if the system continued to grow more robust, it could one day threaten Russia's deterrent. Moscow demanded legally binding guarantees from Washington that the system would not threaten the Russian deterrent. However, the U.S. side explained that congressionally approved legally binding guarantees were impossible.

During the November 2011 Valdai Club meeting, Putin reiterated what had become Russia's central message: "we believe," he said, "that the establishment of a missile defense system represents a danger to Russia." "Don't threaten us," he warned, adding that Russia would deploy its own system to counter the U.S. system if need be. Putin quoted Rogozin, who claimed that key Republican senators in the spring of 2011 had told him that missile defense was indeed aimed at Russia, adding, "The ball is in your court. Will you change?" In a curious coda, Putin remarked that the United States and the Soviet Union had successfully "shared" data on nuclear technology in the 1940s and that this could be a model for future cooperation. Needless to say, Americans were puzzled by the use of the word "share" for the espionage activities of Julius Rosenberg and his colleagues, who passed U.S. nuclear secrets to the USSR.[57]

In late November 2011, Medvedev announced that the yearlong negotiations on cooperative missile defense were over. Moscow had not been able to secure written guarantees that the system would not be used against Russia. He repeated the threat to deploy Iskander missiles in Kaliningrad that he had made the day after Obama's election—he also warned that Russia might withdraw from the New START treaty and rescind its cooperation on Afghanistan. He held out the possibility for more negotiations if the United States were willing to take Russia's "legitimate security interests" into account.[58] Former U.S. chairman of the Joint Chiefs of Staff Admiral Michael Mullen attributes these reactions to Russian officials' fear that Missile Defense will ultimately threaten their strategic forces, which is their last guarantee for them to remain a major power.[59]

The U.S. side stressed its interest in continuing to negotiate a cooperative missile defense agreement, but it appeared that this part of the reset had failed. According to former national security advisor Stephen Hadley, "The outlines for a deal are there. The ways to cooperate have been clear for twenty years. Bush 41, Clinton, Bush 43, and Obama have all tried. But you can't overcome the politics."[60] Putin confirmed this in his remarks after his meeting with Obama at the June 2012 G-20 summit in Mexico: "I think the problem of the missile shield will not be solved regardless of whether Obama is re-elected or not."[61] Deputy Foreign Minister Sergei Ryabkov sounded a sober note: "We hope that problems in the area of missile defense will not reach the scale when a rollback, a deep cooling, not to say an ice age, begins in our relations."[62]

In a curious coda to the MD stalemate, President Obama was caught on an open microphone at the March 2012 Seoul nuclear summit a few weeks after Putin's reelection confiding to outgoing President Medvedev his future plans for missile defense: "After my election I will have more flexibility." Medvedev responded in English: "I understand. I will transmit this information to Vladimir."[63] Needless to say, this evoked caustic comments from Obama's challenger in the 2012 election, Governor Mitt Romney.

In March 2013, Defense Secretary Chuck Hagel announced that the Obama administration had decided to abandon phase four of the missile defense program, which entailed deploying land-based interceptors in Poland and Romania. The reason given was that the danger of a possible missile launch from North Korea had grown, and thus more interceptors needed to be deployed in Alaska.[64] The Russians had objected to phases three and four of the 2010 plan, but they greeted the news with restraint. Deputy Foreign Minister Ryabkov said he felt "no euphoria."[65]

Afghanistan

In contrast to the missile defense impasse, the United States engaged Russia much more productively on two security priorities: Afghanistan and Iran. For the Obama administration, winning the war in Afghanistan and withdrawing as soon as was possible was both a campaign promise in 2008 and a top policy focus once in office. Russia could play a key role facilitating or hindering that goal. Although Putin had thrown Russia's support behind the initial phase of the Bush administration's Afghan campaign, the Kremlin's attitude toward the war remained ambivalent the longer it went on. On the one hand, Russia feared the impact on its neighborhood's stability if NATO withdrew before Afghanistan was able to govern itself and fend off Islamic extremism. On the other hand, the longer the United States retained its military presence in Central Asia, the more difficult it was for Moscow to consolidate its "sphere of privileged interests" there. Moreover, a U.S. failure in Afghanistan would provide some *Schadenfreude* for a country still suffering the fall-out from its own Afghan loss that had precipitated the collapse of the USSR. Thus, the desire to cooperate with NATO was tempered by the impulse to contain Western influence in Central Asia.[66] Nevertheless, the Kremlin's ambivalence began to recede as the situation on the ground deteriorated, increasing the prospect of renewed insurgency and Islamic extremism on its borders. The USSR had stayed in Afghanistan for ten years, and Donald Rumsfeld had predicted the United States would be there for no more than ten weeks. Now America had ended up fighting in Afghanistan longer than had the Soviet Union.

The Obama administration announced a troop surge shortly after it came into office, eventually sending an extra 50,000 troops to Afghanistan. However, it faced a daunting logistical challenge as it contemplated how to transport the troops and materiel to land-locked Afghanistan, which is flanked by hostile or wary neighbors. Until 2009 most of the equipment and fuel was transported from the port of Karachi in Pakistan through the Khyber Pass and inhospitable terrain into eastern Afghanistan. However, this was not far from an area of intense insurgent activity in Pakistan, and attacks on and theft of supplies increased as the war went on. In early 2009, NATO opened the Northern Distribution Network to provide alternative routes from Europe across Central Asia into Afghanistan from the north. These were commercially based logistical arrangements for road, rail, and air connecting Baltic and Caspian ports with Afghanistan via Russia, Central Asia, and the Caucasus. There was a rail route from the Latvian port of Riga through Russia and Kazakhstan carrying nonlethal material, and an air transit route for lethal material over Russian air space was established.

At the July 2009 Moscow summit, Obama and Medvedev signed an agreement for the transportation of lethal and nonlethal goods. America needed more reliable supply routes for Afghanistan. The implementation of the agreement was painfully slow, with fewer than twenty flights completed by the end of 2009, owing to politically motivated foot-dragging on the part of the Russian bureaucracy, reflecting the continuing ambivalence about the U.S. role in Afghanistan.[67] However, as the situation in Pakistan deteriorated, Russian ambivalence appeared to diminish. By the end of 2012, more than 70,000 containers of supplies had crossed over Russian territory.[68] As the timetable for U.S. withdrawal in 2014 was announced, it became clear that the NDN would also be used to transport supplies back to the United States and Europe.

U. S.-Russian cooperation on Afghanistan extended to joint efforts to counter the heroin trade. The Russian side complained that Afghan heroin production and drug use in Russia had greatly increased since the war began, and there were some successful joint operations that destroyed heroin production and interdicted drug flows. Likewise, although counterterrorist intelligence cooperation was sporadic, it continued. The Pentagon also signed a contract with Rosoboronexport to purchase 21 Mi-17 helicopters for use in Afghanistan.[69] By the end of the first term of Obama administration, U.S.-Russian cooperation in Afghanistan was the most important reset achievement after New START. U.S.-Pakistani relations—fragile at the best of times—deteriorated severely after the 2011 killing of Osama Bin Laden by U.S. Navy SEALS on Pakistani soil. As Chairman of the Joint Chiefs of Staff Admiral Mike Mullen said in his valedictory testimony to the Senate armed Services Committee, parts of Pakistan's intelligence services supported the Taliban and had aided and abetted insurgent attacks on U.S. targets.[70] The less reliable an ally Pakistan became, the more important was Russia's role in facilitating the Afghan campaign.

In an ironic reversal of Cold War stereotypes, Russia agreed to the establishment of a NATO transit hub to transport material out of Afghanistan in Ulyanovsk, which happened to be the birthplace of Vladimir Ilyich Lenin. While communists in Ulyanovsk staged demonstrations with the Soviet-sounding slogan "NATO—Hands off

Russia!" former ambassador to NATO and frequent U.S. critic Dmitry Rogozin countered that the transit hub would bring billions of rubles and employment opportunities to the city. Indeed, as the year 2014 approached, Russia became increasingly concerned about a possible U.S. withdrawal. At a Valdai Club meeting Putin had said that there should be "no artificial timetable" for a U.S. withdrawal and Russia and the United States should continue to cooperate there. In a speech in Ulyanovsk opening the transit hub in 2013, Putin reiterated that NATO was "a throwback to the past, to the times of the Cold War," but added, "We need to help them."[71]

Iran

When he came into office, Obama promised that he would try to engage Iran in a dialogue, instead of isolating it as had the Bush administration. He placed this in the broader context of a new U.S. outreach to the Islamic world. In June 2009 he gave what was meant to be a landmark speech at Cairo University in which he said, "I come to Cairo to seek a new beginning between the United States and the Muslim world."[72] Russian commentators responded favorably to these moves, stressing that it was important to talk to the Iranians. However, that same month, Iran held presidential elections and in the aftermath, protestors challenging the election results were violently crushed. Washington criticized Iranian government actions against the population. If there had been a hope for a dual-track Iranian diplomacy, it petered out quickly. The White House had to focus on the major problem in U.S.-Iranian relations—Iran's nuclear program. As in the case of Afghanistan, Iran was an issue on which Russia could obstruct vital U.S. and European national security interests, or it could facilitate American goals. The reset policy aimed to secure Russian support for measures to limit Iran's nuclear program and reduce its ambivalence about how to deal with Tehran.

During Medvedev's term in the Kremlin, Russia took measures to increase cooperation with the United States in reining in Iran's nuclear program. The decisive moment came in September 2009 when Obama's national security advisor General James Jones showed Sergei Prikhodko, Medvedev's national security advisor, satellite imagery of a secret underground uranium enrichment facility in Qom. The Russian shook his head, saying, "This is bad, really bad."[73] At the G-20 summit in Pittsburgh two days later, Obama discussed with Medvedev the facility at Qom—which Russian intelligence had apparently failed to pick up. This influenced Medvedev's views on sanctions. In October 2009 he modified Russian policy, saying that "in some cases, sanctions are unavoidable," even though he pronounced himself against sanctions in general.[74]

For the next few months, Washington engaged Moscow in a series of intense discussions to win the Kremlin over to a new round of sanctions. At the April 2010 Prague summit where New START was signed, Obama and Medvedev spent the bulk of their time discussing Iran and sanctions. In June 2010, Russia joined other P-5 countries in voting for UNSC Resolution 1929, the fourth major sanctions legislation that the UN had passed. It imposed a new, broad-based set of sanctions on Iran, including tougher financial controls and an expanded arms embargo.[75] Equally important for the White House was Moscow's cancellation of its $ 800 million contract to sell S-300 air defense systems to Tehran.[76] These air defense systems were of particular concern to both Washington and Tel Aviv, and Iran accused Russia of capitulating to American and Israeli pressure. Medvedev may have agreed to the cancellation because he wanted to press on with the reset; but it is also likely that Russia itself was becoming more concerned about Iran's nuclear program.

Yet Russia's attitude toward Iran remained ambivalent. Officials continued to insist that Iran had the right to a peaceful nuclear program and reiterated that there was no proof that Iran was on the way to acquiring a nuclear weapons capability. Meanwhile, the Bushehr nuclear power plant was completed in 2010, after many delays, and became operational in 2011.[77] Moreover, when the IAEA released a report in November 2011 claiming that Iran was working in a new facility in which it was designing an atomic bomb, Russia said the report contained no new evidence and said that further sanctions advocated by the United States and its European partners would be counterproductive.[78] Media close to the government accused the United States of fabricating evidence about Iran's program and warned of the dangers of an Israeli or American attack on Iran's nuclear facilities.[79] Putin, in his 2012 preelection article on foreign policy, said that a military attack would have "disastrous" consequences.[80] As the situation with Iran became more contentious, with discussions about Iran closing the straits of Hormuz and possible Western retaliation, Moscow sought to maintain its relationship with Tehran. The Obama administration, like the Bush administration, found out that there were limits to how far Russia would distance itself from one of its few remaining partners in the Middle East.

The Obama team realized that, although the United States and Russia were able to agree on a number of key issues during the reset, disagreements on other issues remained. This became even more apparent as the 2012 Russian presidential election approached.

Chapter Ten

From Berlin to Damascus:
Disagreements Old and New

THE FORMER SOVIET SPACE

The Obama administration came into office determined that U.S. relations with Russia's neighbors not undermine the U.S.-Russian reset. Whereas the Bush administration had elevated Ukraine's and Georgia's integration into Euro-Atlantic structures into a policy priority, the Obama White House took a different tack. It approached the post-Soviet space by taking into account Russian concerns, while insisting that this was no longer a zero-sum game. Developments on the ground also ensured that the post-Soviet space ceased to be a major problem in U.S.-Russian relations, although fundamental differences of interest remained. Bureaucratic obstacles to a coordinated American policy also continued to complicate decisions, as they had during the Bush years. NSC senior director for Russia Michael McFaul had responsibility for all of the former Soviet space during the election campaign but, once in the White House, was given responsibility for Russia only, with the Western NIS and Caucasus going to the senior director for Europe and with Central Asia going to the South Asia senior director. In 2009 McFaul succeed in reincorporating Central Asia into his portfolio, but these bureaucratic divisions complicated the creation of a holistic policy toward Russia and its neighbors.

Events in Kyiv largely removed Ukraine as a U.S.-Russian issue. In the presidential election of February 2010, Viktor Yanukovych—rejected by the population during the Orange Revolution in 2004—defeated his opponent and Orange Revolution victor, former prime minister Yulia Tymoshenko. Despite years of American and European efforts to promote democracy and rule of law in Ukraine, the Orange Revolution was dead, a victim of the constant infighting between former president Yushchenko and Tymoshenko and of unabated corruption at the top that alienated much of the original Orange forces and led to widespread popular disillusionment. Said one Ukrainian observer, "People want democracy, but they also want a strong leader who will provide for them."[1] Ironically, Ukraine in 2010 was one of the more democratic countries in Eurasia because it was impossible to predict the outcome of the election. Western observers declared it by and large free and fair, leaving Washington and Brussels no choice but to accept the outcome and hope that Yanukovych would chose a path of Western integration. He did not.

Two months after his election, Yanukovych renewed the Russian lease on the Black Sea fleet, allowing the Russian navy to remain in the Crimea until 2042. He also declared that Ukraine would remain a neutral country and was not interested in NATO membership. He jailed Tymoshenko, initially on charges that the 2009 gas agreement that she signed with Russia forced Ukraine to pay too high a price for gas. Although he continued to insist that he favored a Deep Free Trade and an Association Agreement with the EU, the jailing of Tymoshenko created a major obstacle to closer ties with Brussels. U.S.-Ukrainian relations were adversely affected by the domestic crackdown on Yanukovych's opponents. Indeed, U.S. officials complained of Washington's "Ukraine fatigue" as Kyiv resisted calls for great transparency and rule of law. But with the NATO issue off the table, U.S. policy toward Ukraine no longer aroused Russia ire.

If Ukraine receded as a contentious U.S.-Russia issue, events in Kyrgyzstan provided an unanticipated venue for U.S.-Russian cooperation. When the Obama administration first took office, President Bakiyev began a bidding war with Russia and the United States for basing rights. After the 2005 loss of the K-2 base in Uzbekistan, the U.S. military base at Manas had become the main transit hub for U.S. troops going to Afghanistan, and fifteen thousand troops, planes, and five hundred tons of cargo a month passed through the base. Moscow had been pressuring Bakiyev to eject the Americans, and, in February 2009 he announced the base closure. On the same day, Russia, which already had its own Kant base near Bishkek, offered a $2 billion loan to Kyrgyzstan. Nevertheless, the United States began to renegotiate its agreement with Bakiyev, and in June 2009 Kyrgyzstan reversed its decision after Washington agreed to triple the rent for the base, now called the Manas Transit Center. Moscow was clearly angry at what it saw as Bakiyev's betrayal.

A year later, the Kremlin had its revenge. Bakiyev was ousted in a popular uprising in April 2010, and some speculated that the Russians had a hand in his ouster.[2] His son was accused of directly profiting from the fuel contracts at Manas. Bakiyev fled to Belarus, and an interim government took over. However, ethnic clashes between Kyrgyz and Uzbeks broke out in the south, and, amid the growing violence, Washington and Moscow worked together to try to stabilize the situation. The United States proposed a joint peace-keeping force with Russia, but Moscow demurred. Nevertheless, the Obama administration viewed cooperation in the Kyrgyz crisis as a success of the reset.[3]

The reset did little to remove Georgia as an issue of contention between Washington and Moscow. However, among the "dogs that did not bark" were another Russia-Georgia war, which some had feared would break out.[4] Nevertheless, Russian officials continued to criticize the Obama administration for its support of Saakashvili. Both Putin and Medvedev excoriated the Georgian president in meetings with the Valdai Discussion Club, insinuating that he was mentally unstable. Russia also warned that any rearmament of Georgia would be viewed as a hostile act. This question—the extent to which the United States should resupply the Georgian army—became an issue both within the Obama administration and between Russia and the United States.

Georgia continued to send troops to fight in Iraq and Afghanistan. There were one thousand troops there in 2011, making Georgia the largest per capita troop contributor to the Afghan War. Pentagon officials argued that it was important both to maintain the military training program and to refurbish military equipment that Georgia had lost in the 2008 war. Other officials, focusing on the sensitivity of the issue for U.S.-Russian relations because of questions about how Georgia might use the equipment, were reluctant to support rearming Georgia. Moreover, Georgia and Russia accused each other of supporting separatist groups on each other's territory. The Obama administration urged restraint on both sides, while it refused to recognize South Ossetia and Abkhazia.

In October 2012, President Mikheil Saakashvili's party suffered an unexpected electoral defeat in parliamentary elections, leading to the appointment of opposition leader billionaire Bidzina Ivanishvili as prime minster. Ivanishvili, who had made his money in Moscow, pledged to improve relations with Russia, began to arrest and put on trial Saakashvili-connected officials, and accused the president of behaving "inadequately" during the 2008 war.[5] The United States reached out to Ivanishvili and observed with both interest and concern attempts to mend Georgian-Russian relations and moves to de-legitimize Saakashvili and the Rose Revolution. The Georgian situation was essentially a stalemate. It symbolized the larger issue of how to reconcile Russian and U.S. interests in the post-Soviet space, part of the broader question of how to improve Euro-Atlantic security architecture two decades after Cold War's end.

EURO-ATLANTIC SECURITY ARCHITECTURE

The United States and its allies were unable, despite the reset, to make any breakthrough on the larger issue confronting NATO, namely how to bridge the gap between Russian and Western perspectives on Euro-Atlantic security. The Russo-Georgia War had exposed the vulnerability of the states "in between," those countries in the common neighborhood of the EU and Russia but outside both NATO and EU structures. Two months before the war, President Medvedev had made his maiden foreign speech in Berlin, in which he declared that the current system was broken and the OSCE was unable to engage effectively in rejuvenating it. He called for a new, legally binding treaty on European security that would be signed by all the parties in the region.[6]

Medvedev offered his draft European Security Treaty in November 2009. It contained the typical elements of an international treaty—legally binding articles dealing with rules and decision-making processes.[7] At the same time, Lavrov offered the NRC a draft of a new treaty between NATO and Russia, which was quite similar to the Med-vedev Treaty.[8] The Western response ranged from lukewarm to hos-tile. From the U.S. point of view there was no need for another legally binding Euro-Atlantic super-treaty. The OSCE had already taken care of that. Several clauses in the proposed Medvedev treaty particularly worried NATO because they implied that NATO's commitment to col-lective defense should be superseded by an all-European commitment to collective defense. But how was one to define a threat or an attack? The Russians claimed that Georgia had attacked them. As the proposal stood, NATO countries could conceivably be called on to defend Rus-sia if it became engaged in military hostilities with a neighboring state. Moreover, the treaty would effectively limit NATO's ability to invoke Article 5 for its own members.

The Medvedev treaty was a nonstarter. As Secretary Clinton said in Paris in 2010, the United States shared Russia's goal of a more secure Europe, but "we believe that these goals are best pursued in the con-text of existing institutions such as the OSCE and the NATO-Russia Council rather than negotiating new treaties."[9] Nevertheless, the "old" European states had more at stake on this issue than did the United States. Washington viewed Moscow as less central to the resolution of global security problems than did Europe, for whom Russia was the key to guaranteeing stability in the region. Germany, France, and Italy viewed Russia as a primary security partner and were significantly more forward looking in engaging Russia on Euro-Atlantic security than were the United States or its Central European allies. As Theo Sommer, long-time editor of *Die Zeit* and respected German establishment figure put it:

> No-one in Germany would still consider Putin a "flawless demo-crat." But the demonstrations shaking Russia after the recent elec-tions show that there is great potential for change, albeit slow, in the right direction. Propagating a new Cold war—on the grounds that Putin transformed his country from a threadbare economy and fragile democracy into an autocratic state hostile to the Unit-ed States and Europe is not something Berlin will subscribe to.[10]

The United States and its allies responded by suggesting that the issue of Euro-Atlantic security be taken up in the OCSE, an organization with which Russia had increasingly become disenchanted because of its emphasis on human rights and electoral transparency. The OSCE in 2009 began discussing improving Euro-Atlantic security under the Greek presidency during a summit in Corfu, hence it became known as the Corfu Process, whose mission was to "review the state of play in European security and renovate our mechanisms to deal with traditional and new challenges."[11] The Russians continued to complain that the United States and its allies refused to respond seriously to their initiatives, and were dismissive of the Corfu Process.[12]

The NATO-Russia relationship experienced a modest improvement under the reset policy. Russia had broken off all contact with NATO after the Georgia War, but contacts resumed at the ministerial level at a NATO–Russia Council meeting in December in 2009.[13] Shortly thereafter, NATO secretary general Anders Fogh Rasmussen went to Moscow, the first such visit since the Russo-Georgia War. He met with both members of the tandem as well as other top officials. He announced that Russia was one of his top priorities, and he was committed to improving NATO-Russia ties. The issues of Georgia's territorial integrity and of possible further NATO enlargement also came up, and in his video blog, Rasmussen called his visit "a new beginning" despite some "disagreements and differences." Medvedev described the NATO-Russian relationship as moving to a "new level."[14]

A familiar pattern reemerged. NATO and Russia cooperated quite effectively on practical issues such as search and rescue, antipiracy, counternarcotics in Afghanistan, and counterterrorist exercises. But the differences between Russian and NATO views remained a fundamental obstacle to cooperation. After all, Russia's 2010 military doctrine named NATO the number one external danger to Russia, whereas NATO's new strategic concept talked about the desire for further cooperation and a "strong partnership" with Russia.[15] From Washington's point of view, the only way forward was to continue to engage Russia in the NRC format and try to overcome Moscow's antipathy toward the organization. But there were limits to how long the Obama administration would wait. In November 2011, it announced that the United States would cease honoring its obligations under the Conventional Forces in Europe Treaty with regards to Russia. After three years of trying to induce Russia to recommit to the CFE regime, the United States realized that Putin's 2007 decision to withdraw from the treaty was final. Reset had its limits.

SPIES AND LEAKS

The scene might have come from a new version of the 1950 Hollywood Cold War classic thriller *The Third Man*. An American and a Russian plane landed within minutes of each other at Vienna's Schwechat airport. They taxied down the runway to an isolated part of the tarmac where they parked nose to tail. Ten Russian "sleeper" agents who had operated in the United States for the previous decade and four Russians who had been jailed in Russia for spying for the United States descended from their respective aircrafts and quickly switched planes. Within minutes, the planes had taken off again—one to Washington via London and the other to Moscow.

The Russian agents were long-term plants who had studied in the United States and had blended into American suburban life, most of them assuming false identities. One New Jersey couple had complained to their Moscow control officer that they needed a larger house with a swimming pool to keep up with their neighbors. Anna Chapman, the glamorous Mata Hari of the group, exchanged surreptitious emails with her colleague from a Starbucks in New York. Mikhail Semenko worked in a small travel agency in Arlington, Virginia, and became an aggressive networker who managed to get on the invitee lists of major Washington, D.C., think tanks.[16] They joined Parent Teacher Associations at local schools. Their children lived the American dream. At least one of their children, a student at George Washington University, was being groomed as a next-generation spy.[17] They used old espionage techniques such as invisible ink and shortwave radio broadcasts and high-tech ones such as steganography, which involved inserting hidden messages on websites that only the sender and intended recipient could understand. It was less clear what useful secrets they sent back to Moscow that were not readily available from the websites of think tanks and elsewhere on the Internet. Perhaps, it was speculated, the SVR's intention was to plant them in the United States so that they could insinuate themselves into elite commercial and political circles that would give them access to people who might eventually rise to the top of the U.S. political system. The comic aspects of the spies' surreptitious lives tended to obscure the consistent efforts and considerable expenditures that the SVR expended to implant the sleeper agents.

Spying was not exactly a new phenomenon in U.S.-Russian ties; after all, it had been a perennial feature of the relationship. Powell's first act as secretary of state had been to expel fifty Russian intelligence agents. But, for Obama, the discovery of this spy ring came at an awkward time. Medvedev was due to visit the United States on June 24, 2010. On June 11, the FBI, which had been monitoring the agents for many years, informed the president that they wanted to move swiftly to arrest them. They feared that one or more of the spies suspected that they had been unmasked and would flee the United States before they could be apprehended. Obama was determined that the spy affair not derail the reset His idea was to engage Medvedev on his modernization plan by having him visit Silicon Valley and promoting the U.S.-Russian business relationship as a key to the enhancement of the reset. Given the imminence of President Medvedev's visit, the FBI held off making the arrests until after the Russian leader had left.[18] By then, the prisoner swap had already been arranged and Medvedev's visit had gone off without a hitch.[19] This was the largest U.S.-Russian spy swap in decades. National Security Advisor James Jones emphasizes that the spies "hadn't done any real damage."[20] Soon after the Russians returned, Vladimir Putin, the former KGB agent, met and sang patriotic songs with them and bestowed awards on them for their service to their country.[21]

The Medvedev visit was deemed a great success. But the juxtaposition of the cheeseburger summit and sleeper spies highlighted the contradictions in the reset and the inevitability of what could at best be a selective partnership.

U.S.-Russian relations were further tested by the WikiLeaks affair. In late November 2010, Julian Assange, founder of the WikiLeaks site, released thousands of classified cables from the U.S. Embassy in Moscow and from other U.S. embassies where Russian issues were discussed. The cables ranged from descriptions of an extravagant wedding in Dagestan at which Chechen strongman Ramzan Kadyrov wielded a golden pistol and threw $100 bills around to an assessment of the tandem: "Medvedev plays Robin to Putin's Batman." There were also discussions of Russia's slide toward autocracy and allegations of widespread and high-level corruption, including assessments from foreigners who told U.S. officials that Russia was a "virtual mafia state."[22] In an interview with CNN's Larry King, Putin commented on the Batman-Robin quote: "Statements of this kind are, of course, aimed at insulting one of us, at snagging our self-confidence, pushing us toward certain steps that would destroy our productive cooperation in running the country."[23] Nevertheless, despite the inflammatory nature of material in some of the leaked cables, WikiLeaks appeared not to have had a major impact on U.S.-Russian relations.[24]

SUBSTANCE VERSUS PROCESS

One of the key American goals in the reset was to increase the number of stakeholders in the U.S.-Russian relationship, creating a broader-based network of people in both countries who would develop a long-term interest in improved ties. The U.S.-Russia bilateral presidential commission was a means to that end. By the beginning of the second Obama term it consisted of the following long list of working groups: agriculture, arms control and international security, military technical cooperation, cyber security, business development and economic relations, civil society, counternarcotics, counterterrorism, defense relations, education, culture, sports and media, emergency situations, energy, environment, health, innovation, intelligence, military cooperation, nuclear energy and nuclear security, policy steering, rule of law, science and technology, and space cooperation.[25] The most controversial was the civil society group. Until 2011 it was cochaired by Michael McFaul, the president's senior advisor on Russia, and Vladislav Surkov, deputy head of the Presidential Administration. Critics in the United States and Russia pointed out that Surkov was the author of "sovereign democracy," the architect of managed elections, creator of the youth group *Nashi* that had harassed the British and Estonian ambassadors, and an opponent of autonomous civil society. Russians outside the government also complained about the closed selection process for those who were permitted to participate in its meetings. This highlighted a major asymmetry in a bilateral commission that involved a country with an independent civil society pursuing a dialogue with one in which the authorities discouraged civic activity that was not approved by the state. The Civil Society working group was disbanded at the end of 2012. Surkov, by then deputy prime minister, was fired in May 2013 ostensibly in connection with a corruption investigation into the Skolkovo innovation village project that had been partly launched during Medvedev's 2010 visit to Silicon Valley.[26]

The other groups were less controversial and there was a flurry of activity for all of them.[27] Groups dealing with energy and education, for instance, were able to make progress. Cultural groups were very active, and youth exchanges grew. A senior State Department official who had been involved in the Gore-Chernomyrdin Commission compared the Bilateral Presidential Commission favorably to its 1990s incarnation saying some groups work better than others, but that unexpected headway had been made even in the civil society groups. However, it would take a long time to measure how successful the bilateral commission had been in creating a larger group of stakeholders. Even if measurable outcomes were elusive, one could make the argument that the process itself was important. Given the limited number of venues for U.S.-Russian interaction and the continuing mutual suspicion on both sides, an ongoing endeavor that involved hundreds of people could one day become the nucleus of a broader platform for something more extensive.

THE END OF THE TANDEM: PUTIN RETURNS TO THE KREMLIN

On September 24, 2011, ending months of speculation, Dmitry Medvedev strode up to the podium at the Congress of the United Russia party to make a startling—but not totally unexpected— announcement: "I think it's right that the party congress support the candidacy of the head of the government, Vladimir Putin, in the role of the country's president."[28] To loud applause, Putin accepted, adding that he and Medvedev had years ago agreed that they would reverse roles.[29] The tandem was to all intents and purposes over, and then fifty-nine-year-old Putin could theoretically stay in power for two more terms—until 2024.

But 2011 was not 2007, and in the four years since the tandem was first announced, the Medvedev presidency had opened up greater political space in Russian society. A younger, more affluent, urban Internet generation was no longer willing to accept the previous social compact involving exchanging material well-being for political quiesence. The blogosphere went into overdrive comparing Putin to Brezhnev in his dotage and announcing that Russians wanted a voice in their political system and real choices. A significant segment of the increasingly educated middle class felt insulted by what they termed the castling move (a chess move involving the king and a rook changing places). Following the December 4 Duma elections in which widespread fraud was reported by independent monitoring groups, a large crowd—estimates ran from 30,000 to 100,000—gathered peacefully in Bolotnaya Square in the bitter cold demanding that Putin go. They wore white ribbons. Putin's response was to mock them, saying that the white ribbons reminded him of condoms.[30] White or not, he was determined that this not evolve into another color revolution. The protests continued after the presidential election on March 4, 2012, when Putin was declared the winner and into 2013, albeit in dwindling numbers.

Before his 2012 reelection Putin published a series of articles outlining his vision for the future. In one of them he essentially declared mission accomplished, stressing how he had brought Russia back from the brink of chaos: "We restored basic state governance. We had to restore the authority and power of the state itself. [We] helped deliver Russia from the blind alley of a civil war."[31] He views himself as a leader who embodies the Russian tradition of *derzhavnost'*, the belief that Russia is destined to be a strong state and a great power.[32] His message to protestors and to the outside world was that he had saved Russia from the abyss.

The mobilization of the urban elites and the rise of an active opposition had a direct impact on U.S.-Russian relations and made it more difficult to continue the reset. After Putin's initial shock at the protests, he recouped and immediately began to tie the protests to nefarious foreign influences, particularly the United States—"they want to show us that they can rock the boat." The demonization of America appealed to an important segment of Putin's base—the provincial working class—although it evoked ridicule among the urban opposition. Because

Secretary Clinton had criticized the vote fraud, she came in for special invective. Putin accused her of paying protestors to go into the streets, which she vigorously denied.[33] When the new U.S. ambassador (and former NSC senior director) Michael McFaul—the first U.S. ambassador to Russia to engage in active tweeting—arrived in February 2012, he was initially subject to relentless criticism.[34]

Putin articulated his ideas about the United States more systematically in a lengthy article on foreign policy that he published during the election campaign. "Russia and the Changing World" was vintage Putin, resonating with his 2007 Munich speech. He accused the Americans of being "obsessed with the idea of ensuring their absolute invulnerability." But according to Putin, "Absolute invulnerability for one means absolute vulnerability for all the others." He repeated all his arguments against unilateralism, NATO enlargement, and disregard for the United Nations.[35] Nevertheless, he held out the possibility for improved relations if Washington could rid itself of its Cold War stereotypes.

Putin had returned to the Kremlin, but with more uncertainty surrounding the future of the system he had created. Obama had based the reset on his relationship with Medvedev. Several senior U.S. officials admitted that the September 24 "castling" maneuver had come as a disappointment to the White House. What would the new Putin presidency bring for U.S.-Russian relations? The initial clues were not encouraging. The first Obama-Putin meeting since July 2009 had been scheduled to take place before the G-8 summit at Camp David. At the last moment, Putin apparently decided that he did not want his first foreign trip as president to be to the United States. He announced that he was not coming and dispatched Medvedev instead. The official reason was that Putin had to work on forming his new cabinet, but many believed it was a deliberate snub.

The Putin-Obama meeting on the sidelines of the G-20 summit in Los Cabos Mexico a few weeks later was difficult. The presidents could barely muster a smile for the assembled reporters. Michael McFaul tried to give it a positive spin: "I thought the chemistry was very businesslike and cordial." Then he commented on Putin's dour demeanor: "That's the way he looks, that's the way he acts."[36] The issue that prompted the frosty smiles and was to dominate U.S.-Russian relations after Obama's reelection was the upheaval in the Arab world and specifically the civil war in Syria.

THE UNITED STATES, RUSSIA, AND THE ARAB SPRING

The ferment that began to engulf the Arab world early in 2011 in many ways represented the Freedom Agenda redux, albeit in a different setting—the Middle East as opposed to the Near Abroad. As the United States supported popular uprisings against autocratic Middle Eastern regimes—some of which it had resoltuely backed for decades—Russia, once again, became increasingly unsettled by Washington's advocacy of regime change. The Arab uprisings highlighted the ideological and philosophical gap between the United States and Russia. The United States and its allies emphasized the primacy of two core principles, informed by the bitter lessons of the Balkan conflicts in the 1990s: the responsibility to protect and humanitarian intervention. Russia, by contrast, embraced a classical nineteenth-century worldview, stressing the primacy of absolute sovereignty and noninterference in the affairs of other states.

Moreover, evoking the example of an Iraq that remained plagued by violence and instability, Moscow was skeptical about how these uprisings would end. It feared the unintended consequences of regime change in the Middle East. Given Russia's proximity to the Arab world and its own Muslim population that was becoming more religious and reproducing much faster than the Slavic population, the underlying fear of contagion from Islamist movements was understandable.[37] The United States, by contrast, was far away, had a Muslim population that was by and large well-integrated into society, and realized that it would have to work with these movements when they came to power.

The revolts in the Arab world began in December 2010 with a Tunisian fruit seller immolating himself to protest against police harassment then spread in 2011 to Egypt, Libya, Syria, and other countries in the region. The cascading upheaval caught most of the world by surprise. The Obama administration hesitated before abandoning its longtime ally Hosni Mubarak in Egypt, but it eventually came down on the side of populations demanding the ouster of dictators and the introduction of greater democracy. The Arab spring introduced the specter of instability and Islamist rule in the region, but the West decided that it could no longer continue basing its policies on the predictability of unpopular authoritarian leaders.

Moscow's reaction was entirely different. Russia had productive ties with the region's rulers and feared that ousting these leaders would usher in instability and Islamist fundamentalism that could threaten Russia and its neighbors. Some officials saw the hand of the United States and its special services in the Egyptian revolution, apparently not persuaded by the fact that Mubarak had for decades been a close ally and the recipient of billions of dollars of U.S. aid. But the Arab spring also had implications for Russia's domestic situation. As opponents of the tandem argued and countless Russian bloggers pointed out, what happened in Tahrir Square could also happen in Red Square.

The Obama administration's first issue with Russia came after the Libyan uprising against Muammar Qaddafi began. NATO and some Arab nations agreed to impose a no-fly zone in Libya to assist the rebels, and Washington wanted this to go through UN channels to legitimize the action. Russia had a considerable economic stake in Libya. After forgiving Tripoli's Soviet-era $4.5 billion debt in April 2008, Russian firms signed lucrative oil and construction deals, amounting to $10 billion, and arms sales remained an important part of the relationship. Moscow had traditionally been reluctant to engage in punitive actions in that part of the world for fear of jeopardizing its remaining post-Soviet political and economic influence. However, after listening to Vice President Biden's arguments about the importance of supporting the rebels, Medvedev agreed that Russia would abstain from—rather than veto—United Nations Resolution 1973, which authorized the use of air power to impose a no-fly zone. There has been considerable speculation about whether the tandem disagreed on this policy. Some American officials believe that Medvedev did not fully comprehend what a no-fly zone meant. Others believe that Medvedev's decision to abstain influenced Putin's decision to return to the presidency. Putin described the UN resolution as a "mediaeval call for a crusade, when someone would call someone to go to a particular place and liberate something" and consistently criticized NATO's actions.[38] Indeed, a month after the resolution, Lavrov claimed that NATO had overstepped its mission in Libya.[39] Qaddafi's bloody death was heavily criticized by most Russian officials, and Vladimir Putin called the Libyan dictator's end—he was shot as he emerged from hiding in a drainage pipe—"barbaric." Russia's halfhearted support of the Libyan campaign and its reluctance to recognize the new government left its position in Libya considerably diminished after the end of the war.[40]

Syria was a much more contentious issue than Libya. The long drawn-out uprising against Syria's Bashar Al'Assad which began in March 2011 confronted Russia with the prospect that its last ally in the Arab world—and the major source of its influence in the region—might too be removed with the help of NATO. Russia's one remaining foreign naval base (and only warm-water port) was in the Syrian town of Tartus, although it was by all accounts not that significant and in a state of disrepair.[41] Syria is one of the top five foreign buyers of Russian defense equipment.[42] Russian companies also have around $20 billion invested in Syria, primarily in natural gas extraction. Indeed, as the international community prepared to impose tough sanctions on Syria, Russia sent an aircraft carrier to Tartus and announced the sale of YAK-30 fighter jets to Syria.[43] It continued to supply Syria with a variety of sophisticated military hardware as the conflict raged on.

Russia refused to cooperate on any action against its last remaining ally in the region. It vetoed a UNSC resolution that called for Assad to step aside, describing it as "unbalanced."[44] It consistently blocked UN action—supported by most Arab states and Turkey—that could have helped the opposition forces.[45] Its banks helped Syria evade financial sanctions. When former UN secretary-general Kofi Annan resigned his position as special envoy for Syria, he blamed Russia for obstructing action to halt the carnage.[46] His successor Lakhdar Brahimi also resigned for similar reasons. There was increasing pressure from both the West and regional powers such as Turkey to undertake a UN-sanctioned intervention in Syria to respond to the use of chemical weapons and halt the killing of tens of thousands of people.

As Putin told the Valdai group, the West should be careful about what it wished for. His warnings were consistent with the Russian position going back to the run-up to the Iraq War a decade earlier. The Arab uprisings (he, like all other Russian officials, did not use the word "spring") could well lead to the rise of Islamist parties with radical agendas. Indeed, Russia feared the spread of radical Sunni Islamist governments that would destabilize the region and appeal to restive Muslims in the north Caucasus. The Assad regime, in its view, was a bulwark against the radical Islamist threat. While the United States and its European allies worked hard to craft a UN, resolution that was acceptable to Moscow, Russia called instead for dialogue between the government and protestors.

After Obama's reelection in November 2012, U.S.-Russian tensions over Syria (as well as the Magnitsky bill and its aftermath) increased. For a few months Putin was unavailable to meet with any American official. Finally, having received the message that Russia was willing to reengage, National Security Advisor Thomas Donilon traveled to Moscow in April 2013 bearing a letter from Obama to Putin outlining an agenda and two planned presidential meetings for the year.[47] Secretary of State John Kerry, who had been chairman of the Senate Foreign Relations Committee, by all accounts enjoyed a more cordial relationship with Lavrov than his two predecessors. He traveled to Moscow in May amid evidence that chemical weapons had been used in Syria.[48] He and Lavrov announced that they would coconvene an international conference on Syria designed to bring all the warring factions to the table and reach a negotiated settlement.[49] It was unclear whether these efforts would succeed or indeed whether Russian and American views of how best to handle the Syrian crisis could become more closely aligned. Russia continued to believe that the United Nations Security Council should not be in the business of regime change.[50] Putin pointedly summarized his views on Syria during a marathon press conference: "Undoubtedly change is needed. We are worried about something else: what happens next."[51]

THE RESET IN PERSPECTIVE

By the time of the November 2012 U.S. election, the fourth U.S.-Russian reset had already run its course. Bill Clinton had believed that, with a new Kremlin leader, it would be possible to create a qualitatively new U.S.-Russian relationship. George W. Bush initially believed the same of Vladimir Putin. Barack Obama's reset had been based on the presumption that, with two younger, post-Cold War leaders, Russia and the United States might be able to reframe their relationship. All three U.S. presidents initially saw something in their Russian counterpart that gave them hope. By the time their first terms ended, however, the U.S.-Russian relationship was in trouble. In Clinton's and Bush's case, bilateral ties deteriorated further during their second terms. The Obama reset began to falter when Putin announced his decision to return to the Kremlin and was over by the summer of 2013.

When Obama first entered the White House, it was still possible to believe that the tandem might evolve in a direction that enabled Medvedev to become the de facto as well as the de jure president. The Obama administration had come into office believing that improving the U.S.-Russian relationship could help to "empower" Medvedev. The two presidents had worked on the most difficult issues in the bilateral relationship together; but the reality was that Putin had continued to run Russia throughout the Medvedev interlude. The assumption in the White House was that Medvedev could not have taken any major decisions without Putin's assent. Thus, Putin had bought into the reset. The accents were different—Medvedev was, on the whole, more positive about relations with the United States than was Putin, and occasionally, as with the UN vote on Libya, the two men seemed to have disagreed—but there was consensus on support for better U.S.-Russian relations. Nevertheless, the September 24, 2011 announcement of the tandem job switch, the toughening of rhetoric during the Duma and presidential election campaigns, and Putin's actions once he was back in the Kremlin raised questions about the durability of the reset. The concrete accomplishments—New START, cooperation on Afghanistan and Iran, and Russia's WTO membership—would remain. But would there be a reset 2.0? How dependent would it be on personal dynamics?

The White House had assumed, that, because Medvedev could not have taken any major actions without Putin's approval, there would be continuity in Russian policy once Putin returned to the Kremlin. Indeed, senior officials explicitly conveyed this hope to their Russian colleagues. Once it became clear that this was not to be the case, they struggled to understand the sources of discontinuity in the Kremlin's America policy.

Putin's policy toward the United States appeared to be increasingly tied up with domestic political developments in both countries. U.S.-Russian relations further deteriorated in late 2012 when both Houses of Congress adopted legislation designed to punish Russian officials and businesses involved in human rights abuses. The Justice for Sergei Magnitsky Act was adopted as a response to the death in a Russian prison of thirty-seven-year-old lawyer Sergei Magnitsky, who had uncovered large-scale embezzlement on the part of Russian law enforcement and tax collection officials. It was alleged that he had been denied medical care and tortured, and yet no one was brought to justice.[52] Indeed, the authorities put him on trial posthumously.

In December 2012, despite the White House's reservations about the impact that this legislation might have, President Obama signed into law the Sergei Magnitsky Accountability and Rule of Law Act. It specifies that individuals connected to Magnitsky's death should be placed on a visa ban list and their assets in the United States should be frozen. It also leaves open the possibility for other individuals deemed guilty of "extrajudicial killings, torture, or other gross violations of human rights" to be added to the list.[53]

The Russians argued hard against the Magnitsky bill and threatened retaliation with their own lists. Russian ambassador to the United States Sergei Kislyak wrote of the Magnitsky Act that "unwillingness to show respect, to hear arguments, to work on building normal relations is of course frustrating. Our two countries deserve better."[54] When the bill came into law, Putin said, "This is very bad. This, of course, poisons our relations with the United States."[55]

The subsequent Russian reaction to the Magnitsky bill surprised American officials. The Duma passed the Dima Yakovlev Law, named after a Russian child who had died in the custody of his adoptive American parents. This legislation banned all future adoptions by Americans of Russian children.[56] Americans had adopted 60,000 Russian children prior to this ban. Moreover, the Kremlin announced that it had its own blacklist of U.S. officials guilty of violating human rights who could not enter Russia and began denying visas to them.[57] In a highly unusual move, Russia also expelled a diplomat whom they accused of being a spy and showed his arrest on TV, including his supposed blond wig.[58]

In the aftermath of the demonstrations against him and the fact that Moscow and some other urban areas had apparently not reelected him (he won the presidential election because of his support among the provincial working class), Putin apparently decided to use anti-Americanism to appeal to his base and reassert political control. After his reelection, Russia encated a series of measures clamping down on civil society, the opposition, and their foreign supporters. Any Russian NGO that received foreign funding was required to register as a "foreign agent," a term that carried sinister connotations from the Soviet era. This law was so broad in scope that it jeopardized funding for established NGOs such as the Moscow Helsinki Group and the internationally acclaimed human rights group Memorial.[59] As a result, the National Democratic Institute and the International Republican Institute moved their operations to the Baltic states. Russia canceled its agreement on law enforcement and counternarcotics cooperation with the United States.[60] It ordered the closure of the United States Agency for International Development (UDSAID),- which had operated for more than two decades and given Russia a total of $2.6 billion in assistance.[61] It passed laws restricting Internet freedom in the name of "combating extermism," recriminalized slander, and imposed high fines for participation in illegal protests. It passed a controversial law outlawing "homosexual propaganda." And it broadened the defintion of treason to encompass providing asssistance to foreign organizations.[62]

Russia also announced that it was not interested in renewing the Nunn-Lugar Cooperative Threat Reduction legislation, a cornerstone of U.S.-Russian relations for the previous twenty years. Claiming that the agreement reflected an unequal relationship that dated back to the early 1990s, it subsequently agreed to begin talks on a follow-on agreement where Russia would have a different role. The Obama administration was committed to securing a new agreement whereby Russia and the United States would work together on nonproliferation issues in third countries.[63]

The 2013 Russian Foreign Policy Concept reflected Russia's priorities. Arguing that the West was becoming weaker and was destabilizing the international system, it highlighted Russia's unique role in a multipolar world. Stressing that its top foreign policy priority was the CIS and the creation of a Eurasian Economic Union of former Soviet states, it advocated building a "solid economic foundation" for Russian-American relations.[64] In a speech to senior Defense Ministry staff, Putin accused the United States of undermining the strategic balance of forces through its missile defense programs and further NATO enlargement and argued for a new Russian military buildup.[65]

Rhetorical invective against the United States was on the rise. In addition to stifling civil society and closing down foreign democracy-building efforts that went back to the collapse of the Soviet Union, Putin was determined to show that Russia, as a fully sovereign state whose economy was performing better than many countries, no longer needed any American financial assistance.

The Obama administration responded to these developments in a low-key manner. During the presidential election campaign, Russia had played only a minor part. Republican candidate Mitt Romney's campaign—in a surprising and anachronistic salvo—faulted Obama for treating the Kremlin with kid gloves when Russia was, according to Romney, the United States "number one geopolitical foe," because it "fights every cause for the world's worst actors."[66] During the year preceding the election, the Obama administration had become more vocal about the Russian government's clampdown on opposition protests because critics from the right and left accused it of ignoring Putin's repression of civil society. But it reacted to Russian rhetorical provocations after the U.S. election with restraint. The consensus was that the United States could have little impact on what the Putin administration did at home and Washington had important international business that it had to conduct with Russia.

After Obama's reelection, the chief task was maintain the post-reset status quo, especially vis-à-vis Afghanistan and Iran, and to secure a more cooperative Russian stance on Syria. The United States would continue to seek a missile defense deal and further arms control agreements, but expectations were modest. As long as attitudes in Washington and Moscow toward each other ranged from ambivalent to antagonistic, avenues for a qualitative improvement in relations would be constrained.[67]

Chapter Eleven
The Limits of Partnership

Why has it been so difficult for the United States and Russia to create a productive post–Cold War partnership? With the demise of the USSR and the end of a bipolar world, it appeared that the major obstacles to an improved relationship had disappeared. Russia and the United States no longer faced each other across an ideological divide competing for power and influence in the global arena. There were compelling reasons for Washington to reach out to Moscow and redefine bilateral ties. Yet the initial hopes for a new partnership had all but disappeared by 1999, although they were temporarily revived after 9/11 and then again after Obama's election—only to evaporate after the fourth reset had reached its limits. The two countries share important interests—including counterterrorism and counterproliferation—but the gap between both interests and values has constrained their ability to agree on how to cooperate on key global challenges.

A major reason for the chronic difficulties is that the way in which Russia was reborn after 1991 created inequalities between Washington and Moscow that Russia has found hard to accept and that Putin is determined to reverse. What the United States viewed as a triumph for freedom—the end of the Soviet system—many Russians have come to see as a humiliating defeat for a mighty superpower. They blame the

United States for treating Russia as a defeated rival, not a potential partner. The concept of an "equal partnership of unequals" may appeal to Russians, but that is not the way that Washington approaches dealing with Moscow. Add to the implosion of the USSR other key factors: the traditional Russian wariness of the West, decades of isolation, lingering consciousness of relative economic backwardness, and the chaos and immiseration that accompanied the collapse of the Soviet Union— all of this set the stage for an accumulation of resentments on the Russian side and of incomprehension and frustration on the American side.

This book has argued that there has been far more continuity in Russia policy between Democratic and Republican administrations than many would publicly admit. Moreover, the U.S. Congress has, for more than two decades, has often been skeptical about deeper engagement with Russia and this has further complicated relations. Many of the key issues with which both countries have dealt have remained the same: missile defense, arms control and nonproliferation, Afghanistan and counterterrorism, Iran, Russia's WTO accession and regulating U.S.-Russian relations in the post-Soviet space. In view of the differences between the American and Russian political systems and worldviews, the range of possible ways of dealing with these issues is limited. Moreover, because of the disparities in power and influence between Washington and Moscow, the United States has until recently played a disproportionate role in determining which issues would dominate the relationship. The U.S.-Russian relationship remains a structural anachronism given the focus on hard security issues. As the world's two nuclear superpowers, Russia and the United States are caught in a time warp that is difficult to unravel.

History continues to shape the future of the relationship. U.S.-Russian relations are still influenced by the different ways in which the United States and Russia view the 1990s. Many Russians believe that the United States has been unable to understand the extent of the trauma and chaos of the Soviet collapse. With hindsight one can point to the undoubted progress that was made in the 1990s as Russia dealt with triple transitions from communism to a quasi-democracy, from state control over the economy to a quasi-market system, and from an imperial to a postimperial state—albeit with a lingering imperial mindset.[1] The Clinton administration viewed the denuclearization of Russia's neighbors, the beginnings of a market economy, competitive elections, greater freedom of expression, and securing Russia's cooperation in the Balkans as part of its achievements. The United States was, however, unable to provide for Russia a meaningful role—or stake—in the new Euro-Atlantic security architecture. The problem is that many Russians look back at the 1990s as a time of chaos, poverty, weak leadership, ruthless and opaque oligarchic capitalism, and international humiliation by the United States. Since 2000, order has been restored, people's standard of living has risen, life has become more predictable, and Russia is once again a major player on the world stage. Needless to say, this is a narrative that Putin has championed. A decade and a half after the end of the Yeltsin era, these very different perceptions continue to evoke strong emotions, particularly in Russia.

There is a recurring—and unresolved—debate in the United States about how best to handle Russia. It is a divide that cuts across partisan lines. Those favoring an approach based on realism and national interest attribute many of the problems in the U.S.-Russian relationship to what they see as a misplaced emphasis on trying to reengineer Russian society and bring democracy to Russia. They argue that the relationship is most productive when Washington concentrates on pragmatic foreign policy cooperation with Moscow, limits criticism of its domestic system, focuses on the resolution of common problems, and treats Russia with respect. Critics of Realpolitik on the right and left—including some members of U.S. Congress—argue that the United States should link its foreign policy cooperation to Russia's domestic system and should penalize Moscow for what it sees as its growing authoritarianism.[2]

At the heart of these debates is the difficult question of how far the United States should factor into its policies considerations of Russia's unique postimperial preoccupations and continuing suspicion of American intentions. The question that George Kennan raised in his 1947 "Mr. X" article—To what extent does Russia's domestic system create a unique foreign policy that makes dealing with Moscow unlike dealing with any other power?—remains alive today.[3] Advocates of greater engagement with Russia argue that, as the stronger power, the United States, following Germany's example, can afford to tailor its policies to Russia's special concerns and demonstrate more "empathy."

Many of these arguments exaggerate the amount of influence the United States has over Russia's internal evolution. The U.S. ability to shape what happens inside Russia is at best marginal. Even when Russia was at its weakest in the 1990s it developed along its own political and economic trajectory, tailoring the advice of U.S. NGOs and private-sector consultants to Russia's unique situation—one that was very difficult for outsiders to fully comprehend. The Russia of the second decade of the twenty-first century is a far cry from that of the 1990s. Hence it is much more difficult for the United States to influence what happens inside Russia at a time when the Kremlin is determined to eradicate foreign involvement in its internal affairs—except for trade and foreign investment in certain sectors.

A persistent theme in U.S.-Russian relations has been the asymmetry in each side's stakes in the bilateral relationship. Since the Soviet collapse, Russia has represented a second-order priority for the United States, although it has been important to seek Russian cooperation on the first-order priorities, such as nonproliferation, Afghanistan, Iran, and the upheavals in the Arab world. Russia is important instrumentally for the United States in terms of Washington's broader foreign policy goals, but it is not an issue in U.S. domestic politics—except for a small group of members of Congress, émigrés and experts. By contrast, the United States—at least until recently—represented a top priority for Moscow and was seen as the key to Russia's return to great-power status.

However, Moscow today views the United States as a declining power because of its challenging economic situation. Russia believes that its international choices have widened. This was very much on display when China's new president Xi Jinping visited Moscow in March 2013. Russia was his first overseas destination after taking office. The trip was intended to highlight Russia's "pivot to Asia" and the reality that China and Russia together offer the world a model that is different from America's with its emphasis on absolute sovereignty.[4] Putin stressed that both presidents would like to "shape a new, more just world order."[5]

The United States has become increasingly important instrumentally—in a negative sense—in terms of Russian domestic politics. In his April 2013 five-hour call-in show, Putin argued that U.S-Russian relations had begun to deteriorate in 2003 after the Iraq war.[6] Blaming the United States for Russia's problems and accusing Washington of aiding and abetting the political opposition and threatening Russia's territorial integrity by tacitly supporting Chechen separatists has become a major theme in Putin's increasingly strident narrative. Putin's rhetoric and actions since he returned to the Kremlin have reinforced the challenges of achieving a more full-fledged partnership.

LESSONS FROM FOUR RESETS

A consistent lesson from the past decade is that reset lies in the eye of the beholder and that Russia's view of the four resets is different from the U.S. view. George H. W. Bush's modest attempt to recalibrate relations after the Soviet collapse occurred during a time of maximum Russian weakness and raised questions about whether more should have been done to support the Yeltsin government economically. Clinton's more full-fledged attempt to create a partnership with Yeltsin produced some successes from the U.S. point of view but is largely discredited among the current Russian ruling elite. Putin's post-9/11 reset foundered because both sides had different expectations of what it would accomplish. Putin believed that by reaching out to Bush and facilitating the establishment of U.S. bases in Central Asia, the United States would view Russia as a partner, recognize its sphere of influence in the post-Soviet space, treat it as an equal, and give it the respect that had been lacking during the Yeltsin era. From Moscow's perspective, Washington refused to treat Russia as an equal, did not accept the legitimacy of its struggle against terrorists in the North Caucasus, and subsequently pursued policies that were inimical to its interests, particularly in the former Soviet space. The bottom line is that Putin and his colleagues continue to believe that the United States never appreciated the importance of their post-9/11 attempts to create a strategic partnership.

The fourth reset was an Obama administration initiative and, from Washington's point of view, accomplished much of what it set out to do—New START, Iran, and Afghanistan. But missile defense cooperation and joint solutions to the Syria crisis have proved more challenging.

Part of the reason for this reset's success was the reduction in American attention to the post-Soviet space and the explicit delinking of foreign policy from Russia's domestic situation. The Russian side is generally more cautious about the Obama reset, viewing it as a U.S. course correction and an admission of previous American errors. Moscow believes, however, that there are limits to *perezagruzska* if the United States insists on implementing its missile defense program, refuses to consider a new European Security treaty, and supports regime change in the Arab world.[7]

The past two decades also highlight the disproportionate role of personal ties between the Russian and American leaders. Both Democrats and Republicans have, during election campaigns, accused the other side of "over-personalizing" relations with Russia while they were in office; but both have repeated their predecessor's pattern when they themselves entered the White House. Quite simply, the institutional basis of the relationship remains thin and, in the absence of a broader group of stakeholders, ties between the two presidents remain very important, as was clear from 2009 to the end of 2011. The disadvantage of the personalization of relations was evident when the Kremlin changed hands and the Obama White House had to adjust to its new interlocutor.

The domestic politics of America's Russia policy has also been a source of continuity. Officials from the Bush 41, Clinton, Bush 43, and Obama administrations agree that it has been an uphill struggle to interest Congress in improving ties with Russia. For more than two decades, it has generally been a challenge to find any congressional leader who has been willing to champion a more constructive U.S.-Russian agenda. It took two decades after the end of the USSR and the end of the ban on Jewish emigration to rescind the Jackson-Vanik amendment, and Congress has done little to encourage U.S.-Russian economic relations. Jackson-Vanik was rescinded only because Congress passed substitute legislation—the Justice for Sergei Magnitsky Act—which was hardly conducive to closer commercial ties. Russian officials understand that Congress has been an impediment to moving the relationship forward but have difficulty comprehending the complex relationship between the executive and legislative branches of the U.S. government, perhaps because there is no real separation of power in Russia. The Russian government has also been singularly ineffective in making its case to Congress.

How have politics and economics interacted with each other since the Soviet collapse? The general consensus among the American private sector is that, while the deterioration of U.S.-Russian political relations under Bush did not affect business that much, the improvement of ties under Obama has made a positive difference.[8] Certainly congressional restrictions imposed largely for political reasons had not encouraged the commercial relationship, but neither had the absence of PNTR made much difference before Russia entered the WTO. The major impediments to a more substantial economic relationship appeared to be economic and legal, rather than political. The U.S. and Russia did not have the necessary economic complementarity to foster a robust economic relationship as long as Russia remained primarily a raw materials and arms exporter. Moreover, the absence of the rule of law was a constant challenge, even though Russia under Putin and Medvedev made significant strides in improving the application of commercial law. Were Russia to implement the ambitious modernization program promoted rhetorically by both Putin and Medvedev and diversify its economy, the opportunities for expanding U.S.-Russian economic ties would grow appreciably.

Conversely, if the economic relationship were to improve significantly, could that affect the political relationship? The German experience suggests that it could. Germany's economic interdependence with Russia has affected its approach to political relations. With Russia as an important energy supplier and thousands of medium and small German businesses active in Russia, the imperative of engaging Russia and maintaining good political relations is constant. Angela Merkel discovered that soon after becoming chancellor. Bilateral trade totals 52 billion euros and is important for a trade-dependent economy.[9] Nevertheless, the German-Russian relationship experienced strains in 2013, particularly after the Kremlin targeted German political foundations working with civil society in Moscow in their crackdown on NGOs.[10] Of course, the United States is a large country for whom foreign trade is not nearly as important as it is for Germany. U.S.-Russian bilateral trade amounts to $41 billion. However, propinquity counts. Canada is the United States' largest trading partner. But if there were a larger group of stakeholders on both sides, then the situation would change. Former ambassador to Russia John Beyrle claims that "we need more deals that create stakes on both sides."[11] China is the obvious counterexample to Russia. Despite the administration's sometimes testy political relations with China and concerns about its human rights record, U.S. business advocates successfully for its interests because China is such an important economic partner. It ranks second after Canada. There is no legislation similar to the Magnitsky Act for China, despite documented cases of corruption and prison abuse. This fact is, of course, particularly galling to the Russians and reinforces their narrative about double standards.

Within the executive branch, Russia policy has sometimes been inconsistent and fragmented. The bureaucratic reorganizations during the Bush era—abolishing the State Department's Office for the Newly Independent States, moving the post-Soviet states to the European Bureau, and then the Central Asian states to the Bureau of South Asia, and similarly dividing Eurasia up into different offices in the National Security Council and the Defense Department—meant that officials who dealt with Russia policy no longer had an overview of or responsibility for policy toward Russia's neighbors, and there was little coordination between those focusing on Russia and those dealing with its neighborhood. The National Intelligence Council is the one remaining major government institution where Russia and Eurasia remain under one rubric, facilitating a more integrated view of the region. The intent of these government reorganizations was political—to deemphasize the concept of a post-Soviet space where Russia still plays a disproportionate role. The principle of denying that Russia should have a "sphere of privileged interests" in Eurasia was understandable, but reality suggests otherwise—at least for the foreseeable future, as Putin pursues his number one foreign policy priority, a Eurasian Economic Union. The ties that bind remain strong—a common language, trade connections, educational links, family ties, business ties, and a shared history and culture. Many of Russia's neighbors understand that they need to achieve a fine balancing act between Moscow and other external powers, especially in challenging economic times when Moscow retains considerable economic clout in the region.

SELECTIVE PARTNERS

U.S.-Russian relations have also been affected by Moscow's and Washington's broader foreign policy preoccupations. Under Vladimir Putin, Russia has pursued four major foreign policy goals.[12] The first—increasingly on display as upheavals in the Middle East spread— was to ensure that no major international decision can be taken without Russian participation. Russia is entitled to its seat at the table, Russia's views should be respected and taken into account, and the United Nations Security Council should be the decisive venue for all important decisions. Moreover, American officials have observed that the Russians often focus on process rather than progress. Multinational negotiations on two frozen conflicts—Nagorno-Karabakh and Transnistria— have been going on for more than two decades, but Russia seems to be in no hurry to see these disputes resolved. As long as these disputes are unresolved, Russia has leverage. The preference for talks rather than action has also been apparent in Russia's handling of the situation in in Syria. It remains to be seen what the joint U.S-Russian sponsored moves to resolve the Syrian crisis will accomplish.

The second goal has been to maintain the status quo in the Euro-Atlantic arena and ensure that there is no more eastern enlargement of either NATO or the European Union in the former Soviet states. The successful creation of a Eurasian Union that includes Ukraine would ensure the success of that strategy. Another goal has been to contain and push back Western democracy-promotion efforts in Russia and its neighbors and minimize the possibility of regime change or instability in Eurasia. Russia offers itself as a defender of the autocratic rulers in its neighborhood. The final set of goals—as was made clear in a series of Foreign Ministry documents—has been to promote Russia's economic interests and, by implication, those of its political elite by enlisting Western investment and technology in Russia's modernization project.[13]

America plays a key role—both negative and positive—in all of these Russian goals. By acting without Security Council sanction—as it did in Kosovo and Iraq because it knew Russian would veto the resolutions—it can exclude Russia from having a seat at the table. The United States must also continue to deal with the consequences of failing to include Russia in the enlarged Euro-Atlantic security system in the 1990s. Some Clinton and Bush-era officials believe that the United States should have taken up both Yeltsin's and Putin's enquiries about NATO membership.[14] By denying Russia the prospect of eventual NATO membership while Central Europe and the Baltic States joined, America reinforced the Kremlin's belief that it remains outside of Euro-Atlantic structures and hence has no responsibility to them.[15]

U.S. foreign policy goals have, since 9/11, focused on counter-terrorism, ousting the Taliban in Afghanistan and stabilizing the situation there, ousting Saddam Hussein in Iraq, containing Iran's nuclear program, global nonproliferation, and, since 2011, support for a stable transition away from autocracy in the Middle East. Russia has been a partner—albeit sometimes a reluctant one—in most of these endeavors. Washington realizes that Russia has the ability to thwart U.S. policies on these issues—hence, the attempts to secure Russian support for Iran sanctions, the Northern Distribution Network, and joint action on Libya and Syria. The U.S.-Russian agenda going forward is long and complex.

Thus, the U.S.-Russian relationship remains a selective partnership, where Moscow and Washington cooperate on some issues and disagree on others. Deep currents of mutual mistrust remain, although constructive partnership on issues of mutual interest has also worked. The Clinton, Bush, and Obama administrations all encountered the anti-Americanism that former Ambassador to Russia and Deputy Secretary of State William Burns describes as "part of Russia's deep historical sensibility and suspicion of outsiders."[16] But they have also experienced more forward-looking Russian views and Putin's pragmatism and willingness to make deals if he believes they are in Russia's interest.

Part of the enduring Russian resentment against U.S. policies has been the U.S. government and NGO involvement in democracy-promotion efforts. This is an important element of American foreign policy, although, as we have seen, it has not always been consistently applied. Nevertheless, Russia (unlike China, for instance) signed agreements when it joined the OSCE, the Council of Europe, and other bodies committing it to observe basic Euro-Atlantic norms such as the rule of law, due process, human rights, and freedom of speech and assembly. It is, therefore, entirely legitimate for the United States to hold

Russia accountable for implementing commitments it made when it joined these bodies.

After more than two decades of modern U.S.-Russian relations and four resets, there is a strong argument to be made that the United States should have moderate expectations, define its foreign policy priorities with Russia, and systematically and consistently try to advance its agenda on these issues without over-emphasizing Russia's domestic trajectory. That was the theory behind the Obama administration's two-track diplomacy, and it worked quite well until Russia entered its election season with unexpected opposition to Putin, who then blamed the United States for aiding and abetting the protestors. At a minimum, the United States will have to reassess its engagement with Russian civil society since the crackdown on foreign-supported NGOs.

The experience of the post-Soviet period suggests that the United States should be both modest and realistic about the degree to which its programs can influence the course of Russia's internal development. American officials should have learned in the past two decades that Russia's evolution away from the Soviet system will take several generations, or even the seventy years that the Germans originally predicted. The U.S. timetable may be dictated by four-year election cycles, but Russia's evolution occurs at its own deliberate pace and not in a linear fashion, as developments over the past decades suggest. Paraphrasing George Kennan's 1947 "Mr. X" article, the United States should pursue a long-term, consistent policy of engagement with Russia—but not expect any breakthroughs.

The same cautionary conclusions can be drawn for U.S. policy in the post-Soviet space. Given the challenges the United States faces in Iran and the greater Middle East and Asia, the former Soviet space will likely receive less attention going forward. After the U.S. withdrawal from Afghanistan, Central Asia is likely to decline as a priority. The Bush administration focused considerable attention on Russia's neighbors, viewing its policies through a Russian prism—the more distanced from Russia the country was, the better. It wanted NATO membership for Ukraine more than Ukraine itself wanted it. The Obama administration, too, viewed its policies toward Russia's neighbors partly through a Russian prism—but in a different way from its predecessor. It was alert to Russian concerns about American activities in its neighborhood and calibrated its policies toward Georgia accordingly. The question of how much the United States should be responsive to Russian concerns that it may or may not consider legitimate continues to divide officials and experts and is also a source of disagreement between Washington and some of its key NATO allies.

Of course, Russia generally supports all the Eurasian leaders, presenting itself as the bulwark against regime change and seeks to increase its influence in its "sphere of privileged interest." Putin's project for his third term is his Eurasian Union, an economic association of post-Soviet states. He called for "close integration based on new values and a new political and economic foundation" and described the new Union as a "powerful supranational association capable of becoming one of the poles of the modern world."[17] Irrespective of whether it succeeds or not, Russia still retains considerable influence in much of its neighborhood. The United States is far away and preoccupied elsewhere.

BEYOND RESETS

What does the future hold for the U.S.-Russian relationship? If there is to be another attempt to improve U.S.-Russian ties, it will involve new challenges. The April 15, 2013, bombings at the Boston Marathon highlighted the potential for and the obstacles to U.S.-Russian cooperation on an issue where they ostensibly share similar interests—counterterrorism. On that day—Patriots Day—bombs exploded at the marathon' finishing line, killing three people and severly injuring dozens more. The FBI identified the two brothers who had planted the bombs as Chechen immigrants who had received political asylum in the United States. Reactions in Washington and Moscow were mixed. On one hand, the United States and Russia agreed to step up their cooperation on counterterrorism. On the other hand, the identification of the suspects as Chechens reopened an emotional Russian debate about double standards. All of the senior Russian officials interviewed for this book stressed that a major Russian grievance since the early 1990s has been that the United States has constantly criticized Russia for its actions in the two Chechen wars, refusing to recognize that Russia was dealing with a serious threat that began as a separatist movement and subsequently developed into a terrorist movement. Indeed, after the bombings, the pro-Kremlin Sergei Markov claimed that "the United States had supported Chechen terrorism and now these terrorists are blowing up Americans."[18] Kremlin spokesmen blamed the lack of counterterrorism cooperation between the two countries for leading to the bombings.[19] If only Washington had ackowledged the terrorist threats from Chechens that Russia faced, ceased criticizing Moscow for violations of human rights in the North Caucasus, and worked together with Russia on these issues, so the argument goes, then America would have been less vulnerable to the same threats.

U.S. reactions also highlighted the complexities of counterterrorism cooperation. Officials admitted that the FSB had called attention to one of the brothers some years before and had asked the FBI for information about him. However, the Russian intelligence services themselves had apparently not been forthcoming about what they knew about him, particularly during his six-month sojourn in Dagestan in 2012, raising broader questions about how reciprocal this intelligence sharing was. While both sides declared that they were stepping up their counterterrorism cooperation in the lead-up to the 2014 winter Olympics in Sochi—which borders of the North Caucasus—the wariness about sharing information that had become clear in the months after 9/11 persisted more than a decade later. This was a product not only of Cold War legacies but of different definitions of what constitutes a terrorist threat.

Despite these challenges, U.S. officials continue to seek more effective ways to cooperate with Russia. In April 2013 a group of former U.S. ambassadors to Russia and Russian ambassadors to the United States met to propose new ways forward.[20] Stressing that both countries must recognize that they are operating in a more diverse world with new challenges, they concluded "The world is no longer hostage to tense relations between Moscow and Washington, but the global community is still concerned to see these relations put on a stable foundation."[21] Former ambassador to Moscow John Beyrle has outlined five areas on which the U.S. administration should focus. It should continue carefully to support civil society and greater openness in Russia but in a way that does not play into Russian suspicions about the United States' intentions. It should continue to seek a cooperative solution to missile defense by engaging Russia in such a way that it feels that it is part of the solution, not part of the problem. It should focus on creating more U.S. stakeholders by promoting more bilateral trade and investment. It should try to engage Congress more on Russia issues. And it should also make the most out of the openness that exists in Russia to promote more cultural and educational exchanges.[22]

If the United States were to focus its priorities in the way advocated by Beyrle, the ability to achieve them would largely hinge on whether the Russian side is interested in responding positively to this agenda. So far, the signals have been mixed. Criticism of America continues unabated, but Putin has also on several occasions said that the U.S.-Russian relationship needs to improve. The Kremlin continues to fight its political opponents—divided as they are—and this domestic agenda has influenced its foreign policy activities. Domestic politics will continue to drive foreign policy going forward. Under these circumstances, a prudent U.S. policy would be to focus on protecting those areas where both can cooperate—Afghanistan, nonproliferation, and counterterrorism—and eschew attempts to upgrade the relationship unless Russia indicates that it, too, is seriously interested in an upgrade. The agenda for U.S.-Russian relations remains long, and there are compelling reasons for why both sides have to work together.

At the time of the Boston bombings, both Washington and Moscow, recognizing the need to improve ties, were making plans to reinvigorate the flagging relationship. The focal point was a two-day summit, scheduled for Moscow in September. It would be Obama's first visit to Moscow since 2009 and the first time that the he and Putin had held an extended bilateral meeting. The Kremlin appeared eager to hold a summit for it would serve a larger purpose, both showcasing Russia's role as a major international player and reinforcing Putin's importance as a global leader. The September 2013 summit was to focus on three main issues: The first was arms control and missile defense—in the context of President Obama's June Berlin speech laying out new initiatives involving significant weapons reductions.[23] The second was Syria and its bloody civil war, which had Russia and the United States arrayed on different sides. The third was bolstering U.S. trade and investment in Russia, a theme that Putin had addressed on multiple occasions. As the summit date neared, however, there was some unease at the White House and in the State Department because of what seemed to be a slow Russian response to U.S. proposals for concrete deliverables. Despite the Kremlin's strong desire for the meeting, Moscow did not seem to be pushing the agenda forward.[24] But that may have been the result of uncertain decision making in Moscow, and it was certainly expected that a high-profile summit was still in the making.

However, the relationship was always vulnerable to external surprises. And that is exactly what happened on June 23, when an Aeroflot flight from Hong Kong arrived at Moscow's Sheremetyevo airport. On board was Edward Snowden, a disgruntled contractor for the U.S. National Security Agency, carrying several computers full of top-secret documents. He had begun releasing information to journalists about highly classified NSA programs and had aligned himself with Wikileaks, which had previously released a vast amount of confidential U.S. diplomatic cables. Snowden had surfaced first in Hong Kong, but after a few days the Chinese authorities, apparently deciding to pass the problem on to Russia, put him on the flight to Moscow. He was carrying with him a trove of files about U.S. surveillance programs of international communications and was threatening to release much more.

The volatile nature of the U.S-Russian relationship was once more on display. The White House revoked his U.S. passport and insisted that Snowden be extradited to the United States to face criminal charges for leaking classified information. The Russians demurred, citing the lack of an extradition treaty. Tense discussions continued for five weeks while Snowden remained in diplomatic limbo somehow unseen in the airport transit area. Russian officials eventually arranged a press conference for him, at which a group of strange bedfellows—Russian human rights activists and pro-Kremlin officials—praised him as a whistleblower for exposing what they described as nefarious American practices and highlighting Washington's hypocrisy for criticizing Moscow over its human rights violations while the White House allegedly "spied" on its own citizens. Admitting that Snowden had first contacted Russian diplomats in Hong Kong, Putin said that Russia received "no information" from Snowden and implied that he would have preferred not to have this problem. As he said publicly, "I would like not to deal with such issues because it is like shearing a pig. There's lots of squealing and little fleece."[25] But he had also referred to Snowden as a "new dissident" and likened him to Nobel Prize–winning Soviet dissident Andrei Sakharov.[26] Eventually, however, the Russians announced that they would grant Snowden temporary political asylum, although Putin insisted that the leaker was to "stop his work aimed at harming our American partners" as long as he remained in Russia.[27]

Washington's reaction was swift. The anticipated rapprochement was off. Announcing that "there is not enough recent progress in our bilateral political agenda with Russia to hold a U.S.-Russia Summit," the White House admitted that "Russia's disappointing decision to grant Edward Snowden temporary asylum" had been a factor in the cancellation.[28] But there was little question that the cancellation was mainly about Russia's handling of Snowden. Added the White House, "This move by the Russian government undermines a long history of cooperation with Russia, cooperation that's been on the upswing since the Boston bombings."[29] The last time a leader had canceled a U.S.-Russian summit had been more than half a century earlier, in 1960, when Nikita Khrushchev walked out on Dwight Eisenhower in Paris following the downing of an American U-2 spy plane over Soviet territory. Now it was not a spy plane but Edward Snowden who had crashed into U.S.-Russian relations, and once again a summit was off.

After the cancellation, President Obama called for a "pause" in U.S.-Russian relations to "reassess where it is that Russia is going, what our core interests are." Then, in an uncharacteristically personal remark, he described Putin's demeanor this way: "He's got that kind of slouch, looking like the bored kid in the back of the classroom," although he admitted that his meetings with Putin are "often very productive."[30] The Russians wasted no time in snapping back. Foreign Minister Sergei Lavrov, meeting with John Kerry in Washington, admonished the Americans: "We need to work as grown-ups," he said, pointedly adding, "And we hope this will be reciprocal.[31]

Although Obama tried to downplay the importance of the switch from Medvedev to Putin, the body language between Obama and Putin had never been good, going back to their first meeting in Moscow when Putin was prime minister. It was certainly on evidence when they met again in Ireland for the G-8 summit in June 2013. The testy public remarks only reinforced the new reality. The reset had worked well while Medvedev was in the Kremlin because Obama had a good working relationship with him that enabled them to reach agreement on the most contentious of issues. Absent those personal ties, the reset lacked ballast since, as this book has made clear, little gets done in U.S.-Russian relations unless the two presidents themselves move the agenda forward.

The disintegration of the Obama reset highlighted the perennial dilemma of how to deal with Moscow's mixed signals. On the one hand, the Kremlin certainly wanted the presidential meeting because of what the summit would have said about Russia's (and Putin's) place in the world. On the other hand, the Kremlin sent a clear signal by choosing to grant Snowden asylum in Russia. It could have found a way for Snowden to leave Russia for one of the Latin American countries that had offered him political asylum (although Washington had made clear the high costs for any Latin government that would do so). Instead, the Kremlin chose to keep him in Russia and showcase its role as the champion of an underdog fighting America's antiterrorism programs— a rich irony, to say the least, given Russia's own continuing crackdown on opposition forces, accusing them of fueling homegrown extremism. The short-term political gains to be reaped by supporting Snowden apparently ranked above the benefits of holding a summit with the U.S. president, raising questions about Kremlin decision making and Putin's own priorities.

Obama's call for a "pause" in U.S-Russian relations showed that the post-Soviet cycle of U.S.-Russian relations—great expectations followed by disappointment—had repeated itself for a fourth time. The disillusionment phase had accelerated after Putin's return to the Kremlin. Nevertheless, continued engagement at lower levels was imperative, given the international challenges that both countries faced. While the United States will find it difficult to craft a more productive relationship with Russia, the next occupant of the White House will surely be compelled to continue his predecessors' quest, taking into account changes resulting from mistakes of the past and the new landscapes of the future. The reset button may have been disconnected. But pushing a "pause button" is only a temporary expedient.

External factors will also affect the relationship. If the European financial crisis continues or worsens, that will have a negative impact on the Russia economy, since Europe is Russia's most important economic partner. A deteriorating economic situation and falling oil prices could lead Russia to reevaluate its policies toward the United States in pursuit of improved economic ties. However, it is quite possible that Putin believes that the two countries can compartmentalize their relations and that the United States will be interested in closer economic ties irrespective of the political relationship.

Since the collapse of the USSR, countless Russians and foreign experts have developed future scenarios for Russia.[32] There are usually three scenarios. The first is muddling along or muddling up or down—in other words, Russia continues to introduce modest changes, but its basic trajectory does not change, and it does not succeed in modernizing its economy and society. The second is the negative scenario where current trends such as demographic decline, deteriorating infrastructure, corruption, unrest in the North Caucasus, and a possible sustained fall in oil prices lead Russia on a path toward greater weakness and authoritarianism, or more chaos. In neither of these scenarios does Russia become a more productive partner for the United States.[33] The third is the optimistic scenario. Russia really does begin to modernize, diversify its economy, move away from heavy dependence on oil and gas, introduce the rule of law, and tackle corruption. Eventually the political system becomes more competitive and democratic. Russia finally fully embraces the modern world.

Would it be easier for the United States to deal with a more modern and democratic Russia? That would depend on a variety of factors. A Russia with a more diversified, less energy-focused economy would be a more attractive economic partner for the United States. But a more modern, prosperous, and self-confident Russia would also have its own foreign policy interests, and one cannot assume that these would necessarily be any more compatible with those of the United States than they are today. Indeed, the United States and Russia would likely continue to be competitors. Russian polling data suggests that younger Russians are as nationalistic—if not more so—than older Russians, and that could influence a future Kremlin whose leader was not chosen in a "managed" election. Moreover, Russia would continue to focus on its immediate neighborhood. Indeed, a Russia that fully embraces the modern world could ultimately have a beneficial effect on the countries surrounding it. But it not necessarily be a more congenial partner for the United States.[34]

The 2008 financial crisis and its aftermath, the rapid rise of China, the persistent Euro-crisis, and the United States' continuing economic difficulties—all these have already affected the relative influence of Russia and the United States in the world. Russia under Putin has become a stronger international player than it was in the 1990s, but it is not clear that it is a rising power to the same extent that the other BRICs are. Its economic performance still hinges on the price of oil, its working-age population is declining, its male youth mortality rates rival those of sub-Saharan Africa, and its infrastructure is deteriorating.[35] While the West floundered economically, Russia managed its financial crisis reasonably well. But its growth rate is projected to fall in the next years. Nevertheless, Russia believes that the West is in decline and that the drivers of the world are changing to the advantage of the BRICs and the G-20 countries. China remains the great unknown—including its growing role in Russia's sparsely populated Far East—and a possible scenario, which more Westward-oriented Russian advocate, could involve longer-term U.S.-Russian cooperation to contain China's rise. But that still appears to be far off. Nevertheless, both sides understand that the changing global configuration will change the environment in which the bilateral relationship will operate in the future.

Former secretary of state Henry Kissinger, who has regularly met with President Putin, attributes some of the persistent problems in U.S.-Russian relations to the inability of American officials to appreciate Russia's history or geography and to a tendency to assume that Russia's definitions of its needs are similar to those of the United States. He views Putin as a strategic thinker and economic reformer whose vision for Russia is to turn it into a respected, modern power. He believes that Washington should seek a strategic partnership with Russia. However, this would not include discussions about Russia's domestic system. "It is not our job to reorganize their society."[36]

Former national security advisor Stephen Hadley has observed: "Rather than importing the past into the present Russia needs to get to the point where it imports the future into the present. Otherwise it will remain a prisoner of the past."[37] Indeed, America and Russia both have to deal with two legacies—those of the Cold War and of the 1990s when the asymmetries in power were most pronounced. In the second decade of the twenty-first century Russia is much stronger and that more recent legacy needs to be reassessed.

Three U.S. presidents have tried to find the golden key that would unlock the door to a qualitatively better U.S.-Russian relationship since the Soviet collapse. So far no one has found the key. But an internal reset is also vital. Both the United States and Russia need to re-examine the way they think about each other and develop approaches that reflect the realities of the twenty-first century world, a more complex world with new global centers of power. Until and unless Washington and Moscow can move beyond the Cold War and post–Cold War past, the most that any reset—irrespective of whether it originates in the Kremlin or the White House—can do is to manage more effectively what will remain a challenging relationship.

The most productive way for the United States to deal with Russia going forward is to recognize that this is a relationship with a large, still important country that has a hybrid political system and faces serious domestic challenges. Russia's worldview is significantly at odds with that of America and will remain so for the foreseeable future. Washington should exercise restraint in publicly commenting on developments in Russia—either positively or negatively. It should focus on those concrete areas where the two countries can and must work together. If the United States can move away from the pattern of the past two decades, when cycles of great expectations about improving ties with Russia have been followed by periods of disappointments and frustration, then Washington and Moscow may be able to avoid the need for future resets in what is and will remain a limited partnership.

Acknowledgments

The journey that led me to write this book began in 1999. I had written two previous books, one on Russian-German relations and one, as a "recovering Sovietologist," on the rebirth of post-1989 Russia and Germany. Then Gregory Craig, director of the State Department's Office of Policy Planning, invited me to join the policy-making world. He gave me a portfolio that included both Russia and Eastern and Central Europe. I would like to thank him, Morton Halperin, and Richard Haass, directors of the Office of Policy Planning under whom I served, and Daniel Hamilton, for enabling me to participate in this process.

My second opportunity to participate in the formation of U.S. policy toward Russia came when Robert Hutchings, chairman of the National Intelligence Council, asked me to join the NIC and gave me a portfolio that covered all of Eurasia. I am grateful to him and my colleagues at the National Intelligence Council for enabling me to work with them on a range of issues. Particular thanks go to my predecessor, the late George Kolt and to David Gordon, Martin Swartz, and Steedman Hinckley. My two stints in government gave me invaluable insights into U.S. policy toward Russia—and into the limits of partnership. It also reinforced my respect for the dedicated public servants who work on challenging issues.

For many years, Georgetown University has been my academic home, and in this century I have led its Center for Eurasian, Russian, and East European Studies. As a scholar-practitioner, my academic research has been essential to the writing of this book. I would like to thank the leadership of Georgetown University—President John J. DeGioia and two deans of the School of Foreign Service, Robert Gallucci and Carol Lancaster—for providing a supportive environment for policy-relevant academic work. I am indebted to my colleague Marcia Morris for twice taking over the directorship of the center while I was on leave, and to Jennifer Long, the associate director, for steering the program so expertly in my absence. I am also grateful to those who have helped make CERES such a congenial place to work: Benjamin Loring, Christina Watts, and Eugene Imas. Special thanks go to my colleagues in the Department of Government, particularly Thane Gustafson and Robert Lieber, for their insights and broader perspectives on these issues.

I am grateful to those individuals and organizations that supported my research for this book. A Fulbright fellowship enabled me to spend time in Moscow teaching at the Moscow State Institute of International Relations and conducting research. I would like to thank Aleksei Bogaturov and Tatiana Shakleina for giving me the opportunity to teach a course on U.S.-Russian relations at MGIMO. Thanks also to Rose Gottemoeller and the Moscow Carnegie Center for hosting me during that time. I have also appreciated working with Alexander Dynkin, director of the Institute for World Economy and International Relations. The American Academy in Berlin also supported my research and housed me in its beautiful Wannsee villa. Thanks to its President Gary Smith for organizing such interesting discussion sessions. Thanks also to Deana Arsenian and the Carnegie Corporation of New York for funding the Working Group on US.-Russian Relations that I cochaired, first with Eugene Rumer and then with Fiona Hill, both good colleagues from whom I have learned a great deal over the years. Our discussions in Washington with academics and policy makers over a three-year period enhanced my understanding of many of the issues at the heart of this book.

Special thanks go to Strobe Talbott, president of the Brookings Institution and former deputy secretary of state, for his font of wisdom about Russia and his encouragement over many years both when I served in the Department of State and while I was writing this book.

I am particularly grateful to those who read all or part of this manuscript and gave me excellent comments: Fiona Hill, Robert Nurick, Eugene Rumer, Bobo Lo, Lilia Shevtsova, Steven Weisman, and Thane

Gustafson. Thanks also to the Brookings Institution and to Martin Indyk and Steven Pifer for enabling me to cochair the Hewett Forum on Post-Soviet Affairs, whose monthly discussions have enhanced my understanding of Russia and Eurasia.

I express my deep appreciation to all of the people whom I interviewed for the book, both in and out of government. Your insights were essential for this project, and you gave generously of your time.

Thanks also to my intrepid research assistants: Anita Kondoyanidi, Nick Naroditski, Liberty Tillemann-Dick, and Martina Bozadzieva. The staff at the IHS-CERA office in Moscow, led by Irina Zamarina, has been very supportive over the years when I have made research trips there. Thanks to Ruth Mandel for finding the photographs.

I would also like to thank Svetlana Mironyuk and Sergei Karaganov for inviting me to participate for the past decade in the annual sessions of the Valdai International Discussion Club. The meetings with the top Russian leadership and with other Russian colleagues have been most illuminating. Our extended dinners with Vladimir Putin have provided insights into his vision and assessment of U.S.-Russian relations.

I would like to express my gratitude to my two editors at Princeton University Press—Chuck Myers and Eric Crahan—for all their support. Chuck's willingness to provide advice and editorial counsel is particularly appreciated. Thanks also to my production editor, Nathan Carr. And special appreciation goes to my agent Georges Borchardt and to Valerie Borchardt.

I also want to remember two people whose ideas have influenced me in important ways. First and foremost was my mentor and thesis advisor Adam Ulam, whose insights about Russia were always penetrating and prophetic and whose humor and cultured skepticism about most things have informed my understanding of this part of the world. The other is my friend and former student Joyce Lasky Reed, with whom I spent countless hours discussing things Russian and who invited me, via board membership of the Faberge Arts Foundation, to participate in promoting closer U.S-Russian relations through the medium of culture.

Special thanks go to my family, which has supported me throughout this process. My children Alexander and Rebecca always provide a fresh perspective on all issues and enable me to keep a sense of proportion about what is and is not important. My deepest gratitude goes to my husband, Daniel Yergin, my greatest supporter—and toughest editorial critic--who read several drafts, challenged assumptions, and whose wisdom and insights over many years have been invaluable.

List of Interviewees

Madeleine Albright: U.S. Ambassador to the United Nations 1993–1996; Secretary of State, 1997–2001.

Richard Armitage: Deputy Secretary of State, 2001–2005.

John Beyrle: Deputy Director State Department Office of Newly Independent States, Deputy Chief of Mission, U.S. Embassy Moscow, U.S. Ambassador to Russia, 2008–2012.

John Bolton: Undersecretary of State for Arms Control and International Security, 2001–2005; U.S. Ambassador to United Nations, 2005–2006.

Joshua Bolten: White House Chief of Staff, 2006–2009.

Matthew Bryza: Director for Europe and Eurasia, National Security Council, 2001–2005; Deputy Assistant Secretary of Europe and Eurasia, 2005–2009; U.S. Ambassador to Azerbaijan, 2010–2011.

William Burns: U.S. Ambassador to Russia, 2005–2008; Undersecretary of State for Political Affairs, 2008–2011; Deputy Secretary of State, 2011–present.

Anatoly Chubais: First Deputy Prime Minister of Russia, 1992–1998.

James Collins: U.S. Ambassador to Russia, 1997–2001.

Ivo Daalder·: U.S. Ambassador to NATO, 2009–2013.

Paula Dobriansky: Undersecretary of State for Democracy and Global Affairs, 2001–2009.

Thomas Donilon: National Security Advisor, 2010–2013.

Eric Edelman: Under Secretary of Defense for Policy, 2005–2009.

Donald Evans: Secretary of Commerce, 2001–2005.

John Evans: Consul General in St. Petersburg, 2001–2004; Ambassador to Armenia, 2004–2006.

Julie Finley: U.S. Ambassador to OSCE, 2005–2009.

Rosemarie Forsythe: Director for Russian, Ukrainian and Eurasian Affairs at the National Security Council, 1992–1995.

Daniel Fried: Senior Director for Europe, National Security Council, 2001–2005; Assistant Secretary of State for European and Eurasian Affairs, 2005–2009.

Rose Gottemoeller: Director for Russian and Eurasian Affairs, 1993–94; Assistant Secretary of State and Acting Undersecretary of State for Arms Control, Verification, and Compliance, 2008–2013.

Thomas Graham: Associate Director, Office of Policy Planning, U.S. State Department, 2001–2002; Director and Senior Director on Russia, National Security Council, 2002–2007.

Drew Guff: Managing Director, Siguler Guff and Company, 1995–present.

Richard Haass: Senior Director for Middle East and South Asia, National Security Council, 1989–1992; State Department Director of Policy Planning 2001–2005.

Stephen Hadley: Deputy National Security Advisor, 2001–2005; National Security Advisor, 2005–2009.

Fiona Hill: National Intelligence Officer for Russia and Eurasia, 2006–2009.

Igor Ivanov: Minister of Foreign Affairs of the Russian Federation, 1998–2004.

Elizabeth Jones: Assistant Secretary of State for Europe, 2001–2005.

Sergei Karaganov: Chairman, Russian Council on Foreign and Defense Policy, 1992–2012.

Mikhail Kasyanov: Prime Minister of Russia, 2000–2004.

Henry Kissinger: National Security Advisor, 1969–1975; Secretary of State, 1973–1977.

Andrey Kortunov: President, New Eurasia Foundation, Moscow, 2004–present.

David Kramer: Policy Planning Staff, Department of State, 2002–2005; Deputy Assistant Secretary of State for Russia and Eurasia, 2005–2008; Assistant Secretary for Democracy, Human Rights, and Labor, 2008–2009.

Fyodr Lukyanov: Chairman, Russian Council on Foreign and Defense Policy, 2012–present; editor, *Russia in Global Affairs*.

James MacDougall: Deputy Assistant Secretary of Defense for Eurasia, 2003–2007.

Michael McFaul: Senior Director for Russia (and Central Asia) National Security Council, 2008–2011; U.S. ambassador to Russia, 2012–present.

David Merkel: Deputy Assistant Secretary of State for Eurasia, 2008–2009.

Richard Miles: U.S. Ambassador to Georgia, 2002–2005.

Richard Morningstar: State Department Special Envoy for Caspian Basin Energy Diplomacy 1998–2001; Special Envoy for Eurasian Energy, 2009–2012; Ambassador to Azerbaijan, 2012–present.

Mike Mullen: Admiral, U.S. Chairman of the Joint Chiefs of Staff, from, 2007–2011.

Victoria Nuland: Deputy Director, Office of Newly Independent States, Department of State , 1997–1999; Principal Deputy National Security Advisor, Office of the Vice President, 2003–2005; U.S. Ambassador to NATO, 2005–2008.

Thomas Pickering: U.S. Ambassador to Russia 1993–1996, Undersecretary of State for Political Affairs, 1997–2000.

Steven Pifer: U.S. Ambassador to Ukraine 1997–2000; Deputy Assistant Secretary of State for Russia and Eurasia, 2001–2004.

Daniel Poneman: Senior Director for Non-Proliferation, National Security Council, 1993–1996; Deputy Secretary of Energy, 2009–present.

Evgeny Primakov, Russian Foreign Minister 1996–1998, Prime Minister 1998–1999.

Steven Rademaker: Assistant Secretary of State for International Security and Non-Proliferation, Head of Bureau of Arms Control, 2002–2006.

Sergey Rogov: Director, Institute of USA and Canada.

Eric Rubin: Deputy Chief of Mission, U.S. Embassy Moscow, 2008–2011; Deputy Assistant Secretary of State for Eurasian Affairs, 2011–present.

Daniel Russell: Deputy Chief of Mission, U.S. Embassy Moscow, 2005–2008; Deputy Assistant Secretary of State for Russia and Eurasia, 2009–2013.

Brent Scowcroft: National Security Advisor, 1989–1993.

Strobe Talbott: Ambassador at Large, Special Advisor to the President for the Newly Independent States, 1993–1994; Deputy Secretary of State, 1994–2001.

Dmitri Trenin: Director, Carnegie Moscow Center, 2008–present.

Yuri Ushakov: Russian Ambassador to the United States, 1999–2008; Foreign Policy Advisor to Prime Minister and President Putin, 2008–present.

Edward Verona: President of the U.S.-Russia Business Council. 2008–2013.

Alexander Vershbow: U.S. Ambassador to Russia, 2001–2005; Assistant Secretary of Defense for International Security Affairs, 2009–2012; Deputy Secretary-general of NATO, 2012–present.

Alexander Voloshin: Head, Russian Presidential Administration, 1997–2003.

Celeste Wallander: Deputy Assistant Secretary of Defense for Russia/Ukraine/Eurasia, 2009–2012.

Damon Wilson: Senior Director for European Affairs at National Security Council, 2004–2006.

Grigory Yavlinsky: Head of the Yabloko Party. 1993–2008.

Igor Yurgens: Director Insor, Institute for Contemporary Development, 2008–present.

Chronology of Major Events
in U.S.-Russian Relations

1991

July 31: START I is signed by Presidents Gorbachev and Bush.

Aug. 18–21: Soviet hard-liners stage an abortive coup is against Gorbachev.

Dec. 8: Boris Yeltsin meets with Ukrainian and Belarus presidents in hunting lodge outside Brest to create the Commonwealth of Independent States.

Dec. 12: Bush signs in to law the Cooperative Threat Reduction (Nunn-Lugar) legislation.

Dec. 25: Gorbachev announces the dissolution of the USSR.

1992

Feb. 1: Russian president Yeltsin visits the U.S. and meets George H. W. Bush at Camp David.

May 23: Lisbon Protocol signed for the denuclearization of Ukraine, Belarus, and Kazakhstan.

Nov. 3: Bill Clinton elected president of United States.

1993

Jan. 2–3: George H. W. Bush and Boris Yeltsin sign START II treaty.

Mar. 28: Russian parliament tries unsuccessfully to impeach President Yeltsin.

Apr. 3–4: First Clinton-Yeltsin summit at Vancouver.

Sept. 21: Yeltsin calls for elections in December.

Oct. 4: Yeltsin orders shelling of his armed opponents in the parliament.

Dec. 12: Vladimir Zhirinovsky's Liberal Democratic Party wins an unexpected 22.9 percent of the Russian vote.

1994

Jan. 15: Clinton, Yeltsin and Ukraine's President Kravchuk sign the trilateral accord to remove nuclear weapons from Ukraine.

Sept. 27: Clinton and Yeltsin hold a summit in Washington.

Dec. 11: Russian military launches offensive in Chechnya , which has declared its secession from Russia.

1995

May 9–10: Clinton and Yeltsin begin NATO-Russia dialogue.

Aug. 28–30: Bosnian Serbs shell Sarajevo, initiating NATO airstrikes as a response.

Oct. 23: Clinton and Yeltsin meet in Hyde Park, and agree on Russia's role in peace settlement in Bosnia.

Nov. 1–21: At Dayton, Ohio, talks to end the war result in Bosnian peace settlement.

1996

Jan. 9: Evgeny Primakov becomes the Russian foreign minister, replacing Andrei Kozyrev.

Jan.: "Davos Pact". Key oligarchs agree to give substantial financial support for Yeltsin's reelection campaign against communist Gennady Zyuganov.

April 19–21: Clinton, at St. Petersburg, attends nuclear safety conference and explains the NATO enlargement timetable to Yeltsin.

June–July: In first round presidential elections, Yeltsin wins with only a slight lead over Communist leader Zyuganov. In the second round Yeltsin defeats Zyuganov convincingly.

Nov. 5: Clinton wins reelection.

1997

Mar. 20–21: Yeltsin tries to convince Clinton not to admit former Soviet states into NATO at Helsinki.

May 27: Yeltsin signs the NATO-Russia Founding Act at a NATO Summit in Paris.

June 20–21: Yeltsin promises to investigate Russian weapons sales to Iran.

1998

Mar 23: Yeltsin replaces Prime Minister Viktor Chernomyrdin with Sergei Kiriyenko.

May 16–17: Russia officially joins the G-8.

Aug. 14–17: Russian engulfed in financial crisis.

Sept. 10: Yeltsin appoints Evegeny Primakov prime minister. Igor Ivanov becomes foreign minister.

Oct. 13: Kosovo crisis escalates.

1999

Feb. 6–23: United States leads peace talks on Kosovo in Rambouillet, France.

Mar. 23–24: NATO begins airstrikes against Serbia. Primakov, en route to meeting Gore in Washington, turns his plane around midair and returns to Moscow.

Apr. 23–24: Poland, Hungary, and Czech Republic join NATO.

May 12: Prime Minister Primakov replaced by Sergei Stepashin.

June 3: Finnish president Ahtisaari and Chernomyrdin agree to plan for ending the Kosovo War.

June 11–12: Russia troops rush the Pristina airport in defiance of agreements signed by Moscow.

June 16: Russia and United States agree on Russian role in NATO peace-keeping force in Kosovo.

Aug. 2: Chechen rebel forces invade Dagestan.

Aug. 9: Vladimir Putin becomes prime minister of Russia.

Sept.: Apartment bombings in several Russia cities, including Moscow, attributed to Chechen terrorists.

Sept. 23: Russia begins a ground invasion of Chechnya.

Nov. 18: Clinton and Yeltsin meet at OSCE Istanbul summit for a tense last summit.

Dec. 31: Yeltsin resigns Russian presidency early.

2000

Feb. 6: Russian troops capture Grozny, retake control of Chechnya.

Mar. 26: Putin wins Russian presidential election.

July: Putin meets with oligarchs, telling them to eschew further political activities.

2001

Jan. 20: George W. Bush inaugurated as president.

June 16: First Bush-Putin Summit, in Ljubljana, Slovenia.

Sept. 11: Al Qaeda terrorist attacks on World Trade Center and Pentagon kill three thousand people. Putin is first to call Bush with condolences.

Nov. 14–15: At Crawford, Texas, Bush and Putin have their second summit.

Dec. 13: United States announces withdrawal from ABM Treaty.

2002

May 24: Treaty on Strategic Offensive Reduction (SORT) signed.

May 29: At the Rome NATO Summit, the NATO-Russia Council is founded.

Oct 23: Chechen militants storm Moscow's Dubrovka Theater taking 850 people hostage; 130 die as a result of the gas pumped in to the theater by Russian security forces.

2003

Feb. 5: Secretary of State Colin Powell accuses Iraq of developing WMD in a speech to the UN Security Council.

Feb. 10: The Russian, French, and German leaders issue a joint statement opposing military intervention in Iraq.

Mar. 20: U.S.-led coalition invades Iraq.

Apr. 11–12: Putin, Chirac, and Schroeder meet in St. Petersburg to voice dissent against U.S. war in Iraq.

Sept. 26–27: Bush and Putin meet in Camp David.

Oct. 25: Mikhail Khodorkovsky arrested, charged with tax evasion and fraud.

Nov. 22: Georgian president Eduard Shevardnadze ousted in blood-less Rose Revolution by Mikheil Saakashvili.

2004

Jan. 4: Mikheil Saakashvili elected Georgian president.

Feb. 12: Putin calls Soviet collapse a "national tragedy."

Mar. 9: Sergei Lavrov becomes Russian foreign minister.

Mar. 14: Putin reelected to second term.

Mar. 29: Seven countries, including the three Baltic states, join NATO—Bulgaria, Estonia, Latvia, Lithuania, Romania, Slovakia, and Slovenia.

Sept. 1: Beslan school hostage crisis. Militants in North Caucasus take children and teachers hostage. At least 380 die.

Sept. 13: Putin consolidates power, with regional governors to be appointed from center, not elected regionally.

Nov 2. George W. Bush reelected president.

Nov. 21: Ukrainian's Orange Revolution begins after falsified election results.

Dec 26: A revote ordered by Ukraine's Supreme Court elects Viktor Yushchenko as president.

2005

Jan. 20: George W. Bush inaugurated for second term. Announces his Freedom Agenda.

Jan. 23: Viktor Yushchenko inaugurated as Ukraine's president.

Feb. 23–25: Third Bush-Putin summit, Bratislava. The two spar over democracy.

Feb.–Mar.: Kyrgyz president Askar Akayev ousted during Tulip Revolution and is replaced by Kurmanbek Bakiyev.

2006

Jan 1: Gazprom temporarily shuts off gas to Ukraine in dispute over price.

May 4: Vice President Dick Cheney gives controversial Vilnius speech attacking Russia.

Oct. 7: Outspoken journalist Anna Politkovskaya is assassinated.

Dec. 23: UNSC Resolution 1737 passed, sanctioning Iran.

2007

Feb.: United States begins negotiations to develop missile defense emplacements in Poland and Czech Republic. The Russian government opposes it strenuously.

Feb. 10: Putin gives confrontational speech attacking U.S. foreign policy at Forty-Third Munich Security conference.

Mar. 24: UN Security Council Resolution 1747 expands sanctions on Iran.

July 1–2: George H. W. and George W. Bush meet Putin for "Lobster Summit" in Kennebunkport, Maine.

2008

Feb. 18: United States recognizes Kosovo's independence from Serbia.

Mar. 2: Dmitry Medvedev elected president of Russia.

Mar. 3: UN Security Council Resolution 1803 passed, toughening language on Iran's nuclear program.

Apr. 4: Putin addresses NATO Conference at Bucharest, speaking out against membership action plans for Ukraine and Georgia and declares Ukraine "is not a real country."

Apr. 6: Bush and Putin's last summit in Sochi produces the Strategic Framework Declaration.

May 7: Medvedev sworn in as president of Russian Federation, and Putin becomes prime minister. They announce a new "tandem."

Aug. 7: Russian-Georgian war over South Ossetia begins.

Aug. 11: Bush and Putin meet for last time at Beijing Olympics.

Aug. 20: Poland and United States sign an agreement to deploy missile defense interceptors in Central Europe.

Sept. 15: Lehman Brothers goes under, unleashing a global financial crisis and prompting Russia to develop an economic safeguarding plan.

Sept. 27: UN Security Council passes a resolution pressuring Iran to comply with international efforts to monitor its nuclear program.

Nov. 4: Barack Obama elected president.

Nov. 5: Medvedev announces plans to install Iskander missiles in Kaliningrad, partially in response to U.S. missile defense emplacements to be set in Poland or Czech Republic.

Nov. 22: Bush holds last meeting with Medvedev at the APEC Summit in Peru.

2009

Jan. 1: Russia shuts off gas to Ukraine again.

Jan. 20: Obama inaugurated as U.S. president.

Mar. 6: Lavrov and Clinton meet in Geneva, at which Clinton gives Lavrov a "reset" button in Russian, except it is misspelled to say "overload."

Apr. 1: Medvedev and Obama meet in London.

July 7–8: U.S.-Russia Summit, takes places in Moscow. The Bilateral Presidential Commission is established.

Sept.: Obama announces that missile defense installations in Poland are to be scrapped.

Sept. 24–25: At the G-20 Pittsburg summit, Obama and Medvedev discuss Iran's secret nuclear enrichment site at Qom.

Nov. 29: Medvedev submits a proposed European Security Treaty.

2010

Feb. 14: Viktor Yanukovych defeats Yulia Tymoshenko to become the president of Ukraine.

Apr. 8: Obama and Medvedev sign New START in Prague.

Apr. 10: A Polish aircraft crashes near Smolensk, killing President Lech Kaczynski and other leading Polish figures.

Apr. 15: Kurmanbek Bakiyev resigns his presidency of Kyrgyzstan in response to a popular uprising.

June 3: Ukrainian parliament states that it will belong to no military bloc.

June 9: UN Security Council Resolution 1929 passes, with Russian support, imposing further sanctions on Iran for its nuclear program.

June 24: Medvedev and Obama meet in the United States, visiting a famous D.C. burger joint. Medvedev tours Silicon Valley and opens his first Twitter account.

June 27: Anna Chapman and nine other Russians are arrested for espionage.

Oct. 30: Lavrov and Clinton meet in Hanoi at the East Asia summit.

Nov. 19–20: NATO-Russia Council meets for the first time since the August war with Georgia.

Nov. 28: U.S. diplomatic papers published online at WikiLeaks.

2011

Mar. 17: Russia abstains from UN Security Council Resolution 1973, refusing to use its veto to prevent military action in Libya and support for the ouster of Qaddafi.

May 2: Osama Bin Laden killed in Abbottabad, Pakistan.

July 4: NATO-Russia Council meets at Sochi.

Sept. 4: Bushehr nuclear plant in Iran goes online.

Sept. 6: First line of Nord Stream goes online.

Sept. 24: Putin and Medvedev announce "castling move" to switch places in 2012.

Sept. 26: Finance Minister Alexei Kudrin resigns.

Oct. 4: Russia and China block UN Security Council Resolution to intervene in Syria's civil conflict.

Nov.: Medvedev announces that cooperative missile defense negotiations have broken down.

Nov. 23: United States withdraws from CFE Treaty cooperation.

Dec. 10: Thousands of Russian protesters reacting to what they consider fraudulent parliamentary elections rally in Bolotnaya Square.

2012

Feb. 5: Russia and China veto UN Security Resolution on Russian protests.

Mar. 4: Putin wins reelection as president of Russia.

Mar. 26–27: Seoul Nuclear Summit occurs, at which Obama promises Medvedev "increased flexibility" after U.S. presidential election.

Apr. 16: ExxonMobil and Rosneft signed an agreement to jointly explore Russia's Arctic.

Apr. 20–21: NATO Summit meets in Chicago, but the NATO-Russia Council does not meet, because of the impasse over missile defense.

May 6: Large protests occur the day before President Putin's inauguration.

May 7: Putin inaugurated for third presidential term.

May 18: Putin cancels trip to United States for G-8 summit, sends Medvedev instead.

June 18–19: Putin and Obama meet at the G-20 meeting in Mexico.

Sept. 18: Russia ejects United States Agency for International Development.

Oct. 8: Second line of Nord Stream goes online.

Nov. 6: President Obama is reelected to second term.

Dec. 14: Justice for Sergei Magnitsky Bill passed into law, imposing visa and financial sanctions on some Russian officials.

Dec. 21: Duma, in response, passes the Dima Yakovlev law, ending U.S. adoptions of Russian children.

2013

Jan. 20: Obama, in inaugural speech, highlights global democracy promotion as key goal.

Mar. 16: Obama administration abandons phase four of missile defense plans, citing new dangers from North Korea.

Apr. 14: National Security Advisor Thomas Donilon visits Moscow and delivers a letter from Obama to Putin with suggestions for resuming engagement on a range of issues. Two presidential summits are planned for 2013.

Apr. 15–19: Chechen brothers Tsarnaev detonate bombs at the Boston Marathon killing three and injuring dozens. Putin and Obama pledge to increase counterterrorist cooperation.

May 7: Secretary of State John Kerry visits Moscow and meets with Putin and Lavrov. Russia and the United States agree to convene a multilateral conference to explore ways of resolving the Syrian crisis.

Aug. 8: The White House cancels the planned Moscow Summit.

Sept. 5: At the G-20 meeting in St. Petersburg, Obama and Putin clash over intervention in Syria's civil war.

Notes

INTRODUCTION

1. The summit is graphically documented in the BBC documentary, *Putin, Russia and the West* (2011), part 4.

2. The G-20, the Group of Twenty Finance Ministers and Central Bank Governors, represents the world's twenty leading economies. It was founded during the 2008 global financial crisis to manage international economic problems.

3. Russia Today, June 20, 2012, http://rt.com/politics/putin-obama-mexico-g20-us -293/.

4. Remarks by President Obama and President Putin of Russia after Bilateral Meeting, The White House, June 1819, 2012, www.whitehouse.gov/the-press-office/2012/06 /18/remarks-president-obama-and-president-putin-rusia-after-bilateral-meetin.

5. *Moscow Times*, September 9, 2013.

6. Remarks by Senator Sam Nunn at Carnegie Corporation of New York Conference "The Future of Western-Russian Intellectual Cooperation," Washington, DC, May 1, 2013.

7. Inaugural address by President Obama, www.whitehouse.gov/the-press-office/2013 /01/21/inaugural-address-president-barack-obama.

PROLOGUE: GEORGE H. W. BUSH AND RUSSIA REBORN

1. www.nytimes.com/1991/12/26/wolrd/end-of-the-soviet-union-text-of-gorbachev's -farewell-address.html?pagewanted+print&src=pm.

2. "End of The Soviet Union," text of Bush's address to nation on Gorbachev's resignation, December 25, 1991, http://www.nytimes.com/1991/12/26/world/end-soviet -union-text-bush-s-address-nation-gorbachev-s-resignation.html.

3. Interview with Brent Scowcroft.

4. Robert Gates, *From the Shadows* (New York: Simon and Schuster, 1996), ch. 26.

5. See in particular the piece by George Kolt, head of the CIA's Office of Soviet Analysis, "The Soviet Cauldron," reprinted in Eugene Rumer and Celeste Wallander, ed., *Russia Watch: Essays in Honor of George Kolt* (Washington, DC: CSIS Press, 2007), p. 84.

6. Interview with Rosemarie Forsythe.

7. George Bush and Brent Scowcroft, *A World Transformed* (New York: Vintage Books, 1999), p. 505.

8. Ibid., p. 515.

9. Interview with Brent Scowcroft.

10. Bush and Scowcroft; James A. Baker, *The Politics of Diplomacy* (New York: Putnam, 1995).

11. Bush and Scowcroft, p. 564.

12. Gates, p. 552.

13. When the author taught at MGIMO in 2008, none of her students accepted that the Soviet Union had collapsed because of its internal weaknesses. They were convinced that outside forces—particularly the United States and its "special services" had caused the collapse.

14. Angela Stent, *Russia and Germany Reborn: Unification, the Soviet Collapse and the New Europe* (Princeton: Princeton University Press 1999), p. 74.

15. Gates, chs. 27–29.

16. Interview with senior Bush administration official.

17. For an instructive justification of the policies of one of the chief reformers, see Yegor Gaidar, *Collapse of An Empire* (Washington, DC: Brookings Institution Press, 2007). He describes the dire straits of the Russian economy in the fall of 1991.

18. Ibid.

19. James M. Goldgeier and Michael McFaul, *Power and Purpose: U.S. Policy toward Russia after the Cold War* (Washington, DC: Brookings Institution Press), p. 53.

20. Interview with Ambassador Richard Gardner.

21. "The Lisbon Protocol at a Glance," www.armscontrol.org/print/3289; Amy Wolf, "Nuclear Weapons in the Former Soviet Union: Location, Command and Control," Congressional Research Service Brief, November 27, 1996, www.fas.org/spp/svarious /crs/91-144.htm.summ.

22. http://www.youtube.com/watch?v=NRY1DBLUJaw.

23. For a detailed discussion of the evolution and accomplishments of the program, see "Changing Threats in the Post-Cold War World," speech by Senator Sam Nunn at the Monterey Institute of International Studies, August 20, 1995.

24. "Nunn-Lugar Cooperation Initiative," www.dtra.mil/Missions/nunn-lugar/nunn -lugar-hom.aspx.

25. Interview with Daniel Poneman, Deputy Secretary of Energy, who worked in George H. W. Bush's White House.

26. Yegor Gaidar interview in Daniel Yergin and Joseph Stanislaw, *The Commanding Heights* (New York: Simon and Shuster, 1998), pp. 280–281.

27. See for instance Angela Stent and Daniel Yergin, "Send Help before It's Too Late," *New York Times,* December 15, 1991. They suggested a Strategic Food Initiative to ensure that enough food reached Russia and the other republics. http://www.nytimes .com/1991/12/15/opinion/send-help-before-it-s-too-late.html.

28. "Nixon Urges More Aid to Russia," Associated Press, January 6, 1992.

29. Goldgeier and McFaul, p. 79.

30. Interview with Brent Scowcroft.

31. Interview with Richard Armitage.

32. Angela Stent, "Russia's Economic Revolution and the West," *Survival* 37, no.1 (Spring 1995): 121–143.

33. Interview with Armitage.

34. Interview with Anatoly Chubais.

CHAPTER ONE: THE BILL AND BORIS SHOW

1. Cited in Strobe Talbott, *The Russia Hand: A Memoir of Presidential Diplomacy* (New York: Random House, 2002), p. 42.

2. Interview with Richard Haass.

3. Talbott, p. 5.

4. Talbott had devoted much of his prior professional career as a journalist to writing about the USSR and Soviet-U.S. relations.

5. Interview with Strobe Talbott.

6. Remarks by President Clinton to the American Society of Newspaper Editors, The White House, April 1, 1993, http://clinton6.nara.gov/1993/04/1993-04-01-presidents-speech-to-am-soc-of-newspaper-editors.html.

7. Yegor Gaidar *Collapse of an Empire* (Washington, DC: Brookings Institution Press, 2007).

8. Cited in Daniel Yergin and Joseph Stanislaw, *The Commanding Heights* (New York: Simon and Shuster, 1998), p. 281.

9. Thane Gustafson, *Capitalism Russian Style* (Cambridge: Cambridge University Press, 1999).

10. See Peter Reddaway and Dmitri Glinsky, *The Tragedy of Russia's Reforms* (Washington, DC: Carnegie Endowment for International Peace 2001); Stephen Cohen, *Failed Crusade: America and the Tragedy of Post-Communist Russia* (New York: Norton, 2001).

11. Edward Keenan, "Moscovite Political Folkways," *Russian Review* 45 (1986): 125–181.

12. Information from Strobe Talbott.

13. Interview with Rosemarie Forsythe.

14. Information from Strobe Talbott.

15. Interview with senior Yeltsin-era official.

16. Bill Clinton, *My Life* (New York: Vintage, 2005), p. 508.

17. "At least Yeltsin's not a mean drunk," Clinton said after the Vancouver summit. Talbott, p. 65.

18. Clinton, p. 882.

19. Boris Yeltsin, *Midnight Diaries* (New York: Public Affairs, 2000), p. 134.

20. Aleksandr Korzhakov, *Boris Eltsin: Ot Rassveta do Zakata* (Moscow: Interbook, 1997), p. 236.

21. For an insider's account of Yeltsin's changing views, see *Epokha Iel'tsina* (Moscow: Bagrus, 2001), ch. 5.

22. Clinton, p. 549.

23. Interview with Thomas Pickering.

24. Lilia Shevtsova, *Yeltsin's Russia* (Washington, DC: Carnegie Endowment for International Peace, 1999), p. 91.

25. Talbott, p. 205.

26. David E. Hoffman, *The Oligarchs: Wealth and Power in the New Russia* (New York: Public Affairs, 2002); Chrystia Freeland, *Sale of the Century: the Inside Story of the Second Russian Revolution* (London: Abacus, 2006).

27. Interview with Strobe Talbott.

28. For a semifictional account, see Yuri Zeltser and Grace Cary Bickley, *Spinning Boris*, TV film, dir. Roger Spottiswoode (New York: Showtime Networks, 2003).

29. Talbott interview.

30. Angela Stent, *Russia and Germany Reborn: Unification, the Soviet Collapse and the New Europe* (Princeton: Princeton University Press 1999), p. 188.

31. Pickering interview.

32. *Epokha Ie'ltsina,* p. 471.

33. Interview with Sergei Karaganov.

34. See Jack Matlock, *Superpower Illusions* (New Haven: Yale University Press, 2010); Stephen Cohen, *Soviet Fates and Lost Alternatives* (New York: Columbia University Press, 2009).

35. Interview with Alexander Voloshin.

36. Evgeny Primakov, *Gody v Bol'shoi Politike* (Moscow: Kollektsia "Sovershenno Sekretno," 1999), p. 212.

37. Talbott, pp. 194–195.

38. Interview with Daniel Poneman.

39. Talbott, p. 114.

40. Interview with Daniel Poneman.

41. Interview with Rose Gottemoeller.

42. The billionaire financier George Soros made a contribution to alleviating this situation by creating the International Science Foundation, which gave grants to Russian scientists to continue their research in new directions.

43. Goldgeier and McFaul, p. 293.

44. Interviews with Thomas Pickering, Eric Edelman.

45. *Los Angeles Times*, June 22, 1989.

46. Mark Katz, "Iran and Russia," in Robin Wright, ed., *The Iran Primer: Power, Politics and U.S. Policy* (Washington, DC: United States Institute of Peace, 2010).

47. Anthony Cordesman and Adam Seitz, *Iranian Weapons of Mass Destruction* (Washington, DC: Center for Strategic and International Studies, 2009), pp. 209–210.

48. Goldgeier and McFaul, p. 301.

49. Talbott, pp. 65–66.

50. Goldgeier and McFaul, pp. 176–177.

51. Anton Khlopkov and Anna Lutkova, *The Bushehr NPP: Why did it Take so long?* (Moscow: Center for Energy and Security Studies, August 21, 2010), p. 7, www.ceness-russia.org.

52. Talbott, pp. 255, 258, 265, 294–295.

CHAPTER TWO: RETHINKING EURO-ATLANTIC SECURITY

1. Angela Stent, "Reluctant Europeans: Three Centuries of Russian Ambivalence toward the West," in Robert Legvold, ed., *Russian Foreign Policy in the Twenty-First Century in the Shadow of the Past* (New York: Columbia University Press, 2007), ch. 5.

2. See Jack Matlock, *Autopsy on an Empire: The American Ambassador's Account of the Collapse of the Soviet Union* (New York: Random House, 1995); Mary Elise Sarotte, *1989: The Struggle to Create Post–Cold War Europe* (Princeton: Princeton University Press, 2011).

3. Angela Stent, "Gorbachev's Reagan," *Weekly Standard*, October 28, 1996, p. 22.

4. Stent, *Russia and Germany Reborn,* p. 225.

5. Ibid., pp. 113–114.

6. George Kennan, "A Fateful Error," *New York Times,* February 5, 1997.

7. "America and Europe: Common Challenges and Common Answers," lecture by Volker Ruehe, Georgetown University, March 2, 1993, pp. 9–10.

8. http://usa.usembassy.de/etexts/ga6-890531.htm.

9. Article 5 of the 1949 Washington Treaty commits all NATO member states to collective defense. If one member is attacked, it is considered an attack on all. In fact, the only time that Article 5 was invoked was after the September 11 terrorist attacks on the United States.

10. Clinton, p. 750.

11. Interviews with Ambassadors James Collins and Thomas Pickering.

12. Ronald Asmus, *Opening NATO's Door* (Washington, DC: Council on Foreign Relations, 2004).

13. Interview with Brent Scowcroft.

14. Interview with Madeleine Albright.

15. Primakov, *A World Challenged*, p. 242.

16. Interview with Anatoly Chubais.

17. Ivo Daalder, *Getting to Dayton: The Making of America's Bosnia Policy* (Washington, DC: Brookings Institution Press, 2000), p. 16.

18. Richard Holbrooke, *To End A War* (New York: Modern Library, 1999), p. 117.

19. Talbott, p. 76.

20. Holbrooke, p. 117.

21. Yeltsin, *Midnight Diaries*, p. 259.

22. Interview with Igor Ivanov.

23. At the height of this crisis came one of the more notable moments in U.S.-Russian relations, when Yeltsin proposed to Clinton that they should meet on a submarine and solve the problem themselves. Interview with Strobe Talbott.

24. Yeltsin, *Midnight Diaries*, p. 266.

25. Ibid., p. 349.

26. Talbott, pp. 361–362.

27. Interview with senior Russian official; Talbott, pp. 362–363.

28. *Washington Post,* April 22, 1996.

29. Clinton, p. 869.

30. Interview with Voloshin.

CHAPTER THREE: BUSH AND PUTIN IN THE AGE OF TERROR

1. Fiona Hill and Clifford Gaddy, *Vladimir Putin: Operative in the Kremlin* (Washington DC: Brookings Institution Press, 2013), ch. 5.

2. Ibid., p. 183.

3. Ibid., p. 201.

4. Allen C. Lynch, *Vladimir Putin and Russian Statecraft* (Washington, DC: Potomac Books, 2011), pp. 22–24.

5. Vladimir Putin, *First Person* (New York: Public Affairs, 2000), pp. 69, 80.

6. Alexander Rahr, *Wladimir Putin: Der "Deutsche" im Kreml* (Munich: Universitaets Verlag, 2000).

7. Lynch, pp. 34–37.

8. According to Kissinger, Putin early on told him that they shared the background of an intelligence officer—Putin in the KGB and Kissinger in army intelligence during the war.

9. Interview with John Evans.

10. Interviews with Ambassadors James Collins, Thomas Pickering, and Deputy Secretary of State Richard Armitage.

11. Putin, p. 178.

12. "Rossiia Na Rubezhe Tysiachletii," *Nezavisimaia Gazeta*, December 30, 1999; http://ww.ng.ru/politics/1999-12-30/4_millenium.html.

13. Hill and Gaddy, ch. 3.

14. Bobo Lo, "Evolution or Regression? Russian Foreign Policy in Putin's Second Term," in H. Blakkisrud, ed., *Towards a Post-Putin Russia* (Oslo: Norwegian Institute of International Affairs, 2006), p. 63.

15. *Foreign Policy Concept of the Russian Federation*, reprinted in Igor Ivanov, *The New Russian Diplomacy* (Washington, DC: Brookings Institution Press, 2000), appendix.

16. Peter Baker and Susan Glasser, *Kremlin Rising* (New York: Simon and Schuster, 2005), ch. 2.

17. George W. Bush, *Decision Points* (New York: Crown Publishers, 2011).

18. Condoleezza Rice, *Extraordinary, Ordinary People* (New York: Crown Archetype, Random House, 2010), p. 163.

19. Elisabeth Bumiller, *Condoleezza Rice: An American Life* (New York: Random House, 2007), pp. 57–58.

20. Condoleezza Rice, *No Higher Honor* (New York: Random House, 2011), p. 262.

21. James Mann, *The Rise of the Vulcans* (New York: Penguin, 2004), pp. 204–205.

22. Bob Woodward, *Bush at War* (New York: Simon Schuster, 2002), p. 6.

23. Condoleezza Rice, "Promoting the National Interest," *Foreign Affairs* 79, no. 1 (2000): 45–62.

24. George Bush, "A Distinctly American Internationalism," speech at Ronald Reagan Presidential Library, November 19, 1999, http://www.mtholyoke.edu/acad/intrel/bush/wspeech.htm.

25. Bush Newsmaker interview on PBS' *Newshour with Jim Lehrer*, February 16, 2000, www.pbs.org/newshour/bb/election/jan-june00/bush_2-16.html.

26. The Second Presidential Debate between Gov. Bush and Vice President Gore, October 11, 2000, The Commission on Presidential Debates, http://www.debates.org/?page=october-11-2000-debate-transcript.

27. Baker and Glasser, p. 126.

28. Donald Rumsfeld, *Known and Unknown* (New York: Penguin, 2011), pp. 306–307.

29. Members of the Speaker's Advisory Group on Russia, *Russia's Road to Corruption*, www.fas.org/news/russia/2000/russia/part00-cover.htm.

30. National Intelligence Council, *Global Trends, 2015: A Dialogue about the Future with Nongovernmental Experts* (Washington, DC, December 2000).

31. Powell interview in BBC documentary, *Putin, Russia and the West*, episode 1, "Taking Control."

32. Interview with senior Russian official.

33. Interview with Deputy Secretary of State Richard Armitage.

34. Interview with Igor Ivanov.

35. "Vyisyilka rossiskikh diplomatov iz SSHA," Agentura.ru 2001.

36. See State 100169, June 8, 2001 (Unclassified telegram): "We have two terrific bureaus coming together." The author was working in the State Department's Office of Policy Planning at the time, and supported S/NIS's arguments that it was premature to close the bureau. Russia and the post-Soviet states still had much more in common with each other than with any European country. The new administration wanted to make the point that Russia did not deserve special attention and that the United States did not recognize its unique relationship with the post-Soviet states. In the second Bush administration, the Central Asian countries were taken out of the European bureau and put in the South Asian Bureau.

37. Interview with A. Elizabeth Jones.

38. http://www.washingtonpost.com/wp-srv/onpolitics/transcripts/bushtext022701.htm.

39. Bush, *Decision Points*, p. 195.

40. Rice, *No Higher Honor*, p. 63.

41. Bush, *Decision Points*, pp. 195–196.

42. In the BBC documentary, *Putin, Russia and the West*, Ivanov and Rice recount how, when they were attending the May 2002 Moscow summit, they slipped out of the Bolshoi Ballet's production of *The Nutcracker*, which bored them, and instead attended an avant-garde modern dance performance.

43. Rice, *No Higher Honor*, pp. 62, 174.

44. Transcript of Bush and Putin news conference, June 18, 2011, http://cnn.worldnews.printhtis.clickability.com/pt/cpt?expire=-1&title=CNN.com+-+Transcript%3A+Bush.

45. Interview with State Department official who attended the talks.

46. Bush, *Decision Points,* p. 196.

47. Rice, *No Higher Honor*, p. 63.

48. Powell interview in BBC documentary *Putin, Russia and the West*, part 1.

49. "Bush I Putin: Idealnaia para," *Kommersant Vlast'*, no. 25 (June 26, 2001).

50. Interviews with senior Bush administration officials.

51. Peggy Noonan, "A Chat in the Oval Office," *Wall Street Journal,* June 26, 2001.

52. Baker and Glasser, p. 121.

53. Steve Coll, *Ghost Wars* (New York: Penguin Press, 2004), p.185.

54. See Report of the 9/11 Commission, http://www.9-11commission.gov/report/911 Report.pdf.

55. Evgeny Primakov, *A World Challenged* (Washington, DC: Brookings Institution Press, 2004), p. 76.

56. Bush, *Decision Points,* p. 196; Woodward, p. 118.

57. *Putin, Russian and the West*, part 1.

58. http://www.ng.ru/politics/2001-09-20/insider.html.

59. Primakov, *A World Challenged,* p. 69.

60. *Putin, Russia and the West.*

61. Baker and Glasser, p. 130. Ivanov, who in some ways resembled Putin, had complained to a U.S. official after Putin's 1999 selection by the Yeltsin family, "I don't understand why he was chosen. I was a general, and he was only a KGB lieutenant-colonel."

62. Interview with Mikhail Kasyanov, who was then Putin's prime minister.

63. Woodward, p. 118.

64. Interview with Grigory Yavlinsky.

65. "Putin to Offer vision of Europe," CNN online, September 25, 2001, http://edition .cnn.com/2001/WORLD/europe/09/25/gen.russia.germany1050/index.html.

66. Rumsfeld, pp. 372, 382–384.

67. Interview with John Bolton.

68. *Nezvisimaia Gazeta*, December 21, 2001; January 15, 2002.

69. Andrew Jack, *Inside Putin's Russia* (Oxford: Oxford University Press, 2004), p. 260.

70. Cited in Baker and Glasser, p. 138.

71. Putin's speech to the Bundestag, www.freerepublic.com/focus/f-new/532647 /posts.

72. Rumsfeld, p. 397.

73. George Tenet, *At the Center of the Storm* (New York: Harper Collins, 2007), pp. 275– 276.

74. Conversations with several officials involved in counterterrorism cooperation, including Richard Armitage.

75. Text of Bush-Putin press conference, *PBS Newshour*, November 13, 2001, www.pbs .org/newshour/bb/terrorism/july-dec01/excerpts_11-13.html.

76. Interview with Ambassador Steven Pifer. The Russian ambassador told him that going to Crawford would be "a slight."

77. Remarks by President Bush and President Putin to Russian exchange students and students of Crawford High School, November 15, 2001, George W. Bush Archives, http://georgewbush-whitehouse.archives.gov/news/releases/2001/11/20011115-4.html.

78. According to one senior official, when the advance Russian team arrived in Crawford and was shown the ranch, the members asked, "When are we going to see the real home?"

79. Interview with Don Evans.

80. Interview with Dmitri Trenin.

81. Interview with John Beyrle.

82. Interview with Igor Ivanov.

83. Interview with Alexander Voloshin.

84. Angela Stent and Lilia Shevtsova, "America, Russia and Europe: A Realignment?" *Survival* 44, no. 4 (Winter 2002–2003): 21–31.

85. Rumsfeld recalls in his memoirs that in August 2001, General Yuri Baluevsky, the country's second-ranking military officer, had told him that they believed that the brains behind the missile defense program was none other than Lyndon LaRouche. Rumsfeld, p. 309.

86. John Bolton, *Surrender Is Not an Option* (New York: Simon and Shuster, 2008), p. 74.

87. Secretary Rumsfeld Joint Press Availability with Russian Defense Minister, December 17, 2001, http://avalon.law.yale.edu/sept11/dod_brief132.asp.

88. Jack, pp. 2–3.

89. Text of President Bush's 2002 State of the Union Address, January 29, 2002, www.washingtonpost.com/wp-srv/onpoliyics/transcripts/sou012.

90. Interview with Steven Pifer.

91. Bolton, p. 77.

92. Treaty between the United States of America and the Russian Federation on Strategic Offensive Reductions, May 24, 2002, www.state.gov/avc/trty/127129.htm.

93. Goldgeier and McFaul, p. 323; Victor Yesin, "Nuclear Disarmament: Problems and Prospects," *Russia in Global Affairs* 6, no. 1 (January–March 2008), http://eng.global affairs.ru/number/n_10357.

94. Primakov, *Gody v Bol'shoi Politike*, p. 67.

95. For a full text of the "Joint Declaration on a New Strategic Partnership," see http://www.state.gov/avc/try/127129.htm.

96. *Putin, Russia and the West*, interviews with Lord Robertson and Chancellor Schroeder.

97. "Why NATO Should Invite Russia to Join," memo from Richard Haass, Director of Policy Planning, to Secretary Colin Powell, July 27, 2001. Memo in author's possession with permission of State Department.

98. Interview with Richard Haass.

99. James A. Baker, "Russia in NATO?" *Washington Quarterly* 26 (Winter 2002): 95–103.

100. For the collection of speeches and provisions, see *NATO-Russia Council, Rome Summit, 2002*, NATO, www.nato.int/docu/basictext/b020528e.htm.

101. "The Transatlantic Partnership at the Crossroads: Meeting NATO's Five Challenges," speech by U.S. Ambassador to NATO Alexander Vershbow at the Netherland Institute of International Relations, March 23, 2001, http://european-security.com/index.php?id=868.

102. Primakov, *Gody v Bol'shoi Politike*, p. 64.

103. Author's discussions while serving in the State Department's Office of Policy Planning and discussions with United States–NATO and at the Riga meeting of the Euro-Atlantic Partnership and Cooperation Council, 2001.

104. "Prague Summit Declaration," www.nato.int/docu/pr/2002/p02-127e.htm.

105. Baker and Glasser, p. 221.

106. Hill and Gaddy, pp. 198–199.

107. *Putin, Russia and the West*, part 1; Baker and Glasser, p. 87.

108. Lilia Shevtsova, *Putin's Russia* (Washington, DC: Carnegie Endowment for International Peace, 2005), pp. 114–120; Olga Khryshtanovskaia, *Anatomiia Rossiskoi Elity* (Moscow: Zakharov, 2004), pp. 372–376.

CHAPTER FOUR: THE IRAQ WAR

1. http://www.bartleby.com/124/pre67.html.

2. George W. Bush, *Decision Points* (New York: Crown Publishers, 2011), pp. 397, 430, 435.

3. Condoleezza Rice, *No Higher Honor* (New York: Random House, 2010), pp. 325, 328.

4. Bush, *Decision Points*, p. 233.

5. For Khodorkovsky's speech at the Russian Industrialists' meeting, see *Putin, Russia and The West*, episode 1.

6. Quoted in Daniel Yergin, *The Quest* (New York: Penguin 2012), p. 40.

7. Newsru, December 2005.

8. Putin's remarks were made at the Valdai Club discussion meeting in Moscow, September 6, 2004.

9. The author attended the meeting with Putin, which lasted well into the night.

10. *Nezavisimaia Gazeta*, September 11, 2004.

11. Bush, "President's Address to the U.N. General Assembly," *New York Times*, September 21, 2004, http://www.nytimes.com/2004/09/21/international/21WEB-PTEX.html.

12. Prior to this, Russia had a mixed electoral system. Half of the members of the Duma were elected in single member districts—similar to the U.S. House of Representatives, and half from party lists using proportional representation. Henceforth only the latter system would be used.

13. Interview with Stephen Hadley.

14. Mr. Rather was fired for inaccurate comments he had made about President Bush's National Guard record.

15. *Washington Post*, February 24, 2005, http://www.washingtonpost.com/wp-dyn/content/article/2005/03/23/AR2005032300625.html.

16. Peter Baker and Susan Glasser, *Kremlin Rising* (New York: Simon and Schuster, 2005), p. 377.

17. Daniel Treisman, *The Return* (New York: Free Press, 2010), p. 113.

18. *Putin, Russia and the West*, part 11.

19. Stephen Sestanovich, *At Odds with Iran and Iraq: Can the United States and Russia resolve their differences?* (Washington, DC: Century Foundation and Stanley Foundation, February 2003).

20. See Donald Rumsfeld, *Known and Unknown* (New York: Penguin, 2011), ch. 30.

21. Dick Cheney, *In My Time* (New York: Threshold Editions, 2012); Rumsfeld; Paul Pillar "Intelligence, Policy and the War in Iraq," *Foreign Affairs* 26 (March–April 2006).

22. John Bolton, *Surrender Is Not an Option* (New York: Simon and Shuster, 2008), pp. 442–447.

23. Rumsfeld, p. 441.

24. Bush, *Decision Points*, p. 245.

25. Rumsfeld, p. 444.

26. CNN, *"Old Europe" Hits Back at Rumsfeld*, January 24, 2003, http://www.cnn.com/2003/WORLD/europe/01/24/france.germany.rumsfeld/.

27. Interview with Richard Haass.

28. Interviews with Richard Armitage, Richard Haass.

29. For the speech, see http://www.cnn.com/2003/US/02/05/sprj.irq.powell.transcript/.

30. Colin Powell in *Putin, Russia and the West*, part 1.

31. Gazeta.ru, February 10, 2003; *Izvestiia*, February 11, 2003.

32. Baker and Glasser, pp. 224–225.

33. Interview with Alexander Voloshin.

34. Primakov, *A World Challenged*, pp. 91–93.

35. Interview with Daniel Fried.

36. James M. Goldgeier and Michael McFaul, *Power and Purpose: U.S. Policy toward Russia after the Cold War* (Washington, DC: Brookings Institution Press), p. 328.

37. Bush, *Decision Points*, p. 233.

38. Rice, *No Higher Honor*, p. 212.

39. Interviews with Don Evans.

40. Interview with Richard Haass.

41. Goldgeier and McFaul, pp. 106–328.

42. Baker and Glasser, p. 223.

43. Lilia Shevtsova, *Putin's Russia* (Washington, DC: Carnegie Endowment for International Peace 2005), p. 267.

44. Evgeny Primakov, *Gody v Bol'shoi Politike* (Moscow: Kollektsia "Sovershenno Sekretno," 1999), *p. 240.*

45. Andrew Jack, *Inside Putin's Russia* Oxford: Oxford University Press, 2004), p. 290; Baker and Glasser, p. 220.

46. PBS, "Putin, Chirac, Schroeder Discuss Post-Saddam Iraq," *Online Newshour*, April 11, 2003, PBS.org, http://www.pbs.org/newshour/updates/meeting_04-11-03.html; Lenta.ru, April 12, 2003.

47. Grani.ru, September 24, 2003; newsru.com, September 23, 2003.

48. *Nezavisimaiia Gazeta*, August 8, 2004.

49. Woodward quoted in Baker and Glasser, p. 228.

50. Interviews with Richard Armitage, Steven Pifer.

51. Rice, *No Higher Honor*, pp. 212–214.

52. Jack, pp. 294–295.

53. This remark was made during a conversation with the author.

54. Baker and Glasser, pp. 229–230.

55. Shevtsova, *Putin's Russia*, p. 272.

CHAPTER FIVE: THE COLOR REVOLUTIONS

1. Charles King, "The Benefits of Ethnic War," *World Politics* 53, no. 4 (2001): 524–552.

2. Lincoln Mitchell, *The Color Revolutions* (Philadelphia: University of Pennsylvania Press, 2012), p. 15.

3. Interview with Matthew Bryza.

4. Interview with Thomas E., Graham.

5. *Washington Post*, November 11, 2003.

6. Interview with James MacDougall.

7. Interview with Ambassador Richard Miles.

8. Evgeny Primakov, *A World Challenged* (Washington, DC: Brookings Institution Press, 2004), p. 127.

9. Charles King, *The Ghost of Freedom* (New York: Oxford University Press, 2008), p. 230.

10. Interview with Matthew Bryza.

11. *Putin, Russia and the West*, part 11.

12. Ibid.

13. Interview with Ambassador Richard Miles.

14. Ibid.

15. Rice, *No Higher Honor*, p. 356.

16. Ronald D. Asmus, *A Little War That Shook The World* (New York: Palgrave Macmillan, 2010) pp. 56–57.

17. *Putin, Russia and the West*, part 11.

18. Interview with Miles. He was also critical of Saaskahvili's inner circle, including his American advisor Daniel Kunin.

19. http://www.eurasianet.org/departments/insight/articles/eav022404.shtml.

20. Angus Roxburgh, *The Strongman in the Kremlin: Vladimir Putin and the Struggle for Russia* (London: I. B Taurus, 2012), pp. 114–117.

21. "Johnson's Russia List," transcript of September 6, 2004, Valdai meeting, RussiaList.org, http://www.russialist.org/8369-putin.php.

22. "On the 'Orange Revolution' the U.S. has Spent Tens of Millions," http://obozrevatel.com/news/2007/4/161/165939.htm.

23. Polit.ru, May 6, 2004.

24. For a discussion, see Timothy Snyder, *The Reconstruction of Nations: Poland Ukraine and Belarus, 1569–1999* (New Haven: Yale University press, 2003); Andrew Wilson, *The Ukrainians: Unexpected Nation* (New Haven: Yale University press, 2002).

25. Daniel Yergin *Shattered Peace: The Origins of the Cold War and the National Security State* (Boston: Houghton Mifflin 1976), ch. 2.

26. Paul D'Anieri, *Orange Revolution and Aftermath* (Washington, DC: Woodrow Wilson Center Press, 2010).

27. Pavlosvky was a former Soviet dissident who became close to Putin's Kremlin, a "political technologist" in the Russian terminology. Nikonov, the ambitious grandson of Soviet foreign minister Vyacheslav Molotov, headed his own think tank in Moscow. Markov, a former liberal who had worked at the Moscow Carnegie Center, had become a staunch Putin backer.

28. *Putin, Russia and the West*, part 11.

29. Rice, *No Higher Honor,* p. 358.

30. Roxburgh, p. 133.

31. Oleksandr Sushko and Olena Prystayko, "Western Influence," in Anders Aslund and Michael McFaul, *Revolution in Orange* (Washington, DC: Carnegie Endowment For international Peace, 2006).

32. www.novgaz.ru/data/2005/17/06.html.

33. Sushko and Prystayko, p. 134.

34. Conversation with President Alxander Kwasniewski. Kwasniewski told the BBC that Putin had first suggested sending Yeltsin as mediator, but the Polish president rejected the suggestion.

35. *Putin, Russia and the West*, part 11.

36. Ivan Kravtsev, "Russia's Post-Orange Empire," www.opendemocracy.net/2947.

37. Interview with Andrei Kortunov who at that point worked for George Soros in Russia.

38. Comment by Sergei Markov at conference held at the Deutsche Gesellschaft fuer Auswaertige Politik, Berlin, March 22, 2005. The author was on a panel with Mr. Markov.

39. Press conference with Stanislav Belkovsky, Federal News Service, May 17, 2005, in Aslund and McFaul, p. 159.

40. Eric McGlinchey, "Autocrats, Islamists and the Rise of Radicalism in Central Asia," *Current History* 104, no. 684 (October 2005): 336–342.

41. www.newsru.ru/world/28Feb2005/vote/html; Associated Press, "Kyrgyz President Akayev Flees," Fox.com, http://www.foxnews.com/story/2005/03/25/report-kyrgyz-president-akayev-flees/; http://www.newsru.ru/world/28Feb2005/vote/html.

42. Martha Olcott, "Lessons of the Tulip Revolution," Testimony, Commission of Security and Cooperation in Europe, Hearing on Kyrgyzstan's Revolution: Causes and Consequences, April 7, 2005.

43. RIA Novosti, "Kyrgyzstan: Central Asian domino effect," RIA.ru. http://en.ria.ru/analysis/20050330/39700822.html.

44. Rumsfeld, p. 633.

45. Alexander Cooley, *Great Games, Local Rules* (New York: Oxford University Press, 2012), p. 102.

46. Interview with James MacDougall.

47. McGlinchey, pp. 337–338.

48. Cooley, p. 38.

49. Rice, *No Higher Honor*, p. 458.

50. Rumsfeld, pp. 635–636.

51. Putin's remarks to Valdai Club, Moscow, September 5, 2005.

52. Rumsfeld, p. 640.

53. George W. Bush, speech at International Republican Institute, Washington, DC, May 18, 2005, http://www.iri.org/sites/default/files/President%20Bush's%20speech.pdf.

54. Cooley, p. 2.

CHAPTER SIX: THE MUNICH SPEECH

1. Interview with Daniel Fried. The conversation took place when Bush was in London for his address to the British Parliament.

2. Interview with Stephen Hadley.

3. Interview with Thomas Graham. On September 28, 2004, the neoconservative think tank Project for a New American Century published a bipartisan Open Letter to Heads of State criticizing Russia for its democratic backsliding. Thereafter, Bush made his first negative statement on Russia, which, according to Graham, he did not want to do.

4. Interview with Joshua Bolten. Bush visited Ukraine in April 2008 and apparently found the political situation there opaque and challenging for an outsider to decipher.

5. Interview with Joshua Bolten.

6. Two notable examples were Bruce Jackson, head of the Project on Transitional Democracies, who lobbied hard for NATO enlargement to Ukraine and Georgia, and Randy Scheunemann, a lobbyist for Georgia, who became Senator John McCain's foreign policy advisor in the 2008 campaign. Those in the administration favoring a less confrontational policy toward Russia sometimes felt that these lobbyists had more clout that they did.

7. For instance, David Merkel, deputy assistant secretary of state of Central Asia and the Caucasus told the author that, in order to get his material cleared, he was not allowed to mention Russia.

8. Dick Cheney, *In My Time* (New York: Threshold Editions, 2012), p. 428.

9. Dick Cheney, speech at Vilnius Conference, Vilnius, 2006, http://georgewbush-whitehouse.archives.gov/news/releases/2006/05/print/20060504-i.html.

10. The author received contradictory accounts from Bush officials in the White House and State Department about whether the Cheney speech was coordinated with anyone outside the OVP.

11. http://oneworld.blogsome.com/2006/04/29/bush-meets-alieyv-in-washington.

12. Ilan Greenberg and Andrew Kramer, "Cheney, Visiting Kazakhstan, Wades into Energy Battle," *New York Times*, May 6, 2006, http://www.nytimes.com/2006/05/06

/world/europe/06cheney.html?pagewanted. Reinforcing the structural problems about coordinating policy toward Russia and Eurasia, Daniel Fried told the author that, although he had seen the Vilnius speech, he was not privy to what was planned for the vice president's speech in Kazakhstan.

13. Interview with David Merkel.

14. Interview with Stephen Hadley.

15. Newsru, "US Vice President Cheney Criticizes Russia for Limiting Freedoms," May 4, 2006, http:www.newsru./com/Russia/04may2006/cheyne.html.

16. Newsru, "Media Call Cheney's Speech on Russia 'Return of the Cold War,'" May 5, 2006, http://www.newsru.com/russia/05may2006/coldwar.html.

17. Phillippe Naughton, "Putin Takes Swipe at Hungry America's 'Comrade Wolf,'" *The Times,* May 10, 2006, http://www.thetimes.co.uk/tto/news/world/europe/article 2602032.ece .

18. Interview with Andrei Kortunov.

19. Vladislav Surkov, "Natsionalizatsia Budushchego," *Ekspert* online 43, November 20, 2006.

20. Surkov Press conference, G-8 Summit, Saint Petersburg, June 2006, http://en.g8 russia.ru/news/20060704/1168817.html.

21. Lenta, "Путин предпочел российскую демократию иракской," lenta.ru, http:// lenta.ru/news/2006/07/15/democracy/.

22. Bush, press conference, the White House, Washington, DC, October 17, 2007. This phrase greatly irked Russian opposition figures because Bush was implying that Russians were incapable of becoming democratic.

23. Putin, speech to members of the Valdai International Discussion Club, Sochi, September 14, 2007, www.kremlin.ru/eng/text/speeches/2007/09/14/1801_type82917 type84779_144106.html.

24. *Nezavisimaia Gazeta,* June 29, 2006.

25. Lenta.ru, July 14, 2006, http:/lenta.ru/news/2006/07/14/html.

26. Interview with Joshua Bolten.

27. Interview with Thomas Graham.

28. Interview with Yuri Ushakov.

29. Baker and Glasser, p. 384.

30. Angus Roxburgh, *The Strongman in the Kremlin: Vladimir Putin and the Struggle for Russia* (London: I. B Taurus, 2012), p. 178.

31. Alexander Goldfarb and Maria Litvinenko, *Death of a Dissident* (New York: Free Press, 2007).

32. Condoleezza Rice, *No Higher Honor* (New York: Random House, 2011), p. 363.

33. Putin, speech to members of the Valdai International Discussion Club, Sochi, September 14, 2007, www.kremlin.ru/eng/text/speeches/2007/09/14/1801_type82917 type84779_144106.shtml.

34. Vladimir Putin, speech, 43rd Munich Conference on Security Policy, Munich, February 12, 2007, http://www.washingtonpost.com/wp-dyn/content/artucle/2007/02/12 /AR2007021200555_pf.html.

35. Newsru.com. February 12, 2007, www.newsru.com/world/12Feb2007/putin.html.

36. Robert Gates, speech, Munich Security Conference, Munich, February 11, 2007, http://www.defense.gov/transcripts/transcript.aspx?transcriptid=3888.

37. Tony Snow, press briefing, The White House, Washington, DC, February 12, 2007, http://georgewbush-whitehouse.archives.gov/news/releases/2007/02/20070212-3.html.

38. *Economist*, "Not a Cold War, but a Tiff," February 15, 2007, http://www.economist .com/node/8703054/.

39. Some members of the audience clearly supported Putin's views.

40. Andrew Kramer, "Putin Is Said to Compare U.S. Policies to Third Reich," *New York Times,* May 9, 2007, http://www.nytimes.com/2007/05/10/world/europe/10russia.html.

41. Adi Ignatius, "A Tsar Is Born," *Time Magazine,* December 19, 2007, http://www.time.com/time/specials/2007/article/0,28804,1690753_1690757_1690766,00.html.

42. Dmitri Trenin, "Russia Leaves the West," *Foreign Affairs* 85, no. 4 (July–August 2006): 87–96.

43. Daniel Yergin, *The Quest* (New York: Penguin 2012), p. 302.

44. Robert S. Litwak, "Living with Ambiguity: Nuclear Deals with Iran and North Korea," *Survival* 50, no. 1 (February–March 2008): 91–118.

45. Director of National Intelligence, "Iran: Nuclear Intensions and Capabilities," National Intelligence Council, Washington, DC, November, 2007, http://www.dni.gov/files/documents/Newsroom/Press%20Releases/2007%20Press%20Releases/20071203_release.pdf.

46. *Kommersant,* March 12, 2001.

47. smi.ru/text/02/02/04/11455.html.

48. Hannes Adomeit, *Russlands Iran-Politik unter Putin* (Berlin: Stiftung Wissenschaft und Politik, 2007).

49. *Nezavisimaia Gazeta,* October 19, 2000.

50. Grani.ru, August 24, 2008.

51. Interview with John Bolton.

52. Gazeta.ru, June 20, 2007.

53. Adomeit, pp. 30–41; Yury Federov, "Russian Policy on Iran," *World Today* 63, no. 2 (February 2007): 4–6.

54. Interview with John Bolton.

55. Mark Fitzpatrick, "Iran and North Korea: The Proliferation Nexus," *Survival* 48, no. 1 (Spring 2006): 70; Eugene Rumer, *Russian Foreign Policy Beyond Putin,* Adelphi Paper 390 (London: Routledge, 2007), pp. 36–38.

56. Rice and Lavrov, press conference, U.S. Embassy Moscow, October 15, 2005.

57. Elaine Sciolino, "Russia and West Split on Iran Nuclear Issue," *New York Times,* March 7, 2006, http://www.nytimes.com/2006/03/07/international/europe/07iran.html?pagewanted=print.

58. Steven Lee Myers, "Russia Says It Opposes UN Sanctions on Iran," *New York Times,* August 26, 2006, http://www.nytimes.com/2006/08/26/world/middleeast/26russia.html.

59. UN resolutions 1737, 1747, 1803, http://www.un.org/sc/committees/1737/. UN Ambassador John Bolton told the author that it was much easier to negotiate with Andrei Denisov, Russia's UN ambassador until 2006, than with his successor Vitaly Churkin, whom Bolton characterizes as a "most unhelpful, Cold-War style emissary."

60. Rice, *No Higher Honor,* pp. 626–627.

61. Kommersant, 32, August 20, 2007.

62. Interviews with Stephen Rademaker, Eric Edelman.

63. Luke Harding, "Russia Threatening New Cold War over Missile Defence," *The Guardian,* April 10, 2007, http://www.guardian.co.uk/world/2007/apr/11/usa.topstories3.

64. RIA Novosti, "Putin, Rice Agree to Tone Down Rhetoric, Turn to Real Issues," en.ria.ru, May 15, 2007, http://en.ria.ru/world/20070515/65534640.html.

65. Condoleezza Rice, speech with Russian Foreign Minister Sergey Lavrov, Embassy of the United States, Moscow, May 15, 2007, http://iipdigital.usembassy.gov/st/english/article/2007/05/20070516083633idybeekcm0.501919.html#axzz2UjTgLQ4L.

66. Rice, *No Higher Honor*, pp. 577–578. Rice describes the CSTO as "a pitiful attempt to create a Warsaw-Pact like structure."

67. Wade Boese, "Bush, Putin Leave Arms Dispute Unsettled," Arms Control Today, May 2008, http://www.armscontrol.org/act/2008_05/BushPutin.

68. C. J. Chivers, "Putin Proposes Alternatives to Missile Defense," *New York Times*, June 9, 2007. http://www.nytimes.com/2007/06/09/world/europe/09azerbaijan.html.

69. Roxburgh, p. 203.

70. Fred Kaplan, "Putin's Clever Missile-Defense Gambit," Slate.com, July 5, 2007, http://www.slate.com/articles/news_and_politics/war_stories/2007/07/how_putin _played_bush_in_kennebunkport.html.

71. Rice, *No Higher Honor,* p. 580.

72. http://www.nytimes.com/2007/07/02/us/02cnd-putin.html?_r=0.

73. Interview with Eric Edelman.

74. Roxburgh, p. 204.

75. Peter Baker, "No Pact, but Bush, Putin Leave a Map," *Washington Post*, April 7, 2008, http://www.washingtonpost.com/wp-dyn/content/story/2008/04/07/ST20080407 00729.html .

CHAPTER SEVEN: FROM KOSOVO TO GEORGIA: THINGS FALL APART

1. Oksana Antonenko, "Russia and the Deadlock Over Kosovo," *Survival* 49, no. 5 (Autumn 2007): 93.

2. Ibid., p. 94.

3. Rice, *No Higher Honor,* p. 579.

4. Interview with James MacDougall.

5. www.rian.ru/wrorld/euorpa/20070608/66931903.html.

6. Strategic Survey 2008 (London: IISS Press, 2008), pp. 200–201.

7. RIA Novosti, February 22, 2008; *Kommersant*, January 25, 2007.

8. Nicholas Kulish and C. J. Chivers, "Kosovo Is Recognized, but Rebuked by Others," *New York Times*, February 19, 2008, http://www.nytimes.com/2008/02/19/world /europe/19kosovo.html?pagewanted=all.

9. Interview with Fiona Hill.

10. Rice, *No Higher Honor*, p. 636.

11. U.S.-Russia Strategic Framework Declaration, April 6, 2008, http://moscow.us embassy.gov/sochi-declaration-040608.html.

12. "President Bush Participates in Joint press Availability with President Putin of Russia," www.whitrehouse.gov/news/repeases/2008/04/print/200080406-3.html.

13. Rice, *No Higher Honor*, pp. 678–679.

14. Interview with Joshua Bolten.

15. George W. Bush, *Decision Points* (New York: Crown Publishers 2005), p. 434.

16. Rice, *No Higher Honor*, p. 670.

17. Interview with Victoria Nuland.

18. Ronald Asmus, *A Little War That Shook the World* (New York: Palgrave Macmillan, 2010), p. 244; interview with Eric Edelman.

19. Interview with Damon Wilson.

20. Interview with Fiona Hill. At one meeting she was asked, "Are you opposed to freedom and democracy?"

21. Rice, *No Higher Honor,* p. 672.

22. *Putin, Russia and the West*, part 3.

23. Eugene Rumer and Angela Stent, *Repairing U.S.-Russian Relations: A Long Road Ahead* (Washington, DC: Institute for National Strategic Studies and Georgetown University, 2009).

24. Angela Stent, *Russia and Germany Reborn: Unification, the Soviet Collapse and the New Europe* (Princeton: Princeton University Press, 1999).

25. Angela Stent, "Berlin's Russia Problem," *National Interest* 88 (2006).

26. Asmus, *A Little War That Shook the World*, p. 120.

27. Roxburgh, p. 224.

28. The author attended the late-night session on April 1, 2008, at which U.S. Deputy Assistant Secretary for the South Caucasus Matthew Bryza also spoke.

29. Interview with Stephen Hadley.

30. Rice, *No Higher Honor*, pp. 673–675. In *Putin, Russia and the West*, part 3, Steinmeier alludes to the fact that some Central Europeans made direct comparisons between Germany's actions and those of Nazi Germany.

31. Asmus, *A Little War That Shook the World*, pp. 133–134.

32. Bucharest summit Declaration, April 3, 2000, http://www.nato.int/cps/en/natolive /offical_texts_8443.htm?mode_pressrelease; conversation with Steven Hadley; *Putin, Russia and the West*, part 3.

33. Putin, speech, NATO Summit, Bucharest, 2008, www.unian.net/rus/news/news -247139.html.

34. Kommersant, "NATO Was Sold to a Blocking Stake," April 7, 2008, http:www .kommersant.ru/doc/877224.

35. Rice, *No Higher Honor,* pp. 675–676; Asmus, *A Little War That Shook the World*, pp. 135–136.

36. Grani.ru, "Saakashvili: Georgia Bucharest gave guarantees entry into NATO," April 5, 2008, www.grani.ru/War/m.135278.html.

37. News.bbc.co.uk/2/hi/europe/4534267.stm.

38. Interviews with Joshua Bolten and Richard Miles.

39. President Bush, speech, Freedom Square, Tbilisi, May 10, 2005, http://armenia .usembassy.gov/news051005.html.

40. Asmus, *A Little War That Shook the World*, pp. 147–148.

41. *Putin, Russia and the West*, part 3.

42. Rice, *No Higher Honor*, pp. 685–686.

43. Asmus, *A Little War That Shook the World*, p. 154.

44. Independent International Fact-Finding Mission on the Conflict in Georgia, www .ceiig.ch/report.html.

45. Roxburgh, p. 241.

46. You Tube, August 16, 2008, http://www.youtube.com/watch?v=syKMsDS2OzE.

47. Asmus, *A Little War That Shook the World*, p. 168; U.S. Cyber Consequences Unit, *Overview by the US-CCU of the Cyber Campaign against Georgia in August of 2008* (Washington, DC: August 2009).

48. Saakashvili called the report a "diplomatic victory for Georgia," www.ria.ru/world /20091001/187164307.html. Duma Foreign policy spokesman Konstantin Kosachev said the report identified Georgia as the aggressor, www.ria.ru/politics/20090930 /1870350.html.

49. Independent International Fact-Finding Mission on the Conflict in Georgia official website, www.ceiig.ch. The most comprehensive book on the war is Asmus's. He has been criticized for a pro-Georgia bias, but it remains the most extensive account of the

events leading up to and during the war. The real unknown is the Russian side, about which we still know very little.

50. Interview with Joshua Bolten.

51. Bush, *Decision Points*, p. 434.

52. Interview with Mike Mullen.

53. Asmus, *A Little War That Shook the World*, p. 199.

54. *Putin, Russia and the West*, part 3.

55. Interview with Stephen Hadley.

56. Rice, *No Higher Honor,* pp. 686–693; Rice, speech to German Marshall Fund, Washington, DC, September 18, 2008.

57. Asmus, *A Little War That Shook the World*, p. 203.

58. Russian media accused the United States of launching another Cold War. See *Trud* 151 (August 14, 2008).

59. Igor' Naumov, *Nezavisimaia Gazeta* 168 (August 12, 2008).

60. Transcript of the Meeting with the Participants of the International Club Valdai, September 12, 2008, www.kremlin.ru.

61. When the author taught a course on U.S.-Russian relations at MGIMO in the fall of 2008, her students set up stalls to collect humanitarian assistance for the "victims of genocide" in South Ossetia.

62. *Ekonomicheskie Novosti*, August 16, 2008.

63. Interview with Stephen Hadley.

64. Interview with Daniel Fried.

65. Dan Eggen, "Bush Reflects on Russian Relations," *Washington Post*, November 23, 2008, http://www.washingtonpost.com/wp-dyn/content/article/2008/11/22/AR2008 112200502.html?nav=hcmodule.

CHAPTER EIGHT: ECONOMICS AND ENERGY: THE STAKEHOLDER CHALLENGE

1. IMF Direction of Trade database.

2. Economist Intelligence Unit 15 March 2012, "Russia business Environment at a Glance," http://country.eiu.com.

3. Valdaiclub.com/economy/50600.html.

4. For a discussion of this point of view, see Andrei Shleifer and Daniel Treisman, "Russia as a Normal Country," *Foreign Affairs*, March–April 2004.

5. One of the more provocative commentators doing business in Russia is Eric Kraus, whose newsletter consistently praises Putin's economic policies, contrasting them to the ineptness of Western policies, and ridicules Western criticism of Russia. See for instance "Enter Dragon, Smoking," Truth & Beauty (& Russian Finance), January 31, 2012. http://www.truthandbeauty.ru/global-macro/enter-dragon-smoking/.

6. Edward Keenan, "Moscovite Political Folkways," *Russian Review* 45 (1986): 125–181.

7. Fiona Hill and Clifford D. Gaddy, *Mr. Putin: Operative in the Kremlin* (Washington, DC: Brookings Institution Press, 2013), ch. 9.

8. Clifford Gaddy and Andrew Kuchins describe Putin as "The CEO of Russia Incorporated." "Putin's Plan," *Washington Quarterly* 31, no. 2 (Spring 2008): 122.

9. Dmitri Trenin, *Getting Russia Right* (Washington, DC: Carnegie Endowment for International Peace, 2007).

10. Hill and Gaddy, ch. 9.

11. RIA Novosti, January 12, 2011.

12. Vladimir Putin, "Russia Muscles Up to the Challenges We Must Face," January 16, 2012, archive.premier.gov.ru/eng/events/news/17755/.

13. For details, see Angus Roxburgh, *The Strongman in the Kremlin: Vladimir Putin and the Struggle for Russia*. London: I. B. Taurus), pp. 284–295.

14. The TNK-BP case is discussed later in this chapter.

15. Jim O'Neill, "Building Better Global Economic BRICs," Goldman Sachs, New York, November 30, 2001, http://www.goldmansachs.com/our-thinking/archive /archive-pdfs/build-better-brics.pdf.

16. Clifford G. Gaddy and Barry W. Ickes, "Russia after the Global Financial Crisis," *Eurasian Geography and Economics* 51, no. 3 (2010): 281–311; Anders Aslund and Andrew Kuchins, *The Russia Balance Sheet* (Washington, DC: Peterson Institute, April 2009), ch. 3.

17. Speech at the 12th Petersburg International Forum, June 8, 2008, www.archive .kremlin.ru/eng/speeches/2008/06/07/1338_type82914type127286_202288.shtml.

18. Bobo Lo, "Russia's Crisis—What It Means for Regime Stability and Moscow's Relations with the World," Center for European Reform Policy Brief, February 2009.

19. Dmitri Medvedev, "Russia-U.S. Relations and Russia's Vision for International Affairs," speech, Brookings Institution, Washington, DC, April 13, 2010, http://www .brookings.edu/events/2010/04/13-medvedev#ref-id=20100413_medvedev1.

20. Newsru, "Putin: the Crisis—a Consequence of the Integration of the World Economy for Which He Fought," December 29, 2008, www.newsru.com/finance/29dec2008 /putincrisis.html.

21. He reiterated these charges in his 2012 article, "Russia Muscles Up to the Challenges We Must Face."

22. Roxburgh, p. 274.

23. Putin, address to World Economic Forum, Davos, January 28, 2009, http://fora .tv/2009/01/28/2009_World_Economic_Forum_Opening_Plenary.

24. Gaddy and Ickes, p. 282.

25. www.rt.com/news/st-petersburg-world-economic-forum-day-2.

26. *Komsomolskaia Pravda*, January 18, 2010.

27. Roxburgh, pp. 272–273.

28. *Putin, Russia and the West*, part 4.

29. Sergei Guriev and Aleh Tsyvinski, "Challenges Facing the Russian Economy after the Crisis," in Anders Aslund, Sergei Guriev and Andrew Kuchins, ed., *Russia after the Global Economic Crisis* (Washington, DC: Brookings Institution, June 2010), ch. 1.

30. Thane Gustafson, *Capitalism Russian Style* (Cambridge: Cambridge University Press, 1999), pp. 64–65.

31. Joseph Berliner, *Factory and Manager in the USSR* (Cambridge, MA: Harvard University Press, 1957).

32. Interview with Drew Guff.

33. Andrew McChesney, "Investing Millions of Dollars with Texan Sense," *Moscow Times*, September 23, 2011, http://www.themoscowtimes.com/business/article/qa -investing-millions-of-dollars-with-texan-sense/444185.html.

34. Interview with Thomas Pickering.

35. *New York Times*, December 25, 2012.

36. Reuters, February 13, 2013.

37. *Moscow Times*, June 3, 2008.

38. Thane Gustafson, *Wheel of Fortune: The Battle for Oil and Power in Russia* (Cambridge, MA: Harvard University Press, 2012), p. 6.

39. www.bp.com/livebp_internet/globalbp/globalbp_uk_english/reporets_and _publicaitons/statistical_enery_review___2011/STAGING/local_assets/pdf/statistical _reveiw_of_world_energy_repor_2012.pdf.

40. "The Evolution of Global Energy Markets," *Russia in Global Affairs* 5, no. 1 (January–March 2007).

41. Daniel Yergin, *The Quest* (New York: Penguin Books, 2012).

42. For a translation of the thesis, see the *Journal of Eurasian Law* 2, no. 1 (2009): 27–174. Brookings scholar Clifford Gaddy has argued that substantial parts of this dissertation were plagiarized from a 1978 book by two American business school professors, whose work is cited in Putin's dissertation. See *Chronicle of Higher Education*, March 26, 2006.

43. See Harley Balzer, "Vladimir Putin's Academic Writings and Russian Natural Resource Policy," *Problems of Post-Communism* (January–February 2006): 48–54.

44. www.kremlin.ru/eng/speeches/2006/09/09.

45. The 2011 Valdai meeting with Mr. Putin took place at Le Cheval Blanc, an elegant equestrian club outside Moscow. In a wide-ranging discussion, the only subject that appeared to animate the Prime Minister was the shale gas issue.

46. Marshall Goldman, *Petrostate: Putin, Power and the New Russia* (New York: Oxford University Press, 2008), pp. 58–60, 139–144.

47. Yergin *The Quest*, pp. 335–336.

48. Remarks to Valdai Discussion Club, September 4, 2006.

49. Angela Stent, *From Embargo to Ostpolitik: The Political Economy of West German-Soviet Relations, 1955–1980* (New York: Cambridge University Press, 1981); Angela Stent *Soviet Energy and Western Europe* (New York: Praeger, 2003).

50. Yergin, *The Quest,* p. 337.

51. Robert Larsson, *Russia's Energy Policy: Security Dimensions and Russia's Reliability as an Energy Supplier* (Stockholm: Swedish Defense Research Agency, 2006).

52. For a detailed analysis, see Margarita Balmaceda, *Energy Dependency, Politics and Corruption in the former Soviet Union* (New York: Routledge, 2008).

53. Interview with Igor Ivanov.

54. Agence France Press, January 1, 2009.

55. Yergin, *The Quest,* p. 413. All of Germany's nuclear power plants are scheduled to be closed by 2022.

56. The author was present at a discussion in Europe when a senior U.S. official criticized an EU member state for its close energy ties with Russia only to be rebuffed by the European official.

57. Yergin, *The Quest*, ch. 16.

58. At the 2009 Forum, Miller told the assembled heads of all the major international energy companies that, if they did not like dealing with Russia, it could sell its gas elsewhere. He then stalked off the stage without listening to their responses. The author was present at both sessions.

59. Interview with Ambassador Richard Morningstar.

60. Yergin, *The Quest*, p. 47.

61. Interview with Richard Morningstar.

62. Yergin, *The Quest*, p. 60.

63. Interview with Richard Morningstar.

64. *Kommersant*, no. 169 (2538), September 19, 2002; *Ekho* no. 208, October 31, 2002; Centrasia.ru, April 14, 2002.

65. Interview with Richard Morningstar.

66. www.centrasia.ru/newsA.php?st=1254129360 .

67. For a timeline, see www.gazprom.ru/production/projects/pipelines/south-stream.

68. Interview with senior EU official.

69. Interview with Richard Morningstar.

70. Richard Sakwa, *The Quality of Freedom: Putin, Khodorkovsky and the Yukos Affair* (Oxford: Oxford University Press, 2009).

71. Interview with Donald Evans.

72. Gustafson, *Wheel of Fortune.*

73. Evans told the author that U.S. business "discounted Khodorkovsky's arrest."

74. Gustafson, *Wheel of Fortune*, pp. 424–426.

75. www.rosneft.com/printable/news/pressrelease/30082011.html.

76. Yergin, *The Quest,* p. 43.

77. *Wall St. Journal*, April 18, 2012; Andrew Kramer, "In Bid for BP's Stake of Venture, Russia Seeks to Boost Energy Assets," *New York Times,* July 25, 2012, http://www.nytimes.com/2012/07/25/business/global/rosneft-opens-talks-on-buying-bps-stake-in-oil-joint-venture.html?pagewanted=all.

78. Yergin, *The Quest,* p. 42.

79. For a full report of the conference, see "U.S.-Russia Commercial Energy Summit," Baker Institute Study, no. 21, February 2003.

80. Interview with Donald Evans.

81. Interview with Daniel Poneman.

82. Scott Borgerson, "The Scramble for the Arctic," *Foreign Affairs* 87, no. 2 (March–April 2008).

83. Wojciech Lorenz, "Could the Arctic Warm Up NATO-Russia Relations?" Policy Paper no. 4 (52), February 2013, PISM (Warsaw: Polish Institute of international Affairs).

84. Katarzyna Zysk, "Russia's Arctic Strategy," *JFQ,* no. 57 (2010): 103–110.

85. National Intelligence Council, *Russia: The Impact of Climate Change to 2030*, Special Report NIC 2009-04 (Washington, DC, April 2009).

86. "The Agreement between the Government of the United States of America and the Government of the Russian Federation," www.state.gov/r/pa/prs/2011/01/153418.htm.

87. For a detailed discussion, see Anton Khlopkov, "US-Russian 123 Agreement Enters into Force: What Next?" *Center for Energy and Security Studies*, January 11, 2011, www.ceness-russia.org.

88. Interview with Daniel Poneman.

89. Viatcheslav Evseev, "WTO Accession and Its Implications for the Russian Economy," talk at Georgetown University Center for Eurasian, Russian and East European Studies, April 11, 2012.

90. *Kommersant*, May 31, 2012.

91. Putin, speech in the Duma, Moscow, May 8, 2012, Rossiya 24 TV station.

92. Rusiko Machaidze "SGS to Monitor Goods across Russia-Georgia Border," *Democracy & Freedom Watch*, November 9, 2011, http://dfwatch.net/sgs-to-monitor-goods-across-russia-georgia-border-71587; *Eurasia Daily Monitor*, December 5, 2011.

93. Anders Aslund and Gary Clyde Hufbauer, *The United States Should Establish Normal Trade Relations with Russia* (Washington, DC: Peterson Institute for International Economics, 2012).

CHAPTER NINE: RESET OR OVERLOAD?
THE OBAMA INITIATIVE

1. http://rt.com/usa/news/clinton-and-lavrov-hit-the-peregruzka-button/.

2. In fact, Russian newspapers had used the word *perezagruzka* to describe Biden's speech in Munich, but apparently no one in Washington had noticed.

3. Cited in Susan Glasser, "Minister No," *Foreign Policy*, May–June 2013, p. 60.

4. http://vz.ru/politics/2009/3/6/262919.html.

5. Ryabkov interview with Aleksei Venediktov, *Ekho Moskvy*, January 26, 2012.

6. Interview with Michael McFaul.

7. English.ruvr.ru.2012_12_19/Putin_to_give_Big_Press_Conferernce.

8. Barack Obama, *The Audacity of Hope* (New York: Vintage, 2006), p. 370.

9. www.debates.org/index.php?page=2008-debate-transcript.

10. www.debates.org/index.php?page=october-7-2008-debate-transcrip.

11. http://lenta.ru/artciles/2008/09/29/debate/; http://ria.ru/analytics/20080929/151678101.html.

12. The Russia and Eurasia Working group was led by Michael McFaul, a Stanford professor who became Senior Director for Russia at the White House in 2008 and then Ambassador to Russia in 2012. The author was a member of this group.

13. Interview with Thomas Donilon.

14. Henry A. Kissinger and George P. Shultz, "Building on Common Ground with Russia," *Washington Post*, October 8, 2008.

15. http://archive.kremlin.ru/eng/speeches/2008/11/05/2144_type70029type82917trpe127286_208836.shtml.

16. . The Ketchum public relations firm that was advising the Kremlin urged Medvedev to acknowledge Obama's election in his November 5 speech and say something forward-looking, but its advice fell on deaf ears. Angus Roxburgh, *The Strongman in the Kremlin: Vladimir Putin and the Struggle for Russia* (London: I. B. Taurus), 260.

17. Interview with Yuri Ushakov.

18. According to a senior State Department official the Obama administration tried on several occasions to invite Putin to come to the United States with a business delegation, but he declined.

19. http:www.securityconference.de/Sergej-B-Iwanow.224+M52087573ab0.0.html.

20. For text of Biden's speech, see http://germany.usembassy.gov/events/2009/feb-biden-security/.

21. "Russian Officials, Media Welcome Biden Munich Speech," (Washington, DC: Open Source Center, February 9, 2009). See also *Nezavisimaia Gazeta*, February 9, 2009.

22. Keynote speech by Michael McFaul, Peterson Institute for International Economics, Washington, April 15, 2011.

23. *Putin, Russia and the West*, part 4; interview with Michael McFaul.

24. www.nytimes.com/2009/04/02/world/euopre/02arms.html.

25. www.Kremlin.ru, April 1, 2009.

26. www2.lse.ac.uk/publoicevents/pdf/20090602RussianPMTtranscript.

27. Russian commentators remarked that this meant that Obama knew who the real boss was. www.ng.ru/politics/2009-07-08/1_obama.html. Russians made the same mistake. The author was present at the St. Petersburg Economic forum in June 2008, when Medvedev walked onto the stage and the announcer, in his flowery basso profundo, began to say "President Vla—," quickly changing it to Dimitri.

28. *Putin, Russia and the West,* part 4.

29. http://feautres.csmonitor.com/globalnews/2009.07/07in-moscow-obama-charms-russians-%E2%80%93-but-not-Putin/.

30. Discussion with Prime Minister Putin, Novo-Ogarevo, September 11, 2009.

31. Obama-Medvedev, press conference, White House, Washington, DC, http://transcripts.cnn.com/TRANSCRIPTS/0907/06/cnr.04.html.

32. Interview with senior State Department official.

33. Obama, speech at New Economic School, Moscow, July 7, 2009, http://www.nytimes.com/2009/07/07/world/europe/07prexy.text.html?pagewanted=all .

34. Obama, speech, Parallel Civil Society Summit, Moscow, July 7, 2009, http://www.whitehouse.gov/the-press-office/remarks-president-parallel-civil-society-summit.

35. The Valdai Discussion Club also raised questions about the tandem. Medvedev met twice with the group, in 2008 and 2009, but then was "too busy" to meet with it in 2010 and 2011. His name was associated with the Yaroslavl Forum, a meeting of political and cultural leaders at which Medvedev presided.

36. Medvedev, speech, Brookings Institution, Washington DC, April 13, 2010, http://www.brookings.edu/events/2010/04/13-medvedev#ref-id=20100413_medvedev1.

37. Interview with Rose Goettemoeller.

38. Interview with Admiral Michael Mullen.

39. Patrick Goodenough, "Putin Impedes Obama's Plan for a World without Nuclear Weapons," CNS News, December 30, 2009, http://cnsnews.com/news/article/putin-impedes-obama-s-plan-world-without-nuclear-weapons.

40. Roxburgh, pp. 267–268; *Putin, Russia and the West,* part 4.

41. Interview with senior administration official.

42. Obama and Medvedev, press conference, Prague Castle, Prague, March 26, 2010, http://www.whitehouse.gov/the-press-office/remarks-president-obama-and-president-medvedev-russia-new-start-treaty-signing-cere.

43. Treaty between the United States of America and the Russian Federation on Measures for the Further Reduction and Limitation of Strategic Offensive Arms. www.state.gov/documents/organization/140035.pdf.

44. Congressional Digest, "Senate Ratifies New START Treaty" December 22, 2010, http://congressionaldigest.com/senate-ratifies-new-start-treaty/.

45. *Kommersant,* February 6, 2012; http://eng.mil.ru/en/science/publications/more.htm?id=11730484@cmsArticle.

46. www.america.gov/st/peacesec-english/2010/April/20100413153843esnamfuako.2951624.html.

47. Obama, State of the Union Address, U.S. Capitol, Washington, DC, February 12, 2013, http://www.nytimes.com/2013/02/13/us/politics/obamas-2013-state-of-the-union-address.html?pagewanted=all.

48. Steven Pifer, *The Next Round: The United States and Nuclear Arms Reductions after New START* (Washington, DC: Brookings Institution, November, 2010).

49. For further discussion, see *Missile Defense in Europe-The Political and Security Dimensions* (Paris: EU Institute for Security Studies, February 2008).

50. "An Open Letter to the Obama Administration from Central and Eastern Europe," *Gazeta Wyborcza,* July 15, 2009, http://wyborcza.pl/1,76842,6825987,An_Open_Letter_to_the_Obama-Administrsation_from_central.html.

51. For details, see Tom Collina, "The European Phased Adaptive Approach at a Glance," http://www.armscontrol.org/print/4392; http://www.state.gov/t/avc/rls/162447.htm.

52. "Open Letter to President Obama on Central Europe," Foreign Policy Initiative, October 2, 2009, http://www.foreignpolicyi.org/content/open-letter-president-obama-central-europe.

53. *Spiegel Online*, September 17, 2009.

54. Interview with Ivo Daalder.

55. http://www.nato.int/cps/en/natolive/news_68876.htm.

56. Richard Weitz, "Illusive Visions and Practical Realities: Russia, NATO and Missile Defense," *Survival* 52, no. 4 (August–September 2010): 99–120.

57. Discussion with Vladimir Putin, November 7, 2001, Le Cheval Blanc, Moscow.

58. Josh Rogin, "Medvedev announces failure of U.S.-Russia missile defense talks; threatens to withdraw from New START" Foreign Policy, November 23, 2011, http://thecable.foreignpolicy.com/posts/2011/11/23/medvedev_announces_failure_of_us_russia_missile-defense.

59. Interview with Admiral Michael Mullen.

60. Interview with Stephen Hadley.

61. "Putin Voices Pessimism on Missile Defense," *Moscow Times,* June 20, 2012. http://www.russialist.org/russia-putin-pessimism-missile-defense-512.php.

62. Moscow. Interfax in Russian 1451 GMT 21 December 11.

63. http://articles.washingtonpost.com/2012-03-26/politics/35449106_1_missile-defense-president-obama-russian-president-dmitry-medvedev.

64. http://rt.com/news/us-cancels-missile-interceptors-350/.

65. *Moscow Times,* March 19, 2013.

66. For an extensive discussion of these issues, see Uwe Halbach "Afghanistan in der Politik Russlands und Zentralasiens" (Berlin: SWP-Studie S31 November 2011).

67. Samuel Charap, *Assessing the "Reset" and the Next Steps for U.S. Russian Policy* (Washington, DC: Center for American Progress, 2010), pp. 10–11.

68. Information from Alice Wells, Senior Director for Russia and Central Asia at the National Security Council, March 8, 2013.

69. "US Helicopter Contract 'In Place' Says Russian Arms Firm," December 3, 2012. http://en.rian.ru/world/20121203/177886242.html.

70. Elizabeth Bumiller and Jane Perlez, "Mullen—Pakistan's Spy Agency Supported US Embassy Attack," *New York Times,* September 22, 2011, http://www.nytimes.com/2011/09/23/world/asia/mullen-asserts-pakistani-role-in-attack-on-us-embassy.html?pagewanted=all.

71. *Moscow Times,* August 2, 2012.

72. http://www.whitehouse.gov/the-press-office/remarks-president-cairo-university-6-04-09.

73. Roxburgh, p. 266. When Lavrov demanded to know why the Russians had not been informed before, McFaul responded, "We thought you knew. I mean these are your guys, not ours."

74. *New York Times,* October 14, 2009.

75. www.whitehouse.gov/the-press-office/fact-sheet-new-un-security-council-sanctions-iran.

76. "On Measures for the Fulfillment on UN Security council Resolution 1929 of 9 June 2010," *President of Russia,* September 22, 2010, http://eng.kremlin.ru/news/980.

77. Putin offered fulsome congratulations to the Iranian and Russian specialists who had built the plant. www.km.ru/v-mire/2011/09/13/yadernaya-programma-irana/putin/pozdravil-iran-s-puskom-pervoi-atomnoi-elektrstan.

78. www.reuters.com/assets/print?aid=USTRE7A857620111109.

79. http://nvo.ng.ru/concepts/2011-11-25/1_bomb_html.

80. *Moscow News,* February 27, 2012.

CHAPTER TEN: FROM BERLIN TO DAMASCUS: DISAGREEMENTS OLD AND NEW

1. Paul D'Anieri, ed., *Orange Revolution and Aftermath: Mobilization, Apathy and the State in Ukraine* (Washington, DC: Woodrow Wilson Center Press, 2010), p. 127.

2. Alexander Cooley, *Great Games, Local Rules* (New York: Oxford University Press, 2012), pp. 127–129.

3. Jim Nichol, *Central Asia: Regional Developments and Implications for US Interests* (Washington, DC: Congressional Research Service), pp. 19–20.

4. McFaul, speech, Peterson Institute, Washington, DC, March 12, 2012, http://www.iie.com/publications/papers/transcript_20120312mcfaul.pdf.

5. http://www.channelnewsasia.com/news/world/georgia-pm-backs-inquiry-into -president-/634584.html.

6. President Medvedev's Speech at Meeting of German Political, Parliamentary and Civic Leaders, Berlin, June 5, 2008, www.ln.mid.ru/brp_4.nsf/0/C080DC2FF8D93629 C3257460003496C4.

7. President of Russia, *European Security Treaty,* November 29, 2009, http://eng.kremlin .ru/news/275.

8. *Agreement on Basic Principles Governing Relations among NATO-Russia Council Member States in Security Sphere,* December 4, 2009.

9. Hillary Clinton, remarks, L'Ecole Militaire, Paris, January 29, 2010, http://www .state.gov/scertary/rm/2010/01/136273.htm.

10. Theo Sommer, "Germany's Foreign and Security Policy," address to the American Council on Germany, New York, December 12, 2011; Margarete Klein and Solvieg Richter, *Russland und die euro-atlantische Sicherheitsordnung* (Berlin: SWP-Studie, December 2011).

11. Julie Finlay, ambassador to the OSCE from 2005 to 2008, believes that, despite its problems, Washington could use the OSCE much better than it has to date. Interview with Julie Finlay.

12. Isabelle François, *Whither the Medvedev Initiative on European Security?* (Washington, DC: National Defense University, December 2011).

13. NATO press release, "Meeting of the North Atlantic Council at the Level of Foreign Ministers Held at NATO Headquarters, Brussels, December 4, 2009."

14. "Russian Leaders Hail NATO Secretary General's Visit; Media Less Positive," Open Source Report, December 18, 2009.

15. "The Military Doctrine of the Russian Federation," February 5, 2010, NATO Strategic Concept, www.natoint/lisbon2010/strategic_concept 2010-eng.pdf.

16. Michael Gaynor, "My Landlord Was a Russian Spy," *Washingtonian,* September 2010.

17. *Moscow Time,* August 8, 2012.

18. Peter Baker, "Despite Arrests, Working to Rebuild Ties with Russia," *New York Times,* June 30, 2010, http://www.nytimes.com/2010/07/01/world/europe/01reset.html.

19. It is highly unlikely that one of the Russians who was released from a Moscow jail was a spy.

20. *Putin, Russia and the West,* part 4.

21. "Putin Meets and Praises Agents After Swap with US," *New York Times,* July 24, 2010, http://www.nytimes.com/2010/07/25/world/europe/25russia.html.

22. Luke Harding, *Mafia State* (London: Guardian Books, 2011), pp. 225–244. Harding read the entire file and wrote about the cables for his newspaper.

23. Simon Shuster, "WikiLeaks' Russian Cables: Bad for Reset, Good for Putin?" *Time Magazine,* December 2, 2010, http://www.time.com/time/world/article/0,8599 ,2034670,00.html.

24. According to Ambassador John Beyrle, "The Russians decided to ignore it and they got over it pretty quickly." Interview with John Beyrle.

25. Military-technical cooperation and cyber security were added at the 2012 G-20 summit. Whitehouse.gov, June 18, 2012.

26. http://www.upi.com/Top_News/World-News/2013/05/08/Putin-dismisses -Deputy-Prime-Minister-Vladislav-Surkov/UPI-90181368053544/.

27. For details, see http://www.state.gov/p/eur/ci/rs/usrussiabilat/index/html.

28. http://www.guardian.co.uk/world/2011/sep/24/purin-proposed-russian-president -medvedev.

29. Many observers—both Russian and foreign—have questioned whether this was indeed the case and believe that Putin may well not have known in 2007 that he wanted to return to the presidency.

30. *Putin, Russia and the West*, part 4.

31. "Russia Muscles Up the Challenges We Must Rise to Face," http://premier.gov
.ru/eng/events/news/17755/print/.

32. See Fiona Hill and Clifford Gaddy, *Mr. Putin: Operative in the Kremlin* (Washington, DC: Brookings Institution Press, 2012).

33. Kommersant, "It's Not in the United States and the Russian People," Kommersant.ru, December 15, 2011, http://kommersant.ru/doc/1838682.

34. McFaul, the former senior director for Russia, had written a great deal about Russia's democratic deficits as a Stanford professor and had many contacts among the opposition.

35. Vladimir Putin, "Russia and the Changing World," *Moscow News*, February 27, 2012, http://mn.ru/politics/20120227/312306749.html.

36. Helene Cooper, "Face to Face, Obama Tries To persuade Putin on Syria," *New York Times*, June 18, 2012, http://www.nytimes.com/2012/06/19/world/syria-dominates-as
-obama-and-putin-meet.html.

37. "Russia's Young Muslims Especially Devout," *Moscow Times*, August 10, 2012, http://www.themoscowtimes.com/news/article/russias-young-muslims-especially-devout
/466349.html. A Pew Research Center study found young Muslims in Russia more devout than their parents.

38. *RBC.ru*, March 21, 2011, http://www.rbc.ru/fnews.open/20110321190605.shtml.

39. Andrew Osbourn, "Russia Denounces Libya Group as 'illegitimate,'" *Telegraph*, May 13, 2011, http://www.telegraph.co.uk/news/worldnews/africaandindianocean
/libya/8512454/Russia-denounces-Libya-contact-group-as-illegitimate.html.

40. Margarete Klein, *Russland und der arabische Fruehling* (Berlin: SWP Aktuelle, January 2012).

41. *Economist*, "Wait and Sea," economist.com, January 14, 2012, www.economist
.com/node/21542793.

42. For details see www.izvesia.ru/news/499505.

43. "Why Russia Protects Assad," *Financial Times*, January 26, 2012; http://globalpublic
square.blogs.cnn.com/2012/01/26.

44. www.mid.ru, February 5, 2012.

45. Margaret Cocker and Jennifer Valentino-Devries, "Syria's Russia Connection," *Wall St. Journal*, August 14, 2012, http://online.wsj.com/article/SB1000087239639044413
0304577560810962055348.html.

46. Colum Lynch "Kofi Annan resigns as envoy to Syria," *Washington Post*, August 3, 2012. http://www.washingtonpost.com/world/national-security/kofi-annan-resigns-as
-envoy-to-syria/2012/08/02/gJQAABj4RX_story.html.

47. Interview with Thomas Donilon.

48. *New York Times*, May 18, 2013.

49. www.state.gov/pa/prs/ps2013/05/209000.htm.

50. Samuel Charap, "Russia, Syria and the Doctrine of Intervention," *Survival*, 55, no 1 (February–March 2013): 35–41.

51. Tom Parfitt, "Vladimir Putin Goes on Offensive against US," *Telegraph*, December 20, 2012, http://www.telegraph.co.uk/news/worldnews/vladimir-putin/9759260
/Vladimir-Putin-goes-on-offensive-against-US.html.

52. For a discussion of the case, see Roxburgh, pp. 288–291.

53. http://www.frefl.org/articleprintview/24898980.html.

54. Sergei Kislyak, "On Normal Trade Relations and the Deficit of Normality," *The Hill*, July 23, 20012.

55. *New York Times*, December 20, 2013.

56. Rt.com/politics/official-word/dima-yakovlev-law-full-995/.

57. *The Cable*, February 27, 2013.

58. http://abcnews.go.com/blogs/headlines/2013/05/russia-unmasks-cia-station-chief-in-moscow/.

59. http://rt.com/politics/russia-issues-first-foreign-951/print/.

60. *Moscow Times*, January 30, 2013.

61. *Washington Post*, September 18, 2012.

62. Freedom House, *Contending with Putin's Russia: A Call for American Leadership* (Washington DC: Freedom House, February 2013).

63. http://www.itar-tass.com/c154/747324.html?utm_medium=twitter&utm_source=ITAR-TASS.

64. Witold Rodkiewicz, "Russian Foreign Policy Concept" (Warsaw: Center for Eastern Studies, February 20, 2013), www.osw.waw.pl/en/publikacje/eastweek/2013-02-20/russian-federation-s-foreign-policy-concept.

65. RIA Novosti, "Putin Orders Defense Ministry to get House in Order," en.ria.ru, February 27, 2013, http://en.ria.ru/military_news/20130227/179715673/Putin-Orders-Defense-Ministry-to-Get-House-in-Order.html.

66. Jonathan Earle, "Romney: Russia Is America's 'No. 1 Foe,'" *Moscow Times*, March 28, 2012, www.themoscowtimes.com/mobile/news/article/455607.html.

67. Angela Stent, "US-Russian Relations in the Second Obama Administration," *Survival* 54, no. 6 (Winter 2012–13): 123–139.

CHAPTER ELEVEN: THE LIMITS OF PARTNERSHIP

1. Angela Stent, "The Return of a Great Power," in Daniel Yergin and Thane Gustafson, *Russia 2010: And What It Means for the World* (New York: Vintage, 1995), pp. 210–233.

2. See for instance Robert Kagan and David J. Kramer, "A Bill That Cracks Down on Russian Corruption," *Washington Post,* June 6, 2012, http://articles.washingtonpost.com/2012-06-06/opinions/35459957_1_sergei-magnitsky-rule-law-accountability-act-human-rights.

3. Mr. X, "The Sources of Soviet Conduct," *Foreign Affairs*, no. 4 (July 1947): 566–582.

4. http://www.nytimes.com/2013/03/23/world/asia/xi-jinping-visits-russia-on-first-trip-abroad.html?pagewanted=all&_r=0.

5. http://rt.com/news/xi-jinping-visit-moscow-642/.

6. http://www.itar-tass.com/en/c142/720570.html.

7. Dmitri Trenin, "After the 'Reset'" (Moscow: Carnegie Moscow Center) March 23, 2011, http:www.carnegie.ru/publications/?fa=43228.

8. Interview with Drew Guff.

9. *Der Spiegel,* March 12, 2012.

10. http://www.nytimes.com/2013/04/08/world/europe/08iht-putin08.html?_r=0.

11. Interview with John Beyrle.

12. We have to assume that, when Medvedev was president and negotiated with Obama, he was implementing policies of which Putin approved—with the exception of Libya. He did not have his own independent foreign policy base.

13. *Russkii Newsweek*, April 2012. The Russian version of Newsweek published a "leaked" document from the Ministry of Foreign Affairs that argues that Russia must build "modernizing alliances" with the West and that this argues for improving ties with the United States and Europe. See "Program for Effective Use of Foreign Policy in the Long-Term Development of Russia"; Russian Ministry of Foreign Affairs, "Kontseptsiia Vneshnei Politiki Rossiskoi Federatsii," February 12, 2013.

14. Interviews with several officials who were involved in these issues in both administrations.

15. Dmitri Trenin, *Post-Imperium* (Washington, DC: Carnegie Endowment for International Peace 2011).

16. Interview with William Burns.

17. Putin, *"A New Integration Project for Eurasia—the Future Is Being Born Today,"* interview, *Izvestiya*, October 4, 2011.

18. *Ekho Moskvy*, April 19, 2013.

19. http://www.interfax.ru, April 19, 2013.

20. *Moscow Times*, April 1, 2013.

21. http://carnegieendowment.org/2013/04/12/priorities-for-russia-u.s.-relations -statement-by-former-ambassadors-to-washington-and-moscow/fza1.

22. Interview with John Beyrle.

23. The text of Obama's Berlin speech is at http://www.whitehouse.gov/the-press -office/2013/06/19/remarks-president-obama-brandenburg-gate-berlin-germany.

24. Interview with senior administration official.

25. http://www.newrepublic.com/article/113615/putin-wont-extradite-snowden-wont -shear-pig.eng.news.kremlin.ru/news/5935/print.

26. http://www.cbsnews.com/8301-202_162-57591783/putin-snowden-must-stop -damaging-our-american-partners/.

27. http://www.reuters.com/video/2013/07/01/putin-calls-on-snowden-to-stop -harming-o?videoId=243705385.

28. http://www.whitehouse.gov/the-press-office/2013/08/07/statement-press-secretary -president-s-travel-russia.

29. http://www.npr.org/blogs/thetwo-way/2013/08/01/207831950/snowden-has-left -moscows-airport-as-russia-grants-asylum.

30. www.whitehouse.gov/the-press-office/2013/08/09/remarks-president-press -conference.

31. http://www.telegraph.co.uk/news/worldnews/europe/russia/10234189/Russian -foreign-minister-tells-US-to-behave-like-grown-ups.html.

32. The author was involved in several of these, beginning before the Soviet collapse in the Shell Group Planning office and continuing with the World Economic Forum in several iterations of Russia scenarios.

33. *Russia and the World, 2025 (Geneva:* World Economic Forum, 2005).

34. Ivan Kravtsev, "Would Democratic Change in Russia Transform Its Foreign Policy?" www.opendemocracy.net/print/70826.

35. Nicholas Eberstadt, "The Dying Bear: Russia's Demographic Disaster," *Foreign Affairs* 90, no. 6 (November–December 2011): 95–109.

36. Interview with Henry Kissinger.

37. Interview with Stephen Hadley.

Bibliography

BOOKS AND ARTICLES

Adomeit, Hannes. *Russlands Iran-Politik unter Putin*. Berlin: Stiftung Wissenschaft und Politik, 2007.

Albright, Madeleine. *Madam Secretary*. New York: Hyperion, 2003.

Antonenko, Oksana. "Russia and the Deadlock over Kosovo." *Survival* 49, no. 5 (Autumn 2007): 91–105.

Aslund, Anders, and Gary C. Hufbauer. *The United States Should Establish Normal Trade Relations with Russia*. Washington, DC: Peterson Institution for International Economics, 2012.

Aslund, Anders, and Michael McFaul. *Revolution in Orange*. Washington, DC: Carnegie Endowment for International Peace, 2006.

Asmus, Ronald. *A Little War That Shook the World*. New York: Palgrave Macmillan, 2010.

———. *Opening NATO's Door*. Washington DC: Council on Foreign Relations, 2004.

Baker, James. *The Politics of Diplomacy*. New York: Putnam,1995.

Baker, Peter, and Susan Glasser. *Kremlin Rising*. New York: Simon and Schuster, 2005.

Balzer, Harley. "Vladimir Putin's Academic Writings and Russian Natural Resource Policy." *Problems of Post-Communism* 58, no. 1 (January–February, 2006): 48–54.

Berliner, Joseph. *Factory and Manager in the USSR*. Cambridge, MA: Harvard University Press, 1957.

Bolton, John. *Surrender Is Not an Option*. New York: Simon and Schuster, 2008.

Borgerson, Scott. "The Scramble for the Arctic." *Foreign Affairs* 87 (March–April 2008). http://www.foreignaffairs.com/articles/63222/scott-g-borgerson/arctic-meltdown.

Bumiller, Elizabeth. *Condoleezza Rice: An American Life*. New York: Random House, 2007.

Bush, George W. *Decision Points*. New York: Crown Publishers, 2011.

———. Newsmaker Interview. *Newshour with Jim Lehrer*, February 16, 2000. Edited by Jim Lehrer. www.pbs.org/newshour/bb/election/jan-june00/bush_2-16.html.

———. Speech at International Republican Institute, May 18, 2005. http://connection.ebscohost.com/c/speeches/17275067/remarks-international-republican-institute-dinner.

Bush, George, and Brent Scowcroft. *A World Transformed*. New York: Vintage Books, 1999.

Charap, Samuel. *Assessing the "Reset" and the Next Steps for U.S. Russian-Relations*. Washington, DC: Policy Center for American Progress, 2010.

Cheney, Dick. *In My Time*. New York: Threshold Editions, 2012.

Clinton, Bill. *My Life*. New York: Vintage, 2005.

Cohen, Stephen. *Failed Crusade: America and the Tragedy of Post-Communist Russia*. New York: Norton 2001.

———. *Soviet Fates and Lost Alternatives*. New York: Columbia University Press, 2009.

Coll, Steven. *Ghost Wars*. New York: Penguin Press, 2004.

Collina, Tom. "The Lisbon Protocol at a Glance." Arms Control Association. http://www.armscontrol.org/print/3289.

Commission on Security and Cooperation in Europe. *Lessons of "The Tulip Revolution": Kyrgyzstan's Revolution; Causes and Consequences*. 2005.

Cooley, Alexander. *Great Games, Local Rules*. New York: Oxford University Press, 2012.

Cordesman, Anthony, and Adam Seitz. *Iranian Weapons of Mass Destruction*. Washington, DC: Center for Strategic and International Studies, 2009.

Council on Foreign Defense Policy. *US-Russian Relations at the Turn of the Century*. Washington, DC: Carnegie Endowment for International Peace, 2000.

Daalder, Ivo. *Getting to Dayton: The Making of America's Bosnia Policy*. Washington, DC: Brookings Institution Press, 2000.

D'Anieri, Paul, ed. *Orange Revolution and Aftermath: Mobilization, Apathy and the State in Ukraine*. Washington, DC: Woodrow Wilson Center Press, 2010.

Epokha Iel'tsina. Moscow: Bagrus, 2001.

Federov, Yury. "Russian Policy on Iran." *World Today* 63, no. 2 (February 2007): 4–6.

Fitzpatrick, Mark. "Iran and North Korea: The Proliferation Nexus." *Survival* 48, no. 1 (2006): 70.

Francois, Isabelle. *Whither the Medvedev Initiative on European Security?* Washington, DC: National Defense University, 2011.

Freeland, Chrystia. *Sale of the Century: The Inside Story of the Second Russian Revolution*. London: Abacus, 2006.

Gaddy, Clifford D., and Barry W. Ickes. "Russia after the Global Financial Crisis." *Eurasian Geography and Economics* 51, no. 3 (2010): 281–311.

Gaidar, Yegor. *Collapse of an Empire*. Washington, DC: Brookings Institution Press, 2007.

Gates, Robert. *From the Shadows*. New York: Simon and Schuster, 1996.

Gessen, Masha. *The Man without a Face*. New York: Penguin, 2013.

Global Trends, 2015: A Dialogue about the Future with Nongovernment Experts. Washington, DC: National Intelligence Council, 2000.

Goldfarb, Alexander, and Maria Litvinenko. *Death of a Dissident*. New York: Free Press, 2007.

Goldgeier, James, and Michael McFaul. *Power and Purpose: U.S. Policy toward Russia after the Cold War*. Washington, DC: Brookings Institution Press, 2003.

Goldman, Marshall. *Petrostate: Putin, Power and the New Russia*. Oxford: Oxford University Press, 2007.

Guseinov, Vagif, Alexei Denisov, and Alexander Goncharenko. "The Evolution of the Global Energy Market." *Russia Global Affairs* 5, no. 1 (2007): 8–24.

Gustafson, Thane. *Capitalism Russian Style*. Cambridge: Cambridge University Press, 1999.

———. *Wheel of Fortune: The Battle for Oil and Power in Russia*. Cambridge, MA: Harvard University Press 2012.

Harding, Luke. *Mafia State*. London: Guardian Books, 2011.

Hill, Fiona, and Clifford D. Gaddy. *Mr. Putin: Operative in the Kremlin*. Washington, DC: Brookings Institution Press, 2013.

Hoffman, David E. *The Oligarchs: Wealth and Power in the New Russia*. New York: Public Affairs, 2002.

Holbrooke, Richard. *To End a War*. New York: Modern Library 1999.

Ivanov, Igor. *The New Russian Diplomacy*. Washington, DC: Brookings Institution Press, 2000.

Jack, Andrew. *Inside Putin's Russia*. Oxford: Oxford University Press, 2004.

Katz, Mark. "Iran and Russia." In *The Iran Primer: Power, Politics, and U.S. Policy*, edited by Robin Wright, pp. 186–190. Washington, DC: United States Institute of Peace, 2010.

Keenan, Edward. "Moscovite Political Folkways." *Russian Review* 45 (1986): 125–181.

Khlopkov, Anton, and Anna Lutkova. "The Bushehr NPP: Why Did It Take So Long?" *Center for Energy and Security Studies*, no. 20 (August 21, 2010).

Khryshtanovskaiia, Olga. *Anatomiia Rossiskoi Elity.* Moscow: Zakharov, 2004.

King, Charles. "The Benefits of Ethnic War." *World Politics* 53, no. 4 (July 2001): 524–552.

———. *The Ghost of Freedom.* New York: Oxford University Press, 2008.

Klein, Margarete. *Russland und der Arabische Fruehling.* Berlin: SWP Aktuelle, 2012.

Klein, Margarete, and Solvieg Richter. *Russland und die euro-atlantsiche Sicherheitsordung.* Berlin: SWP-Studie December 2011.

Korzhakov, Aleksandr. *Boris Eltsin: Ot Rassveta do Zakata.* Moscow: Interbook, 1997.

Kravtsev, Ivan. "Russia's Post-Orange Empire." Open Democracy, http://www.open democracy.net/2947.

Kuchins, Andrew, and Anders Aslund. *The Russia Balance Sheet.* Washington, DC: Peterson Institute for International Economics, 2009.

Larsson, Robert. *Russia's Energy Policy: Security Dimensions and Russia's Reliability as an Energy Supplier.* Stockholm: Swedish Defense Research Agency, 2006.

Litwak, Robert S. "Living with Ambiguity: Nuclear Deals with Iran and North Korea." *Survival* 50, no. 1 (February–March, 2008): 91–118.

Lo, Bobo. "Evolution or Regression? Russian Foreign Policy in Putin's Second Term." In *Towards a Post-Putin Russia*, edited by H. Blakkisrud. Oslo: Norwegian International Affairs, 2006.

———. *Russia's Crisis—What It Means for Regime Stability and Moscow's Relations with the Word.* Policy Brief. London: Center for European Reform, 2009.

Lynch, Allen. *Vladimir Putin and Russian Statecraft.* Washington, DC: Potomac Books, 2011.

Mann, James. *The Rise of the Vulcans.* New York: Penguin Press, 2004.

Matlock, Jack. *Autopsy on an Empire: The American Ambassador's Account of the Collapse of the Soviet Union.* New York: Random House, 1995.

———. *Superpower Illusions.* New Haven: Yale University Press, 2010.

McGlinchey, Eric. "Autocrats, Islamists and the Rise of Radicalism in Central Asia." *Current History* (October 2005): 336–342.

Medvedev, Dmitry. "Russia-U.S. Relations and Russia's Vision for International Affairs." Speech at Brookings Institution, April 13, 2010. www.brookings.edu/media /events/2010/4/13%20/medvedev/20100413/pdf.

Mitchell, Lincoln. *The Color Revolutions.* Philadelphia: University of Pennsylvania Press, 2012.

National Intelligence Council. *Global Trends, 2015: A Dialogue about the Future with Nongovernmental Experts.* Washington, DC, December 2000.

NATO. *Agreement on Basic Principles Governing Relations among NATO-Russia Council Member States in Security Sphere.* Brussels, 2009.

———. *Bucharest Summit Declaration.* Brussels, 2008.

———. *Meeting of the North Atlantic Council at the Level of Foreign Ministers Held at NATO Headquarters.* Brussels, 2009.

———. "Prague Summit Declaration." Press release. November 21, 2002.

———. *Strategic Concept for the Defense and Security of the Members of the North Atlantic Treaty Organization.* Brussels, 2010.

Nicholl, Jim. *Central Asia: Regional Developments and Implications for US Interests.* Washington, DC: Congressional Research Service, 2012.

Obama, Barack. *The Audacity of Hope.* New York: Vintage, 2006.

——. "Inaugural Address by President Barack Obama." The White House. http://www
.whitehouse.gov/the-press-office/2013/01/21/inaugural-address-president-barack
-obama.
——. "Second Inaugural Address." The White House, 2013. http://www.whitehouse
.gov/the-press-office/2013/01/21/inaugural-address-president-barack-obama.
O'Neill, Jim. *Building Better Global Economic BRICs*. New York: Goldman, Sachs, 2001.
Pifer, Steven. *The Next Round: The United States and Nuclear Arms Reductions after New START*.
Washington, DC: Brookings Institution Press, 2010.
Pillar, Paul. "Intelligence, Policy and the War in Iraq." *Foreign Affairs* 26 (March–April,
2006).
Primakov, Evgeny. *Gody v Bol'shoi Politike*. Moscow: Kollektsia "Sovershenno Sekretno,"
1999.
——. *A World Challenged*. Washington, DC: Brookings Institution Press, 2004.
Putin, Vladimir. *First Person*. New York: Public Affairs, 2000.
Putin, Russia and the West. TV film. Directed by Paul Mitchell and David Alter. BBC, 2011.
Rahr, Alexander. *Wladimir Putin: Der "Deutsche" im Kreml*. Munich: Universitaets Verlag,
2000.
Reddaway, Peter, and Dmitri Glinsky. *The Tragedy of Russia's Reforms*. Washington, DC:
Carnegie Endowment for International Peace, 2001.
Rice, Condoleezza. *Extraordinary, Ordinary People*. New York: Crown Archetype, Random
House, 2010.
——. *No Higher Honor*. New York: Random House, 2011.
——. "Promoting the National Interest." *Foreign Affairs* 79, no. 1 (2000): 45–62.
Roxburgh, Angus. *The Strongman in the Kremlin: Vladimir Putin and the Struggle for Russia*.
London: I. B. Taurus.
Ruehe, Volker. "America and Europe: Common Challenges and Common Answers."
Speech at Georgetown University, March 2, 1993.
Rumer, Eugene. *Russian Foreign Policy beyond Putin*. Adelphi Paper. London: Routledge,
2007.
Rumer, Eugene, and Angela Stent. *Repairing U.S.-Russian Relations: A Long Road Ahead*.
Washington, DC: Institute for National Strategic Studies and Georgetown Univer-
sity, 2009.
Rumer, Eugene, and Celeste Wallander, eds., *Russia Watch: Essays in Honor of George Kolt*.
Washington, DC: CSIS Press, 2007.
Rumsfeld, Donald. *Known and Unknown*. New York: Penguin, 2011.
Russia and Eurasia Working Group. Policy Memos 1, 2, and 4, 2008. Memos in author's
possession.
Russia and the World, 2025. Geneva: World Economic Forum, 2005.
Russia: The Impact of Climate Change to 2030. Washington, DC: National Intelligence Council,
2009.
Sarotte, Mary Elise. *1989: The Struggle to Create Post–Cold War Europe*. Princeton: Princeton
University Press, 2009.
Schroeder, Gertrude, and Philip Hanson. *The System versus Progress: Soviet Economic Problems*.
London: Centre for Research into Communist Economies, 1986.
Sestanovich, Steven. "At Odds with Iran and Iraq: Can the United States and Russia
Resolve Their Differences?" Washington, DC: Century Foundation and Stanley
Foundation, 2003.
——. "Where Does Russia Belong?" *National Interest* 62 (Winter 2000–2001).
Shevtsova, Lilia. *Putin's Russia*. Washington, DC: Carnegie Endowment for International
Peace, 2005.

——. *Yeltsin's Russia*. Washington, DC: Carnegie Endowment for International Peace, 1999.

Simis, Konstantin. *USSR: Secrets of the Corrupt Society*. London: J. M. Dent & Sons, 1982.

Stent, Angela. "Berlin's Russia Problem." *National Interest* 68 (2006).

——. *From Embargo to Ostpolitik: The Political Economy of West German-Soviet Relations, 1955-1980*. Cambridge: Cambridge University Press, 1981.

——. "Germany and Russia." In *Russia and Europe*, edited by Kjell Engelbrekt and Bertil Nygren, 156-167. London: Routledge, 2010.

——. "Reluctant Europeans: Three Centuries of Russian Ambivalence toward the West." In *Russian Foreign Policy in the Twenty-First Century in the Shadow of the Past*, edited by Robert Legvold, pp. 393-443. New York: Columbia University Press, 2007.

——. "The Return of a Great Power." In *Russia 2010: And What It Means for the World*, edited by Daniel Yergin and Thane Gustafson, pp. 210-233. New York: Vintage, 1995.

——. "Russia and Europe." In *The Global Politics of Energy*, edited by Kurt Campbell and Jonathon Price, pp. 65-94. Washington, DC: Aspen Institute, 2008.

——. *Russia and Germany Reborn: Unification, the Soviet Collapse and the New Europe*. Princeton: Princeton University Press, 1999.

——. "Russia's Economic Revolution and the West." *Survival* 37, no. 1 (Spring 1995): 121-143.

——. *Soviet Energy and Western Europe*. New York: Praeger, 2003.

——. "US-Russian Relations in the Second Obama Administration." *Survival* 54, no. 6 (Winter 2012-2013): 123-139.

Stent, Angela, and Lilia Shevtsova. "America, Russia and Europe: A Realignment?" *Survival* 44, no. 4 (Winter 2002-2003): 121-134.

Surkov, Vladislav. "Natsionalizatsiia Budushchego." *Ekspert*, no. 43 (November 20, 2009). http://www.expert.ru/printissues/expert/2006/43/nacionalizaciya_buduschego /print.

Talbott, Strobe. *The Russia Hand: A Memoir of Presidential Diplomacy*. New York: Random House, 2003.

Tenet, George. *At the Center of the Storm*. New York: Harper Collins, 2007.

Trenin, Dmitri. *Getting Russia Right*. Washington, DC: Carnegie Endowment for International Peace, 2007.

——. "Posle 'Perezagruzki.'" Washington, DC: Carnegie Endowment for International Peace, 2011.

——. *Post-Imperium*. Washington, DC: Carnegie Endowment for International Peace, 2011.

——. "Russia Leaves the West." *Foreign Affairs* 85, no. 4 (July–August 2006): 87–96.

Treisman, Daniel. *The Return*. New York: Free Press, 2010.

U.S. Cyber Consequences Unit, Overview by the US-CCU of the Cyber Campaign against Georgia in August of 2008. Washington, DC, 2009.

Vershbow, Alexander. "The Transatlantic Partnership at the Crossroads: Meeting NATO's Five Challenges." Speech at the Netherland Institute of International Relations, Amsterdam, 2001.

Woodward, Bob. *Bush at War*. New York: Simon Schuster, 2002.

Yeltsin, Boris. *Midnight Diaries*. New York: Public Affairs, 2000.

——. *The Struggle for Russia*. New York: Random House, 1994.

Yergin, Daniel. *The Quest: Energy, Security, and the Remaking of the Modern World*. New York: Penguin Press, 2012.

——. *Shattered Peace: The Origins of the Cold War and the National Security State*. Boston: Houghton Mifflin, 1976.

Yesin, Viktor. "Nuclear Disarmament: Problems and Prospects." *Russia in Global Affairs* 6, no. 1 (January–March 2008). http://eng.globalaffairs.ru/number/n_10357.

Zeltser, Yuri, and Grace Cary Bickley. *Spinning Boris*. TV Film. Directed by Roger Spottiswoode. New York: Showtime Networks, 2003.

Zysk, Katarzyna. "Russia's Arctic Strategy." *Joint Forces Quarterly* 57, no. 2 (2010): 103–110.

MEDIA RESOURCES

"Agentura.Ru." Relcom, accessed March 16, 2013. http://agentura.ru/.

"Biden's Munich Speech: Obama Administration Foreign Policy Projects Weakness and Confusion." Heritage Foundation, accessed March 20, 2013. http://herit.ag/vvtMlp.

"Bush I Putin: Idealnaia Para." *Kommersant Vlast* 25 (June 26, 2001).

Christian Science Monitor, 2013. http://feautres.csmonitor.com.

"CNS News." CNS News, accessed March 25, 2013, http://www.cnsnews.com.

"Commission on 9/11." *The 9/11 Commission Report*. Washington, 2004. http://www.9-11commission.gov/report/911Report.pdf.

"Commission on Presidential Debates." Commission on Presidential Debates, accessed March 27, 2013. http://www.debates.org/index.php?page=2008-debates.

Congressional Digest.

Guardian.

"Meeting with President of the United States of America Barack Obama." President of Russia, accessed March 25, 2013. http://eng.kremlin.ru/news/4045.

Moscow Times.

Newsru. Television, Moscow, 2005.

New Times Moscow.

Nezavisimaya Gazeta.

"Nunn-Lugar Global Cooperation Initiative." U.S. Department of Defense DTRA, accessed March 27, 2013. http://www.dtra.mil/Missions/nunn-lugar/nunn-lugar-home.aspx.

"Open Letter to President Obama on Central Europe." The Foreign Policy Initiative, accessed March 27, 2013. http://www.foreignpolicyi.org/node/12519.

"President of Russia." The Kremlin, accessed March 27, 2013. http://eng.kremlin.ru/.

"Putin to Offer World Vision." CNN, accessed March 27, 2013. http://edition.cnn.com/2001/WORLD/europe/09/25/gen.russia.germany1050/index.html.

RIA Novosti.

"Russia Business Environment at a Glance." Economist Intelligence Unit, accessed March 26, 2013, http://country.eiu.com/Russia.

Russia Today.

"September 26, 2008, Debate Transcript." Commission on Presidential Debates, accessed March 27, 2013, http://www.debates.org/index.php?page=2008-debate-transcript.

Washington Post.

"Why Russia Protects Assad." *Financial Times,* January 26, 2012.

Die Zeit Online, accessed March 27, 2013, http://www.zeit.de.

Credits for Illustration Section
(pages 124–34)

Figure 1. Mikhail Gorbachev calls George H. W. Bush on December 25, 1991. Source: © ITAR-TASS / Yuri Lizunov/Sovfoto

Figure 2. George H. W. Bush and the new Russian leader, Boris Yeltsin, tour Camp David in February 1992. Source: AP Photo/ Doug Mills

Figure 3. At Vancouver, April 1993, Yeltsin meets Bill Clinton. Source: © Larry Downing/Sygma/Corbis

Figure 4. Clinton plays a saxophone just given to him by Yeltsin. Photo by Bob McNeely. Source: Courtesy of the William J. Clinton Presidential Library.

Figure 5. Boris Yeltsin dances his way to victory during his uphill 1996 Presidential campaign. Source: AP Photo/Alexander Zemlianichenko.

Figure 6. Coal miners stage a sit-in in Red Square during Russia's August 1998 financial meltdown. Source: AP Photo/Czarek Sokolovski.

Figure 7. George Bush meets Vladimir Putin in Slovenia in July 2001. Source: REUTERS/Michael Leckel

Figure 8. French president Jacques Chirac, Vladimir Putin, and German chancellor Gerhard Schroeder early 2003. Source: Vladimir Rodionov/RIA Novosti

Figure 9. Yulia Tymoshenko and Viktor Yushchenko, November 2004. Source: Victor Drachev/AFP/Getty Images.

Figure 10. George W. Bush and Georgian President Mikheil Saakashvili and their wives in Freedom Square in Tbilisi in May 2005. Source: REUTERS/Kevin Lamarque KL/TW

Figure 11. German chancellor Angela Merkel argues in April 2008 with Secretary of State Condoleezza Rice and George W. Bush against near-term NATO membership for Ukraine and Georgia. Source: REUTERS/Benoit Doppagne/Pool

Figure 12. Russian tanks rolled across Georgia in August 2008. Source: © Yuri Kozyrev/NOOR

Figure 13. "Lenin" and "Stalin," taking a break from posing with tourists in Red Square, buy hamburgers at a McDonalds in Moscow. Source: Mikhail Fomichev/RIA Novosti

Figure 14. Igor Sechin, former Russian deputy prime minister and now CEO of Rosneft, the largest listed oil company in the world, signs newly installed oil pipeline. Source: © ITAR-TASS/Grigory Sysoyev/Sovfoto

Figure 15. In March 2009, Russian foreign minister Sergei Lavrov and U.S. secretary of state Hillary Clinton pressed the "reset" button to symbolize a new start in the U.S.-Russian relationship. Source: REUTERS/Fabrice Coffrini/Pool

Figure 16. "The Cheeseburger Summit." Demonstrating the "reset" in 2010, President Barack Obama and Russian president Dmitry Medvedev enjoyed a meal at Ray's Hell Burgers in suburban Virginia. Source: REUTERS/Kevin Lamarque

Figure 17. Ten Russian "sleeper spies" are expelled from the United States in June 2010. The most glamorous, Anna Chapman, is featured on the left. Source: Emmanuel Dunand/AFP/Getty Images

Figure 18. Tens of thousands of protestors challenged the results of the December 2011 parliamentary elections. Source: Photo © Yuri Timofeyev, www.ytpage.com

Figure 19. Putin rides his Harley-Davidson to victory in the run-up to the 2012 Presidential election. Source: Sergei Karpukhin/AFP/Getty Images

Figure 20. A Russian nuclear ice-breaker cuts through the Arctic. Source: Photo archive of Rosatomflot

Figure 21. Obama and Putin meet at the 2013 Northern Ireland G-8 Summit. Source: REUTERS/Kevin Lamarque

Index

Abkhazia: color revolutions and, 99,
103–5, 109, 161, 168–71, 175, 208,
238; Georgia and, 99, 103–5, 109, 161,
168–71, 175, 208, 238; U.S. refusal to
recognize, 175
Adamkus, Valdis, 114
Adjaria, 103, 109
adoptions, 252–53, 291
Afghanistan: Al Qaeda and, 47; Bin
Laden and, 47; erosion of Russian
influence and, 98; foreign policy issues
and, xi, 123, 135–37, 218–20, 228–32,
237–38, 240, 252, 254, 256, 258–59,
264–65, 268; George W. Bush and, 80,
117, 148; Georgia and, 109, 169, 172,
237–38; Iran and, 149; K-2 military
base and, 66, 119–22, 236; Khyber
Pass and, 230; lessons from reset policy
and, 259; Manas military base and,
236–37; Mi–17 helicopters and, 231;
Mujaheddin and, 63; NATO and,
168, 240; Northern Alliance and, 32;
Northern Distribution Network and,
168, 230; Obama and, 218–20, 228–32,
254; Operation Enduring Freedom
and, 66, 71; South Caucasus and, 107;
Soviet withdrawal from, 31; Taliban
and, 32, 62–63, 135, 264; terrorism and,
47, 62–71, 75, 78, 135–36, 139, 264;
transportation agreement and, 230–32;
Uzbekistan and, 121; Voloshin on, 94;
Zawahiri and, 47
Afghan War, 21, 80, 149, 237
Ahmadinejad, Mahmoud, 150
Ahtisaari, Martii, 44, 160–61, 285
Akayev, Askar, 64–65, 116–18, 287
Akhmadov, Ilyas, 60

Akramiya, 120, 122
Al'Assad, Bashar, 249
Albright, Madeleine, 40, 43, 55, 113, 199,
215, 279
Alekperov, Vagif, 204
Aleksei II, 187
Al Qaeda: Bin Laden and, 47, 63, 86, 231,
290; Mujaheddin and, 63; Pentagon at-
tack and, 49, 286; terrorism and, 47, 49,
61, 63–64, 67, 70, 86, 88, 90, 231, 286,
290; World Trade Center and, 49, 286;
Zawahiri and, 47
Amerada Hess, 200
Ames, Aldrich, 59
Andijon crisis, 120–22
Annan, Kofi, 249–50
anti-American sentiment, 44, 73, 88, 135,
215, 253, 264
Anti-Ballistic Missile (ABM) Treaty:
Brezhnev and, 30; Clinton and, 30;
George W. Bush and, 60, 69, 72–75, 78,
80, 286; Nixon and, 30
anti-ballistic missiles (ABMs), 223
antiterrorist programs, x, 62–66, 81, 139,
271
Antonov, Anatoly, 222, 224
Apple, 189
Arab spring, 247–50
Arctic, xiii, 291; China and, 205; gas and,
193, 205; natural resources of, 193,
203–6, 291; Northern Sea Route and,
205; UN convention on the Law of the
Sea and, 205; U.S.-Russian cooperation
in, 133, 291
Arctic Council, 205
Arlington, Virginia, ix, 241
Armavir radar station, 156–57

Armenia, 99, 169
Asian-Pacific Economic Cooperation (APEC), 73, 143, 289
Asmus, Ronald, 170–71, 308n49
Assange, Julian, 242–43
assassinations: Gongadze and, 112; Khlebnikov and, 87; Litvinenko and, 145–46; Massoud and, 62–63; Politkovskaya and, 145, 288; Shevardnadze and, 104–5; Tatum and, 186; tsarist system and, 144
"atoms for peace" program, 31
Auschwitz-Birkenau death camp, 138
Austro-Hungarian Empire, 5, 111
authoritarianism, 2, 8, 15, 17, 38, 84, 94, 99, 116, 248, 257, 272
automobile industry, 188
Axis of Evil, 72, 78, 81, 83, 150
Axis of the Unwilling, 91, 94, *127*
Azerbaijan, 31; Armenians and, 99; Caspian littoral states and, 198; Cheney and, 139–40; color revolutions and, 99; democracy and, 141; energy issues and, 199–200, 201; Gabala radar station and, 156; George W. Bush and, 139; GUUAM and, 118, 122; missile defense (MD) and, 156; Morningstar and, 199; Putin and, 156; radar sites and, 225; Tbilisi exercises and, 169
Azeris, 31, 99, 139

Baker, James: Georgia and, 105–6; Gorbachev and, 4, 37; NATO and, 37, 75–76; post-Soviet era embassies and, 7; as realist, 8; START protocols and, 9; Yeltsin and, 4
Bakiyev, Kurmanbek, 117–18, 236–37, 289
Baku-Tbilisi-Ceyhan (BTC) oil pipeline, 108, 139, 199–200
Balkans: Ahtisaari Plan and, 44, 160–61, 285; foreign policy issues and, xiii–xiv, 17, 41–46, 159–61, 200, 247, 257; humanitarian crisis of, 44–45; NATO and, 25. *See also* specific country
Baltic states: Cheney and, 138–39; color revolutions and, 97, 99; Commonwealth of Independent States (CIS) and, 97; energy and, 165, 196; human rights and, 62; independence of, 4; International Republican Institute and, 253;

NATO and, 14–15, 62, 77–78, 164, 230, 264, 287; Nord Stream pipeline and, 196; "post-Soviet syndrome" and, 99; transportation issues and, 230; Vilnius Conference and, 138; Yeltsin and, 4
Baluevsky, Yuri, 300n85
Beethoven, Ludwig van, 108
Beijing Olympic Games, 172, 288
Belarus: Bakiyev and, 237; Clinton and, 17; Commonwealth of Independent States (CIS) and, 97; George W. Bush and, 27; nuclear power and, 9, 27, 283; Shushkevich and, 5; Yeltsin and, 5, 283
Belgrade, 41, 43
Berezovsky, Boris, 23, 79, 85, 145–46, 181
Beria, Lavrenti, 104
Berliner, Joseph, 187
Berlin Wall, 7
Beslan school hostages, 85–86, 145, 287
Beyrle, John, 175, 262, 267–68
Biden, Joseph, 217, 248, 312n2
bilateral trade, 261, 268
Bin Laden, Osama, 47, 63, 86, 231, 290
Black Sea, 65, 110, 138, 157, *169*, 174, 193, 215, 236
Blair, Tony, 135, 202
Boeing, 187–88
Bolton, John, 66, 73, 150–53, 279, 306n59
Bosnia, 26, 41–43, 159, 284
Boston Marathon bombings, 266–68, 270, 291
BP, 181, 200–203
Brahimi, Lakhdar, 249
Brezhnev, Leonid, 25, 30, 245
BRIC countries (Brazil, Russia, India, and China), 136, 148, 182, 185, 273. *See also* specific country
Brzezinski, Zbigniew, 113
Bulgaria, 78, 154, 287
Bureau of Democracy, Labor and Human Rights, 119
Burjanadze, Nino, 106–7
Burns, Nicholas, 121, 162
Burns, William, 264
Bush, George H. W., x; Camp David and, 8, *124*, 283; Chicken Kiev speech and, 3; Cold War issues and, 2, 5, 7–8, 11, 105, 156; Gorbachev and, 2–4, 55, 92, *124*; lobster summit and, 156; Mainz speech and, 38; missile defense (MD) and, 229;

nonproliferation and, 9, 16; Obama and, 217; Operation Desert Storm and, 88–89; reset policy and, 7–9, 217, 259; Shevardnadze and, 105; START I and, 283; START II and, 29, 283; Ukraine and, 304n4; U.S. aid and, 10–12; Yeltsin and, 4, 8, 12, *124*

Bush, George W., x, xvi; as accidental president, 54; Afghanistan and, 80, 117, 148; Anti-Ballistic Missile (ABM) Treaty and, 60, 69, 72–75, 78, 80, 286; arms control and, 49, 53, 55–57, 60, 70, 72–81; Axis of Evil and, 72, 78, 81, 83, 150; Azerbaijan and, 139; background of, 54; Belarus and, 27; Brdo summit and, 60–62; Camp David and, 95–96, 283; China and, 73; Cold War issues and, 56, 60, 72–73, 76, 81, 98, 163, 222; color revolutions and, 98, 101–2, 105, 107–10, 113, 116–22; conservatives and, 80; Crawford ranch of, 66–69, 157, 286, 299n76; democracy and, 78, 83, 141–44; economic issues and, 177, 193–203, 207, 209; energy issues and, 177, 193–203, 207, 209; Extraordinary Rendition Program and, 119; Florida ballot debacle of, 54; Freedom Agenda and, 82–84, 86, 97, 101, 109, 115–17, 121–23, 136, 138–42, 164, 176, 247, 287; Gabala radar station and, 156–57; gas and, 193–98; Georgian War and, 175; Global War on Terror and, 70, 107, 119; Gore-Chernomyrdian Binational Commission and, 28; human rights and, 78–80, 143; India and, 73; International Monetary Fund (IMF) and, 56; Iran and, 72–73, 83; Iraq and, 80–96, 141–44, 148, 212; Jackson-Vanik strictures and, 102; Kosovo and, 160; Kyrgyzstan and, 117; Ljubljana summit and, 162, 286; lobster summit and, 156; Medvedev and, 163, 289; Merkel and, *129*, 168; missile defense (MD) and, 56, 60–61, 69, 72–75, 78, 81, 136, 148, 155–58, 163, 214, 225–26, 229; NATO and, 61–62, 72, 75–78, *129*, 136, 154–55, 163, 165, 264; nonproliferation and, 74; nuclear power and, 68, 207; Obama and, 217; Putin and, 60–81, *127*, 135–44, 148–57, 172, 176, 220; reelection of, 287; reset policy

and, 70, 74, 81, 86–87, 149, 176, 217–18, 235, 251; Rice and, 55–57, 61–62, 64, 66, 80; Russian-American Consultative Group on Strategic Stability and, 74–75; Saakashvili and, *128*, 168–71; Shanghai APEC conference and, 73; Soros and, 102, 106, 110, 113, 122, 296n42; stakeholder issues and, 60, 81; START and, 73–74; Strategic Offensive Reductions Treaty (SORT) and, 74, 78, 96, 222, 286; terrorism and, 56, 62–66, 119, 163; 2000 electoral campaign of, 54–58

Bushehr nuclear power plant, 31–33, 78, 151–53, 207, 233, 290

Camp David, 8, 95–96, *124*, 246, 283, 286

Canada, 204–5, 261–62

capitalism: communism and, xiii; Gaidar and, 16; oligarchic, 180–81, 257; Putin and, 180–81; Russian-style, xiii, 16, 183–84, 257; Wild East, 16

Caspian Guard program, 139

Caspian resources, 198–201

Caucasus, 304n7; Chechnya and, 22 (*see also* Chechnya); color revolutions and, 99, 101, 103, 107, 119; foreign policy issues and, xiv, 230, 235; North, xiv, 32, 47, 67, 70–71, 86, 91, 119, 145, 151, *169*, 170, 250, 259, 267, 272, 287; Northern Distribution Network and, 230; Obama and, 213; pipeline of, 200; South, 99, 101, 103, 107, 176, 200, 308n28; terrorism and, 47, 67, 70–71, 86, 250, 259, 267; Uzbekistan and, 119; Zawahiri and, 47

Central Election Commission, 106, 113–14

Central Intelligence Agency (CIA): Ames and, 59; Chernomyrdin and, 58; Cold War and, 5, 59; color revolutions and, 110, 115, 122; Gates and, 5, 148; Tenet and, 67; terrorism and, 63, 67

Chapman, Anna, *132*, 241, 290

Chechnya, 186; Boston Marathon bombings and, 266–68, 270, 291; Dagestan invasion and, 285; Dubrovka Theater hostages and, 70, 85, 286; foreign policy issues and, 160–61; Georgia and, 105, 107–8; Kadyrov and, 145, 242; NATO

Chechnya (*continued*)
and, 160; Pankisi Gorge and, 105, 107–8; Primakov and, 105, 108; Russian incursion into, xiv, 22, 25–26, 32, 36, 45–48, 56, 60, 63, 67, 70–71, 78–80, 90, 93, 284–86; separatists and, 60, 259; terrorism and, 46–47, 67, 70–71, 85–86, 90, 107, 266–68, 270, 285–86, 291; truce of, 46

"cheeseburger summit," ix, *131*, 242, 290

Cheney, Dick: Azerbaijan and, 139–40; Baltic states and, 138–39; color revolutions and, 101; Freedom Agenda and, 138–41; gas and, 139; Georgia and, 139, 141, 173; Kazakhstan and, 140–41, 304–5n12; Kosovo and, 148; Milošević and, 56; NATO and, 138–39; oil and, 139; Putin and, 56, 101, 137–41, 147; Russian energy blackmail and, 196; tough stance against Russia by, 101, 137–41, 148, 196, 287, 304–5n12; Ukraine and, 139, 141; Vilnius speech of, 138–41, 148, 196, 287, 304–5n12; Yeltsin and, 4

Chernomyrdin, Viktor: Ahtisaari and, 44; CIA report on, 58, 285; Gazprom and, 192; George W. Bush and, 57–58; Gore and, 18, 28, 33, 57, 59, 74, 78, 150, 221, 244; Iran and, 33; Kosovo and, 160; private equity funds and, 187; Serbia and, 160

Chicken Kiev speech, 3

Chilingarov, Artur, 204

China, 18; as Arctic power, 205; BRIC AND, 136, 148, 182, 185, 273; carbon dioxide emissions of, 206; color revolutions and, 121; corruption and, 262; George W. Bush, 73; human rights and, 262; Iraq War and, 87, 92; Kazakhstan and, 140; limits of partnership and, 262, 264, 273; NATO and, 76; nuclear power and, 225; Primakov and, 26; Putin and, 136, 258; Shanghai Cooperation Organization and, 151; Snowden and, 269; South Ossetia and, 175; sovereignty and, 137, 143; stakeholder issues and, 262; Syria and, 290; Turkmenistan pipeline and, 201; U.S. trade with, 178, 188; Xi Jinping and, 258

Chirac, Jacques, 89–91, 93, 95, *127*, 286

Christopher, Warren, 14–15, 21, 41

Chubais, Anatoly, 12, 22

Cisco, 189

Civil Society working group, 243–44

clans, 17, 100, 112, 116, 180–81

Clark, Wesley, 44

climate change, 190, 204, 206–7

Clinton, Bill, x, xvi; Albright and, 55, 215; Anti-Ballistic Missile (ABM) Treaty and, 30; Azerbaijan and, 139–40; Baku-Tbilisi-Ceyhan (BTC) oil pipeline and, 108; Belarus and, 17; bilateral policy framework and, 27–34; Cold War issues and, 11, 13, 26–27, 37, 55–56, 98, 238–39; communism and, 13, 15, 17–24; creating bilateral policy framework and, 14, 27–34; democracy and, 13–15, 17, 19; energy issues and, 177, 198–99; Euro-Atlantic security and, 36–48; Freedom Agenda and, 82–83; G-7 and, 16–17; G-8 and, 16; Gore and, 18, 28 (*see also* Gore, Al); impeachment of, 20, 47; independent post-Soviet states and, 16; International Monetary Fund (IMF) and, 56; interventionist policy of, 15; Iran and, 17, 26, 30–34, 46, 50; Istanbul summit and, 45–46, 285; Jackson-Vanik strictures and, 102; Kazakhstan and, 17, 27; Kosovo and, 17, 20, 26, 159; large-scale societal transformation and, 16–17; Lewinsky and, 20; liberalism and, 15, 82–83; limits of partnership and, 256–57; missile defense (MD) and, 29–30, 46–47, 72, 220, 229; NATO and, 14, 16–17, 20, 25, 29, 45, 59, 75–76, 264, 284; Naval Academy speech of, 15; Newly Independent States ambassador and, 15; new Washington/Moscow vistas and, 17–20; nonproliferation and, 28–29; nuclear power and, 15–16, 27–34, 256–57; Nunn-Lugar program and, 60; offered incentives of, 16; Office of the Newly Independent States and, 59; Operation Desert Fox and, 87; OSCE and, 285; Partnership for Peace (PfP) Program and, 39; Putin and, 46–47; reset policy and, 13, 17, 27, *131*, 159, 212, 217–18, 229, 250–51, 259–60, 264; as Russia's hand, 14–17; shock therapy and, 16; sovereignty and, 16, 18; stakeholder issues and, 17–18, 29; START II and, 29; terrorism and, 119; Tripartite Accord and, 28; Ukraine and, 111–12, 284; U.S. aid and, 11; Uzbekistan and, 119; Washington's Russian interlocutors and, 24–27; weapons of mass destruction (WMD) and, 15–16; Yeltsin and, 14–15, 19–34, 39–49, 60, *125, 126*, 220, 259, 264, 283–85, 297n23

Clinton, Hillary, *131*, 211, 220, 239, 246, 289–90

coal miner strike, *126*

Coca-Cola, 188

Cold War issues, 1, 6, 172, 204; ABM Treaty and, 72–75, 80; Ames and, 59; Baker and, 76; Churchill and, 141; CIA and, 5, 59; Clinton and, 11, 13, 26–27, 37, 55–56, 98, 238–39; color revolutions and, 98, 105; economic issues and, 177–78, 191; energy and, 194; espionage and, 67 (*see also* espionage); Euro-Atlantic security and, 14, 26–27, 29, 31, 34, 36–37, 41, 44, 238; foreign policy issues and, ix–xv; Gates and, 5, 148; George H. W. Bush and, 2, 5, 7–8, 11, 105, 156; George W. Bush and, 56, 60, 72–73, 76, 81, 98, 163, 222; Germany and, 36, 167; Hollywood and, 241; "How to Lose the Cold War" memo and, 11; Iran and, 31; iron curtain and, 141; Kosovo and, 44; legacies of, 3, 163, 177, 267; limits of partnership and, 255, 267, 274; NATO and, 41, 231–32; Nixon and, 11; Obama and, 214, 216, 219, 222, 251; Putin and, 53, 65, 67, 69, 72, 191, 212, 239; Rice and, 56–57, 64, 80–81; Soviet global regime change and, 83; START and, 29, 222, 224–25; stereotypes and, 178, 231, 246; void left by end of, 34; Yeltsin and, 55–56

Collective Security Treaty Organization (CSTO), 122, 155

color revolutions: Abkhazia and, 99, 103–5, 109, 161, 168–71, 175, 208, 238; Andijon crisis and, 120–22; Azerbaijan and, 99; Baltic states and, 97, 99; Bishkek and, 98, 117–18; Caucasus and, 99, 101, 103, 107, 119; Central Intelligence Agency (CIA) and, 110, 115, 122; Cheney and, 101; China and, 121; clans and, 100, 112, 116; Cold War

issues and, 98, 105; Commonwealth of Independent States (CIS) and, 97; communism and, 99–103, 123; corruption and, 100–101, 106–7, 236; cronyism and, 106; democracy and, 99–100, 102, 105, 108–12, 115, 119; European Union (EU) and, 108, 114, 121; Freedom Agenda and, 97, 101, 109, 115–17, 121–23; frozen conflicts and, 98–99, 105, 167, 171, 263; George W. Bush and, 98, 101–2, 105, 107–10, 113, 116–22; Georgia and, 99, 102–13, 117–18, 121–23, *129*; Karshi-Khanabad and, 119–22; *Kmara* and, 106; Kyiv and, 98, 102, 110–11, 113, 118; Kyrgyzstan and, 116–18, 121–23; Nagorno-Karabakh and, 98–99, 263; near abroad and, 98; Newly Independent States (NIS) and, 98–99, 102; nongovernmental organizations (NGOs) and, 101–6, 110, 113–14, 116, 120, 140; oligarchs and, 100, 111–12; Orange Revolution and, 110–16, 118, *128*, 138, 142, 195, 236, 287; perspective on, 122–23; personal ties and, 100; "post-Soviet syndrome" and, 99–103; Powell and, 108, 114–15, 119; Putin and, 100, 104, 109, 112–15, 122–23; republics and, 97–98, 102–3, 111, 122; Rose Revolution and, 103–10, 168, 238, 287; South Ossetia and, 99, 103–5, 109, *129*, 161, 168–71, 175, 208, 238, 288, 309n61; spheres of influence and, 97; statelets and, 98–99; Tbilisi and, 98–99, 104–5, 108–9, 118, 123; text messaging and, 100–101; Transnistria and, 99, 263; Tulip Revolution and, 116–18, 120, 287; Ukraine and, 97–98, 101–2, 110–18, 121–23, *128*, 138, 142, 195, 236, 287; Uzbekistan and, 116, 118–22; Yeltsin and, 104, 110

commercial ties, 52, 100, 102, 151, 177–78, 260

Committee on Foreign Investments in the United States (CFIUS), 189

Commonwealth of Independent States (CIS), 5, 18, 39, 94, 97, 197, 254, 283

communism: capitalism and, xiii; Clinton and, 13, 15, 17–24; Cold War issues and, 13 (*see also* Cold War issues); color revolutions and, 99–103, 123; Cuba

communism (*continued*)
and, 67, 94; Euro-Atlantic security and, 36–39; fall of Berlin Wall and, 7; France and, 11; Gorbachev and, 3–4, 83; Iran and, 32; Italy and, 11; Lenin and, 231; limits of partnership and, 256; Marshall aid and, 11; postcommunist Russia and, x, 2, 7, 10, 12–13, 21, 24, 32, 36, 144; "post-Soviet syndrome" and, 99–103; Putin and, 52, 85; Stalin and, 3, 8, 55, 98, 103–4; Tudeh party and, 31; Turkmen Republic and, 2; Yeltsin and, 8, 284; Yugoslavia and, 6, 12
Communist Party, 3, 17, 22, 31
Comrade Wolf, 141
Conference on Security and Cooperation in Europe (CSCE), 36, 45
Congressional Freedom Support Act, 119
Congress of Peoples' Deputies, 8, 21
Conoco, 200–201
conservatives: George W. Bush and, 80; Helms and, 59; Kudrin and, 182; neoconservatives and, 80, 304n3
Constitutional Conference, 20–21
Consultative Group on Strategic Stability, 81
Contact Group, 42–43, 48, 159–60
Cooperative Threat Reduction Program, 10, 28, 213
Copenhagen conference, 206–7
Corfu Process, 240
corruption: China and, 262; color revolutions and, 100–101, 106–7, 236; cronyism and, 106, 181; economic issues and, 179, 181; Georgia and, 141; ITS index and, 181; Medvedev and, 221, 242–43; North Caucasus and, 272; oligarchs and, 16, 23; patronage and, 106; Putin and, 53; Republicans and, 57; Skolkovo and, 244; Ukraine and, 141, 236; weak rule of law and, 179; Wild East capitalism and, 16
Council of Europe, 36, 147, 264
Council on Foreign Relations, 215
coups: Gorbachev and, 3–4, 21, 46, 110, 283; Khrushchev and, 144
Crawford summit, 66–69, 157, 286, 299n76
Crimea, 3, 110, 236
cronyism, 106, 181
Cuba, 67, 94
cyber security, 171, 243, 316n25
Cyprus, 161

Czech Republic: Havel and, 40, 226; Korbel and, 55; missile defense (MD) and, 154–58, 225–27, 288–89; NATO and, 39–40, 77, 285; Rice and, 55; Schwarzenberg and, 148

Daeubler-Gmelin, Herta, 89
Dagestan, 47, 243, 267
David the Builder, 108
Davos Pact, 22–23, 184, 284
Dayton Accords, 41–42
Deep Free Trade, 236
DEFCON (defense readiness condition), 64
democracy: Arab spring and, 247–50; Azerbaijan and, 141; Cheney and, 138–39, 141; Clinton and, 13–19; collapse of Soviet Union and, 1–11; color revolutions and, 99–100, 102, 105, 108–12, 115, 119; Euro-Atlantic security and, 38, 45, 47–48; Freedom Agenda and, 82–83, 142; Freedom Support Act and, 12; George W. Bush and, 78, 141–44; Georgia and, 141; Gorbachev and, 1–2; human rights and, xiiv (*see also* human rights); Iraq and, 94, 142; Kazakhstan and, 141; limits of partnership and, 256–57, 263–64; Obama and, xiii, 214, 218, 221, 291; promotion of, xiii–xv, 11, 65, 83, 102, 119, 138, 142, 218, 236, 263–64, 291; Putin and, 56, 65, 84–86, 96, 141–44, 147, 178, 239, 287; Soros and, 102, 106, 110, 113, 122, 296n42; sovereign, 141–44, 178, 243, 254; Ukraine and, 141, 236; Uzbekistan and, 119; Western-style, 13, 99, 119
Democrats, 14, 87, 102, 209, 213, 215, 256, 260
Deripaska, Oleg, 185
Dima Yakovlev Law, 252–53
dioxin, 113
Donetsk clan, 112
Donilon, Thomas, 250
Druzhba pipeline, 194
Dubrovka Theater, 70–71, 85, 286
Dudley, Robert, 203
Dyachenko, Tatiana, 23

eavesdropping, 100–101
economic issues: abandonment of state-run socialism and, 177–78; Asian-Pacific Economic Cooperation (APEC) and,

73, 143, 289; automobile industry and, 188; Baku-Tbilisi-Ceyhan (BTC) oil pipeline and, 108, 199–200; bilateral trade and, 261, 268; climate change and, 190, 204, 206–7; coal miner strike and, *126*; Cold War issues and, 177–78, 191; commercial ties and, 52, 100, 102, 151, 177–78, 260; corruption and, 179, 181; Davos Pact and, 23, 284; democracy and, 38; energy and, 177–210; Freedom Support Act and, 12, 119; free market and, 38; G-7 countries and, 16–17, 36, 40, 182; G-8 countries and, 16, 48, 87, 136, 142–43, 147, 156, 161, 196, 246, 271, 285, 291; G-20 countries and, ix, *134*, 185, 215, 218, 229, 233, 247, 273, 289, 291, 293n2; Gaidar and, 10, 16, 294n17; gas and, xii, 191 (*see also* gas); GDP growth and, xii, 182, 205; George W. Bush and, 177, 193–203, 207, 209; global financial crisis and, 183–85, 215, 218–19, 222, 288; Gorbachev reforms and, 3; Great Depression and, 183; International Monetary Fund (IMF) and, 22, 56, 182; investors and, xi, 53, 64, 177–79, 183, 186–90, 201, 204; Jackson-Vanik Amendment and, 27, 68, 71, 94, 102, 123, 163, 209–10, 260; Kazakhstan and, 140; Lehman Brothers and, 183, 184, 288; macroeconomic policies and, 16, 136, 178; Magnitsky Act and, 210, 250, 252, 260, 262, 291; Marshall Plan and, 11; Medvedev and, 181, 183–84, 186–88, 192–93, 206–8; minerals and, 23, 169, 191, 205; monopolies and, 139, 189–93; most-favored nation (MFN) status and, 27; New Economic School and, 220–21; Obama and, 177, 199, 201, 203–4, 207, 214; oil prices and, 49, 91, 136, 157, 178, 182–84, 204, 272 (*see also* oil); oligarchs and, 48, 53, 181, 185, 189, 202–3; Operation Provide Hope and, 11; pensions and, 23, 48, 136, 183; permanent normal trading relations (PNTR) and, 209–10, 261; poverty and, xii, 48, 79, 182, 257; private equity funds and, 187; privatization and, 15, 20, 22, 79, 186, 189, 192; production sharing agreements (PSAs) and, 201; Putin and, 49, 53, 71, 84, 177–96, 201–3, 206–9; reset policy and, 210; rogue states and, 83–84; ruble collapse and, 24; Russia Inc., and, 180–81; Russian MTV and, 187; Russian networks and, 180–81; Russian Orthodox Church and, 187; St. Petersburg International Economic Forum and, 183; sanctions and, 33, 82, 88, 90, 104, 150–53, 233, 249, 263–64, 288–89, 291; shock therapy and, 16; state ownership and, 16; unemployment and, 9–10, 29, 48, 51, 183, 194, 208; U.S. business in Russia and, 186–89; U.S. Chamber of Commerce and, 102, 209; U.S.-Russia Business Council and, 102, 186, 209; Valdai group and, 174, 179, 191–93, 195; Wild East and, 16, 186; World Bank and, 53; World Economic Forum and, 22, 184, 310n23, 319n32; World Trade Organization (WTO) and, 61, 71, 74, 123, 143–44, 208–10, 252, 256, 261; Yeltsin and, 180–81, 186, 201

EDF, 201

Egypt, 47, 59, 84, 111, 247–48

Eisenhower, Dwight, 270

energy: Arctic and, 204–6; Azerbaijan and, 199–200; Baku-Tbilisi-Ceyhan (BTC) oil pipeline and, 108, 199–200; Baltic states and, 165, 196; Caspian and, 198–201; climate change and, 190, 204, 206–7; Clinton and, 177, 198–99; Cold War issues and, 194, 196; European Union (EU) and, 192, 196–97, 201, 236; gas and, 191 (*see also* gas); George W. Bush and, 177, 193–203, 207, 209; Georgia and, 108, 199–200; Great Game and, 198; International Atomic Energy Agency (IAEA) and, 34, 152, 233; Kazakhstan and, 140; Molotov-Ribbentrop Act and, 197; monopolies and, 189–93; Munich speech and, 148–49; Nord Stream pipeline and, 196–97; oil and, 165 (*see also* oil); oligarchs and, 181, 185, 189, 202–3; Poland and, 192, 196–98; public sector cooperation and, 203–8; Putin and, 177–96, 201–3, 206–9; Ukraine and, 111, 138, 190, 194–96, 198, 200, 236, 287; U.S. business in Russia and, 201–3; U.S.-Russia Commercial Energy Summit and, 204

Energy Working Group, 204

ENI, 200

Eritrea, 181

espionage, 253, 316n19; Ames and, 59; assassinations and, 62–63, 87, 104–5, 144–46, 288; Chapman and, 290; Gates and, 148; Hanssen and, 59; invisible ink and, 241; Ivanov and, 58–59; Litvinenko and, 145–46; Obama and, 242; poisonings and, 87, 113, 145–46; Powell and, 58–59, 242; Putin and, 148, 242; Rosenberg and, 228; Semenko and, 241–42; shortwave radio and, 241; sleeper agents and, *132*, 241–42, 290; Snowden and, 269–71; steganography and, 241–42; Tenet on, 67; U-2 plane and, 270; U.S.-Russian swap of, 242; WikiLeaks affair and, 242–43, 269, 290

Estonia, 77, 214, 243, 287

ethnic cleansing, 12, 38, 41, 44, 104, 160

Euro-Atlantic security: Balkans and, 41–45; Clinton/Yeltsin era and, 14, 24, 264; Cold War issues and, 14, 26–27, 29, 31, 34, 36–37, 41, 44, 238–39; color revolutions and, 109; communism and, 36–39; Conference on Security and Cooperation in Europe (CSCE) and, 36, 45; Contact Group and, 42–43, 48, 159–60; Corfu summit and, 240; Dayton Accords and, 41–42; democracy and, 38, 45, 47–48; France and, 239; Freedom Agenda and, 176; George W. Bush/Putin era and, 75, 142, 147, 170–71, 176, 264, 300n103; Germany and, 239; Gorbachev and, 37; Istanbul summit and, 45–46, 285; Kosovo and, 41–45; limits of partnership and, 257, 263–64; NATO and, xiv–xv, 36–47, 238–40, 254 (*see also* North Atlantic Treaty Organization (NATO)); Obama/Putin era and, 235, 238–40; OSCE and, xiv, 45, 106, 140, 147, 238–40, 264, 316n11; rethinking, 35–48; sovereign democracy and, 142; sovereignty and, 48; terrorism and, 45–48 (*see also* terrorism); United Nations (UN) and, 42; Warsaw Pact and, 36, 39; Yeltsin and, 36, 39–44

Euromoney magazine, 185

European Bureau, 7, 15, 119, 137, 262, 298n36

European Security Treaty, xv, 238–39, 260, 289

European Union (EU): Association Agreement and, 236; color revolutions and, 108, 114, 121; energy and, 196–97, 201, 236; EU3 and, 152; Gazprom and, 192; Georgia and, 168; Germany and, 165, 196–97; Iraq War and, 93; Kosovo and, 161–62; Lithuania and, 139; membership action plans (MAPs) and, 165; Russia and, 36, 93, 192, 196, 238, 311n56; Yanukovych and, 236

Evans, Donald, 68, 202, 204, 279

Extraordinary Rendition Program, 119

Exxon-Mobil, 201–3, 291

Facebook, 188

Federal Bureau of Investigation (FBI), 59, 242, 266–67

Federal Security Service (FSB), 145, 202, 267

fentanyl, 71

Finland, 44, 226

Finley, Julie, 316n11

Fischer, Joschka, 90

Forbes magazine, 87

Ford, Gerald, 57

Ford Motor Company, 179, 188

Foreign Affairs journal, 55–56

Fradkov, Mikhail, 84

France, 239; Axis of the Unwilling and, 91, 94, *127*; Chirac and, 89–91, 93, 95, *127*, 286; communism and, 11; EU3 and, 152; EU presidency and, 173; Euro-Atlantic security and, 239; Iraq War and, 87, 89–90, 92–95; NATO and, 37, 77; Russian citizens in, 165; Sarkozy and, 173, 175–76; Sobchak and, 51

Freedom Agenda: Arab spring and, 247–50; Cheney and, 138–41; Clinton and, 82–83; color revolutions and, 97, 101, 109, 115–17, 121–23; democracy and, 82–83, 142; divisiveness of, 97; Euro-Atlantic security and, 176; foreign policy issues and, 136; George W. Bush and, 82–84, 86, 97, 101, 109, 115–17, 121–23, 136, 138–42, 164, 176, 247, 287; Georgia and, 164; Kazakhstan and, 140–41; Kyrgyzstan and, 117–18; liberal internationalist view and, 82–83;

NATO and, 83; Putin and, 86, 138; Rice and, 83; Ukraine and, 115–16, 164

freedom of assembly, 264

freedom of expression, 48, 79, 100, 122, 138, 257

freedom of speech, xii, 264

Freedom Support Act, 12, 119

Fridman, Mikhail, 203

Fried, Daniel, 102

frozen conflicts, 98–99, 105, 167, 171, 263

Fulda Gap, 34

G-7 (Group of Seven Countries), 16–17, 36, 40, 182

G-8 (Group of Eight Countries), 16, 48, 87, 136, 142–43, 147, 156, 161, 196, 246, 271, 285, 291

G-20 (Group of Twenty Countries), ix, *134*, 185, 215, 218, 229, 233, 247, 273, 289, 291, 292, 293n2

Gabala radar station, 156–57

Gaidar, Yegor, 10–11, 16, 294n17

Gamsakhurdia, Zviad, 104

gas: Arctic and, 193, 205; Azerbaijan and, 200; Baltic states and, 165; Caspian, 108, 193, 198–201; Cheney and, 139; economic recovery and, 191; Finland and, 165; Gazprom and, 192–96, 198, 200, 216, 287; George W. Bush and, 193–98; Georgia and, 108; Germany and, 196; global financial crisis and, 184; as intimidation tool, 139, 195–96; Iran and, 32; limits of partnership and, 272; Morningstar and, 199; Nabucco pipeline and, 200; Nord Stream and, 196, 290–91; Putin and, xii, 190, 201; RosUkrEnergo (RUE) and, 195; Saudi Arabia and, 190; Shah Deniz field and, 200; shale, 192, 197–98, 311n45; shutting off supply of, 138, 190, 193, 195–96; South Caucasus Pipeline and, 200; South Stream and, 200–201; Soviet Ministry of Gas Industry and, 192; as strategic sector, 203; Syria and, 249; Turkey and, 200; Turkmenistan and, 200–201; Turkmen Republic and, 2; Tymoshenko and, 112, 236; Ukraine and, 110, 138, 190, 194–96, 236, 289

gas centrifuges, 33

Gates, Robert, 2, 5, 148, 164–65, 184

Gazprom, 192–96, 198, 200, 216, 287

General Motors, 179, 188

genocide, 171, 175, 309n61

Georgetown University, xvi

Georgia, 213; Abkhazia and, 99, 103–5, 109, 161, 168–71, 175, 208, 238; Adjaria and, 103, 109; Afghanistan and, 109, 169, 172, 237–38; Baker Plan and, 105–6; Baku-Tbilisi-Ceyhan (BTC) oil pipeline and, 108, 199–200; Beria and, 104; Burjanadze and, 106–7; Burns and, 162; Chechnya and, 105, 107–8; Cheney and, 139, 141, 173; color revolutions and, 99, 102–13, 117–18, 121–23, *129*; corruption and, 141; David the Builder and, 108; democracy and, 141; energy and, 108, 199–200; European Union (EU) and, 168; Freedom Agenda and, 164; frozen conflicts and, 105; Gamsakhurdia and, 104; gas and, 108; GUUAM and, 118, 122; Helsinki Final Act and, 226; Iraq and, 109, 169, 172–73, 237; Ivanishvili and, 238; *Kmara* and, 106; Lermontov and, 103; liberalism and, 175; limits of partnership and, 266; McCain and, 174; Medvedev and, 174–75, 220, 237; military exercises and, 169–70; mineral water of, 169; Mullen-Makarov channel and, 173; NATO and, 163–68, 240, 290, 304n6; Obama and, 174, 214, 220, 237–38; oil and, 199; Pankisi Gorge and, 105, 107–8; Persians and, 103; Primakov and, 105, 108; Pushkin and, 103; Rice and, 107, 170–71; Rose Revolution and, 103–10, 168, 238, 287; Saakashvili and, 106–10, 123, *128*, 137, 164–75, 237–38, 287, 308n48; Shevardnadze and, 104–10; South Ossetia and, 99, 103–5, 109, *129*, 161, 168–71, 175, 208, 238, 288, 309n61; as stalemate, 238; Stalin and, 103–4; support of United States by, 122–23; Tbilisi and, 98–99, 104–5, 108–9, 118, 123, *128*, 139, 167–71, 174, 176, 199; terrorism and, 107–8, 169; Tolstoy and, 103; Turks and, 103; United Nations (UN) and, 173; U.S.-Russia Strategic Framework Declaration and, 162–63, 288; war with Russia and, 170–76, 200, 214, 220, 238, 240, 288; wine of, 169;

Georgia (*continued*)
World Trade Organization and, 208;
Zhvania and, 106–7
Georgia Train and Equip Program
(GTEP), 107, 169
German Democratic Republic (GDR), 37,
50–51, 104
Germany: automobile industry and, 188;
Axis of the Unwilling and, 91, 94, *127*;
Cold War issues and, 167; East, 6,
12, 37; EU3 and, 152; Euro-Atlantic
security and, 239; Fulda Gap and,
34; G-8 chairmanship and, 136, 196;
gas and, 196; Hitler and, 69, 89, 175,
308n30; Iraq War and, 92–95; Kohl
and, 6; lessons from reset policy and,
257, 261; limits of partnership and,
261; Merkel and, *129*, 165–67, 196, 227,
261; Molotov-Ribbentrop Act and, 197;
NATO and, 77, 165–67; nuclear power
and, 197, 311n55; old/new Europe
and, 89–90, 155; OSCE and, 239–40;
pipeline issues and, 194–97; Putin and,
50–51; reunification of, 6, 36, 36–37;
Rice on, 95; Ruehe and, 38; Rumsfeld
on, 89; Russian citizens in, 165–66;
sovereignty and, 167; Soviet withdrawal
from, 51; Stasi and, 51; Two-Plus-Four
Agreements and, 37; UN Security
Council and, 89; West, 34, 167, 194
Getty Oil, 188
glasnost', 3
global financial crisis, 183–85, 215,
218–19, 222, 288
Global Threat Reduction Initiative, 224
Global Trends, 2015 (U.S. National Intelligence Council), 58
Global War on Terror, 70, 107, 119
Goldman Sachs, 182
Gongadze, Hihory, 112
Google, 189
Gorbachev, Mikhail: Baker and, 4, 37;
breakup of Soviet Union and, 1–7, 21,
104, 283; coup against, 3–4, 21, 46, 110,
283; Euro-Atlantic security and, 37;
George H. W. Bush and, 2–4, 55, 92,
124; German unification and, 37; glasnost' and, 3; house arrest of, 3; interna-
tional communist mission and, 83; Iraq
War and, 92; Jewish emigration and,

27; Kuwait and, 92; liberalism and, 21,
27; oil prices and, 182; perestroika and,
3, 50; Primakov and, 92; Putin and, 50,
182; reforms of, 3–4, 7, 27, 50, 83; resignation of, 1, 5, *124*, 144; Rice and, 55;
Shevardnadze and, 104; START I and,
283; Two-Plus-Four Agreements and,
37; weakened authority of, 4–5; Yeltsin
and, 4–5, 110
Gore, Al, 51, 285; Chernomyrdin and,
18, 28, 33, 57, 59, 74, 78, 150, 221, 244;
Putin and, 51; Republican attacks on,
57–58; 2000 electoral campaign and,
57–58
Gosudarstvennik (statist), 52
Gottemoeller, Rose, 29, 222, 276, 280
Graham, Lindsay, 120, 148
Graham, Thomas, 101–2, 136–37, 144,
280, 304n3
Great Depression, 183
Great Game, 198
Greece, 161, 240
gross domestic product (GDP), xii, 182,
205
Gryzlov, Boris, 114
Guff, Drew, 187
Gulf War, 4, 6, 26, 87–88, 92
Gusinsky, Vladimir, 23, 79, 85, 192
GUUAM (Georgia-Ukraine-Uzbekistan-
Azerbaijan-Molodova), 118, 122

Haass, Richard, 92
Hadley, Stephen, 86, 121, 135, 137, 164,
167, 172–75, 229, 274
Hamas, 175
Hanssen, Robert, 59
Havel, Vaclav, 40, 226
Helms, Jesse, 59
Helsinki Final Act, 226
Heusgen, Christof, 167
Hewlett Packard, 189
highly enriched uranium (HEU), 29
Hitler, Adolf, 69, 89, 175, 308n30
Hizb ut-Tahrir (HT), 119–20
Holbrooke, Richard, 42–43, 113
Hong Kong, 269
hostages: Akramiya protest and, 120;
Beslan school and, 85–86, 145, 287;
Dubrovka Theater and, 70–71, 85, 286;
fentanyl and, 71; Iran and, 31

House International Affairs Committee, 209

"How to Lose the Cold War" (memo), 11

humanitarian interventions, xiii, 44–45, 88, 247, 309n61

human rights: Andijon crisis and, 120–21; Baltic states and, 62; China and, 262; Council of Europe and, 36; Dima Yakovlev Law and, 252–53; Freedom House and, 87; freedom of assembly and, 264; freedom of expression and, 48, 79, 100, 122, 138, 257; freedom of speech and, xii, 264; George W. Bush and, 78, 143; Iraq and, 94; Magnitsky Act and, 209–10, 250, 252, 260, 262, 291; Office of Democratic Initiatives and Human Rights (ODIHR) and, 106; Politkovskaya and, 145; Russia and, xiv–xv, 36, 48, 62, 78–80, 100, 118, 143, 145, 221, 240, 252–53, 264, 267, 269; United Nations and, 87–88; Uzbekistan and, 66, 118–22

Human Rights Watch, 120

Hungary, 39–40, 77, 285

Hussein, Saddam, 84; Axis of Evil and, 81; Gulf War and, 4, 6, 26, 87–88, 92; hanging of, 173; Iran and, 149; Iraq War and, 87–95, 172, 264; Primakov and, 93; Republican Guard and, 88; Shiites and, 150; weapons of mass destruction (WMD) and, 90–91, 94

impeachment, 20, 47, 283

Implementation Force (IFOR), 43

Independent International Fact-Finding Mission on the Conflict in Georgia (EU report), 172

India: BRIC and, 136, 148, 182, 185, 273; carbon dioxide emissions of, 206; George W. Bush and, 73; nuclear power and, 31; Primakov and, 26; sovereignty and, 137

Institute of World Economy and International Relations (IMEMO), 26

intercontinental ballistic missiles (ICBMs), 213

International Atomic Energy Agency (IAEA), 34, 152, 233

International Monetary Fund (IMF), 22, 56, 182

International Republican Institute, 102, 253

Internet freedom, 253

invisible ink, 241

Iran, xi, 84, 135; ABM Treaty and, 72; Afghanistan and, 149; Ahmadinejad and, 150; air defense contract with Russia and, 233; "atoms for peace" program and, 31; Axis of Evil and, 150; Bushehr plant and, 31–33, 78, 151–53, 207, 233, 290; Caspian littoral states and, 198–99; Caspian summit and, 153; Clinton and, 17, 26, 30–34, 46, 50; Cold War issues and, 31; cooperation of, 149–50; foreign policy issues and, 136–37, 139, 149–53, 207, 218–19, 229, 252, 254, 256, 258–59, 264–65; gas and, 32; George W. Bush and, 72–73, 83; hostage crisis of, 31; improving Russian ties and, 31–32; Khamenei and, 153; Khatami and, 150; lessons from reset policy and, 259; limits of partnership and, 256, 258–59, 264; Medvedev and, 232–33; missile defense (MD) and, 72, 153–57, 225–28; Munich speech and, 148, 150; National Intelligence Council and, 150; National Intelligence Estimate on Iran and, 150; nuclear power and, xiv, 30–34, 78, 123, 148–53, 232–33, 264, 288–90; Obama and, 218–19, 225–29, 232–34, 289; observer status of, 151; oil and, 32; Pahlavi and, 31; Putin and, 72–73, 148, 150–51, 153, 233–34, 315n77; Qom facility and, 232–33; Resolution 1737 and, 152; Resolution 1747 and, 152; Resolution 1803 and, 152; Resolution 1929 and, 233, 289; Rice and, 153; as rogue state, 92; Russia as Little Satan and, 31; Russian weapons to, 73; sanctions and, 152–53, 288; Shanghai Cooperation Organization and, 151; straits of Hormuz and, 234; terrorism and, 83, 149–50; Tudeh party and, 31; United States as Great Satan and, 31; Yeltsin and, 26, 30–34, 285

Iraq: Axis of the Unwilling and, 91, 94, *127*; Cheney and, 101; China and, 87, 92; Clinton and, 87, 92; democracy and, 94, 142; European Union (EU) and, 93; foreign policy issues and, xi, 75, 98, 123, *127*, 135–36, 247, 250, 259; France and, 87, 89–90, 92–95; George W. Bush and, 80–96, 141–44, 148, 212; Georgia and,

Iraq (*continued*)
  109, 169, 172–73, 237; Germany and,
  92–95; Gorbachev and, 92; Gulf War
  and, 4, 6, 26, 87–88, 92; human rights
  and, 94; Kurdistan and, 200; Kuwait
  and, 4, 88, 92; "mission accomplished"
  and, 135; nuclear power and, 286; oil-
  for-food program and, 88; Operation
  Desert Fox and, 87; Operation Desert
  Storm and, 88–89; Operation Iraqi
  Freedom and, 91; Powell and, 90, 94,
  286; Primakov and, 91–92; Republican
  Guard and, 88; Resolution 687 and, 88;
  Resolution 1441 and, 89; Rice and, 91,
  95; road to war in, 87–96; as rogue state,
  92; Saddam Hussein and, 6, 26, 81, 84,
  87–95, 149–50, 172–73, 264; sanctions
  and, 263; Shiites and, 150; terrorism
  and, 83; United Nations (UN) and, 82,
  84, 86–94; weapons of mass destruction
  (WMD) and, 83, 87–88, 91, 94, 96, 286;
  Yeltsin and, 87, 94
Ireland, 271
iron curtain, 141
Iskander missile system, 215, 228, 289
Islam: Akramiya and, 120; Andijon crisis
  and, 120–21; Arab spring and, 247–50;
  Azeris and, 31, 99, 139; Balkans and,
  41–45; extremists and, 63, 119–20, 122,
  230; fundamentalism and, 47, 61–62,
  67, 151; Hizb ut-Tahrir (HT) and,
  119–20; Karimov and, 118; Kosovars
  and, 43, 46, 160–61, 288; Muslim com-
  munities and, 247; Obama and, 232;
  radicalism and, xiii, 32, 91, 118, 250;
  Russia and, 31, 247–48, 250; Shiites
  and, 31–32, 150; suicide bombers and,
  63; Sunnis and, 250; terrorism and,
  60–63, 67, 70, 91, 120, 122, 151, 230;
  U.S. experience with, 247; United
  States as Great Satan and, 31; Uzbekistan and, 119–20
Islamic Movement of Uzbekistan (IMU),
  119
Israel, 27, 33, 81, 111, 150, 153, 170, 209,
  233
Italy, 11, 239
Ivanishvili, Bidzina, 238
Ivanov, Igor, 26, 43, 52, 58–60, 69, 107–9,
  195, 199, 285

Ivanov, Sergei, 61, 65, 73, 78, 146, 150,
  155–56, 160, 217, 298n42, 299n61

Jackson, Michael, 44
Jackson-Vanik Amendment, 27, 68, 71, 94,
  102, 123, 163, 209–10, 260
Japan, 197
Jews: Gorbachev and, 27; Jackson-Vanik
  Amendment and, 27, 68, 71, 94, 102,
  123, 163, 209–10, 260
Jones, Elizabeth, 59
Jones, James, 232–33, 242
Justice for Sergei Magnitsky Act, 210,
  250, 252, 260, 262, 291

Kaczynski, Lech, 289
Kadyrov, Ramzan, 145, 242
Karimov, Islom, 64–66, 118–22
Karshi-Khanabad (K-2) military base, 66,
  119–22, 236–37
Kasyanov, Mikhail, 84, 280
Kazakhstan: Akayev and, 117; Caspian
  littoral states and, 198; Cheney and,
  140–41, 304–5n12; Clinton and, 17,
  27; democracy and, 141; energy and,
  140; Freedom Agenda and, 140–41;
  Nazarbayev and, 64–65, 140; North-
  ern Distribution Network and, 230;
  nuclear power and, 9–10, 27, 222, 283;
  oil and, 140
Keenan, Edward, 180
Kennan, George, 257, 265
Kerry, John, 250–51, 270, 292
KGB (Committee on State Security), 48,
  50–51, 53, 62, 65, 68, 104, 145–46, 163,
  216, 242, 297n8, 299n61
Khamenei, Ayatollah, 153
Khatami, 150
Khlebnikov, Paul, 87
Khodorkovsky, Mikhail, 85, 87, 93, 142,
  181, 183, 202, 204, 209, 286
Khrushchev, Nikita, 14, 144, 270
Khudaynatov, Eduard, 203
Kim Jong Il, 78
King, Larry, 243
Kipling, Rudyard, 198
Kislyak, Sergei, 173–74, 252
Kissinger, Henry, 51, 215, 273, 297n8
Kmara, 106
Kohl, Helmut, 6

Kokoshin, Andrei, 141
Kommersant newspaper, 192–93, 211
Korbel, Josef, 55
Korzhakov, Alexander, 20
Kosovo: Ahtisaari Plan and, 44, 160–61, 285; Burns and, 162; Cheney and, 148; Clinton and, 17, 20, 26, 159; Cold War issues and, 44; European Union (EU) and, 161–62; foreign policy issues and, 44, 158–62, 170; George W. Bush and, 160; independence of, xv, 160–62, 170, 288; Islam and, 43, 46, 160–61, 288; limits of partnership and, 263; Munich speech and, 148; NATO and, 159–60; North Atlantic Treaty Organization (NATO) and, 160; political importance of, 158; Putin and, 159, 161–62; rethinking Euro-Atlantic security and, 41–45; self-determination and, 161; Serbia and, 20, 160–62; Stabilization Force and, 159–60; United Nations (UN) and, 89, 160–61; violent crisis of, 159–62, 170, 285; Wisner and, 160–61; Yeltsin and, 17, 20, 26
Kosovo Force (KFOR), 160
Kosovo Liberation Army, 160, 162
Kouchner, Bernard, 174
Kozyrev, Andrei, 18, 24–26, 42–43, 284
Kramer, David, 102
Kraus, Eric, 309n5
Kravchuk, Leonid, 5, 28, 110, 284
Kremlin. *See* Russia
Kuchma, Leonid, 111–14
Kudrin, Alexei, 52, 182, 184–85, 290
Kurdistan, 200
Kursk disaster, 79
Kuwait, 4, 88, 92
Kwasniewski, Alexander, 114, 138, 226, 303n34
Kyoto Protocol, 206–7
Kyrgyzstan: Akayev and, 64–65, 116–18, 287; Bakiyev and, 117–18, 236–37, 289; Bishkek and, 98, 117–18, 237; color revolutions and, 116–18, 121–23; ethnic clashes and, 237; Fergana Valley and, 116–17; Freedom Agenda and, 117–18; George W. Bush and, 117; Jalal-Abad and, 117; Obama and, 236–37; Osh and, 117; reset policy and, 236–37; Russian military bases and, 118, 237; Russia's

interest in, 118, 121; support of United States by, 122–23; Tulip Revolution and, 116–18, 120, 287; U.S. military bases and, 66, 117, 219

LaRouche, Lyndon, 300n85
Latvia, 77, 214, 230, 287
Lavrov, Sergei, 315n73; Clinton and, *131*, 211, 220, 289–90; Kerry and, 250, 270, 292; Kosovo and, 160–61; missile defense and, 155; NATO and, 227–28, 238–39, 249; Rice and, 118, 152–53, 160, 173–74; Vilnius meeting and, 141
Lebed, Alexander, 23
Lehman Brothers, 183, 184, 288
Lenin, Vladimir Ilyich, 231
Leningrad, 50, 191, 216
Leningrad State University, 216
Lermontov, 103
Lewinsky, Monica, 20
Liberal Democratic Party of Russia (LDPR), 21, 92, 284
liberal-internationalist view, 15, 82–83
liberalism: Clinton and, 15, 82–83; Georgia and, 175; Gorbachev and, 21, 27; intelligentsia and, 35; Khodorkovsky and, 93; Markov and, 303n27; NATO and, 44, 52; Nemtsov and, 65; Sobchak and, 51; Yabloko and, 85, 93; Yavlinsky and, 65, 93; Yeltsin and, 16, 36
Libya, 264, 318n12; Arab Spring and, 247–49; NATO and, 248–49; no-fly zones and, 248–49; North Atlantic Treaty Organization (NATO) and, 248–49; Qaddafi and, 248–49, 290; Resolution 1973 and, 248–49; Russian business in, 248–49; United Nations (UN) and, 88, 248–49, 251
Lieberman, Joseph, 148
limits of partnership: China and, 262, 264, 273; Cold War issues and, 255, 267, 274; communism and, 256; democracy and, 256–57, 263–64; Germany and, 261; Iran and, 256, 258–59, 264; Kosovo and, 263; missile defense (MD) and, 256, 259–60, 268; NATO and, 263–66; nonproliferation and, 256, 258, 264, 268; reset policy and, 235, 237–38, 240–43, 246, 250–54, 259–60, 263–74; Yeltsin and, 257, 259, 264

Lincoln, Abraham, 46
Lithuania, 77, 114, 138–39, 287
Litvinenko, Alexander, 145–46
lobster summit, 156
London School of Economics, 219
Los Cabos, Mexico, ix, *134*, 246
Lugar, Richard, 9–10, 16, 28, 60, 74, 213, 253, 283
Lugovoi, Andrei, 145–46
Lukin, Vladimir, 18–19
LUKOIL, 188, 200, 201, 204

Maidan Square, 114
Makarov, Nikolai, 173, 222–23
Makhachkala, 47
Mamedov, Yuri, 24, 28
Manas airport military base, 66, 117, 219, 236–37
Manas Transit Center, 237
Markov, Sergei, 112, 115, 267
Marshall Plan, 11
Massachusetts Institute of Technology, 189
Massoud, Ahmed Shah, 62–63
Matlock, Jack, 25
McCain, John, 87, 120, 143, 148, 174, 213, 304n6
McDonalds, *130*, 188
McFaul, Michael, 221, 235, 243–47, 281, 313n12, 315n73, 317n34
Medvedev, Dmitry: background of, ix, 146, 216; changed rhetoric of, 221–22; cheeseburger summit and, ix, *131*, 242, 290; civil society summit and, 221; climate change and, 206–7; commercial law and, 261; corruption and, 221, 242–43; economic issues and, 181, 183–88, 192–93, 206–8; election of, 162, 288; espionage and, 242–43; establishing persona of, 216; Euro-Atlantic security issues and, 238–41; European Security Treaty and, 238–39, 289; first address of, 215; G-8 summit and, 291; Gazprom and, 192, 216; George W. Bush and, 163, 289; Georgia and, 174–75, 220, 237; innovation village and, 188–89; Iran and, 232–33; Iskander missile system and, 215, 228, 289; as lawyer, ix; London School of Economics speech of, 219; Markov and,

112; missile defense (MD) and, 215, 217, 223, 226–29, 233, 289–90; modernization and, 216; Moscow summit and, 231; NATO and, 227, 238–40; Northern Distribution Network and, 219; nuclear power and, 232–33; Obama and, ix, *131*, 215–23, 226–33, 242, 246, 251, 270–71, 289–90, 313n16, 318n12; oil and, 183; Putin's return and, 212, 244–46, 248, 251–52, 290; reset policy and, 215–23, 226–33, 261; Resolution 1973 and, 248–49; Russian Federal Assembly and, 215; Saakashvili and, 172; Silicon Valley and, 189, 244, 290; START and, 217, 223, 228, 233, 289; tandem government of, 147, 215–19, 221, 240, 242–45, 248–49, 251, 288, 290, 313n27, 314n35; transportation agreement and, 230–32; Twitter account of, ix, 290; U.S.-Russia Bilateral Presidential Commission and, 220–21, 243–44, 289; Valdai Discussion Club and, 174–75, 237, 314n35
Medvedev Treaty, 238–39
membership action plans (MAPs), 77, 163–68, 174
Merkel, Angela, *129*, 165–67, 196, 227, 261
Merkel, David, 281, 304n7
Mi–17 helicopters, 231
Microsoft, 189
Miles, Richard, 109
military bases: Bulgaria and, 154; K-2, 66, 119–22, 236–37; Kant, 118; Kyrgyzstan and, 66, 117–18, 219; Manas airport, 66, 117, 219, 236–37; Putin and, 51; Romania and, 154; Russia and, 118; United States and, 64, 66, 117–22, 154, 219, 236–37; Uzbekistan and, 120–22, 236–37
Miller, Alexei, 192
Milner, Yuri, 188
Milošević, Slobodan, 41–43, 56
minerals, 23, 169, 191, 205
missile defense (MD), xi, xiv, 77, 300n85; ABM Treaty and, 30, 60, 69, 72–75, 78, 80, 286; Armavir radar station and, 156–57; Azerbaijan and, 156; Clinton and, 29–30, 46–47, 220, 229; Cold War issues and, 72, 81; Czech Republic and, 154–58, 225–27, 288–89; Gabala radar station and, 156–57; George H. W.

Bush and, 229; George W. Bush and, 56, 60, 72–75, 78, 81, 136, 148, 155–58, 163, 214, 225–26, 229; Iran and, 72, 153–57, 225–28; Iskander missile system and, 215, 228, 289; limits of partnership and, 256, 259–60, 268; lobster summit and, 156; Medvedev and, 215, 217, 223, 226–29, 233, 289–90; Munich speech and, 148, 154–58; National Missile Defense (NMD) and, 30; NATO and, 154; New START and, 217, 222–28, 231, 233, 252, 259, 289; North Korea and, 72, 81, 154, 225, 228–29, 291; Obama and, 215, 219–20, 223–29, 254, 259–60, 289; Poland and, 154–58, 225–29, 288–89; Putin and, 46, 49–50, 56, 60–61, 69, 148, 153–58, 163, 220, 225, 228, 254; Reagan and, 29–30; Rice and, 162; S-300 system and, 150, 233; second-strike capability and, 154; SS-24/SS-25 ICBMS and, 213; Strategic Arms Limitation Treaty (SALT) and, 74; Strategic Arms Reduction Treaty (START) and, 9, 12, 28–29, 73–74, 163, 217, 220, 222–25, 228, 231, 233, 252, 259, 283, 289; Strategic Offensive Reductions Treaty (SORT) and, 74, 78, 96, 222, 286; theater (TMD), 30, 76; Treaty on Conventional Forces in Europe (CFE) and, 155–56; U.S.-Russia Strategic Framework Declaration and, 162–63, 288; Yeltsin and, 29–30

Mitteleuropa, 38

Mobil, 188, 203

Moldova, 118, 122

Molotov-Ribbentrop pact, 197

Mordashov, Alexei, 188

Morningstar, Richard, 199

Morris, Dick, 23

"Moscovite Political Folkways" (Keenan), 180

Moscow Helsinki Group, 253

Moscow State Institute of International Relations (MGIMNO), xvi, 175, 276, 294n13, 309n61

Moscow Summit, 292

Moscow Treaty. *See* Strategic Offensive Reductions Treaty (SORT)

Mossaddeq, Mohammed, 31

most-favored-nation (MFN) status, 27

"Mr. X" (Kennan), 257, 265

MTV, 187

Mubarak, Hosni, 84, 247

Mujaheddin, 63

Mullen, Michael, 172–73, 222–23, 228, 231

Musharraf, Pervez, 61

Nabucco pipeline, 200

Nagorno-Karabakh, 98–99, 263

Nashi youth group, 86, 243

National Democratic Institute, 102, 221, 253

National Endowment for Democracy, 102–3

National Intelligence Council, 150

National Missile Defense (NMD) system, 30

National Security Agency (NSA), 269

National Security Council (NSC), 55, 80, 92, 101–2, 136–37, 165, 235, 246, 262

NATO-Russia Council (NRC), 76, 164, 238–41

Nauru, 175

Naval Academy, 15

Nazarbayev, Nursultan, 64–65, 140

Nemstov, Boris, 65

neoconservatives, 80, 304n3

New Economic School, 220, 220–21

Newly Independent States (NIS), 15, 18, 59, 98–99, 102, 198, 235, 262, 298n36

New York Nets, 188

Nicaragua, 175

Nikonov, Vyacheslav, 112

Nixon, Richard M., 8; ABM Treaty and, 30; Brezhnev and, 25, 30; Cold War and, 11; Kozyrev and, 25; urges George H. W. Bush to do more for Russia, 11; visits Russia, 25

Niyazov, Sapurmurad, 2

NKVD, 104

no-fly zones, 88, 248–49

Nogovitsyn, Anatoly, 175

nongovernmental organizations (NGOs): color revolutions and, 101–6, 110, 113–14, 116, 120, 140; foreign agent status of, 253; grading of Russia by, 87; limits of partnership and, 258, 261, 264–65; Obama and, 218; succession politics and, 144; transparency and, 48. *See also* specific organization

nonproliferation: Baker and, 9; Clinton and, 28–29; George H. W. Bush and, 9, 16; George W. Bush and, 74; International Security and Nonproliferation and, 154; limits of partnership and, 256, 258, 264, 268; nuclear power and, xiv, 9, 16, 28–29, 33, 40, 74, 76, 144, 154, 214, 218, 222, 253, 256, 258, 264, 268; Obama and, 214, 218, 222, 253; Permanent Joint Council and, 40, 76; Putin and, 144; Yeltsin and, 33
Nonproliferation Treaty, 9
Nord Stream, 196–97, 290–91
North Atlantic Cooperation Council, 12, 167
North Atlantic Treaty Organization (NATO): Afghanistan and, 168, 240; Article Five and, 39; Baker and, 37, 75–76; Balkans and, 41–45; Baltic states and, 14–15, 62, 77–78, 164, 230, 264, 287; Big Bang plan of, 77–78; Bosnia and, 159, 284; Bucharest summit and, 167–68; Bulgaria and, 78, 287; Chechnya and, 160; Cheney and, 138–39; China and, 76; Clinton and, 14, 16–17, 20, 25, 29, 34, 59, 75–76, 264, 284; Cold War issues and, 231–32; Czech Republic and, 39–40, 77, 285; Estonia and, 77, 214, 287; Euro-Atlantic security and, xiv–xv, 36–47, 238–40, 254; France and, 37, 77; Freedom Agenda and, 83; George W. Bush and, 61–62, 72, 75–78, *129*, 136, 154–55, 163, 165, 264; Germany and, 77, 165–67; Georgia and, 163–68, 240, 290, 304n6; Jackson and, 44; Kosovo and, 159–60; Latvia and, 77, 214, 287; Lavrov and, 238–39; liberalism and, 44, 52; Libya and, 248–49; limits of partnership and, 263–66; Lithuania and, 77, 287; Medvedev and, 227, 238–40; membership action plans (MAPs) and, 77, 163–68, 174; military bases and, 154; missile defense (MD) and, 291 (*see also* missile defense (MD)); North Atlantic Cooperation Council and, 12; Northern Distribution Network and, 168, 219, 230, 264; Obama and, 215, 218, 227–28, 230–32; OSCE and, 238–40; Partnership for Peace (PfP) Program and, 39; Permanent Joint Council (PJC) and, 40, 44, 48, 76, 164; Poland and, 39–40, 77, 138, 166–67, 285; Powell and, 75; Putin and, 52, 75–78, 95, 148, 167–68, 232, 246, 288; Rasmussen and, 240; reset policy and, 240; Rice and, 83, *129*; Robertson and, 75–76; Romania and, 78, 287; Rumsfeld and, 89; Serbia and, 285; Slovakia and, 78, 287; Slovenia and, 78, 287; Stabilization Force and, 159–60; Ukraine and, 39, *129*, 163–69, 218, 236, 263, 265, 288, 304n5, 304n6; Ulyanovsk demonstrations and, 231–32; Warsaw Pact and, 14; Washington Treaty and, 296n9; Yeltsin and, 39, 41–44, 75, 159–60, 167, 284–85
North Caucasus, 119, 259, 272
Northern Distribution Network (NDN), 168, 219, 230–31, 264
Northern Sea Route, 205
North Korea: ABM Treaty and, 72; foreign policy issues and, 75, 143; Kim Jong Il and, 78; missile defense (MD) and, 72, 81, 154, 225, 228–29, 291; nuclear power and, xiv; Obama and, 225, 228–29, 291; Putin and, 78; Russian weapons to, 73; terrorism and, 83
North Ossetia, 85–86, 145, 287
NTV channel, 192
nuclear weapons: arms control and, xiv, 4, 29–30, 40, 49, 53, 55–57, 60, 70, 72–81, 219, 222–25, 243, 254, 256, 268; "atoms for peace" program and, 31; Belarus and, 9, 27, 283; bilateral policy framework and, 27–34; Bushehr plant and, 31–33, 78, 151–53, 207, 233, 290; China and, 225; civilian nuclear energy and, 207–8; Clinton and, 15–16, 27–34, 256–57, 284; Cooperative Threat Reduction Program and, 10, 28, 213; gas centrifuges and, 33; George W. Bush and, 68, 207; Germany and, 197, 311n55; Global Threat Reduction Initiative and, 224; Gore-Chernomyrdin Binational Commission and, 28, 57–59, 74, 78, 150, 221, 244; highly enriched uranium (HEU) and, 29; India and, 31; intercontinental ballistic missiles (ICBMs) and, 213; International Atomic Energy Agency (IAEA) and, 34, 152, 233; Iran and, xiv, 30–34, 78, 123, 148–53,

232–33, 264, 288– 290; Iraq and, 286; Japan and, 197; Kazakhstan and, 9–10, 27, 222, 283; Medvedev and, 232–33; National Missile Defense (NMD) and, 30; New START and, 217, 222–28, 231, 233, 252, 259, 289; nonproliferation and, xiv, 9, 16, 28–29, 33, 40, 74, 76, 144, 154, 214, 218, 222, 253, 256, 258, 264, 268; North Korea and, xiv; Nunn-Lugar Threat Reduction Program and, 9–10, 16, 28, 60, 74, 213, 253, 283; Obama and, 208; Resolution 1929 and, 233, 289; rogue nations and, 16; Russian-American Consultative Group on Strategic Stability and, 74–75; Russian Ministry of Atomic Energy and, 33; security issues over, 9–10; Seoul summit and, 229, 290; Strategic Arms Limitation Treaty (SALT) and, 74; Strategic Arms Reduction Treaty (START) and, 9, 12, 28–29, 73–74, 163, 217, 220, 222–26, 228, 231, 233, 252, 259, 283, 289; Strategic Defense Initiative and, 29–30; Strategic Offensive Reductions Treaty (SORT) and, 74, 78, 96, 222, 286; terrorism and, 145–46, 224; Tripartite Accord and, 28; Ukraine and, 9–10, 12, 17, 27–29, 214, 222, 283; UN inspections and, 87–88; uranium and, 29, 33, 151–52, 224, 233; U.S. Atomic Energy Act and, 207; weapons arsenals and, xii–xiii, 9, 29, 57, 68, 72, 152, 224–25; weapons of mass destruction (WMD) and, xi–xiv, 15, 83, 87–88, 91, 94, 96, 286; Yeltsin and, 284

Nuland, Victoria, 164

Nunn-Lugar initiatives, xii, 9–10, 16, 28, 60, 74, 213, 253, 283

Obama, Barack: advisory team of, 214–15; Afghanistan and, 218–20, 228–32, 254; Berlin speech of, 268; Biden and, 217, 248, 312n2; body language of, ix, 270–71; call for pause by, 270–72; Camp David and, 246; Caucasus and, 213; cheeseburger summit and, ix, *131*, 242, 290; Civil Society working group and, 243–44; climate change and, 207; Cold War issues and, 214, 216, 219, 222, 251; democracy and, xiii, 214, 218, 221,

291; election of, 213–15, 289; energy issues and, 177, 199, 201, 203–4, 207; Energy Working Group and, 204; espionage and, 242; first term of, 212; foreign policy limitations of, 213–14; former Soviet space and, 235–38; G-8 summit and, 246, 271; G-20 summit and, 247; George H. W. Bush and, 217; George W. Bush and, 217; Georgia and, 174, 214, 220, 237–38; Gore-Chernomyrdian Binational Commission and, 28; Iran and, 218–19, 225–29, 232–34, 289; Islam and, 232; Kyrgyzstan and, 236–37; as lawyer, ix; London meeting of, 218–19; Medvedev and, ix, *131*, 215–23, 226–33, 242, 246, 251, 270–71, 289–90, 313n16; missile defense (MD) and, 215, 219–20, 223–29, 254, 259–60, 289; moderate rhetoric of, 217–18; Moscow summit and, 219–21, 231; Mubarak and, 248; NATO and, 215, 218, 227–28, 230–32; New Economic School speech of, 220–21; New START and, 217, 222–28, 231, 233, 252, 259, 289; nonproliferation and, 214, 218, 222, 253; North Korea and, 225, 228–29, 291; nuclear power and, 208; oil and, 204, 248; Poland and, 214, 226–27; Putin and, ix, x, *134*, 213, 216–17, 219–21, 223, 225, 228–29, 232–33, 237, 246–47, 250–51; reelection of, 250, 254; reset policy and, ix–x, *134*, 211–12, 215–35, 237, 242–43, 246, 251, 253–54, 259–60, 265; Russia's tandem government and, 215–21; second inaugural speech of, xiii; second term of, 243; Sergei Magnitsky Accountability and Rule of Law Act and, 252; Snowden and, 270–71; START and, 222–28; terrorism and, 291; transportation agreement and, 230–32; U.S.-Russia Bilateral Presidential Commission and, 220–21, 243–44, 289; U.S.-Russia Strategic Framework Declaration and, 162–63, 288

Ode to Joy (Beethoven), 108

Office for Democratic Institutions and Human Rights (ODIHR), 106

Office of Central Asian Affairs, 137

Office of Policy Planning, xvi, 75, 92, 101, 275, 298n36, 300n103

Office of the Vice President (OVP), 102, 137, 304n10
oil, xii, 196; Amerada Hess and, 200; Arctic and, 205; Baku-Tbilisi-Ceyhan pipeline and, 108, 139, 199–200; Baltic states and, 165; BP and, 181, 200–203; Caspian reserves and, 108, 198–99; Cheney and, 139; Conoco and, 200–201; *Druzhba* pipeline and, 194; economic recovery and, 191; Energy Working Group and, 204; and, 199; Exxon and, 201–3, 291; Finland and, 165; Georgia and, 108, 199; Getty Oil and, 188; global financial crisis and, 183–84; as intimidation tool, 139; Iran and, 32; Iraq and, 88; Kazakhstan and, 140; Khodorkovsky and, 93, 181, 204; Khudaynatov and, 203; limits of partnership and, 272; LUKOIL and, 188, 201, 204; Medvedev speech and, 183; Mobil and, 188, 203; monopolies and, 190, 193; Obama and, 204, 248; pensions and, 136; price of, 3, 49, 91, 136, 157, 178, 182–84, 204, 272–73; Putin and, xii, 91, 182, 191–92, 202–3; rogue states and, 83, 140; Rosneft and, *130*, 181, 201–3, 207, 291; Russian Orthodox Church and, 187; Saudi Arabia and, 190; Sechin and, 203; as strategic sector, 203; taxes and, 202; Tillerson and, 203; TNK and, 181, 202–3; Turkey and, 199–200; Turkmen Republic and, 2; Unocal and, 200; U.S.-Russia Commercial Energy Summit and, 204; Yukos and, 85, 181, 202–11
oil-for-food humanitarian program, 88
oligarchs: Berezovsky and, 23, 79, 85, 145–46, 181; capitalism and, 180–81, 257; clans and, 17, 100, 112, 116, 180–81; color revolutions and, 100, 111–12; corruption and, 16, 23; Davos Pact and, 23, 284; Donetsk and, 112; economic issues and, 48, 53, 181, 185, 189, 202–3; Gusinsky and, 23, 79, 85, 192; Khodorkovsky and, 85, 87, 93, 142, 181, 183, 201–2, 204, 209, 286; Putin and, 71, 79, 84, 286; Tymoshenko and, 112, *128*, 236, 289; Yeltsin and, 22–23, 84
Olympics, 172, 267, 288
Open Society Institute, 102, 106

Operation Desert Fox, 87
Operation Desert Storm, 88–89
Operation Enduring Freedom, 66, 71
Operation Iraqi Freedom, 91
Operation Provide Hope, 11
Orange Revolution, 110–16, 118, *128*, 138, 142, 195, 236, 287
Organization for Security and Cooperation in Europe (OSCE), xiv, 45, 106, 140, 147, 238–40, 264, 316n11
Organization of the Islamic Conference (OIC), 151
Orthodox Church, 43, 159, 187
Ottoman empire, 5

P-5 (Five Permanent Members of the United Nations Security Council), 233
Pahlavi, Reza, 31
Paine Webber, 187
Pakistan, 61, 135, 230–31, 290
Pankisi Gorge, 105, 107–8
Partnership for Peace (PfP), 39–40
patronage, 16–17
Pavlovsky, Gleb, 112, 303n27
pensions, 23, 48, 136, 183
Pentagon, 49, 80, 231, 237, 286
Pepsi, 188
perestroika and, 3, 50, 216
Permanent Joint Council (PJC), 40, 44, 48, 76, 164
permanent normal trading relations (PNTR), 209–10, 261
Perry, William, 29
Persians, 31, 103
personal ties, 13, 19, 48, 56, 61, 100, 221, 260, 271
Pickering, Thomas, 187–88
poisonings, 87, 113, 145–46
Poland: energy issues and, 192, 196–98; Kaczynski and, 289; Kwasniewski and, 114, 138, 226, 303n34; missile defense (MD) and, 154–58, 225–29, 288–89; Molotov-Ribbentrop pact and, 197; NATO and, 39–40, 77, 138, 166–67, 285; Obama and, 214, 226–27; partitioning of, 111; Putin and, 138; shale gas and, 192, 198; Sikorski and, 167, 197; Walesa and, 40, 226
Politkovskaya, Anna, 145
polonium-210, 145–46

Poneman, Daniel, 29, 204, 208, 281

poverty, xvi, 48, 79, 182, 257

Powell, Colin: Brdo summit and, 60; color revolutions and, 108, 114–15, 119; Iraq War and, 90, 94, 286; Ivanov and, 58–59; NATO and, 75; Security Council speech of, 90, 286; spy scandals and, 58–59, 242

Prikhodko, Sergei, 52, 87, 232–33

Primakov, Evgeny, 281, 284; background of, 26; Christopher and, 41; Georgia and, 105, 108; Hussein and, 91–93; Iraq War and, 91–93; Kozyrev and, 43; Mujaheddin and, 63; NATO and, 77; Putin and, 91–93; Serbian bombings by NATO and, 44; START treaty and, 74; style of, 26; U.S. military bases and, 65; Yeltsin and, 26, 43, 285

private equity funds, 187

privatization, 15, 20, 22, 79, 186, 189, 192

Proctor & Gamble, 179

production sharing agreements (PSAs), 201

Prokhorov, Mikhail, 188

Pushkin, 103

Putin, Vladimir, x, 20; as accidental president, 54; anti-Americanism and, 253, 268; arms control and, 49, 53, 55–57, 60, 70, 72–81; Axis of the Unwilling and, 91, 94, 127; Azerbaijan and, 156; background of, 45, 48, 50–54, 61; Blair and, 135; body language of, 270–71; Brdo summit and, 60–62; Bucharest summit and, 167–68; Bundestag speech of, 67; Camp David and, 95–96, 246, 283; capitalism and, 180–81; Caspian summit and, 153; Cheney and, 56, 101, 137–41, 147; China and, 136, 258; climate change and, 206–7; Clinton and, 46–47; Cold War issues and, 53, 65, 67, 69, 72, 191, 212, 239; color revolutions and, 100, 104, 109, 112–15, 122–23; commercial law and, 261; communism and, 52, 85; corruption and, 53, 85; Crawford summit and, 66–69; democracy and, 56, 65, 84–87, 96, 141–44, 147, 178, 240, 254, 287; Dubrovka Theater hostages and, 70–71, 85, 286; economic issues and, xii, 49, 53, 71, 84, 177–96, 201–3, 206–9; election fraud and, 245; energy issues and, 177–96, 201–3, 206–9; espionage and, 148, 242; five-hour call-in show of, 258–59; Freedom Agenda and, 86, 138; G-8 summit and, 246, 271; G-20 summit and, 247; Gabala radar station and, 156–57; gas and, xii, 190, 192, 195, 201; George W. Bush and, 60–81, 127, 135–44, 148–57, 172, 176; Germany and, 50–51; Gorbachev and, 50, 182; Gore and, 51; growing tensions with, 135–44, 148–57; harassment tactics of, 145–47; Iran and, 72–73, 150–51, 153, 163, 233–34; Iraq War and, 91–96; journalist assassinations and, 87; Khamenei and, 153; Kissinger and, 51, 273, 297n8; Kosovo and, 159, 161–62; Kudrin and, 52, 182, 184–85, 290; Kursk disaster and, 79; Ljubljana summit and, 162, 286; lobster summit and, 156; Magnitsky Act and, 252; military bases and, 51; missile defense (MD) and, 46, 49–50, 56, 60–61, 69, 148, 153–58, 163, 220, 225, 228, 254; mission of, 52–53; Munich speech of, 147–50, 154–56; Nashi youth group and, 86; NATO and, 52, 72, 75–78, 95, 148, 167–68, 232, 246, 288; new world order and, 69; nonproliferation and, 144; North Korea and, 78; Obama and, ix–x, 134, 213, 216–17, 219–21, 223, 225, 228–29, 232–33, 237, 246–47, 250–51, 291; oil and, xii, 91, 178, 182, 191–92, 202, 202–3; OSCE and, 239–40; poisonings by, 145–46; Poland and, 138; politics of succession and, 144–47; power consolidation by, 79, 84–87, 253, 287; as pragmatist, 53; Primakov and, 91–93; Qaddafi and, 249; reelection of, 96, 290; reset policy and, ix, 70, 74, 81–82, 134, 136, 159, 176, 241, 246, 251, 259, 261, 263; return to power of, 244–47, 251–52, 291; Rice and, 57, 62, 112–23, 146, 156–57, 165; Romney and, 254; "Russia and the Changing World" campaign and, 246; Russia Inc., and, 180–81; Russian-American Consultative Group on Strategic Stability and, 74–75; Santiago speech of, 86; Sarkozy and, 173; second term of, 144–47; self-determination and, 161; Shanghai

Putin, Vladimir (*continued*)
APEC conference and, 73; Snowden and, 269–71; Sobchak and, 51–52, 54, 84, 191, 216; social networks and, 188; sovereignty and, 82, 142–43; Soviet national anthem and, 79; START and, 223; as statist, 52; Strategic Offensive Reductions Treaty (SORT) and, 74, 78, 96, 222, 286; Surkov and, 86, 141–42, 243–44; Syria and, ix, 249–50; tandem government of, 147, 215–19, 221, 240, 242–45, 248–49, 251, 288, 290, 313n27, 314n35; terrorism and, 49, 62–66, 163, 291; 2012 Presidential Election and, *133*; U.S.-Russia Strategic Framework Declaration and, 162–63, 288; Uzbekistan and, 65; Valdai Discussion Club and, 109, 142, 146, 179, 191–93, 195, 219–20, 228, 232, 237, 249–50, 301n8, 311n45; vertical of power of, 78–79, 144; World Trade Organization and, 74; worldview of, 53–54; Yanukovych and, 112–13; Yeltsin and, 45–49, 54, 79, 84, 144, 180–81, 186, 257, 303n34
Putinism, 84–87

Qaddafi, Muammar, 248–49, 290

radar stations, 94, 154, 156–57, 225–26
radicalism, xiii, 32, 91, 118, 250
Radisson Slavanskaya, 186
RAND U.S.-Russia Business Forum, 57
Rasmussen, Anders Fogh, 240
Rather, Dan, 86
Raymond, Lee, 202
Ray's Hell Burgers, ix, *131*
Reagan, Ronald, 29, 56, 59, 112, 194
Realpolitik strategy, 71, 141, 221, 257
Red Square, *126*, *130*, 146, 248
Republican Guard, 88
Republicans, 209, 256, 260; Clinton attacks by, 20, 213; congressional losses of, 148; congressional majority and, 26, 33; corruption of Russia and, 14, 87; difficulty of negotiating with, 224; Gore and, 57; missile defense and, 28, 30, 228; Obama and, 227, 254; think tanks of, 215
reset policy, xvi; beyond, 266–74; "cheeseburger summit" and, ix, *131*, 242; Civil Society working group and, 243–44;

Clinton and, 13, 17, 27, *131*, 159, 212, 217–18, 229, 250–51, 259–60, 264; economic issues and, 210; George H. W. Bush and, 7–9, 217, 259; George W. Bush and, 86–87, 149, 176, 217–18, 235, 251; Kyrgyzstan and, 236–37; lessons from, 259–63; limits of partnership and, 235, 237–38, 240–43, 246, 250–54, 259–60, 263–74; meaning of, 211–12; Medvedev and, 215–23, 226–33; NATO and, 240; Obama and, ix–x, *131*, *134*, 211–12, 215–35, 237, 242–43, 246, 251, 253–54, 259–60, 265, 271; *peregruzka* button and, 211–12; in perspective, 250–54; Putin and, ix, 70, 74, 81–82, *134*, 136, 159, 176, 241, 246, 251; substance vs. process and, 243–44; tandem government of Russia and, 147, 215–19, 221, 240, 242–45, 248–49, 251, 288, 314n35; translated as overload, *131*, 211–12; U.S. Congress and, 86–87
RIA Novosti news agency, 85, 118
Rice, Condoleeza: Burns and, 121; Cold War issues and, 56–57, 64, 80–81; Czech Republic and, 55; *Foreign Affairs* article of, 55–56; Freedom Agenda and, 83; Gabala radar station and, 156–57; George W. Bush and, 55–57, 61–62, 64, 66, 80; Georgia and, 107, 170–71; Gorbachev and, 55; on ignoring Germany, 95; Iran and, 152–53; Iraq War and, 91, 95; Ivanov and, 61, 146, 298n42; Karimov and, 121; Korbel and, 55; Kyrgyzstan and, 117–18; Lavrov and, 118, 152–53, 160, 173–74; membership action plans (MAPs) and, 164–65, 167; missile defense (MD) and, 162; National Security Council and, 55, 165; NATO-Russia Council and, 164; normalized relations with Russia and, 56, 66, 95, 137; North Atlantic Treaty Organization (NATO) and, 83, *129*; on punishing France, 95; Putin and, 57, 62, 112–23, 146, 156–57, 165; Rumsfeld and, 121; Saakashvili and, 170, 174; Scowcroft and, 4; September 11 attacks and, 64; Sochi summit and, 162–63; as Soviet expert, 55; Steinmeier and, 170; Tashkent and, 121; terrorism and, 117, 162; Uzbekistan and, 121; Yanukovych and, 112–13; Yeltsin and, 4, 55

Rice University, 204
Robertson, George, 75–76
Rogozin, Dmitry, 228, 232
Romania, 78, 138, 154, 161, 229, 287
Romney, Mitt, 229, 254
Rose Revolution, 103–10, 168, 238, 287
Ros-Lehtinen, Ileana, 209
RosNano, 189
Rosneft, *130*, 181, 201–3, 207, 291
Rosoboronexport, 231
RosUkrEnergo (RUE), 195
Ruehe, Volker, 38
rule of law, xiv, 17, 35, 96, 100, 166, 179, 187, 216, 236, 243, 252, 261, 264, 272
Rumsfeld, Donald, 57, 66–67, 73, 88, 118–22, 148, 230, 300n85
Rumyantsev, Alexander, 151
Russia, 39, 98, 201, 235; Abkhazia and, 99, 103–5, 109, 161, 168–71, 175, 208, 238; air defense contract with Iran and, 233; Anti-Ballistic Missile (ABM) Treaty and, 30, 53, 60, 69, 72–75, 78, 80, 286; Arab spring and, 247–50; Arctic claims of, 204–6; arm sales to Syria and, 249–50; asymmetry of bilateral relationship and, xi–xii, 27, 53, 58, 78, 189, 197, 243–44, 258, 274; authoritarianism and, 2, 8, 15, 17, 38, 84, 94, 99, 116, 248, 257, 272; automobile industry and, 188; Balkans and, xiii–xiv, 17, 25, 41–46, 159–61, 200, 247, 257; Baltic states and, 4, 14–15, 62, 77–78, 97, 99, 138, 164–65, 196, 230, 253, 264, 287; *bezporiadok* and, xii; bilateral trade and, 261, 268; Brahimi and, 249; BRIC and, 136, 148, 182, 185, 273; capitalism and, xiii, 183–84, 257; carbon dioxide emissions of, 206; Chechnya and, xiv, 22, 25–26, 32, 36, 45–48, 56, 60, 63, 67, 70–71, 78–80, 90, 93, 284–86; children adopted in United States and, 252–53, 291; climate change and, 206–7; Cold War issues and, 53 (*see also* Cold War issues); color revolutions and, 97–123; commercial networks of, 180–81; Congress of People's Deputies and, 21; Constitutional Conference and, 20–21; Crawford summit and, 66–69; Crimea and, 3, 110, 236; Cuba and, 67, 94; cuts gas off, 138, 190, 194–96, 287, 289; Dubrovka Theater hostages and, 70, 85, 286; Duma of, 20–22, 29, 65, 85, 87, 96, 114, 141, 146–47, 161, 188, 202, 204, 208, 220, 224, 245, 251, 291, 301n12; as energy superpower, 190–98; European Union (EU) and, 36, 93, 192, 196, 238, 311n56; future scenarios for, 272–74; G-8 chairmanship and, 136, 196; Gore-Chernomyrdin Binational Commission and, 28, 57–59, 74, 78, 150, 221, 244; Great Game and, 198; growing tension with, 135–58; Helsinki Final Act and, 226; human rights and, xiv–xv, 36, 48, 62, 78–80, 87, 100, 118, 143, 145, 221, 240, 252–53, 264, 267, 269; humiliation of, 9, 25, 27, 48, 52, 255–57; image of rising power and, 136; improving Iranian ties and, 31–32; Iranian nuclear power and, 32–34; iron curtain and, 141; Iskander missile system and, 215, 228, 289; Islam and, 247–48, 250; Jackson-Vanik strictures and, 27, 68, 71, 94, 102, 123, 163, 209–10, 260; Jewish emigration and, 27; Kyrgyzstan and, 118; large-scale societal transformation and, 16–17; Leningrad, 50, 191, 216; Lermontov and, 103; Lithuania and, 139; as Little Satan, 31; Magnitsky Act and, 210, 250, 252, 260, 262, 291; military bases and, 118; Molotov-Ribbentrop Pact and, 197; national identity and, 24; near abroad and, 18, 26, 48, 98, 135, 247; New Economic School and, 220–21; new flag of, 1; new Russian Foreign Policy Concept and, 253–54; NKVD and, 104; oligarchs and, 16, 22–23, 48, 53, 71, 79, 84–85, 100, 111–12, 181, 185, 189, 202–3, 257, 284, 286; perestroika and, 3, 50, 216; postcommunist, x, 2, 7, 10, 12–13, 21, 24, 32, 36, 144; poverty and, xii, 48, 79, 182, 257; Primakov and, 26; as protector of Orthodox Serbs, 159; Pushkin and, 103; Red Square and, *126*, *130*, 146, 248; rethinking Euro-Atlantic security and, 35–48; ruble collapse and, 24; Russian-American Consultative Group on Strategic Stability and, 74–75; St. Petersburg International Economic Forum and, 183; Shanghai Cooperation Organization and, 151; shock therapy and, 16; Siloviki and, 79,

Russia (*continued*)
216; Snowden and, 269–71; soft power
and, 100, 142; Soros and, 102, 106, 110,
113, 122, 296n42; South Ossetia and,
99, 103–5, 109, *129*, 161, 168–71, 175,
208, 238, 288; sovereignty and, 137;
Soviet national anthem and, 79; spheres
of influence and, 53, 97, 159; state
ownership and, 16; Strategic Offensive
Reductions Treaty (SORT) and, 74, 78,
96, 222, 286; Syria and, 249–50; tandem
government of, 147, 215–19, 221, 240,
242–45, 248–49, 251, 288, 290, 313n27,
314n35; Tolstoy and, 103; tsars and,
5, 17, 35, 103, 144, 149, 180, 203; U.S.
business in, 186–89, 201–3; as *velikaia
derzhava* (great power), 52–53; Warsaw
Pact and, 14, 36, 39, 154; war with
Georgia and, 170–76, 200, 214, 220,
238, 240, 288; as Wild East, 16, 186;
zero-sum game approach and, 39, 53,
98, 116, 201, 235
Russia Inc., 180–81
Russian-American Consultative Group on
Strategic Stability, 74–75
Russian Ministry of Atomic Energy, 33
Russian Orthodox Church, 187
*Russia's Road to Corruption: How the Clinton
Administration Exported Government Instead of
Free Enterprise and Failed the Russian People*
(Republican report), 57
Russia Today, ix
Russkii Newsweek magazine, 318n13
Rustaveli Square, 106
Rustavi-2, 106–7
Rutskoi, Alexander, 21
Ryabkov, Sergei, 212
Rybachuk, Oleh, 113

S-300 missiles, 150, 233
Saakashvili, Mikheil: Asmus and, 170–71;
color revolutions and, 106–10, 123, 287;
defense spending and, 170; election of,
287; electoral defeat of, 238; George W.
Bush and, *128*, 137, 168–71; Georgian
conflicts and, 164–75, 237, 308n48;
Hitler and, 175; Hussein and, 172;
Ivanishvili and, 238; Medvedev and,
172; Obama and, 237; Rice and, 170,
174; South Ossetia and, 168–71, 175;

temperament of, 169, 172; Valdai Dis-
cussion Club and, 237; war with Russia
and, 170–72
St. Petersburg, G-20 meeting in, 292
St. Petersburg International Economic
Forum, 183
Sakharov, Andrei, 270
sanctions, 33, 82, 88, 90, 104, 150–53, 233,
249, 263–64, 288–89, 291
Sarkozy, Nicolas, 173, 175–76
Saudi Arabia, 190
Schroeder, Gerhard, 61, 75, 89–91, *127*,
165, 196–97, 200, 286
Schwarzenberg, Karel, 148
Scowcroft, Brent, 2, 4, 8, 11, 28, 40, 55
Sechin, Igor, *130*, 181, 203
Semenko, Mikhail, 241–42
Senate Foreign Relations Committee,
250–51
Seoul Nuclear Summit, 229, 291
Serbia, 20, 113, 288; Belgrade and, 41,
43; Chernomydrin and, 160; Euro-
Atlantic security and, 41–44; Kosovo
and, 160–62; Milošević and, 41–43, 56;
NATO and, 285; Orthodox, 43, 159
shale gas, 192, 197–98, 311n45
Shalikhashvili, John, 39
Shanghai APEC conference, 73
Sheremetyevo airport, 269
Shevardnadze, Eduard, 92, 104–10, 287
Shevtsova, Lilia, 21
Shiites, 31–32, 150
shock therapy, 16
shortwave radio, 241
Shultz, George, 215
Shushkevich, Stanislau, 5
Sierra Leone, 181
Siguler Guff, 187
Sikorski, Radoslav,167, 197
Silicon Valley, ix, 188–89, 242, 244, 290
Siloviki (Securocrats), 79, 216
Slovakia, 78, 161, 287
Slovenia, 60, 63, 78, *127*, 174, 219, 286–87
Snow, Tony, 148
Snowden, Edward, ix–x, 269–71
Sobchak, Anatoly, 51–52, 54, 84, 191, 216
Sochi, 65, 95, 157, 162–63, 267, 288, 290
social networks, 188
soft power, 100, 142
Solana, Javier, 114

Sommer, Theo, 239

Soros, George, 102, 106, 110, 113, 122, 296n42

South Caucasus Pipeline, 200

South Ossetia: color revolutions and, 99, 103–5, 109, *129*; Georgia and, 99, 103–5, 109, *129*, 161, 168–71, 175, 208, 238, 288, 309n61; Tskhinvali and, 168, 171–72; U.S. refusal to recognize, 175; World Trade Organization and, 208

South Stream, 200–201

sovereign democracy, 141–44, 178, 243, 254

sovereignty: absolute, xiii, 247, 258; China and, 137, 143; Clinton and, 16, 18; color revolutions and, 97–123; Euro-Atlantic security and, 48; Germany and, 167; India and, 137; Putin and, 82, 142–43; rule of law and, xiv, 17, 35, 96, 100, 166, 179, 187, 216, 236, 243, 252, 261, 264, 272; Russia and, 137

Soviet Ministry of Gas Industry, 192

Soviet Union: Bolshevik Revolution and, 1, 3; breakup of, ix–xv, 1–11, 35, 44, 53, 57, 59, 63, 85, 94, 98, 159, 180, 195, 207, 230, 255–56, 260, 272, 283; Chechnya and, 46 (*see also* Chechnya); Cold War issues and, 37 (*see also* Cold War issues); color revolutions and, 98, 103–4, 107, 109–11, 116; détente and, 218; George W. Bush and, 70, 74, 81; Gorbachev and, 1–7, 21, 37, 104; internal weakness of, 3; Iran and, 32; Jackson-Vanik strictures and, 27, 68, 71, 94, 102, 123, 163, 209–10, 260; KGB and, 48, 50–51, 53, 62, 65, 68, 104, 145–46, 163, 216, 242, 297n8, 299n61; Kozyrev and, 25; lowered flag of, 1; most-favored nation (MFN) status and, 27; national anthem of, 79; nationalities question and, 3; NATO and, 62, 77; Nixon and, 25; nuclear power and, 32, 228; oil and, 182, 190, 194; perestroika and, 3, 50, 216; Rice and, 55; State Department's European Bureau and, 15; Strauss and, 186

Spain, 161

Spiegel, Der (journal), 61

SS-24 missiles, 213

SS-25 missiles, 213

Stabilization Force, 159–60

stakeholder issues: China and, 262; Clinton and, 17–18, 29; energy and, 178–79 (*see also* energy); Euro-Atlantic security and, 36; George W. Bush and, 60, 81; increasing number of stakeholders and, 243–44, 260, 262, 268

Stalinism, 3, 8, 55, 98, 103–4

Stasi, 51

steganography, 241–42

Steinmeier, Frank-Walter, 167, 170

Strategic Arms Limitation Treaty (SALT), 74

Strategic Arms Reduction Treaty (START): Clinton and, 29; Cold War issues and, 29, 222, 224–25; George H. W. Bush and, 29, 283; George W. Bush and, 73–74; Gorbachev and, 283; Medvedev and, 217, 223, 228, 233, 289; missile defense and, 9, 12, 28–29, 73–74, 163, 217, 220, 222–26, 228, 231, 233, 252, 259, 283, 289; New START and, 217, 222–28, 231, 233, 252, 259, 289; Obama and, 222–28; Putin and, 223

Strategic Defense Initiative, 29–30

Strategic Offensive Reductions Treaty (SORT), 74, 78, 96, 222, 286

Strauss, Robert, 186

suicide bombers, 63

Sunnis, 250

Surkov, Vladislav, 86, 141–42, 243–44

SVR (Russian Foreign Intelligence Service), 26, 242

Syria: Al'Assad and, 249; Annan and, 249–50; Arab Spring and, 247–50; limits of partnership and, 254, 259, 263–64, 268; Putin and, ix, 249–50, 292; Russian arms sales to, 249–50; sanctions against, 249; United Nations (UN) and, 249–50, 290

Talbott, Strobe, 3, 14, 22–23, 26, 28, 30, 42, 59, 295n4

Taliban: Afghanistan and, 135; Mujaheddin and, 63; Operation Enduring Freedom and, 66, 71; Pakistan and, 231; terrorism and, 32, 61–64, 66–67, 69–72, 135, 149, 231, 264

Tashkent, 118–21

Tatum, Paul, 186

Tenet, George, 67

terrorism: Afghanistan and, 47, 62–71, 75, 78, 135–36, 139, 264; Akramiya and, 120; Al Qaeda and, 47, 49, 61, 63–64, 67, 70, 88, 90, 286; antiterrorist programs and, x, 62–66, 81, 139, 271; Basic Principles and, 162; Beslan school and, 85–86, 145, 287; Bin Laden and, 47, 63, 86, 231, 290; Boston Marathon bombings and, 266–68, 270, 291; Caspian Guard program and, 139; Caucasus and, 47, 67, 70–71, 86, 250, 259, 267; Central Intelligence Agency (CIA) and, 58–59, 63, 67; Chechnya and, 46–47, 67, 70–71, 85–86, 90, 107, 266–68, 270, 285–86, 291; Clinton and, 119; coalition against, 69–72; counterterrorism efforts and, xii, 67, 70, 74, 76, 107–8, 121, 140, 231, 240, 243, 255–56, 264, 266–68, 291, 299n74; DEFCON 3 and, 64; Dubrovka Theater hostages and, 70–71, 85, 286; Extraordinary Rendition Program and, 119; fentanyl and, 71; George W. Bush and, 56, 62–66, 119, 163; Georgia and, 107–8, 169; grand bargain and, 150; hostages and, 70–71, 85–86, 145, 287; Iran and, 83, 149–50; Iraq and, 83; Islam and, 60–63, 67, 70, 91, 120, 122, 151, 230; Islamic Movement of Uzbekistan (IMU) and, 119; Karimov and, 118–19; Kazakhstan and, 140; Litvinenko assassination and, 145–46; Massoud assassination and, 62–63; Mujaheddin and, 63; as neglected issue, 45–48; new world order and, 69; North Caucasus and, 259; North Korea and, 83; nuclear power and, 145–46, 224; Obama and, 291; Operation Enduring Freedom and, 66, 71; Pankisi Gorge and, 105, 107–8; Pentagon attack and, 49, 286; Putin and, 49, 163, 291; Rice and, 117, 162; September 11 attacks and, x, 47, 49–50, 67, 69, 71, 73–74, 76, 78, 84, 88, 90, 93, 96, 107, 118, 176, 212, 255, 259, 264, 267, 286, 296n19; suicide bombers and, 63; Taliban and, 32, 61–64, 66–67, 69–72, 135, 149, 231, 264; Uzbekistan and, 118–19; war on terror and, 49, 65, 70, 96, 107, 117, 119; World Trade Center and, 49, 63–64, 286

Texas Rangers, 54

text messaging, 100–101

Thatcher, Margaret, 194

theater missile defense (TMD), 30, 76

Third Man, The (film), 241

Time Magazine, 149

TNK, 181, 202–3

Tolstoy, 103

Trans-Adriatic pipeline, 201

Transnistria, 99, 263

transparency, 101, 113, 115, 141, 181, 209, 223, 236, 240

Transparency International, 181

Treaty on Conventional Forces in Europe (CFE) Treaty, xv, 155–56, 240–41, 290

Trenin, Dmitri, 149

Tripartite Accord, 28

Tsarnev brothers, 291

tsars, 5, 17, 35, 103, 144, 149, 180, 203

Tudeh communist party, 31

Tulip Revolution, 116–18, 120, 287

Turkey, 199–200, 249

Turkmenistan, 195, 198, 200–201

Turkmen Republic, 2

Turks, 103

Tuvalu, 175

Twitter, ix, 290

Two-Plus-Four Agreements, 37

Tymoshenko, Yulia, 112, *128*, 236, 289

U-2 spy plane, 270

Ukraine, 235; borders of, 111; Cheney and, 139, 141; Chicken Kiev speech and, 3; Clinton and, 111, 284; color revolutions and, 97–98, 101–2, 110–18, 121–23, *128*, 138, 142, 195, 236, 287; Commonwealth of Independent States (CIS) and, 97; corruption and, 141, 236; Deep Free Trade and, 236; democracy and, 141, 236; energy and, 138, 190, 194–96, 198, 200, 236, 287; as Europeans, 98; foreign policy issues and, 135, 137; Freedom Agenda and, 115–16, 164; gas and, 110, 138, 190, 194–96, 236, 289; government overthrow of, 101; GUUAM and, 118, 122; Jackson-Vanik Amendment and, 27; Kravchuk and, 5, 28, 110, 284; Kuchma and, 111–14; Kyiv and, 28, 98, 102, 110–11, 113, 118, 192, 195, 236; Little Russians and, 111; March Rada elections and, 195; National Security Council and, 102; NATO and, 39, *129*, 163–69, 218, 236, 263, 265, 288, 304n5, 304n6; nuclear power and, 9–12, 17, 27–29, 214, 222, 283; Nunn-Lugar initiatives and, 213; Orange Revolution of, 110–16, 118, *128*, 138, 142, 195, 236, 287; Radio Liberty and, 94; as receding issue, 236; Russia cuts off gas to, 138, 190, 194–96, 287, 289; shale gas resources of, 198; South Stream pipeline and, 200; suicidal nationalism and, 4; support of United States by, 122–23; Tbilisi exercises and, 169; Tripartite Accord and, 28; Tymoshenko and, 112, *128*, 236, 289; Yanukovych and, 112–16, *128*, 197, 236, 289; Yeltsin and, 4–5, 283–84; Yushchenko and, 112–16, *128*, 137–38, 165–66, 195, 236, 287

"Ukraine fatigue," 236

Ukrainian Soviet Socialist Republic, 111

unemployment, 9–10, 29, 48, 51, 183, 194, 208

United Kingdom, 31, 181; Blair and, 135, 202; EU3 and, 152; Great Game and, 198; Litvinenko assassination and, 145–46; Thatcher and, 194

United Nations (UN), 31, 148, 246; Annan and, 249–50; Brahimi and, 249; Commission on Human Rights and, 88; Convention on the Law of the Sea and, 205; Disarmament Commission and, 88; Euro-Atlantic security and, 42; General Assembly and, 86, 89, 94, 174; Georgia and, 173; Gulf War and, 4; human rights and, 87–88; inspections by, 87–88; Iranian nuclear power and, 151–53, 288; Iraq War and, 82, 84, 86–94; Kosovo and, 89, 160–61; Libya and, 88, 248–49, 251; P-5 and, 233; Resolution 687 and, 88; Resolution 1441 and, 89; Resolution 1737 and, 152, 288; Resolution 1747 and, 152, 288; Resolution 1803 and, 152, 288; Resolution 1929 and, 233, 289; Resolution 1973 and, 248–49, 290; sanctions and, 82; Security Council and, 8, 53, 80, 84, 87–90, 92, 152, 173, 233, 249–50, 263, 288; Serbia and, 41, 43; Syria and, 249–50, 290

United Nations Interim Administration Mission in Kosovo (UNMIK), 160

United States: adoption of Russian children and, 252–53, 291; anti-American sentiment and, 44, 73, 88, 135, 215, 253, 264; Anti-Ballistic Missile (ABM) Treaty and, 30, 53, 60, 69, 72–75, 78, 80, 286; Arab spring and, 247–50; asymmetry of bilateral relationship and, xi–xii, 27, 53, 58, 78, 189, 197, 243–44, 258, 274; bilateral trade and, 261, 268; blame against, 255–56; carbon dioxide emissions of, 206; Central Asian military bases and, 64, 66, 117–22, 154, 219, 236–37; Cold War issues and, 53 (*see also* Cold War issues); as declining power, 258; democracy and, xiii (*see also* democracy); Democrats and, 14, 87, 102, 209, 213, 215, 256, 260; Gore-Chernomyrdin Binational Commission and, 28, 57–59, 74, 78, 150, 221, 244; as Great Satan, 31; Gulf War and, 4, 6, 26, 87–88, 92; hostage crisis of, 31; Islam and, 247; Mosaddeq and, 31; post-Soviet era embassies and, 7; Republicans and, 14, 20, 26, 28, 30, 33, 57, 87, 148, 209, 213, 215, 224, 227–28, 254, 256, 260; rethinking Euro-Atlantic security and, 35–48; Russian-American Consultative Group on Strategic Stability and, 74–75; Strategic Defense Initiative and, 29–30; Strategic Offensive Reductions Treaty (SORT) and, 74, 78, 96, 222, 286; trade with China and, 178, 188; Washington's Russian interlocutors and, 24–27; zero-sum game approach and, 39, 53, 98, 116, 201, 235

United States Agency for International Development (USAID), 113, 253

unmanned aerial vehicle (UAV), 170

Unocal, 200

uranium, 29, 33, 151–52, 224, 233

U.S. Atomic Energy Act, 207

U.S. Chamber of Commerce, 102, 209

U.S. Civil War, 46

U.S. Congress, 11–12, 20, 26–27, 86–87, 137, 143, 196, 202, 209, 224, 256–57

U.S. Geological Survey, 205

Ushakov, Yuri, 58, 144, 157, 216, 282

Usmanov, Alisher, 188

U.S. National Intelligence Council, 58
U.S.-Russia Bilateral Presidential Commission, 220–21, 243–44, 289
U.S.-Russia Business Council, 102, 186, 209
U.S.-Russia Commercial Energy Summit, 204
U.S.-Russia Strategic Framework Declaration, 162–63, 288
USSR (Union of Soviet Socialist Republics). *See* Soviet Union
Uzbekistan: Akramiya and, 120; Andijon crisis and, 120–21; arms embargo on, 121; Central Asian bases and, 65–66; Clinton and, 119; color revolutions and, 116, 118–22; democracy and, 119; Extraordinary Rendition Program and, 119; foreign policy issues and, 118–19, 135; Freedom Support Act and, 12, 119; GUUAM and, 118, 122; Hizb ut-Tahrir (HT) and, 119–20; human rights and, 66, 118–22; Islamic extremists and, 119–20; Karimov and, 64–66, 118–22; North Caucasus and, 119; Putin and, 65; Rice and, 121; Russian Treaty of Friendship and, 121; Shanghai Cooperation Organization and, 121; Tashkent and, 118–21; terrorism and, 119; U.S. military bases and, 118–22, 236–37

Valdai International Discussion Club, xvi, 277; Arab spring and, 249–50; economic issues and, 174, 179, 191–93, 195; Medvedev and, 174–75, 237, 314n35; Putin and, 109, 142, 146, 179, 191–93, 195, 219–20, 228, 232, 237, 249–50, 301n8, 311n45; RIA Novosti agency and, 85–86
Vanuatu, 175
Vekselberg, Viktor, 188–89, 203
Venezuela, 175
vertical of power, 78–79, 144
Vilnius speech, 138–41, 148, 196, 287, 304–5n12
Voloshin, Alexander, 25, 52, 70, 91, 94, 185–86, 282
voucher privatization, 22, 186
Vyakhirev, Rem, 192

Walesa, Lech, 40, 226
war crimes, 162

Warlick, Mary, 137
war on terror, 49, 65, 70, 96, 107, 117, 119
Warsaw Pact, 14, 36, 39, 154
Washington Treaty, 296n9
weapons of mass destruction (WMD), xi–xiv, 15–16, 83, 87–88, 91, 94, 96, 286
White House. *See* United States
WikiLeaks affair, 242–43, 269, 290
Wild East, 16, 186
Wintershall, 201
Wisner, Frank, 160–61
Wolfensohn, James, 53
World Bank, 53
World Economic Forum, 22, 184, 310n23, 310n32, 319n32
World Trade Center, 49, 63–64, 286
World Trade Organization (WTO), 36, 61, 71, 74, 123, 143–44, 208–10, 252, 256, 261
World War II era, 11, 31, 122, 146, 149

Xi Jinping, 258

Yabloko, 85, 93, 282
YAK-30 fighter jets, 249
Yakunin, Vladimir, 146
Yanukovych, Viktor, 112–16, *128*, 196–97, 236, 289
Yavlinsky, Grigory, 65, 93, 282
Yeltsin, Boris, x; background of, 4; Baker and, 4; Baltic independence and, 4–5; Belarus and, 5, 283; bilateral policy framework and, 27–34; Camp David and, 8, *124*, 283; Cheney and, 4; Chernomyrdin and, 285; Chubais and, 12; Clinton and, 14–15, 19–34, 39–49, 60, *125*, *126*, 220, 259, 264, 283–85, 297n23; Cold War issues and, 55–56; color revolutions and, 104, 110; Commonwealth of Independent States (CIS) and, 283; communism and, 8, 284; Congress of People's Deputies and, 21; Constitutional Conference and, 20–21; Davos Pact and, 23, 284; decline of, 45–48; Democrats and, 213; dissolves legislature, 21; Duma and, 22, 29; economic issues and, 180–81, 186, 201; election help for, 23–24; estrangement of, 20; Euro-Atlantic security and, 36, 39–44; George H. W. Bush and, 4, 8, 12, *124*;

Gorbachev and, 4–5, 110; impeachment of, 20, 283; Iran and, 26, 30–34, 285; Iraq War and, 87, 94; Istanbul summit and, 45–46, 285; Jackson-Vanik strictures and, 27; KGB restructuring and, 48; Kiriyenko and, 285; Kosovo and, 17, 20, 26; Kozyrev and, 18, 24–26, 42–43, 284; Kravchuk and, 5, 284; as lesser of two evils, 24; liberalism and, 15–16, 36; limits of partnership and, 257, 259, 264; missile defense (MD) and, 29–30; national identity and, 24; NATO and, 39, 41–44, 75, 159–60, 167, 284–85; nonproliferation and, 33; nuclear power and, 284; oil prices and, 182; OSCE and, 285; Partnership for Peace (PfP) Program and, 39; physical condition of, 19, 22, 24, 46–47; political family of, 54, 144; as President of Russian Republic, 4; Primakov and, 26, 43, 285; production sharing agreements (PSAs) and, 201; property ownership and, 22–23; Putin and, 45–49, 54, 79, 84, 144, 180–81, 186, 257, 303n34; reforms of, 4–5, 8, 15–16, 20–22, 36; Republicans and, 213; resignation of, 285; retaining power for, 20–24; rethinking Euro-Atlantic security and, 36, 39, 41–48; Rice and, 4, 55; rising criticism of, 24–27; Rutskoi and, 21; Scowcroft and, 4, 55; shelling of parliament by, 21, 283; Soviet national anthem and, 79; START II and, 29, 283; as stepfather to Clinton, 19; Tripartite Accord and, 28; 24; Ukraine and, 4–5, 283–84; unpredictability of, 4, 19; U.S. aid to, 12; U.S. efforts at keeping him in power, 20–24; Zyuganov and, 22–23, 39, 284

youth groups, 86, 116, 243

Yugoslavia, 6, 12, 15, 38, 41, 43, 45, 60, 159, 162, 176

Yukos, 85, 202–11

Yushchenko, Viktor, 112–16, *128*, 137–38, 165–66, 195, 236, 287

Zawahiri, Ayman Al, 47

Zeit, Die (newspaper), 239

zero-sum game approach, 39, 53, 98, 116, 201, 235

Zhirinovsky, Vladimir, 21, 92, 284

Zhvania, Zurab, 106–7

Zuckerberg, Mark, 188

Zyuganov, Gennady, 22–23, 39, 284